The Assassination of Lincoln:
History and Myth

The Assassination of Lincoln: History and Myth

Lloyd Lewis

With an Introduction by Mark E. Neely, Jr.

University of Nebraska Press
Lincoln and London

Copyright 1929 by Harcourt, Brace and Company
Renewal copyright 1957 by Kathryn D. Lewis
Introduction to the Bison Book Edition © 1994 by the University of
Nebraska Press
Manufactured in the United States of America

First Bison Book printing: 1994
Most recent printing indicated by the last digit below:
10   9   8   7   6   5   4   3   2   1

Library of Congress Cataloging-in-Publication Data
Lewis, Lloyd, 1891–1949.
[Myths after Lincoln]
The assassination of Lincoln: history and myth / by Lloyd Lewis.—Bison
Book ed.
p.   cm.
Originally published: Myths after Lincoln. New York: Harcourt, Brace,
c1929.
"A Bison book."
Includes bibliographical references (p.   ) and index.
ISBN 0-8032-7949-3
1. Lincoln, Abraham, 1809–1865—Assassination.   2. Booth, John
Wilkes, 1838–1865.   I. Title.
E457.5.L67   1994
973.7'092—dc20
94-560
CIP

Published by arrangement with Harcourt, Brace and Company. Originally published under the title *Myths after Lincoln*.

∞

TO THE MEMORY OF
JOSEPH B. *and* JAY LEWIS

INTRODUCTION

by Mark E. Neely, Jr.

I first encountered the work of Lloyd Lewis in the late 1970s, and not a minute too soon, either. In 1972 I had left university teaching to work in a library and museum of Lincolniana located in Indiana. Leaving behind the Abraham Lincoln studied in universities and graduate schools and confronting the Lincoln admired in the forests of Kentucky and Indiana and on the prairies of Illinois is to undergo what in modern street language is called "a reality check." For the new job I had boned up on what I thought was necessary to know about Lincoln, his political career, mostly, and his presidential administration.

I shall never forget the first tour I guided through the museum. At the end of it a patron asked me whether it was true that Abraham Lincoln's body had been moved seventeen times after its initial burial. All of my education failed me at that point. I had no idea that it had ever been moved. And wouldn't have known where Lincoln was finally buried, had I not visited Springfield once and seen the enormous tomb and memorial. My education also failed the public. I was there to answer their questions and I could not.

For me, Lincoln was not a mythic figure. He was a protagonist in history, a Whig, a Republican, a commander-in-chief, and an emancipator. That was partly because I was fresh from the university and partly because of my sectional origins. Growing up in a state that had seceded from the Union in 1861, I knew Lincoln first as an academic subject, not as an object of popular veneration in local lore, the way boys who grew up in the Midwest knew Lincoln in the 1940s.

The most difficult lesson I had to learn on the job was this: Abraham Lincoln belongs to the people and not to the historians.

Eventually Lloyd Lewis, through his influential book *Myths after Lincoln* (titled *The Assassination of Lincoln: History and Myth* for this Bison Book edition) taught me that, and I hope now that I never forget it.

Lloyd Downs Lewis came to Lincoln from the other route. Born in Pendleton, a town in east central Indiana, on May 2, 1891, he was the son of a Quaker farmer and newspaper editor. Lewis earned his B.A. at Swarthmore in 1913 and at first followed in his father's steps as a newspaperman. After working briefly as a reporter in Philadelphia, he moved to Chicago in 1915 to work on the *Record-Herald*. Despite his religious origins, he served in the Navy in World War I. After the armistice, he returned to Chicago to work in public relations for a cinema chain.

All the while his real interest appears to have been history. He had listened as a boy in Indiana to the tales of veterans, old Quaker soldiers who had marched in the Union blue in the ranks of the Army of the Tennessee. Now as a man in his thirties, he read—at night and on weekends after promoting the film industry in Chicago. He read books on the Civil War—and on Lincoln. After all, Pendleton was less than ten miles from Anderson, the home of jumpy Lewis Weichmann, the witness whose testimony hanged Mary Surratt for aiding John Wilkes Booth in the murder of President Lincoln. There was no escaping that atmosphere of veneration and folklore and morbid mystery.

Lewis read other sorts of books as well, among them, James George Frazer's *The Golden Bough*, a study of mythology. There he found the key to understanding if not his own fascination with Lincoln then at least that of the public. Lewis could write, of course; manipulating words constituted his stock in trade. He decided to write a book, not about Lincoln but about the myths surrounding Lincoln after his death—mostly myths about his death. He wrote with great skill and never allowed the theory that held the book together to intrude clumsily on the tale:

> When the colonists in America had cut the cord that tied them to the Old World, they rang the Liberty Bell and threw their hats over the windmills. Independence was a brave and joyous thing for them to have won, yet when the shouting died, they felt a little lonely in the wil-

derness, realizing that in gaining their political freedom they had lost their claim upon the warm folk-traditions of the mother lands. They missed the security of all those national myths upon which a people must lean. . . . It was one thing to have banished King George III from their lives and another to have lost King Arthur.

Any sentient reader realizes exactly where this line of thought is headed and cannot wait to get there. More important, that reader is not encumbered with a sluggish discussion of anthropology or literary myth: the reader has gained the essential insight and is ready—eager, even—to incorporate Lincoln's myth in it. This is good writing and subtle intelligence.

Lloyd Lewis's *Myths after Lincoln* was first published in 1929, but most readers today seem to know the book from its reprinting (in slightly revised form) by the Readers Club in 1941. Even the popular Readers Club edition has now become scarce in used and rare book shops, and that is why this new edition is being produced over a half-century later.

There is another more important reason for reissuing this work. Lloyd Lewis had something that many, many forgotten writers on Lincoln did not. Lewis had an eye for a great story. He was a journalist, and he recognized the two greatest stories of the Civil War: the assassination of Lincoln and the chillingly prophetic genius of William Tecumseh Sherman. One he dealt with in *Myths after Lincoln,* the assassination of the sixteenth president of the United States. The other he wrote about in a book published three years after the Lincoln book, *Sherman, Fighting Prophet.* These were the great stories of the Civil War North (the Confederacy itself may have been the only great story from the other side).

It may seem remarkable that as late as the 1920s the assassination and death of Lincoln remained a story needing to be told. By contrast the assassination of President John F. Kennedy, now only a generation behind us, has already spawned a mountain of books. And in the generations following Lincoln's assassination there appeared to be much to keep the subject alive. Other aspects of Lincoln's biography attracted a myriad of authors. And, unhappily, the history of the republic offered vivid reminders of the relevance of assassination to the continuing course of American history. Each succeeding generation up to Lewis's time experienced an assassination. James A. Garfield, a Civil War veteran, was shot and died slowly, memorably in 1881—with Robert Todd Lincoln, President Lincoln's son and a member of Garfield's cabinet, looking on helplessly, tortured by who knows what horrible memories. In 1901 William McKinley fell victim to an assassin's bullet. The popular mind was transfixed by the subject, apparently. Antique shops still display an occasional curio with the heads of the three martyred Republicans depicted on it—Lincoln, Garfield, and McKinley.

But history—that is, the fledgling history profession—avoided the subject, disdained it in fact. Perhaps the historians, eager to attain the professional status of a "scientific" discipline, saw as their role the study of the steady forces in American history, not the unpredictable ones, the wild cards that changed the course of events but themselves proved exactly how chaotically changeable history was. Whatever the cause, the effect can be readily discerned from the tone of the statement by the greatest academic Lincoln biographer of the twentieth century, roughly a contemporary of Lewis, James Garfield Randall, of the University of Illinois. "This biography knows only the living Lincoln," Randall wrote by way of introduction to the subject of his four-volume work. Interest in the assassination was akin to interest in Lincoln's youthful romance with Ann Rutledge in New Salem as a sign of amateurism or antiquarianism.

Lewis spied the opportunity that historians were blind to and took his place among the chroniclers of Lincoln's assassination. He still holds an undisputed spot as author of the most readable general account of the assassination conspiracy, the murder, death, and funeral of Lincoln. Chapter 19, "The Four Who Were Hanged," makes gripping reading, and Chapter 12, "Half Circus, Half Heartbreak," still seems a more compelling description of the long trip of Lincoln's funeral train than the modern oversized books that reproduce the many photographs of that melancholy ride. Chapter 25, on "The Coney Men" who attempted to steal Lincoln's body from its tomb to exchange it for a counterfeiter in prison, also makes fascinating reading, depicting a slice of life in sharp contrast with the sentimentality and respectable bouquets otherwise associated with Lincoln's entombment (that was the chapter I most needed to have read for my first museum tour). Even as a popular writer, Lewis holds a transitional place in the history of the literature on the Lincoln assassination. William Hanchett, whose *Lincoln Murder Conspiracies*, published in 1983, is the best scholarly study of the crime, writes about Lewis's view of the assassination at some length.

Lewis's interpretation of the events is generally sound, sounder than many of the theories that came after him. "Within a few years," he wrote, "nobody would believe any more that the South had prompted the murder," though that had been the prosecution theory at the trial of John Wilkes Booth's alleged fellow conspirators. In fact, the idea that the assassination was a Confederate Secret Service plot, instigated by Jefferson Davis or other high-ranking Confederate officials, is currently undergoing a revival, but readers would do well to stick with the wisdom of Lloyd Lewis here. The Civil War was singularly free of atrocities and the excesses associated with twentieth-century warfare. It was, as Lewis noted carefully, "singularly free of sex crimes," and targeting civilians, even civilian political leaders, was rare. Even tough-talking old Thad Stevens, the Republican Radical from Pennsylvania, said of Jefferson Davis and other Confederate leaders, "I know these men. They are gentlemen and incapable of being assassins."

Likewise, Lewis wisely dismissed the idea that Booth was a madman. Lewis was very shrewd, indeed prophetic, in his judgment that the efforts of Secretary of War Edwin M. Stanton to keep Booth's physical remains from providing a rallying place for unreconstructed rebels backfired and served only to fuel popular suspicions and fantasies.

. . . [T]he elaborate secrecy boomeranged on Stanton and [U.S. Secret Service head Lafayette C.] Baker. Soon people in all parts of the country were saying the things that Washingtonians had said from the first: that dead man wasn't the assassin, Booth had got away and all the mysterious actions could mean but one thing—the Secret Service had shot the wrong man, and had destroyed the body to hide its mistake, also to collect the reward. Sometimes this whisper insinuated that Stanton had known of the error and had been forced to conceal it to keep from making the government ridiculous; sometimes it said that Stanton had been tricked by Baker and his detectives into believing that the body was really Booth's.

It would not depart much from such reasoning to reach—in a pattern all too familiar to readers of theories about the Kennedy assassination —the conclusion that the man in the best position to investigate the conspiracy was also in the best position to cover it up—that Stanton himself was in on the plot, and that what followed was a baroque cover-up by higher-ups with sinister political motives to kill President Lincoln. Precisely such a conclusion was reached by an amateur historian named Otto Eisenschiml in 1937 and launched a forty-year reign of accusation directed against Edwin M. Stanton and the Republican Radicals that still has considerable currency in popular circles.

Lewis was too smart for that, but it must be admitted that his work did offer fuel for the fires of misplaced suspicion. As William Hanchett points out, Lewis played an important role in tarnishing the reputation of Stanton, and that was a crucial step toward Eisenschiml's ideas. He also perpetuated the idea of the Radical Republicans as bitter political enemies of Lincoln which would underwrite that fanciful theory by providing a motive for Stanton to be interested in the moderate Lincoln's elimination from the political picture. The latter is the worst fault of the book, and it must be stated here that almost nothing he says about Reconstruction can be believed. Moreover, the tone of his writing about the Reconstruction Radicals amounts to character assassination and defamation of the defenseless dead. He virtually equates zeal to end slavery with sadism toward fellow American Southerners. Modern readers should take all of what he says about politics with a grain of salt.

Even in his realm of acknowledged competence, Lewis made a number of errors. Careful readers will notice that Lewis, researching and writing in the time he could spare from his salaried job, allowed inaccuracies in his text that professional historians usually eliminate. A glaring typographical error appears on page

168, for example, where Lincoln's second inaugural ball is dated August 4, 1865, more than three months after the president's death. Edward Spangler on page 164 becomes George Spangler on page 195 (actually his name appears to have been the unusual "Edman," and not many modern authorities include him among Booth's accomplices). What Mrs. Surratt knew and when she knew it are more controversial questions than may appear in these pages, and Lewis's certainty about her guilt may well have been a function of hometown loyalties—the principal witness against her, it will be remembered, came from Anderson, Indiana, and Lewis's father had once edited a newspaper in Anderson. The Kansas senator identified as James S. Lane on page 228 was christened James Henry Lane, and the Reverend J. B. Thompson of Broadway Tabernacle Church mentioned on page 82 was actually Joseph Parrish Thompson, a famous man in an era when churchmen held more sway than they do today (incidentally, Lewis's Chapter 9 on the Lincoln funeral eulogies, "They Knew What God Wanted," put these sometimes neglected sources to good use).

Readers may be surprised to learn, in light of the harsh words Lewis has for abolitionists and their Radical Republican heirs, that he was a political liberal himself. The sketch of Lewis's life in the *Dictionary of American Biography* is particularly good because it was written by Paul Angle, one-time director of the Chicago Historical Society, an able Lincoln scholar himself, and a man who knew Lewis personally (in that era when many Lincoln writers lived in and about Chicago). Angle notes that Lewis supported Franklin Delano Roosevelt for president, Henry Horner for governor of Illinois, and after World War II, Adlai Stevenson for the same post. Most New Dealers and Democrats did not think of themselves as "radicals" in politics, and they did not necessarily identify with the radicals of Lincoln's era—as Lincoln himself did not.

After the publication of *Myths after Lincoln,* Lewis spent most of the 1930s and World War II working for the *Chicago Daily News. Sherman Fighting Prophet* appeared in 1932. In 1945 he retired from full-time journalism and was working on a biography of Ulysses S. Grant when he died in 1949. *Captain Sam Grant* was published posthumously in 1950. Lewis left notes for the next part of Grant's life. He had contemplated a multi-volume biography. His widow, Kathryn, eventually chose another midwestern writer whom she met in Chicago, Bruce Catton, to continue the work from Lewis's notes, and the result was the widely acclaimed and still valuable two-volume work, *Grant Moves South* and *Grant Takes Command.*

The Lewis-Catton link is significant as a symbol of a tradition of great writing on America's Civil War reaching from the 1920s into the 1960s. For more than a generation evocative narrative history has made converts to the study of the Civil War, and if Lloyd Lewis did not found that tradition, he was at least in the forefront of it. To read or reread this book is to realize what good writing can do for history.

ACKNOWLEDGMENT

To TOM PEETE CROSS, Professor of Comparative Literature at the University of Chicago, for the use of his immense and scholarly information on folk-lore and its examination.

To William E. Dodd, Professor of History at the University of Chicago, for the use of his knowledge of American history, his ability to weigh facts with unmatched insight and honesty, and for his remark, "Perhaps no man can ever free himself entirely from prejudice; still, it is interesting to attempt it."

To Mrs. C. O'Crowley and Miss Tillie Weichmann of Anderson, Indiana; E. V. Valentine and William B. Lightfoot of Richmond, Virginia; and John B. Simonton of Washington, D. C., all of whom gave me the interviews quoted on pages that follow.

To Governor Henry Horner of Illinois for the use of his famous collection of Lincolniana; and to Carl Sandburg for items, counsel and promptings.

To the Congressional Library at Washington; to the Public Libraries of New York, Chicago and Richmond, Virginia; and to the Chicago Historical Society for the use of books and manuscripts.

To Edward Lewis and Sanford M. Keltner of Anderson, Indiana; Charles H. Jordan of Wauseon, Ohio; W. C. Woodall of Columbus, Georgia; James Hutton of Chicago, Illinois, and Aubrey Cribb of Springfield, Illinois, for valued items of information.

To Herbert Wells Fay and J. C. Thompson of Springfield, Illinois, for time and thought spent in unearthing facts concerning Abraham Lincoln's tomb.

To Major Willis Crittenberger of the U. S. War Department for assistance in finding original manuscripts in the Department's archives at Washington.

To *Liberty, Plain Talk* and *Century* for the right to reprint, here, as chapters, articles which they originally published.

To certain pioneers such as Joseph Rogers, Ziba Darlington, Noah Haines and T. M. Hardy, veterans of the Army of the Tennessee, who have long been dead under little Union flags in the Friends' graveyard at Spring Valley, Indiana, but who, in their lifetimes, would tell an inquisitive boy what they remembered.

CONTENTS

PART ONE: THE DYING GOD

PART TWO: THE AMERICAN JUDAS

PART THREE: ALTAR SMOKE

EPILOGUE

The Assassination of Lincoln:
History and Myth

PART ONE

THE DYING GOD

✧ ✧ ✧ 1 ✧ ✧ ✧

THREE SILVER STARS

IT WAS STRANGELY QUIET even for Sunday, this ninth day of April, 1865, as Ulysses S. Grant jogged along the Virginia road that led to Appomattox Court House, his head drooping on his stubby little body.

The big guns were still. Through the woods on either side of the white road, two armies sat motionless, waiting.

One of them was his, the bruised but powerful Army of the Potomac, the other was that of his enemies, the Army of Northern Virginia, bled white and exhausted.

Four years of war were done. Eleven States of the South that had been fighting so frenziedly to tear their way out of the United States of America had fallen gasping across their guns. They hadn't the strength to make their get-away. Secession was a gone dream, a lost cause.

Grant, always solemn, more solemn now than ever, was riding to receive Robert E. Lee's surrender, and it made him sad. At Lee and at Lee's desperate Army of Northern Virginia, last hope of the South, he had been pounding all Spring, all the Winter before, and the Summer before that. Now the end had come. He was glad it was over, but compassion for the brave old foe drowned all the elation of his own triumph.

Extraordinary spectacle, this man Grant as he rode to Appomattox. Whatever he was at that moment he owed to war. It had taken him out of squalid failure and hurtled him upward to a success such as no American soldier before or after him could win, yet he hated war, and for all his terrible willingness to fight, he had been scheming and scheming to stop the bloody business — scheming to halt the very thing that was making him immortal. Like his chieftain, Abraham Lincoln, that sad, cool man in the White House, he had wanted peace more than victory.

Into a two-story brick house on the edge of a tiny village he went as to his own surrender, dust and ashes over his mussy uniform, a private's stained overcoat upon his back, looking, as he entered, like a Missouri farmer who had by mistake crawled into a blouse that carried, unnoticed, three little silver stars on its shoulders.

Awaiting him was Lee, who of all men knew that those stars were no mistake, Lee in his own resplendent uniform, handsome, aristocratic, perfect model of the old army manners and professional culture to which both Grant and he had been trained at West Point — ideals which he had remembered and which Grant, luckily for the Union, had so soon forgotten.

The aristocrat wore a sword, the democrat none, and, noticing this, the democrat, with a grave courtesy that somehow shamed the lofty hauteur of the cavalier, explained that he had not had time to bring out his official blade and get fixed up for the ceremony.

As simply and naturally as though at an ordinary meeting of officers, Grant presented his staff, and the Union men, admiring the great Confederate, made gracious attempts to ease the situation with small, pleasant talk. But to them Lee, who had been an officer all his life, could be only stiff and cold, and when his eye fell on Grant's military secretary, Col. Ely S. Parker, full-blooded Indian chief of the Six Nations, he stared in amazement, evidently thinking that the Yankees had brought in a negro officer to humiliate him.

But under the gentle voice of his plain, slouching conqueror, Lee's proud reserve began to thaw. Grant talked of the Mexican War, in which both had served, and would have gone on in such informal fashion if Lee had not brought up the business of the day — surrender.

Grant silently wrote out the terms. They were simple: the enlisted men were to surrender their arms, the officers to retain theirs, all were to give their paroles and go home, not to be disturbed by United States authority so long as they kept their promise not to fight the government again. He handed them to his adversary and waited. Lee wiped his glasses, adjusted them to his nose, and began reading.

The sweeping generosity of the terms, considering what the Southern politicians had told their soldiers about the bloodthirst of the North, must have been plain in their full significance to Lee.

His face lit up when he came to the clause which allowed the officers to keep their property, and when he had finished he said with a little ring in his voice, "This will have a very happy effect upon my army."

Grant wanted the whole thing to be happy and asked if Lee had anything more to suggest. The Confederate wondered if his cavalrymen and artillerymen, who owned their horses, would be permitted to keep them. "No, the terms as written don't permit it," said Grant. He hadn't known the Southern army was thus organized. But he would allow it anyway and do better than that, he said; he would tell his officers to let every man claim a horse or mule and take it home. The Confederate privates were mostly small farmers, that he knew, and with their land overrun by two armies they would find times hard, indeed, without work-horses.

At this Lee melted entirely.

"This will have the best possible effect upon the men," he said, warming to so unmartial a conquistador. "It will be very gratifying and will do much toward conciliating our people."

Then as staff officers copied the letters of surrender and the terms, Lee bent toward Grant, as in embarrassment, and whispered in his rival's ear that his men hadn't had anything but parched corn to eat in several days. It was like one brother confiding in another. Grant turned to his staff officers: "You go to the Twenty-fourth, you to the Fiftieth," and so on, naming his various corps, "and ask every man who has three rations to turn over two of them. Go to the commissaries, go to the quartermasters. General Lee's army is on the point of starvation."

Away rode the officers and Lee's men received the food, which they wanted, almost as soon as the news of the surrender which, exhausted though they were, they did not want.

Through the Union lines went the word like a Spring wind. Guns began to boom salutes of victory. Grant, hearing them, ordered all celebration to stop. "The rebels are our countrymen again; the best sign of rejoicing after the victory will be to abstain from all demonstrations on the field," he said.

Grant rode one way, Lee the other, such a sight as the world never saw before, the victor as depressed as the vanquished. Around Lee pressed his ragged starvelings, weeping, holding his hand, calling upon God to bless him. He wept, too, saying, "I have done the best I could for you."

The surrender itself was quietly done — no ceremonies, no humiliations of ceremonious capitulation. Confederate officers signed paroles for the Army of Northern Virginia, 26,765 men — all that were left from the 49,000 who had begun the Appomattox campaign. Death and desertion had both been busy. A few of the Union fighters felt a little cheated at not being able to behold a formal ceremony such as had been celebrated at Yorktown in 1781, with the defeated enemy marching without guns between long lines of their conquerors, but no such nonsense lived in the mass of Northern troops, who were content to feed the Confederates, slap them on the back, and call "Good-bye" as they crawled on their horses and scattered southward.

Grant, in whose iron face a faint trace of easiness was now apparent, sat down in his camp. He was silent for a time and his staff was silent, too, watching him. At length Grant spoke up, addressing his quartermaster: "Ingalls, do you remember that old white mule that So-and-So used to ride when we were in the City of Mexico?"

Of course Ingalls remembered it. His business was to remember things that his idol wanted. That was what a quartermaster was for.

And as the Spring twilight came down, Grant talked on and on — his officers no doubt squirming with their desire to rehash and gossip about the great surrender — his mind rambling on back across twenty years to center and cling to the antics of an old white mule on the road to Popocatapetl.

MAD MARCH HARES

THROUGH THE NIGHT OF April 9, 1865, the telegraph ticked the gladdest message it had carried since that day, twenty-one years before, when it had stuttered out its first letters, "W-h-a-t h-a-t-h G-o-d w-r-o-u-g-h-t," at Professor Morse's inaugural demonstration of his invention.

Now the dots and dashes spelled out the hysterical words, "Lee has surrendered. The war is over."

The news came smashing into Northern cities and country towns at midnight on the tongues of bells — courthouse bells launched the joyous clangor, and fire-bells, church-bells, dinner-bells took up the refrain.

Out from their houses poured the people to catch the flying news. Cannons on the squares began to boom, rockets began to swish and crack in the air. Men and boys on lathering horses carried the word to villages and farms. Torchlight processions swung into the streets, dancing, swaying, and swelling at each step. People in delirium rushed home to dress up funny and to race back into the parading lines. Dignified old gentlemen pranced and capered, throwing their hats at the moon. Confirmed enemies forgot neighborhood spites and shook hands, then, as emotion struck the backs of their knees, toppled into each other's arms, and snuggled their ludicrous whiskers together. Women laughed wildly, tears of heartsease adding a reckless shine to their faces.

Mobs tore up plank sidewalks for bonfires and then, roaring with happy fury, fell upon the recruiting boxes of the army enlistment forces and tossed them into the fire.

The war was over. The North and South were remarried and this was their *charivari*.

And, as at all proper "shivarees," black bottles came out. Saloons flew open, and the North got howling drunk. Clergymen peeking from their windows shook their heads to see the Sabbath dishonored. Not all of them, however. The more zealous preachers rushed out to address the mass-meetings into which the processions came reeling.

Religious folk said it was wondrous that the news should come on Palm Sunday, the anniversary of Christ's triumphant entry into Jerusalem. Hymns arose in the night air.

"Sing unto the Lord, for he hath triumphed gloriously; the horse and the rider he hath thrown into the sea."

Cities sang with red, white, and blue bunting that broke out on the faces of buildings in the torchlights, and the people sang with ecstasy and wine. They sang "Rally 'round the flag, boys, rally once again, shouting the battlecry of Freedom." They sang "John Brown's body lies a-moldering in the grave" and "Mine eyes have seen the glory of the coming of the Lord." And church hymns, too. All songs were hymns that night. Up on the bar at Willard's Hotel in Washington an old man launched forth the Doxology. No less earnestly because their hearts were expanding under the grape, the drinkers joined with him, making the glasses tinkle with reverberations in their niches up behind the bartender.

To the Union people, Lee's surrender meant that a million men could now come home out of the valley of the shadow of death. Five hundred thousand soldiers, three-fifths of them Northern, two-fifths Southern, were sleeping under the sod and the dew, as the poet mourned. Death, taxes, and the draft were all lifted from the people at one swoop.

The Union felt that rush of relief that comes to all families when the hearse comes back from the graveyard after a long funeral.

At dawn the celebration was only beginning. Thousands of persons had slept through the hubbub and now appeared, adding fresh intoxication to the babel. Into the hearts of towns and cities came men, women, and children who seemed to be walking on their hands. They poured downtown in buggies, surreys, buckboards, carriages, on foot, "and almost on their heads," as the newspapers said. Horses had flags in their bridles, bunting on their reins, and the drivers had flags in their lapels, their whip-sockets, their teeth, and down the backs of their necks.

A stranger coming upon the sidewalks of New York would

have thought himself fallen upon a "carnival of March hares, a bedlam of good cheer, an outbreak of school urchins," exulted the New York *Independent*.

Schools were dismissed before noon, pouring floods of wild children into the white sea of joy.

Business was suspended completely, merchants, bankers, lawyers, doctors, householders crawling out of windows and teetering across ridgepoles to decorate their buildings with flags and bunting. The Chicago Board of Trade sang "Old Hundred" and other hymns, chanted war songs; "bulls" embraced "bears," and "light men carried heavy men." A curious symbol of elation in pioneer America was this thing of lifting people. When a man or boy grew excited, nervous, or confused it was quite the established thing for him to fly at some near-by male and try to lift him off his feet and carry him, kicking and laughing, while the crowd roared. Such frolicsome strugglings and mock wrestlings were accepted as enormously funny and served to break the ice in groups of self-conscious, embarrassed rustics.

Sportive wrestlings and thumpings gave outlet to enormous excitement on this Monday, April 10. Mobs milled in the streets, scrambling out of the way of fire-engines, which, gaily festooned, clanged past, manned by uproarious firemen and civilians. Saloons were jammed. Men who had been total abstainers felt so good that they crowded the bars howling, "Let's have another to Lincoln," then "to Grant," "to Sherman," "to Sheridan," "to Thomas," and on and on as the roll of the Yankee hero-generals was called.

Wounded soldiers were surrounded by shouting crowds who insisted that the veterans tell their war experiences again. They were hugged, their pockets were thrust full of greenbacks, and they were plied with liquor until they toppled into stupor as the celebrants rushed off after other victims.

Effigies of Jefferson Davis, leader of the confederated Southern States, dangled everywhere, from lamp-posts, from shop-signs, from floats in the processions that wound so endlessly round and round the streets. Many of these effigies were burned, often in the buggies or carriages which had borne them in parades. On one truck in a Chicago parade an effigy of the "rebel" leader was being eaten by a large Newfoundland dog — some inventive artist having evidently stuffed the scarecrow with liver.

Mock coffins rode high in the processions with "Jeff Davis" chalked upon them.

Already the news had come that Davis had fled southward from Richmond, the Secession capital, and many parading wagons bore trunks with such labels as "J. Davis, Mexico" and other similar references to the man's general unwelcomeness henceforth in the nation.

Burlesque tableaus satirized the overthrow of the Confederacy. Patent medicine advertisements — then common in all newspapers — were imitated in such placards as "Phil Sheridan's Soothing Syrup for the Johnnies" or "Sherman's Vermifuge for Joe Johnston."

Still, this was all in fun. The people, all at once, had forgiven their Southern brothers for everything, for the years of dole and woe, grief and taxation, which, as they thought, the Secessionists had forced upon them.

Peace and reconciliation were already sweeping the land.

In Trinity Church, New York, the next day, notables of the city led the thankful masses in the hymn, "Glory be to God on high, and on earth peace, good will towards men."

By Monday night this rising spirit of "let the dead past bury its dead" was almost universal in the North. "Praise God from whom all blessings flow" was sung in churches, in town-halls, in saloons, in lodge-rooms, on the street, and in country schoolhouses where farmers gathered. The religious note was mounting. Cannon were booming as steadily as ever, bonfires blazing on the main streets, glasses clinking, parades roaring, orators thundering, Chinese lanterns dancing from house to house, tree to tree, anvils popping in cross-road smithies where no cannon could be had — yet there was something new in the celebrations — rows of candles standing in the windows of the nation, burning with a steady, peaceful fire.

Sunday night had been Hallowe'en; Monday had added the Fourth of July, and now Monday night, as by magic, brought Christmas to the merrymaking.

Fireworks reddened the upper sky. Livery-stable hands in Chicago had thrilling sport shooting rockets and Roman candles at the windows and roof-crowds of the Chicago *Times,* Democratic "copperhead" newspaper which had been once suppressed during the war for vilifying Lincoln.

The uproar passed over prison walls and told thousands of Confederate captives that their release would come soon now. Promptly the prisoners began forming companies and regiments to enlist under the but lately hated Stars and Stripes for the Indian wars of the West.

Here and there could be found Union men who clung to old grudges, refusing to join in the saturnalia of glee. They said the North was weak and foolish to drop war hatreds so quickly. The South, which had treacherously tried to secede from the Union four years before, and which had brought the horrors of war upon the nation, should not be forgiven so soon. It had not been punished enough. Here was General Grant turning loose all his captured enemies; here he was accepting Lee's surrender, then telling him and his hordes to go free. "Rebels" were traitors and should be treated like criminals. In such sour words did a small and sterner group of Northerners protest against the good will that gushed all around them.

Crowds might listen to such "bitter-enders" and under the spell of their oratory feel again for the moment the surge of old blood-lusts, but not for long. It was more fun to run, parade, burn sentry-boxes, sing, holler, and have one drink after another.

Benjamin Butler, tempestuous Union general, trying now in excessive patriotism to forget the scandals of his military career, came out of his Washington hotel to address a passing crowd. Over the heads of his listeners he hurled the words:

"What shall be done with men educated in the military academy (West Point) at public expense, sworn to protect our flag, who without justification, excuse, or palliation even, betrayed the flag and used the knowledge obtained in the nation's school to break down the government that nurtured them?"

Cries of "Hang them — hang them!" "Give them a rope!" came up to him from the listeners.

"Then we are agreed," Butler roared on; "condign punishment for the military traitor who deserts the flag for rebellion, disfranchisement and safekeeping for the civilian using his perjured place to betray his country, right of fellowship for misguided and deceived victims of the rebellion, and equal rights for the black man under the law."

Shouts rang as he concluded, but a few moments later his listeners had been caught up in that larger emotion of jubilee and were going down the street cheering for Lincoln and for Grant, who had disagreed entirely with Ben Butler.

"Forgive and forget" were the watchwords of the day — and tender-hearted Lincoln was the hero. What had been his weakness in the eyes of his critics all through the war, his softness toward the South, now was his strength. His habits of mercy and sorrow now loomed as his superior wisdom, his true greatness. The war President whom thousands, sometimes a majority of Northerners, had abused or distrusted, was now the man of the hour. Hail to the Chief! Hurray for Lincoln! He had been right all along! They had misjudged him. Hadn't he won?

For Grant a hymn of praise scarcely less fervent rocked the North. For him too a wave of gratitude, almost of affection, was sweeping over the South.

Grant had given his conquered foes their freedom back again — and their horses.

☆   ☆   ☆   **3**   ☆   ☆   ☆

IN THE CABIN OF THE "RIVER QUEEN"

BEHIND ALL THAT DRAMA of Grant's victory and Lee's defeat and the ecstasy of 20,000,000 Northerners is a story — a story that must be told if any one anywhere is to understand how the great Republic rocketed Abraham Lincoln, the prairie lawyer, into sainthood.

It is a story that begins with Lincoln leaving Washington eighteen days before this momentous Sunday, leaving the White

House with a guileless, innocent face, and, as one reads history, with something up his sleeve — something sly, deep, subtle, and profound.

With his wife, his youngest son Tad — Thomas, whom Lincoln had nicknamed "Tadpole" because, as a baby, his head had been abnormally large — and a party of friends, the President had set out for the front, starting for City Point on the James River, headquarters of Grant, who was battering Lee back closer and closer on to Richmond, capital of the Confederacy.

On the surface there was nothing unusual in that. Many times he had gone down to the war zone to visit his men — often, too often, these journeys had been discouragingly short, much of the war having been fought perilously close to his own Capitol home. Now it was better; he had to take a steamer and travel twenty-four hours to get to Grant's camp.

Ostensibly this trip was only a sort of vacation from the White House. Some of the President's friends said that he was going to visit his eldest son Robert, who had been a captain on Grant's personal staff for two months. Secretly Lincoln had sent a telegram to Robert on March 21 saying, "We now think of starting to you about 1 P.M. Thursday. Don't make public." Furthermore he took along the girl whom Robert was, in 1868, to marry, Mary Harlan, daughter of James Harlan, newly appointed Secretary of the Interior. Mary's father and mother, old friends from Illinois, were in the party too.

Another explanation of the trip, made by Washingtonians, was that the President was evading Congressmen, those pests who had been begging favors around his desk ever since the beginning of his second term on March 4.

Still others said Lincoln wanted to feast his eyes on the fruits of the long-awaited victory.

People in Washington were always explaining Lincoln's actions like that. He seemed so simple and transparent, so artless and plain in everything he did, that many important dignitaries around him thought him utterly obvious, a good, kind, meandering man. That he could be brooding and hatching plots behind that gentle Oriental face of his was unbelievable to the pretentious schemers of Washington in the '60's.

That he could be going down to City Point on a mission, secretive, shrewd, and extremely practical, was evidently not suspected.

As a matter of fact he had been forced to play practical politics ever since his first election in 1860. Through both terms of office he had been plotting to save the Union. In '61 eleven Southern States were out of the Union, seceding, declaring themselves free from hateful comradeship with Northern commonwealths. As they withdrew, many Yankees had thrown up their hands like frightened spinsters repeating Horace Greeley's editorial theme, "Erring sisters, depart in peace." But not Lincoln. He said that there could be but one nation, not two. If need be, war would hold the Southern States to their rightful places in the Union. Secession was unlawful.

Four border-commonwealths had wavered, looking over the fence at their eleven sisters capering across the hills. To hold these doubting States in the Union, the President had used both war and politics, mostly politics, and had won. War was another man's game to Lincoln; politics was his own old trade, and at it he had worsted, prodigiously, his rival Jefferson Davis, President of the seceded States. Not only had he kept the border States from joining the Confederacy, he had pried loose a great area of Virginia, proudest of those States, splitting it off, draping it with the Stars and Stripes, and giving it Statehood under the name of West Virginia.

At war, however, there was more for Lincoln to learn. It was a new trade for him, who was a conciliator by nature, having been a famous peace-maker, as a youth, among the lusty, pugnacious frontiersmen. As a lawyer, too, he had habitually urged compromise upon litigants, obtaining so many settlements out of court that his own pocketbook had suffered. To become a warrior at fifty-two years of age was a task indeed, and, to make his lot harder, there were no military geniuses ready at hand for him to lean upon. The South had wooed away the most promising soldier of the regular army, Robert E. Lee, winning him over to the service of his State, Virginia. From the start, the Confederacy had leaders who were capable military men, desperate and eager for victory, such men as Lincoln must hunt for hopelessly across two and one half years of wretchedness.

In that time Lincoln had sent three magnificent blue-clad armies down into Virginia to capture Richmond, and three times he had seen them roll back in defeat. Twice he had seen gray armies sweep into the North on terrifying invasions, and twice he had seen his men halt them with carnage, then curiously, perhaps treacherously, mark time, dawdling and waiting while the shattered Confederates made their inexcusable escapes back to the recruiting-grounds of the South once more.

Was this always to go on? Didn't his generals want to win the war? Were they beating around the bush in the hope that the war would somehow come to a compromise, with the South returning to its former place in the Union with slavery preserved intact? Was Stanton, his war minister, right in believing that the regular army leaders did not propose to crush the enemy? Had Stanton been right in telling Senator Wilson, chairman of the Military Committee, that patriotism seemed to be lost at West Point? Was Lincoln always to be surrounded by generals who would blame their defeats upon him and his incompetence?

Behind him, in the North, was a growing disposition to howl him down as a fuddler, a muddler, a "slow-poke," a man of fatal indecisions. From the beginning such critics had kept at this clanging abuse, seeing not at all that a wise leader may sometimes win bold issues by merely muddling through.

In the third year of the war Abraham Lincoln might well have wondered where he was to find generals who would be willing to roll up their sleeves and go in to kill and kill so ruthlessly that the long, wasteful barbarism would be soon and mercifully ended.

Then on the fourth of July, 1863, as though the God to whom he prayed so endlessly might have heard him at last, two such men came out of the West, two who were half Southern, their lives centering around St. Louis, both of them loving the Union, yet not hating slavery; two who had long ago discounted their West Point training and drifted out of the army — two "no-goods" in the eyes of important people, one but lately a bibulous peddler of cord-wood, the other a school teacher suspect of lunacy.

Obscurely these two men had been rising, since 1861, in the Union Army of the Tennessee, that tough and ready legion of midland frontiersmen who cleared the western border, winning victory after victory until at Vicksburg on July 4, '63, they captured 34,000 Confederates and set the Mississippi River, "Father of Waters," going again, as Lincoln observed, "unvexed to the sea."

Here, on the anniversary of the Union's birth, were two generals for Lincoln, Grant and Sherman, the heroes of Vicksburg, two realistic, logical, resolute men who would be willing to take the job of ending the stalemate, seeing clearly that if war was to be outlawed it must be made Hell and nothing else. Quietly Lincoln lifted them to power, slipping them into the seats of his pompous tacticians and remorselessly holding them there against all the roars of the orthodox militarists and moralists, loosing them to smash and wreck as fiercely as they chose, in order that the suicidal wastage might be the quicker ended.

Through '64 they had done their work. Silent, grim little Grant, for all that his tipsiness was national gossip, had proved himself master of the "unconquerable" Robert E. Lee, genius of the Confederacy. Two "rebel" armies Grant had captured in the West, now, in March, 1865, he was about to gobble up a third, the famous Army of Northern Virginia.

And Sherman, in spite of what the newspapers might say about his craziness, had dazzled history for all time with the most daring of military marches, gutting the deep South with fire and sword, marching and fighting, lunging onward ten miles a day through swamps, setting his falcon head ever toward the goal: "Crazy" Sherman, his brain blazing, but, somehow, cool as ice, calling signals so unerringly that his men thrilled and bucked on preposterously — the nucleus of his army still that band of lean brown midlanders, the Army of the Tennessee — marching on, laughing, with victory on their banners, hams on their bayonets, until the leader of their opponents, the shrewd little General Johnston, was, despairing, to say of them, "There has been no such army since the days of Julius Caesar."

As Lincoln looked southward from the White House in March, 1865, the end of the war was visible. Grant was hammering Lee into helplessness, the blue-clad soldiers well fed and afire with victory, the gray soldiers starving and ragged and beginning now to desert by the thousands as they saw themselves outnumbered two to one and over, their Cause doomed. To make the issue doubly certain there was Sherman with his Caesarian warriors, eighty thousand strong, crashing up through the Carolinas to join with Grant in case they should be needed.

It was not to help Grant that Lincoln went down to the battle-front. It was to help Lee.

The question in his mind was not who would win, but what the winner would do with the vanquished.

From the days of '61 Lincoln had been faced with two terrific necessities, one immediate, the other lurking on the horizon. First, he must overthrow the Confederacy, show the Secessionists that their notion about a State having the right to leave the Union was wrong; second, when the Southerners were whipped, he must get them back into the Republic in such a frame of mind as would permit them to become loyal Unionists with all possible speed.

To accomplish his first purpose he must keep the North fighting-mad, but not so angry that it would torture and persecute the Southerners once their armies had collapsed.

It was a delicate job, and to handle it, he, cleverest diplomat of his time, had been forced to make himself to all intents and purposes dictator of the nation. Only a dictator could so marshal the national forces as to win military victory, and, more to the point, no one but a dictator could save the South from spoliation in the hour of its surrender.

In March, 1865, his first necessity was gone. The Confederacy was palpably done. But his second problem, less simple, was upon him.

His first-line enemies now were not the gray-clad armies, but the black-clad Radicals of his own party, a little group of willful Republicans who had banded themselves together to see that the victorious North was not cheated out of the fruits of victory.

This little cabal saw red. In its ranks were fanatical Sadists who wanted to hang the "rebel" leaders; in its ranks, too, were fanatics of a nobler breed, "Abolitionists" who demanded that everything North or South be sacrificed to the great cause of negro citizenship. It was the "dusky brother," not the Union, that claimed their warm hearts.

With the Sadists, in this Radical group, Lincoln had no sympathy; the Abolitionists he understood but distrusted, as they distrusted him.

If he were to make the Union one again, he must outwit both factions of these headstrong zealots who made common cause against him.

Few in numbers were these Radicals, yet powerful in influence with politicians, brilliant of tongue, capable of whipping up dangerous passions.

At their head was Charles Sumner, the learned and august Senator from Massachusetts, who could command, at a word, the opinion of educated and cultured "respectables" of New England. Beside him ranged "Bluff" Ben Wade, Senator from Ohio, brave, narrow, righteously fuming against "traitors," himself a disappointed aspirant for Lincoln's chair — Ben Wade, idol of the Abolitionists who dotted his State. Flanking these two was Zachariah Chandler, Senator from Michigan — Chandler of the hard mouth and passionate sympathies, fearless aid to fugitive negroes as they traveled over "the underground railroad" to Canada — Chandler, who had said before the war, "without a little blood-letting this Union will not be worth a rush." In the House of Representatives sat Thaddeus Stevens, most forceful man in that body, old, crippled, cruel, despising Lincoln's soft heart — Stevens, able to cry Pennsylvania to fury against slaveholders even though he made no concealment of a mulatto mistress in his own Washington home — Stevens, sardonic, mocking at "aristocracy," bold, not caring if his wig be set straight upon his head or not. Close by hovered Henry Winter Davis, Maryland Abolitionist of flaming tongue and scholarly invective, spell-binding, "the master avenger," as his admirers nicknamed him — Davis, ready and competent, for all his known lack of consistency, to juggle mobs and issues like magic. In Lincoln's own Cabinet the Radicals had at least one representative for almost four years, Salmon P. Chase, Secretary of the Treasury, Pecksniffian, contemptuous of Lincoln, yet a rock of strength to the President, with his financial skill and force.

Strong, bitter men were these leaders, skillful enough to convince lesser politicians that Lincoln was not the man for the

Republican party to renominate for President in the convention that would come in June, 1864.

He was too weak, they said; he had fumbled the war, spent oceans of blood, and had accomplished nothing. One term was enough for anybody, said the Radicals as they bullied the lesser politicians into line. No other President in the last generation had tried to succeed himself. Lincoln was trying to be King in the Republic!

But these "leading minds" found, when time came to nominate a candidate, that they led none but the politicians, Congressmen, Senators, and prominent party wheel-horses. The voters were out of hand. The masses wanted Lincoln, insisted upon him with an overwhelming demand, and so there was nothing for the Radicals to do but sneer at the "idiotic people" while the delegates renominated the President on the first ballot, almost unanimously.

Lincoln's enemies had suffered notable casualties, too, in the rout. Henry Winter Davis had been retired from the House of Representatives by his Maryland constituents as penalty for having savagely accused Lincoln's administration with being too gently disposed toward the eventual readmission of Southern States. However, Davis was around the Capitol as a "lame duck" and, later, lobbyist for vengeance, thinking up bitter things for Ben Wade to shout.

Salmon P. Chase, the great Radical of the Cabinet, had been lost to the anti-Lincoln cabal also. While sitting among the President's ministers, Chase had campaigned against his chief for the Presidential nomination, and to his support the "bitter-enders" had brought up their forces. But to no purpose. His own State, Ohio, choosing delegates to the national convention, thumbed Chase down most unmercifully, and in June he resigned his Secretaryship of the Treasury and retired, only to find himself, in December, kicked upstairs into the post of Chief Justice of the United States Supreme Court.

Such a dramatic move as this appointment meant one of two things, perhaps a little of both: Lincoln, in the philosophic largeness of his intellect, knew Chase to be the right man for the judgeship, or he wanted to shift a powerful enemy out of the political arena. At any rate Lincoln lifted his rival up on to the high shelf where he would be no bother in the battle that would come over Reconstruction.

All of these matters enraged the Radicals, but none of these casualties was quite so distressing as the insult Lincoln had given the sacred Republican party at the June convention, when, under his dictatorship, the very name of the party itself had been modified to include the words, "The National Union Party." Careless of the holy traditions of abolition, sectionalism, and anti-slaveryism that enshrined the word "Republican," Lincoln had chosen to emphasize the spirit contained in that new and broader name, making the party one of coalition with conservative Northern Democrats and border-State Unionists. He was out to corral the votes of all men who believed in the Union regardless of previous party affiliation.

To make his coalition plans even plainer he had dictated that his running-mate on the ticket should be a Southern Democrat, Andrew Johnson, military governor of Tennessee, a consecrated Union man, to be sure, but a Southerner — a horrible thing in the eyes of the Radicals.

"Why should they take a man from that damned little rebel territory?" snarled Thaddeus Stevens, stamping his club-foot, and few of his fellow Radicals could feel resentment during the campaign when the Democratic party, fighting for control of the North and a possible peace with the South, assailed the Republican ticket as one of "gawks, rail-splitters, and tailors." Andrew Johnson had been a tailor in his youth, a "poor white" of the Southern under-dog strata, illiterate until his wife had taught him to read.

Furthermore, the "avengers" could not be as angry as were their bed-fellows, the pro-Lincoln Republicans, when the Democrats centered their campaign fire against the President's character — charges which the Rev. Henry Clay Dean, an Iowa Copperhead, epitomized in his speech from the platform of the Democratic Presidential convention in Chicago that August.

"With all his vast armies Lincoln has failed, *failed,* FAILED, FAILED!" screamed the dominie. "And still the monster usurper wants more victims for his slaughter pens. I blush that such a felon should occupy the highest gift of the people. Perjury and larceny are written all over him. Ever since the usurper, traitor and tyrant has occupied the Presidential chair, the Republican party has shouted war to the knife and knife to the hilt. Blood has flowed in torrents, and yet the thirst of the old monster is not quenched. His cry is ever for more blood."

In spite of all the secret pleasure they derived from hearing the opposition denounce Lincoln, the Radicals had not enjoyed the year, 1864, what with the President's consistent flouting of the professional politicians and his indorsement by those fools, the common people. They had one great hope remaining. When the war was over, as it seemed certain to be, they could wreak vengeance upon the vanquished "rebels." The minute Lee was down, they would try to leap upon him and either wring his neck or bundle him off to another St. Helena, far outside the land of that family connection of his, George Washington.

Ever since the days in '61 when Lee, with so many officers of the United States army and navy, had resigned their Federal commissions to go South and join the Secessionists, the Radicals of the North had demanded that such fellows should be hanged or exiled when caught. They had broken their oaths of allegiance to the nation, it was declared, and their defense that they owed a prior loyalty to their States was mere claptrap and buncombe. Unless they were rigorously punished the nation would never be safe from treason.

All through the war Lincoln had let this bloody cry go on, evidently deciding that such transparent nonsense served a useful purpose in keeping up war fervor. But it is even more evident that he had concluded that, when the time should come, he would allow no "treason" trials nor hangings of men like Lee who had merely read the Constitution differently from men like himself. Such men might be political prisoners, but never criminals.

However, as was his way, he said nothing about his lenient views in this regard, obviously perceiving that if he announced any such gentleness of purpose he would weaken himself with the voters and discourage the "war-to-the-finish" sentiment which must be kept at fever-heat if the conflict was to be won and the Union saved.

So, in December, 1863, he compromised, "foxing" the Radicals, jollying them along. In that month he issued an order of amnesty and forgiveness to the "rebels," proclaiming his readiness to pardon all surrendering Secessionists except those of certain specified classes, namely; all who had been officers of the "so-called Confederate Government" above the rank of colonel in the army or of lieutenant in the navy; all civil or diplomatic officials of the rebellion; all persons who had deserted posts in the United States Congress, judiciary, army or navy to aid the enemy; and all who had failed to treat colored soldiers and sailors of the Union as lawful prisoners of war when captured.

What punishment he would deal out to these groups of "rebels," Lincoln didn't say, although the implication was plain that they would not escape so easily as would the rank and file of the "secesh" peoples. As he expected, the matter did not come to a decision, since no Southerners accepted his offer. But he allowed it to stand, a promise to the Union "avengers" that the Confederate leaders should not go scot-free when the end should come. It was still standing in March, 1865, when signs of Southern collapse grew plentiful.

On the third of that month Grant telegraphed Lincoln that Lee was feeling around for terms of surrender. The President, receiving the message in a White House that was jammed with politicians arriving for the morrow's inauguration ceremonies, wrote out a reply which he gave to Stanton, his war minister, to send: "The President directs me to say that he wishes you to have no conference with General Lee unless it be for capitulation of General Lee's army, or on some minor or purely military matter. He instructs me to say that you are not to decide, discuss, or confer upon any political questions. Such questions the President holds in his own hands, and will submit them to no military conferences or conventions. Meanwhile you are to press to your utmost your military advantages."

There could be but one construction put upon this message by the Radicals as they read it or heard it discussed: the President was not going to grant full and immediate immunity to Confederate leaders when they flew the white flag. His telegram hinted that the question as to what would be done with oath-breakers was too important to be decided post-haste at some battlefield surrender.

Like the terms of his amnesty offer in '63, this order obviously reassured the Radicals that something was going to be done about punishing the arch Secessionists. And in his inauguration address on the next day, March 4, there were more signs, clearer and stronger, that he was coming around to a point somewhat nearer their program. Lincoln had begun this speech with his usual calmness, discussing the causes of the war with dispassion and declaring that its progress had been reasonably satisfactory and encouraging. But, in the latter half of this short address, the high, slow voice of the speaker had sent out words that surely comforted the Radicals.

The first hint that Lincoln might be leaning toward their opinion of "rebels" came when he said: "It may seem strange that any men should dare to ask a just God's assistance in wringing their bread from the sweat of other men's faces, but let us judge not that we be not judged."

Despite the gentle ending to the sentence, there was in its body an implication, to the Radicals, that Lincoln might not be so far away from their view of slaveholders, after all.

And there seemed to be no question at all about the President's conversion to a strong, hard peace, when he said a moment later: "Fondly do we hope, fervently do we pray, that this mighty scourge of war may speedily pass away. Yet if God wills that it shall continue until all the wealth piled by the bondsman's two hundred and fifty years of unrequited toil shall be sunk, and until every drop of blood drawn with the lash shall be paid by another drawn with the sword, as was said three thousand years ago, so still it must be said, The judgments of the Lord are true and righteous altogether."

To listening Radicals who hungered for the impoverishment of the South and the spilling of "rebel" blood in payment for the twin crimes of Slavery and Secession, these words of Lincoln's spoke glad volumes.

It was, indeed, the one frank approach that Lincoln had made to the policy of vengeance, and not even his words that followed, asking his hearers to strive on with malice toward none and charity for all, could counteract, for the Radicals, the effect of his solemn mention of "blood" and "the lash" and "the sword." True enough, he had not committed himself to any definite program of Reconstruction, but he had given the avengers hope. It was no time to provoke them. The moment was at hand when peace and conciliation should fill the air.

Lincoln, with the Radicals that day, was like a doctor who fools distraught patients with soothing promises that he knows can never, in wisdom, be kept.

His inaugural over, the President said no more about the issue, letting the Radicals quiet down if they would.

Then on March 23, with his wife and little boy, he sailed for the war front, free, for the time being, as has been said, from politicians.

Also, he wanted to get away from his Cabinet.

That group of men, who could never quite decide whether the President was a very deep man with a simple face or a very simple man with mysterious silences, had, in February, unanimously opposed his kindly plan to pay the Southern States $400,000,000 for their slaves. In the war zone Lincoln intended to be free from these ministers, and in a few days, when Seward, his Secretary of State, came rushing down with some important matters, Lincoln promptly sent him home, at which the other secretaries took the hint, remaining away.

In the "lordly" James River, just off City Point where Grant and his staff had their headquarters, the *River Queen*, the Presidential steamship, anchored, where, in the days and nights that followed, was heard the sound of distant guns.

Down the gangplank each day the tall, stooping President, more enormous than ever in his long coat and high hat, went ashore to visit the soldiers in their camps and trenches, to shake hands with the wounded, and to look at the guns, forts, and prisoners that had been captured. It was plain that he was just wandering around on a visit.

He saw his son Robert, the twenty-two-year-old who had

spent all but three months of the war in Harvard University and who had sat, since January, as a belated captain on Grant's personal staff.

The boy had wanted to enlist all along, and his father, knowing that Lee's three sons were on the battlefront also thought that Robert should go, but the mother objected, saying that he would be more useful to the Cause if he concluded his education before enlisting. Mrs. Lincoln had already lost two sons in infancy, Eddie in Springfield, Willie in the White House, and since her sanity was always a matter of tender concern to her husband, he had feared that her reason would topple altogether if she saw her eldest boy, Robert, in danger. So Lincoln shielded his son, and the North, remembering how many other mothers' sons he had pardoned, held its tongue.

For days Lincoln roamed around the camp, telling anecdotes to roaring officers about the evening fires or riding through acres of cheering soldiers. (He looked strangely graceful on horseback.)

To all intents and purposes he was merely a man feeling good about how things were going.

In reality he was waiting for Sherman. Down in North Carolina, where he was maneuvering wily Joe Johnston and his battered Confederates into a pocket, Sherman had received word to come up to City Point for a conference with Grant. And, although he didn't like to leave his approaching victory, Sherman went.

On the twenty-seventh he was at City Point and, with Grant, came to the *River Queen.*

Lincoln gathered his two trusted warriors in the cabin and shut the door. Exactly what he said to them has never been made plain by history, both Grant and Sherman having been forever after evasive concerning it.

Twice the President and his marshals were closeted, then the two fighting men went back to their work, Sherman to North Carolina to finish Joe Johnston in two weeks' time, Grant to his task of squeezing Lee out of his Richmond trenches onto the road that was to end at Appomattox eleven days later.

From the deck of the *River Queen* Lincoln saw them go, and

sat, biding his time, waiting, to all appearances, not so much like a President of the United States as like some gentle and gigantic Oriental mandarin in whose heart there could be no guile.

In effect, President Lincoln, in the cabin of the *River Queen,* had given secret orders for one of the most cunning examples of the "double-cross" that the whole range of American politics, before or after him, could show. Up in the North, the Radicals and "master avengers," ignorant of this cabin conference, might be licking their chops all they liked, tasting already the blood of "rebel" leaders. Did they but know it, all such dreams were hopeless.

The "gawk" politician had "fixed the case." What happened in the days that followed argued that.

It will be remembered that Lincoln in '63 had exempted certain "rebels" from pardon, and that on the third of March, '64, he had publicly ordered Grant to refrain from deciding any political question; yet when Grant and Sherman, in April, wrote out the terms for Confederate surrender, they nullified the '63 edict entirely and damaged in varying degrees the '64 injunction. The parole given by Grant guaranteed *all* officers, as well as the men, freedom from civil or military prosecution as long as they obeyed the parole and their local laws. Sherman understood this to mean "a pardon," and in his turn guaranteed not only amnesty to soldiers but political, personal and property rights to the Southern people in general.

And each general acted with a confidence that could only have come from a belief that he was carrying out what he had understood Lincoln to mean on the *River Queen.* Both generals were trained military men, exact in executing orders and were, moreover, of proven clarity in grasping the meaning of verbal orders.

To the masses, both South and North, the surrender-terms, as they were first made public, had been apparently coined by Sherman and Grant on their respective battlefields, and Sherman was bitterly denounced for "traitorous leniency" to the defeated foe when his terms reached Washington, arriving, as they did, in an atmosphere of such hysteria over Lincoln's death that they were immediately rejected. To the Radicals of the North, however, it must have been plain that Lincoln was the guilty man; the lawyer-politician of the frontier had, for the occasion, gone back into his past and brought out an old device with which to trick his party foes.

Lee went free as the wind on the ninth of April, and how the Radicals howled to see him go! Even the Vice-President of the Republic, Andrew Johnson, ran to Lincoln, protesting against so weak a peace. Lincoln could do nothing. It was too late. Grant had given Lee his word.

Much good it did the "bitter-enders" to denounce the peace as one without victory. Their clamor for the arrest of Lee and his brother officers was drowned in the rejoicing that swept the North.

Lincoln was to hear the loyal States in hysterical elation hurl his name to the stars, cheering for him, for his man, Grant, for Peace, and for Mercy.

Lincoln was the king of victory, the king who had done no wrong.

"Peace on earth, good will toward men," sang joyous mobs in the streets, nobody listening any more to the ravings of the Radicals who could only gnash their teeth and groan. The enemies of Lincoln and Lee had been cheated of their prey, and all they had left to comfort them was the tragic knowledge that they had, at last, after many lessons, learned how politics was played in the backwoods of Illinois.

☆ ☆ ☆ 4 ☆ ☆ ☆

"JUST A FRIEND FROM ILLINOIS"

THE PRESIDENT OF THE UNITED STATES watched his generals, Grant and Sherman, leave the *River Queen* in those late March days of 1865, and, as has been said, waited, knowing that his wires were laid.

Still, the statesman, embarked now upon the stealthiest political game of his career, could not be idle. He must fix things so that the negro question should be as slight a barrier to Reconstruction as possible. There the sharpest rub would come. Only profound diplomacy could win.

On the first of April, three days after the departure of Sherman, Mrs. Lincoln left the *River Queen*, returning to Washington, where, the moment she arrived, she began assembling a party of guests to accompany her back, on the fifth, to City Point. And the first of all, whom she invited, was Charles Sumner, the leader of the Radicals himself. For years both Mary Todd Lincoln and her husband had plied the great dissenter with flowers and invitations, Sumner taking it as a kindly tribute of backwoods people to his learning and power, others, in the light of history, taking it as a shrewd attempt by the Lincolns to work the New England Senator away from his bitter opposition to the Presidential policy of eventual Reconstruction.

Since long before the war, Sumner had tortured the South with Jehovic taunts and sneers, learned, intellectual sneers that could only be answered with blows. Scholarly and masterly of invective as he was, he had maddened the Southerners with scorching charges that they, the vaunted knights of aristocracy and chivalry, were only wretched decadents and mock Ivanhoes so long as they clung to the institution of slavery, which civilization and morality had long ago outlawed. And here at the end of the war was Sumner still more concerned over justice to the negro than over peace to the Union. From the start of the fighting the Abolitionists, who were consecrated to the freeing of the slaves, no matter if it wrecked the Constitution, had claimed Sumner for their leader and had toward the end of the war found themselves, in spite of their dislike of vengeance toward the Southern people, politically united with the vindictive Radicals.

Just as the bitter-enders feared that Lincoln would fail to punish "traitors," so the more humane Abolitionists feared that he would fail to lift the negro to his full citizenship.

Anti-slavery men felt that the Emancipation Proclamation, which had merely freed the slaves in Secession territory, had not done its work until every ex-slave in the land was marching to the polls. This happy consummation must come at all costs the minute the war was over.

Lincoln, who knew the South, had no such ideas. He felt compassion for the negro, a sense of outrage at the institution of slavery, but he did not propose to let either his sentiments or hatreds complicate his main task, his big job of piecing the Union together again.

Consequently, without much consideration for the slaves or the Abolitionists or for Congress itself, he began, in December, 1863, to dictate the terms under which the South might return to the Republic. These terms he included in that offer of amnesty which pleased the Radicals by excepting from pardon all "rebels" who had broken their oath of allegiance to the national government. But if Lincoln's plan hinted that he might follow the Radicals in dealing with the Confederate chieftains, it broke with them on the negro question.

To each Confederate State Lincoln's offer was clear, saying in substance, "Call an election of your white voters under your old laws of 1860, and if one-tenth of them turn out and vote to establish a State government that will quit Secession, return to the Union, take the oath of allegiance, and abide by the Emancipation Proclamation which freed the slaves, I will recognize you as a State in the Republic again."

It looked simple, but there was a black man, indeed, hidden in its innocent pile of wood.

To the Radicals this portion of Lincoln's offer seemed ruinous, for it neglected to make the Southerners "eat crow" as part of their penalty for having "rebelled." What the Northern "avengers" wanted was for each Southern State to get down on its knees in admission that slavery was wrong and, in that contrite posture, to pass State laws giving citizenship, the vote, and complete equality to its ex-slaves. When those things had been done the "irreconcilables" would consider restoring the erring States to their former places in the Union.

Lincoln, with that instinct for mass-feeling which had served him so well in politics, knew how cruel a revenge it would be to compel each Southern State to enfranchise all its former slaves so soon after defeat on the battlefield. He knew the bitterness that such an iron demand would kindle in Southern hearts and how many delays it would cause. Better to welcome the wandering sisters home without quibbles as to where they had been or in what clothes they presented themselves, and then, once they were at the fireside again, coax them with gentle persuasions to clean their garments. That blot of slavery which stained their skirts had been placed there by the North as well as by the South, he thought.

He was for making reunion easy—too easy, the Radicals cried as they pictured the situation to the voters in something of this fashion:

"Look at Lincoln; he is offering to make peace without victory! This war is not only to free the negro, but to make him the equal of the white man as well. We say that no Southern State shall be allowed back in the Union until it has by its own votes freed the negro and made him the equal of his old master in every way. This man Lincoln is a pro-Southerner at heart, he's pro-slavery under his skin."

Through December and January, 1864, the Radicals massed their forces to drive Lincoln from his merciful position on Reconstruction. To them it was vital that Lincoln be forced to abandon his lenient program before the end of the war should come.

What maddened them was the apparent fact that Lincoln was going to make peace with the South himself, ignoring all the advice and rights of Congress. He frankly said as much, declaring that Congress had no right to dictate what the returning States should do about slavery. That was a matter for himself as commander of the army and navy to decide. He was responsible for the conduct of the war, and this was a war measure just as the Emancipation Proclamation had been a war measure. It was the old battle between Lincoln and the politicians again, Lincoln still not trusting the politicians to deal fairly with the South.

The attack of the "avengers" came with Henry Winter Davis acting as the spear-head. In the House, Davis brought up a bill to knock out Lincoln's amnesty program, for while the Radicals approved of that program's implied hostility toward Southern leaders, they thought that its "pro-slavery" demerits vastly outweighed its good points. Davis' bill said to each Southern State, "Call an election of your white voters, and if a *majority* of them vote to draft a loyal constitution that will abolish slavery forever, we will let you back into the Union."

Where Lincoln's program would readmit a State on the vote of only 10 per cent. of its white voters, Davis' plan required a majority of those suffrages. Lincoln would let a State return without having done anything more for the negro than to admit silently that he was henceforth free; Davis would insist that the State first pass laws giving the ex-slave entire equality.

The difference between the two programs was monumental to the "irreconcilables," and the House, speedily followed by the Senate, passed Davis' bill, bringing it to the President on July 2, 1864, two days before Congress was to adjourn.

Were the Radicals to win? They had whipped the politicians into line against the President, and in a national campaign-time, too.

Lincoln, with a cool indifference that drove his enemies frantic, stuffed the bill in his pocket and let it die, neither signing it nor vetoing it, and not even bothering to argue about the matter, merely saying offhand that there was no time for him to study it properly or give it his decision before Congress adjourned.

Again Lincoln had served notice upon the Radicals and their politician herd that he didn't want to quarrel with them, but the facts were that he and the people were running the government. What were they going to do about it?

Calmly he proceeded along his original plan, just as though Congress had not disagreed.

Down in Louisiana, where his army overran a good third of the State and where considerable pro-Union sentiment had grown, he had been working to set up a sort of sample State which could serve as a working model for all other States when they decided to give up and come home.

He had ordered his soldiers to call an election in February of that year '64. One-fifth of the total number of voters had come to the polls, a response far better than his stipulated one-tenth. They had voted to form a loyal State, take the oath of allegiance, and accept the fact that slaves were free, but had done nothing about awarding the ballot to the colored man.

True enough, at Lincoln's suggestion they had empowered their Legislature, when it should convene, to permit a slender fraction of ex-slaves to vote. Lincoln's idea was to enfranchise the "very intelligent" negroes and those who had served in the Union army, a pitiful number it was true, but still a start along the road of gradual enfranchisement which he hoped the South would take.

This Louisiana plan came up to Congress in February, 1865, begging that the State be admitted on such a basis.

Lincoln, careless how the Southern States got back into the Union so long as they *got* back, pushed the appeal. The main thing with him was to get the defeated States on their feet as fast as they took the oath of allegiance, and here was a beginning. What if it was only a mock State that came begging? It was better than none.

But Charles Sumner, who had been silent the previous summer when Ben Wade and Henry Winter Davis had railed at Lincoln, "the tyrant," for scheming to organize "rebel" States with his army and thus command more votes for his personal political machine — Sumner now unlimbered his guns.

He stormed on to the floor, like a madman, thundering "No" — the main thing was to make the negro a citizen and a voter. No "rebel" State should be allowed to return until it had made every slave equal to his white master in everything.

If you let Lincoln's hand-made State of Louisiana come in as it is now constituted, said Sumner, you will admit that the war has been fought in vain.

Sumner's filibuster worked. Again Congress sided with the Radicals against the President, and Lincoln, seeing that he was whipped, withdrew Louisiana's plea and let it die. He wanted no open fight with a powerful faction of his party at a time when the South was likely any day to fall.

Lincoln had been defeated, but he had weathered defeat before this, and in his bag of prairie tricks were more ways than one to skin this particular political cat. He would wait for some better opening in which to fix upon the South his easy scheme for a partial enfranchisement of the negro.

Although Sumner's victory had cut him sharply, Lincoln hid

his disappointment like the philosopher that he was, and chose to nurse the pompous Abolitionist along with friendship and bouquets. Eight days after the disaster he had picked no one in the world but Sumner himself to escort Mrs. Lincoln, as the second couple in line, at the grand inauguration ball.

And here, five weeks after the affair, he was preparing to entertain the Senator at City Point, possibly thinking that a trip down to the war zone would do the man's bitter mind some good.

On the day that his wife was assembling her party in Washington, Lincoln was keeping close to Grant, visiting him at Petersburgh, where the Union troops had finally sliced through the Confederate breastworks to force Lee out into the open; and on the next day Lincoln entered the abandoned capital of the Confederacy, Richmond, the city toward which he had been spurring his generals since 1861.

With only ten sailors and four officers to guard him, he walked into the burning citadel, leading by the hand Tad, his twelve-year-old, tongue-tied son. A mile and a half he strode through chaos with sobbing, exulting negroes kneeling about him, calling him God. The streets were full of drunken Confederates, but he was unmolested, striding on as easily as when in Illinois he had walked through the woods twenty miles for a book.

In the Secessionists' White House he sat him down, joyous as a boy, in Jefferson Davis' chair, which was as yet scarcely cold from the exasperated body of the executive who had fled from it. He drove for a time about the city, examining the stronghold that had once seemed so impregnable; then he bethought himself of a prairie acquaintance whom he'd like to see again after many years. In Richmond, he recalled, lived General George Pickett, who had sided with the South and who had led that bloodiest, wildest charge of the war at Gettysburg. Lincoln had obtained a West Point cadetship for him in other years. Perhaps Pickett was among the paroled. Lincoln asked to be shown his home, and when it was reached, he walked up and rang the bell.

A woman answered. No, General Pickett was not at home. Who should she say had called?

"Oh," said Lincoln, "just tell him it was a friend of his from Illinois."

So he came back to headquarters. There the assistant Secretary of State for the Confederacy wanted to see him, — Judge J. A. Campbell, one-time justice of the United States Supreme Court, an anti-slavery man who had, like Lee, sadly followed his State out of the Union in '61. Campbell was no man to run away like Jefferson Davis and the rest. He would stay and get his State back into the Union. For months he had been advising surrender, facing the blunt fact that a hundred thousand men had, in hopelessness, deserted the gray ranks.

A frank political deal Campbell offered to Lincoln. Promise not to confiscate Virginia property, deal mercifully with us, he said, and the Old Dominion will quit. Lincoln told him that while it wouldn't be right for him to offer a pardon to Jefferson Davis, almost any other Southerner could have anything of the kind he wanted. Campbell proposed that Lincoln allow the Virginia Legislature to meet in Richmond; there it would repeal the ordinance of Secession and command its troops to lay down their arms. Lee would have to surrender. To such a plan Lincoln agreed, instructing his officers to permit such an assemblage — a rash and ruinous thing to do, according to the Radicals, who tore their hair when they heard of it, damning Lincoln for having recognized a secession form of government. As a matter of fact Judge Campbell, in issuing the call, did give this interpretation to Lincoln's order, and the President was forced to revoke his offer. But it mattered little, since by that time Lee had surrendered, and the incident was remembered only because it pointed the extraordinary lengths to which Lincoln would stretch his power to hasten gentle reconstruction.

During the day and night that Lincoln remained in Richmond he talked to other Virginians besides Judge Campbell and assured them that he would make peace generously.

"You need not love Virginia less, only love the Union more," was the gist of his words to them.

His plan for easing the Southerners back into the Republic was working.

On the following day he returned to the *River Queen* to meet the party that his wife was bringing down from Washington. They must see the captured entrenchments. Into a special car he put them when they had arrived, and without a word of explanation, placed among such distinguished guests the humble negro waiters of the *River Queen*. The colored boys wished to see where their late masters had met Waterloo, and Lincoln included them in his sightseeing party. The elegant Marquis de Chambrun, Sumner's friend whom Mrs. Lincoln had invited to come down to the front, thought this inclusion of the negroes a sample of Lincoln's immense humanity.

More likely it was a sample of Lincoln's political sagacity, his way of showing Abolitionist Sumner how the President really felt toward the black man.

How far did Lincoln plan to go with his merciful schemings? Did he expect to remain on the ground and personally handle the surrender of Lee, who had now been caught a little way outside Richmond in Grant's ring of bayonets, to which he must sooner or later submit?

If so, accident intervened. Up in Washington, Seward, most sympathetic of all the Cabinet toward Lincoln's policy of mercy, had been thrown from his carriage and lay bedfast with a broken jaw. Lincoln must hurry home. Before he went he toured the hospitals, shaking hands with thousands of wounded men, saying afterward that it hadn't tired him at all. Either on that day or shortly before, he took a drive with Mrs. Lincoln along the banks of the James. They stopped at a country graveyard, green with Spring. They walked among the headstones. "Mary," he said, "you are younger than I. You will survive me. When I am gone, lay my remains in some quiet place like this."

Toward evening on April 8 he boarded the *River Queen* with his guests and waited on the deck as the engineers made up steam for the return to Washington. Sundown was in the air. A military band hurried to the pier to serenade the chief, and was asked by Lincoln to play the "Marseillaise" for the Marquis. That done, the President asked the musicians to play "Dixie," which, in amazement, they did.

"The tune is Federal property now and, besides, it is good to show the rebels that with us they will be free to hear it again," said Lincoln to Chambrun.

At ten o'clock they sailed.

All night the *River Queen* steamed up Chesapeake Bay.

The next day was Sunday, full of that same quiet that was surrounding Grant as he jogged along the road out to Appomattox Court House and the gray general who waited for him there. In the sunlight the steamer came up the Potomac that was now more peaceful than in four past years. In the cabin Lincoln sat with his guests, talking not of war nor peace but of William Shakespeare. Beside him sat his wife; near her, Sumner, the handsome bachelor, also the elegant Marquis, and three or four others — friends and political supporters.

"A small family party" Lincoln felt it to be, and he slumped comfortably in his chair, his knees rising before him, his long, dark fingers holding a finely bound copy of Shakespeare's plays, out of which he read hour after hour.

There may have been no reason worth noting for Lincoln's enormous interest in Shakespeare that day. Still, it would have been like him to hold the conversation to some such neutral and impersonal ground as literature. Perhaps he chose this way of keeping Sumner from discussing the Reconstruction upon which they differed so widely. To be shut up in a tiny cabin with so arrogant a personality was a situation requiring tact indeed.

At any rate the great issue between the two men was kept slumbering this whole day while the talk ran on books and what the authors of books had meant to say.

In *Macbeth*, his favorite play, Lincoln read longest, his thin voice coming, in time, to that verse:

> *"Duncan is in his grave.*
> *After life's fitful fever he sleeps well;*
> *Treason has done its worst; not steel nor poison,*
> *Malice domestic, foreign levy, nothing*
> *Can touch him further."*

Lincoln read it, then stopped. The passage had caught him. What thoughts it had set stirring in him no one knows. Still, it is not difficult to guess. To him, too, life had been a fitful fever.

Fifty-six years before, he had been born to grinding poverty, and he had grown up in trouble. Debts, bashful failures at love, pathetic doubts about his mother's and his own legitimacy of birth, political defeats, had tortured his young manhood. "Malice domestic" had never been his, but harassments domestic had clung to him, for the woman whom he loved and who loved him had a fiery scolding way with her that could be managed only with tolerant persuasion. Across four years of war he had listened to the scalding abuse of the people whom he was trying to save, the sneers of foreign nations, libeling him as a baboon, a clown, a bloody monster. He had worn himself thin, his incredible strength was beginning to melt, and — he had never slept well in the White House.

No wonder, now that he had emerged triumphant above his enemies, he stopped and brooded over that verse of Shakespeare's.

But he made no application of the speech to himself when he lowered the book and began to talk to his listeners. Instead he rambled slowly into thoughts about how true it was that a murderer must always come to envy the sleep of his victim.

Then he raised the book and read the passage again.

A natural thing it was, this rereading of these particular words; yet as his guests remembered it afterward, it seemed strange and mysterious, for within a week Lincoln was to be dead with a bullet through the back of his head, life's fitful fever over, and sleeping all too well in the White House at last. And the Marquis de Chambrun, civilized and cultured, would be wondering like any superstitious woodsman whether the President had been caught by the strange beauty of that verse or whether he had sensed in it some vague presentiment of his own doom.

Even in that bright sunshine of April that lay on the *River Queen* the mists had begun to gather around Abraham Lincoln. Soon the altar-fires of the Republic would be kindled in his worship and the American folk in their fancy would be picturing him as a blessed and sorrowful deity who had foreseen his own end with supernatural eye.

Day was dying as the steamer docked off Washington, and the Lincolns, Sumner, and the Marquis de Chambrun drove home together.

Ahead lay the capital, and all at once, Mrs. Lincoln, who had been silent for some time, burst out in that headlong rashness of hers, "That city is full of our enemies!"

Rarely had Lincoln lost his temper with Mary Todd, choosing silence as the one road to marital peace, but he broke out now, evidently provoked beyond endurance that his wife should so easily forget the necessity of wooing Sumner away from all thoughts of "enemies."

In exasperation he raised his arm and his voice: "Enemies! We must never speak of that!"

☆ ☆ ☆ 5 ☆ ☆ ☆

"A SHIP SAILING RAPIDLY"

SOON AFTER ABRAHAM LINCOLN, on this Sunday evening, had returned to the White House from a visit to the bedside of his jaw-broken Secretary of State, a messenger came tumbling in with a telegram from General Grant. The end had come! Grant, probably by way of drawing out Lincoln's last-minute wishes on the matter of capturing Jefferson Davis, added to his telegram the opinion that he might be able to capture the fleeing Confederate President.

Lincoln turned to the people about him in the White House and talked of the difficult position into which such a capture would maneuver the Administration, so busy, now, turning "rebels" loose.

But into his peaceful thoughts came his wife, again bursting out, in fiery thoughtlessness, "Don't allow him to escape the law! He must be hanged."

When his helpmeet had forgotten herself in similar fashion earlier in the evening, Lincoln had snapped her up heatedly, but now he had himself in hand and only turned a long, tragic face upon her, saying quietly, "Let us judge not that we be not judged."

He wanted no decisions to come out of the White House for a time. The people had swung his way. Good feeling was mounting each hour, and with each of these hours his strength grew greater for the battle that would come with the Radicals over Reconstruction. For the present they were cowed, overwhelmed, fearful of the President's tremendous popularity with the voters, but they would strike again when Congress convened in December. By that time mercy must be solidified as a Union policy.

Lincoln must think coolly and carefully before he replied to any of those cheering crowds that swept up to the White House every little while demanding a speech. He must not commit himself, not give his enemies any footing upon which they could crawl back into the limelight out of the pit into which he had tripped them.

He must fall back upon that old trick of his, the trick of muddling, so profound, so shrewd, so successful.

When one throng stormed so loud outside his windows that he could not deny it, he appeared for a moment, joking with them, putting them off, pretending surprise, unpreparedness, and finally slipped out of the situation by setting the band to play "Dixie."

The next night, Tuesday, April 11, the crowd was back, larger and more insistent than ever — "mad March hares" from all over the city pouring in upon the White House lawn.

Slowly the President appeared on the steps, a dark wraith of the Lincoln who had come out of the prairie four years before, his face, in the flaring torchlights, sad with all the deaths his people had died, his clothes hanging on him loosely despite the craft with which he had had them made to hide his loss of thirty pounds.

Sagely, cautiously, like some ancient and humane Chinese philosopher talking to excited children, or like some patient backwoodsman trying to gentle barking dogs with cool words, he began dropping quiet, merciful thoughts into the minds that gaped open on the lawn below him.

He mentioned the joys of peace, saying nothing at all of punishment for "rebels." He spoke of God and thanksgiving, not of vengeance. It was not the cry of a conqueror.

What everybody must do now, he said, was to get the Southerners back into the Union so tactfully that they would feel that they had never been away from home at all.

"We all agree," he said soothingly, "that the seceded States, so called, are out of their proper practical relation with the Union, and that the sole object of the government, civil and military, in regard to those States, is to again get them into that proper relation. I believe that it is not only possible, but in fact easier, to do this without deciding or even considering whether these States have ever been out of the Union, than with it. Finding themselves safely at home, it would be utterly immaterial whether they had ever been abroad."

Then, so deftly and easily that few of his hearers realized what political dynamite he was juggling, he began to bring up into the open his campaign against the Radicals.

He had out-generaled them cleverly with his terms for Lee's surrender, but that victory had been achieved by stealth. Now he would commence taking the issue over their heads to the people.

He worked leisurely around to the question of Louisiana and the admission of its loyal Union minority to the Federal Government, the question upon which the "avengers" had defeated him in February. Wouldn't it be better for the future if Reconstruction were begun in this gentle, tolerant way as the Louisiana plan pointed?

"Concede that the new government of Louisiana is only what it is as the egg is to the fowl, we shall sooner have the fowl by hatching the egg than by smashing it."

The crowd which had, so far, listened in disappointment to the unexciting speech, broke out laughing at the joke about chickens, and Lincoln quickly brought the talk to a close with the good-humored word that he wasn't going to be stiff and stubborn about the question, everything was so new and unprecedented. He might have some new announcement to make to the people of the South. He was thinking things over, and would act when he was satisfied it was proper.

To the South, which had already seen that the Northern soldiers felt kindly toward them, Lincoln's words, signifying that the Northern government was going to be just as considerate, came like a last-minute pardon to a doomed prisoner. The Southerners began to see that the Radicals of the North could never force Lincoln to hang and exile "rebels," nor to take Southern property away in punishment, nor to turn the whole population over to the mercies of the ex-slaves. It dawned upon many of them that these bloody threats had come only from a loud and vicious little group in the North and that the demagogues of their own section had made such fulminations appear to represent the Northern people.

And when it realized that Lincoln, the lenient, was to be in the saddle for almost four years to come, the South felt safe. At the President's right hand sat Seward, full of a kindred generosity.

Across the three days that followed, peace and reconciliation smoothed out Mason and Dixon's line.

Slavery and Secession, those twin danger-reefs, had been blasted out of the way forever. Soon the Southern people, it seemed, could go back to those free divisions of political opinion, joining with this party or that, as they had done for eighty years before the campaign of 1860. They weren't by nature as solidly Democratic as the war had compelled them to be. Deep in them ran the old native American independence, the right of the freeborn citizens to vote as they pleased. Indeed, during the war, the Southerners had shown they had held too much of this inborn American fire for their own good, squabbling and wrangling over States' rights in the embattled Confederacy, quarreling, civil authorities against military, until their bickerings hastened the tragic collapse of their Cause.

In the gray ranks that poured homeward after the surrender were thousands and thousands of men who had loved the Union all along, men like Lee and Stonewall Jackson, who had reluctantly sided with their native States against the Federal government. Now that their debt to States' rights was paid and the issue settled, numbers of these men were ready to align themselves with new parties, perhaps even with the Republican party if it cast off the "bitter-enders" and let bygones be bygones.

Southerners, who had been Whigs before the war forced them into Democratic ranks, were ready now to quit their disagreeable bedfellows and to join some more congenial party.

In the North, too, the war-drawn party lines could loosen and allow voters to return to freer associations.

Everything was ready in the week following Lee's surrender for new line-ups, new affiliations that would speedily destroy sectionalism.

Powerful forces were compelling the masses toward fraternization. General Lee threw his influence toward friendship. So did Alexander Stephens, the adored of Georgia, Stephens with the tiny body and the broad mind, Vice-President of the Confederacy, enemy of the sourer Jefferson Davis and himself an old-time friend of Lincoln's when both had been Whig Congressmen. General Gordon, as white a knight as Lee, put his wide power into the movement.

The idols of the South were reconciled to reunion full and complete, both Lee and Stephens preparing themselves, if not ready that minute, to urge their States to accept Lincoln's plan of Reconstruction with the more intelligent negroes voting.

Only among Southern women and preachers did it seem that hatred would long survive, both classes still resenting the charges of immorality which the Northern Abolitionists had heaped upon the slave-holding civilization.

General Jeff Thompson, dismissing his gray Missouri raiders, charged them: "Go home, work hard at your crops, avoid all political discussions. If any man says 'nigger' to you swear you that you never knew or saw one in your life. We have talked about niggers for forty years and have been outtalked; we have fought about the niggers for four years and have been damned badly whipped, and now it is not your 'put.' The Yankees have won the nigger and will do what they please with him and you will have no say in the matter. Go home, stay there! Don't go anywhere but to mill. Don't go to church, for the ministers will put knots and mischief in your heads and get you into trouble."

Five days of Holy Week passed, Lincoln's policy of mercy sweeping the people along. Even Stanton, jumping up and down with the intoxication of victory, thought to hang over his portico, among other extravagant decorations, a cunning arrangement of gas-jets that spelled "Peace." Many Southern sympathizers were contaminated with the excitement and flew the Stars and Stripes, whooping their joy and overlooking the flaunting excess with which the Union men illuminated Arlington, the home of Robert E. Lee, confiscated since 1861.

Then came Friday the 14th, Good Friday, as it happened.

Friday was the regular Cabinet-meeting day, and this was the happiest Friday either Lincoln or his Cabinet had had in four years and more. On that very day they knew that down in Charleston, South Carolina, General Anderson, whose surrender of Fort Sumter had started the war in 1861, was now raising the Stars and Stripes over the fortress again while bands played and patriots cheered.

Long-legged Lincoln eased back in his White House chair and talked informally—the meeting had not yet begun, since it must wait upon Stanton, Secretary of War, who was still bustling around the telegraph-office. General Grant, who had come up from Appomattox to be Lincoln's guest at the Cabinet conference, was as solemn in victory as in battle and told Lincoln that he was anxious about Sherman, away down in North Carolina there, face to face with General Johnston and the remaining "rebel" army. At this, Lincoln spoke up, saying that things would be all right. He had had a sign.

All of the dignitaries in the room remembered later what it was that Lincoln then went on to say, although some recalled the words a little differently from others. Some remembered that he had been very grave as he spoke, others that he had been sad, still others noted nothing unusual. Secretary of the Navy Welles, less superstitious than most men of his time, and with a memory always alert to catch significant happenings which might be jotted down in his voluminous diary, remembered Lincoln's words like this:

"I have no doubt that favorable news will soon come, for I had, last night, my usual dream that has preceded nearly every important event of the war. I seemed to be in a singular and indescribable vessel, but always the same, and to be moving with great rapidity toward a dark and indefinite shore."

As the secretaries and the general watched, the long man talked on:

"I have had this singular dream preceding the firing on Sumter, the battles of Bull Run, Antietam, Gettysburg, Stone River, Vicksburg, Wilmington, and so on."

Grant, who was no one to believe in dreams, broke in, a little tartly, "Stone River was no victory. A few such victories would have ruined the country, and I know of no other important results from it."

"I shouldn't altogether agree with you," replied Lincoln, "but whatever may be the facts, my singular dream preceded that fight. Victory has not always followed my dream, but the event and the results have been important. I have no doubt that a battle has taken place or is about to be fought and Johnston will be beaten, for I had this strange dream again last night. It must relate to Sherman; my thoughts are in that direction, and I know of no other very important event which is likely just now to occur."

With that the conversation turned off into the problems of reconstructing the South, and none of Lincoln's listeners might have ever remembered the dream if its teller had not been murdered that evening.

When Lincoln was dead, it struck them that there had been some "other very important event" just ahead of the dreaming President, and that the dream itself had been like a premonition, a sign from the beyond.

No warning ghosts walked in Lincoln's mind, however, as the Cabinet meeting drew to its close. He was thinking how like an act of God it was that Congress was out of the way till Fall and the Radicals helpless to disturb his plans. There would be no persecution of Confederate bitter-enders, that he told the Cabinet plainly, "no bloody work."

"Frighten them out of the country, let down the bars, scare them off," he said, making motions with his scarecrow arms like a man shooing sheep. "Enough lives have been sacrificed. We must extinguish our resentment if we expect harmony and union. There is too much desire on the part of our very good friends to be masters, to interfere with and dictate to those

States, to treat the people not as fellow citizens; there is too little respect for the right. I don't sympathize with those feelings."

He felt happy and exhilarated, but not for long. His wife spoiled his fun.

They were riding over the city in the afternoon, the two of them, taking the air before time came to go to the theater, as had been arranged. Mrs. Lincoln kept watching her husband, noting his strange animation and unusual joyousness. Evidently without thinking that he could be elated over the triumph of his merciful program, she broke out in sudden fear: "I have seen you thus only once before; it was just before our dear Willie died."

At the mention of that son whose death, in '62, had staggered him, haunting his sleep until the little boy's face came in dreams to soothe him, Lincoln lost his cheerfulness and slumped back into that melancholy which had, since 1840, seemed "to drip from him as he walked." After a time, however, his spirits rose somewhat, and by evening, when theater time came, he was on the wings of optimism once more.

Northerners, wanting life, laughter, color in the victory madness, rushed to the theater to celebrate. Good Friday, always the worst night of the year in the theater, was one of the best in 1865. Especially was the theater of John T. Ford, in Washington, packed and jammed this evening, for there, it had been announced, both Lincoln and Grant would show themselves to the public. Even that Northern faction which still spat when the name of Lincoln, "that bloody butcher," was mentioned, wanted to see the man who had guided his government so slowly and mysteriously through to overwhelming success.

Ford's Theater was full to the doors as the curtain went up and the play began, but the audience gave only half attention to the actors. With one eye it watched the President's empty box — and waited.

HORRIBLE CARNIVAL

A LITTLE AFTER EIGHT O'CLOCK Mrs. Abraham Lincoln, in her finery, came bustling into the theater-box, with her husband and their guests following. Down on the stage Laura Keane, the star, stopped the dialogue to courtesy toward the arriving party. A roar went up from the crowd; the orchestra crashed into "Hail to the Chief," and the President, his huge, sallow face relaxing a little, bowed and bowed until the tumult died.

The proud wife who, long ago in a frontier town, had married this tall, dark man when he was a penniless lawyer, explaining to her friends that some day she expected him to become President, sat down with rustling skirts. On her left, next the audience, sat her husband, a President indeed and a savior of his country as well, rocking comfortably beside her now in the special chair brought by the management for his long, slumping body. On her right sat their guests, an army officer and his stepsister whom he was engaged to marry, both high enough in Washington society to please the Kentucky notions of their hostess.

They had come to the theater through a city that floated white in the fire of gasoline torchlights, torches that danced the victory dance over the heads of paraders who hailed Lincoln boisterously along the way. Triumphal arches had spanned Pennsylvania Avenue over their heads as the President and his wife rode by. It was an evening of high elation, and as the comedy ran on for the next two hours, laughter washed like a bright sea around the Presidential box. Lincoln's bodyguard, catching the luxurious relaxation of the hour, slipped away from his post at the box door to find himself a seat from which he might enjoy the show.

Along in the third act something happened; just what it was, Mrs. Lincoln, intent upon the stage before her, could not for a moment make out. Some one out of the box had gone down over the rail on to the stage — a form that passed too quickly to be plainly seen. The startled woman sprang to her feet and looked down on to the stage, thinking that her husband had fallen out of the box.

Painful though it would have been for so proud a Southern belle to see her mate, the President of the United States, humiliating himself and her by an awkward tumble in front of everybody, a sight infinitely worse met her eyes.

Down on the stage a strange man was scrambling to his feet, waving a bloody knife and shouting something in a foreign tongue. What could it mean? The frightened woman turned back to the box. Her husband still sat in his rocking-chair, but with his head oddly hanging on his breast. One of their guests, Miss Harris, sat frozen in terror; the other, Major Rathbone, was scrambling off the floor, shouting wildly, blood gushing from his arm. Mrs. Lincoln screamed, clutched at her husband, wheeled around the narrow box in distraction. Major Rathbone fumbled with the box door. It had been barred from within by the assassin just before he shot the President through the back of the head and then, knifing Rathbone to the floor, jumped over the box rail to the stage and away through the wings to a horse and flight.

Every one in the house was on tiptoe, the readier ones screaming "Catch that man!" as the murderer escaped. Walt Whitman described it well:

"A moment's strange incredulous suspense and then the deluge — people burst through chairs and railings and break them up — there is inextricable confusion and terror — women faint — quiet, feeble persons fall and are trampled on — many cries of agony are heard — the broad stage fills to suffocation with a dense and motley crowd like some horrible carnival — two or three manage to pass up water from the stage to the President's box — others try to clamber up.

"In the midst of all this the soldiers of the President's Guard, with others, suddenly drawn to the scene, burst in (some two hundred altogether); they storm the house, through all the tiers, especially the upper one, inflamed with fury, literally charging the audience with fixed bayonets, muskets and pistols, shouting 'Clear out! Clear out!'"

Up in the box, physicians from the audience found the wound in Lincoln's head, knew it to be fatal, refused to let the dying man be jolted over cobblestones back to the White House, approved a resting-place in a lodging-house across the street, and had the unconscious President carried there on a shutter. Crowds on the main floor of the theater jostled each other to see the red stains and at the same time squirmed to keep from stepping on them.

Outside on the streets cavalry sabers cleared a space before the theater, and between the rearing horses, the mob caught glimpses of dark figures crossing in straining, careful haste as they bore the wounded Lincoln into Peterson's lodging-house.

The phantasmagoria had begun. America was launched upon the maddest hour of its history.

Over Washington the word of the disaster went like prairie fire. In mid-air it collided with another fearsome rumor, blended with it, and flew on at redoubled speed. Seward, Secretary of State, was dying, too, the new story ran. An assassin had cut his throat even while Lincoln was being shot.

Through army barracks drums beat the long alarm roll which soldiers had never expected to hear again. Squads of infantrymen dashed away to guard the homes of the Cabinet, the Supreme Court judges, the generals. At military headquarters a hundred men stood in line waiting, as couriers dashed up in swift succession announcing fresh assassinations. To the death-list which had begun with Lincoln were added the names of Seward, Johnson, Stanton, and then Grant — their own Grant. Blindly the soldiers accepted all rumors and stood waving their swords, holding aloft their guns, roaring their vengeance like chained lions, tears on their cheeks.

Through the sleeping residential districts rattled the mysterious danger-signal of the Union League, secret loyalist society, two short staccato raps on the pavement, thrice repeated. Citizens came boiling out to this summons, tossing on their clothes and gripping firearms.

Sleep had gone from Washington that night. Over town

rushed frenzied mobs, howling "Burn the theater!" and another cry still more terrible, "Kill the goddam rebels! Kill the traitors!" The thirty thousand Confederate soldiers who had been turned loose in Washington on parole after Lee's surrender were in awful peril, for to the Union population which had lived for four years in constant dread that the Virginia armies would any day come into Washington with fire and sword, the happenings of the night meant but one thing: the Confederates under cover of their surrender on the battlefield had treacherously crept into town by night and were seeking to capture by assassination the city that they could never win by open assault. The South had risen again, so the mobs believed; the war was on once more.

Calmer men, such as Senator William M. Stewart of Nevada, who were on the streets in the pandemonium, expected any minute to see the mobs of Federal soldiers and Northern civilians start massacring the paroled Confederate veterans. Stewart saw distraught mobs halted just in time by cooler heads who, mounting steps or tree-boxes, cried to the crowds, "What would Mr. Lincoln say if he could talk to you?" Stewart thought only a miracle prevented Yankee soldiers from killing their late adversaries, for the soldiers idolized Lincoln far more universally and consistently than did the civilians.

Back in the lodging-house Lincoln's great length had been stretched catty-corner of a borrowed bed in a little hall room and the bed pulled over to a spot beneath a dismal gas-jet that flickered down upon the cavernous face. Surgeons massed about it. There was no hope. Dignitaries came puffing and wide-eyed, the doctors at the door holding back as many as they could. Up the steps came the imperious Senator from Massachusetts, Charles Sumner, arriving within thirty minutes after the assassination. Physicians advised him to stay out.

"I WILL go in," he thundered, and butted his way clear through to the bedside, where he remained.

Came, too, Lincoln's Secretary of War, Edwin M. Stanton, his nerves jumping like devils. Always erratic, Stanton was now in a panic, for he had been told by the Senators who had summoned him from his home that a skulking figure had fled from

the porch as they came up. Believing this, he had pounced upon
the notion that he, like Lincoln and Seward, had been marked
for slaughter by the Confederate plotters.

For years Stanton had been waging relentless war on the
"rebels" with one hand while with the other he held in check
Northern profiteers, and now, with that decisive energy which
was sometimes brilliant, sometimes merely rash, he rose up to
smash the South again. In the back bedroom of Peterson's
lodging-house he took charge of the Republic. Through the
war this "mad incorruptible" had believed himself to be the real
ruler of the nation, guiding with his superior brain the weaker,
softer will of Lincoln, and now his hour had come. He was
dictator.

He sent for more detectives, more troops, for a judge to sit
down beside him and examine witnesses: he discovered that the
assassin had been recognized to be J. Wilkes Booth, the actor;
he confiscated Ford's Theater, he threw pickets around the
entire city fifty feet apart; he set the telegraphers to notifying
the nation, warning troops to watch the Canadian border for
escaping conspirators. But he was no man to be Caesar in such
a time.

A triumph as first mate, he failed as captain. With cool-
headed Lincoln to guide him, he had been a genius for efficiency
in the war office — "The Great Energy," his friends called him
— but now that he assumed the supreme command his weaknesses glared forth. His health was breaking, cracking up under
the strain of faithful days and nights at his desk — gone as his
money had gone, sacrificed for the nation's business, war. Lincoln
had found superb use for Stanton's talents and had employed
them unsparingly.

Ferocious headaches had racked the secretary for years,
asthma tore at his throat, and, besides, he had a phobia which
unbalanced his brain whenever he was near a corpse.

His biographers tell how in the days when Stanton was a
little boy, in Steubenville, Ohio, his father had hung a skeleton
in the barn for him to study so that when he grew up he would
be a doctor, and how it was his particular delight to terrify

the neighbor children with candles gleaming from inside the skull.

In Columbus, Ohio, where, as a young man, he managed a bookstore, his landlady's daughter died suddenly from cholera one afternoon, and Stanton, coming home for supper, heard the news with disbelief. The girl had been sound and well at noontime, and here at sundown she was dead and buried. His mind would not accept the fact, and with two young friends he hurried to the graveyard and dug the body up to make sure that the girl had not been buried alive.

In later years he had staggered under the blow of a daughter's death, and after the child had been buried a year he had the body exhumed and laid in a special metal container which he kept in his room for another year or more until, at the death of his wife, he was persuaded to rebury little Lucy with her mother.

His phobia gripped him more savagely at the death of this wife, his first, and he cast her wedding-ring and letters into her coffin with the command that they be buried with her. When friends took the articles out, Stanton watched and put them back, trying to hide them in the dead woman's shroud, repeating this performance until time for the funeral. Pitifully he fussed over his wife's burial-clothes, compelling the dressmaker to alter her work over and over so that his "dear Mary" might look precisely as she had upon her wedding-day. In the night he arranged her nightcap and gown beside him in bed and wept.

When his brother, Dr. Darwin Stanton, had killed himself in delirious fever in 1846, Stanton broke away from the casket to run like a hunted thing through the woods, with the mourners in hot pursuit, and when caught, he was watched for days and nights lest he imitate his brother's act.

In March, 1865, with the President dead, the Vice-President drunk, so it was said, and the Secretary of State, next in authority, presumably dying of a cut throat, Stanton seized the reins, performing miracles of organization as well as marvels of imagination.

But he was too close to a dead man.

All along through the war he had leaned toward the Radicals, deploring if not condemning Lincoln's "weak-kneed" sympathy for the "rebels." Now he enlisted in their cause, the humane Gideon Welles, Secretary of the Navy, catching him a day or two later conferring with the "avengers" and evidently relaying to them secrets of Johnson's first Cabinet meetings. A strange man, Stanton, at times a tireless hero, at others a flighty fool—this night of April 14 he was both, driving the bureau of military justice out on a desperate hunt to find evidence which would prove that the Confederacy had plotted Lincoln's murder.

Every few minutes he hurried to the sick-room as the night wore on. So did Mrs. Lincoln, from her place on the sofa in the parlor where Miss Harris tried to keep her. Once they came together, this nerve-wracked pair, the secretary and the wife, beside the dying man. Mrs. Lincoln was pressing her face against her husband's when Lincoln's breath suddenly grew hoarser and louder, and the poor woman, springing back, fell to the floor in a faint. Stanton heard her scream and tore into the room waving his arms and shouting, "Take that woman out of here and don't let her in again!" They bore her away where soothing women waited. Stanton was czar.

Mrs. Lincoln was not in the room when, at 7.20 a.m., the end came, and she moaned because they had not called her. Stanton was there, as he was certain to be, weeping genuine tears. Across the other side of the bed, in a rocking-chair that he had occupied all night long, sat Stanton's ancient rival, Welles, naval minister, silently watching Stanton, we may be sure, as he had been watching him distrustfully throughout the war, and knowing, perhaps, that he was worrying his old enemy by watching him now. Welles in his calm, patriarchal beard, rocking and watching the scene, steadfast, ready for work if work there were to do, but no man to create needless confusion; Welles rocking, watching and rocking—a much safer man to be dictator in that moment, had he owned the rank.

Beside Stanton at the head of the bed was Sumner, sobbing deeply, bending like a Roman tribune over a slaughtered friend, his polished Boston pompadour tangling with the coarse, strong locks of the frontiersman (Lincoln had described his own hair as "horsehair"). Against Sumner leaned Capt. Robert Lincoln, home that day from City Point.

When the doctors said, "He is dead," Stanton did a curious thing. As though he were alone, he slowly, formally raised his hand, put his hat upon his head, then, as majestically, took it off, like an emperor crowning himself. That done, he turned to Lincoln's clergyman, saying, "Doctor, lead us in prayer." The Reverend Gurley's prayer finished, the officials filed out, and Stanton, an executive to the last, went about the room, darkening the windows and saying, "Now he belongs to the ages." Alone of all the eloquent men in the room at that time for eloquence, Stanton said anything whatsoever worth remembering.

Another story, less perfectly authenticated, is that he groaned, "Oh, now there is no one to do me justice." He could have said it, whether he did or not, for Lincoln had defended him often enough during the war, holding him in office against complaints that were, at times, national in volume. That his war secretary was brusque, crude, insolent, rash, Lincoln knew, and he also knew, better than any man, how often he had been the subject of Stanton's impatient sneers, but he said nothing, finding magnificent use for his difficult employee's talents. Lincoln understood how Stanton loved the Union and hated the Confederacy, how he had routed the war profiteers ruthlessly, and how inexhaustible he was, just the man for the Cause, whether Lincoln liked him or he Lincoln.

Every one around the deathbed except the indomitable Secretary of War seemed to be in a daze. Dr. Leale, one of the army surgeons in attendance, was almost exhausted as he closed the dead man's eyes, put coins upon them, and drew up the sheet. For hours, after probing the wound, he had sat in a chair by the bed holding the dying President's hand, a labor of love.

From experience Leale knew that sometimes in such cases recognition and reason came glimmering back to the unconscious mind just before death struck, and if this should happen to the kindly man here on the bed, the doctor didn't want him to find himself all alone.

Now there was no use in staying any longer, and Leale went staggering out on to the street to wander home bareheaded and bloody through the cold Spring rain that had begun to fall.

✧ ✧ ✧ 7 ✧ ✧ ✧

COLD RAIN IN THE MORNING

WHEN LIFE WAS GONE from the President's body, Stanton cleared the lodging-house of mourners, sent Mrs. Lincoln home in a carriage, hurried riders through the capital to start the death-bells tolling, and convened as many Cabinet members as he could find in secret session. He would ride the whirlwind, and he alone.

For the Vice-President, Andrew Johnson, who by law should have been at the helm that night, Stanton had no use; indeed, if Senator Stewart is to be believed, Stanton had not bothered to notify the Vice-President at all. Sumner, however, remembered later that Johnson had spent two minutes by the bedside, and there is other evidence that he came, if only for a few minutes, to the house of death.

According to the Nevada Senator, Stewart, the Vice-President had slept through at least the greater part of that horrible carnival, dead to the world in his bedroom at the Kirkwood House. It was only when Lincoln was dead that Senator Solomon Foot of Vermont, head of the Republican caucus, thought of Johnson and set out through the cold morning rain to awaken him. Bundling Chief Justice Salmon P. Chase into a rattle-trap hack, Foot bounced with him over the cobblestones, saying, "It will not do to be without a President in the White House in times like these."

Repeated poundings on the bedroom door brought Johnson out, blinking, matted mud in his hair, liquor on his breath, his feet bare. Ushering his morning visitors in, Johnson felt around back of him for a chair, found one, and sank into it. The same Senator Stewart tells what happened, and since he was there, his word must stand, for, even though we know how he hated Johnson, he was never a careless liar.

"The President has been assassinated. He died this morning, and I have come to administer the oath of office to you," said the ponderous Chief Justice. Slowly the fact worked through Johnson's mind, and all at once he popped up to his full height, reaching upward extravagantly with his right arm, and thickly announced, "I'm ready."

Chase swore him in as the seventeenth President of the United States, and the minute the work was done Stewart raced away for Stanton and, bringing the war minister up, found the others gone and Johnson down again, flat on his bed. The two men fell to work, dressing the drunken President as respectably as they could, helped him down into Stanton's carriage, and drove him to the White House, where they hid him while attendants ran for a doctor, a tailor, and a barber. With flying fingers the tailor fitted new clothes on Johnson, the doctor dosed him vigorously, and the barber shaved him and cut his muddy hair. Late in the afternoon a few chosen individuals were allowed to see him, as Stewart said, "just to satisfy themselves that there was a President in the White House."

A mad day had followed a mad night, and every man's mind was so jumbled that nobody, in after years, could be exactly sure what had happened. Johnson's partisans always maintained that Stewart had drawn the long bow of his imagination in picturing the new President's condition, for they pointed out that Johnson did not occupy the White House until after Mrs. Lincoln left it weeks later.

Still, Stewart might have been wrong about this detail and right about the others. He was, he said, an eyewitness. And again, Johnson may have been taken to the White House on Saturday for the steadying effect his presence might have on the nation, and may have left within a few hours for other quarters. The fact that his meetings with the Cabinet in the crisis took place in the Treasury Building does not disprove Stewart's picture of that bleak, lunatic Saturday.

At any rate Johnson sat in the President's chair this day, Lincoln lay in the guest-room of the White House where the embalmers had placed him, a room in which he had seldom been (Crook, one of his bodyguards, said "never"), Mrs. Lincoln lay tossing in another room, moaning, "How can it be?" Little Tad, her twelve-year-old son, was crying steadily, saying in his tongue-tied way to the White House attendants, "They've killed my papa," and the cold Spring rain came down.

Tad had been in another Washington theater, Grover's, the night before, when a strange man had come out on the stage, interrupting the performance to announce that the President had been assassinated, and the boy had screamed his heartbreak as they carried him back to the empty White House. There, when it was learned that his father was not yet dead, attendants comforted him with false, soothing hopes so that he might sleep.

But he learned the truth quickly enough on Saturday morning, and wept afresh.

Another little boy, name unknown — just a little boy of Washington — was seen by reporters industriously rubbing bits of white paper on the steps of Peterson's lodging-house some time after nine o'clock when the President's body had been borne to the White House. The boy kept at his task, dropping each piece of paper into his pocket.

A reporter, edging up through the crowd that stood staring at the house of gloom, said to the boy, "What are you doing?"

"Don't you see those dark places on the boards?" the little fellow replied. "That's the President's blood, and I want to save it."

If the trampling feet of the night before and the cold rain of the morning had left no dark stains on the boards for the little boy to rub, what does it matter? There were dark stains enough on the North that Saturday morning, the stains of madness. Across the Union States that "horrible carnival" which had begun in Washington was now being repeated with manifold lunacy.

Through the camps where Union armies rested on their arms, horsemen spurred, spreading the word. Soldiers hardened to killing wept, raved, shrieked demands that the rebels be given back their arms and that the war be started again and fought out to extermination. Burn all the Southern cities! Drive the rebels into the sea!

Just as the joyous news of Lee's surrender had come smashing into the cities of the North on the tongues of bells Palm Sunday night, so did the awful word of Lincoln's death come Good Friday night. And the religious folk who saw in one the triumph of Jesus, saw in the other the crucifixion. Where the bells of Sunday had exulted, the bells of Saturday tolled a funeral song.

By Saturday morning the whole North was in mourning. The flags, the arches, the bunting that had gone up five days before in such intoxication now came down and the buildings were so draped in black that all their life was gone. The same men who had teetered across their ridgepoles, hanging colors, now retraced their steps with crape in their hands. Business was suspended except in dry-goods stores, which kept open while women stripped the shelves of all material dark enough to be used for mourning. And as the sewing women made sable decorations for their windows and porches, they wept, and their menfolks wept, too, clasping hands with each other on the street, or embracing as grief smote the backs of their knees.

When black fabrics gave out and when all the old black dresses were cut up into bunting, paper was dyed with ink and cut into festoons for railings and windows.

Grim death decorations darkened the face of the North.

People looked at the Spring rain falling and said the heavens were weeping, too.

Any one who did not drape his home in black was, of course, a traitor. Mobs took delight in compelling Southern sympathizers to decorate their houses lavishly in mourning. Two ex-Presidents of the United States felt the sting of this compulsion.

Wild eyes saw that the home of Millard Fillmore in Buffalo was not adorned in black, and soon a crowd was seething about his dwelling throwing on it ink, and probably worse, too, if one reads between the lines of the restrained reports of the time. That done, the mourners called on the former President to come out. He did so and explained his lapse rather lamely by saying that his wife was sick and that he hadn't got out to hear the news. Since his wife was known to be an invalid and since he himself proceeded to eulogize Lincoln with enthusiasm, nothing more was done to Millard Fillmore.

Franklin Pierce, too, talked his way out of a similar predicament. To the mob that demanded a speech from him and jeered, "Where's your flag?" Pierce, an old-time Democrat, spoke lengthily in defense of himself and his loyalty, eventually calming his hearers so that no violence resulted.

Still, those bells that called the people to sorrow called them to vengeance, too.

As the face of the North changed from colors that sang to crape that wept, so did its heart change.

Rage followed the first stunning impact of the news. As the word came that the assassination was part of a plot of the defeated Confederacy to win the war by a last-minute outbreak of murder, the Union populations became demented. Grief and anger joined in the hearts of Lincoln's partisans, and Democrats, who could not share the full frenzy of grief for the Republican President, nevertheless boiled with anger at the insult to the nation. Even the great majority of those Northerners who sincerely hated Lincoln were appalled at this turn of events.

Mass meetings sprang up everywhere, and as the word came in that more and more evidence had been uncovered to prove the gigantic scope of the Confederate plot, order vanished and mobs began chasing "rebel sympathizers." No man who had, in other years, spoken his belief in the righteousness of Secession was now safe. Copperheads, as these citizens were called, hid in their homes or police stations.

The mobs that had all week laughed and jeered at the mention of "Jeff" Davis now gritted out "Hang him!" and meant it, too. The slogan rang across the North. In Washington, Vice-President Johnson, General Butler, and John Covode, a Radical Congressman, decided this Saturday that Davis, when caught, should be hanged.

Inferno had come. Pro-Southerners were ridden on rails, tarred and feathered; a few were shot; others were beaten to death with paving-stones. On Monday Joseph Shaw, editor of the Westminster (Maryland) *Democrat*, was killed because he had published abuse of Lincoln on Sunday.

Instances there were of soldiers in the streets of cities shooting to death fools who exulted over the Yankee President's downfall.

In New York, where Southern sympathizers were always on the verge of breaking out into anti-Lincoln riots, Union mobs were busy. On Wall Street angry ears heard a certain Joseph McKenzie of Williamsburg saying on the Post Office steps, "Did you hear Abe Lincoln's last joke?" And a second later Joseph McKenzie was fleeing down the Street of Dollars with a fanged pack at his heels howling, "Secesh." A policeman gathered the fugitive into his arms just in time to prevent him from being torn to pieces. Another Southern sympathizer, George Wells, was heard to say, "Old Abe, the —— ——, he ought to have been killed six months ago." A policeman knocked George down, picked him up, and dragged him to court, where the judge sent him on to prison for six months. Many such sentences were given to citizens who spoke too freely.

Secessionists were penned in buildings by mobs that clawed at doors which owners hastily locked until the overworked police could arrive. Wall Street rang with the howl, "Hang Jeff Davis!" repeated endlessly.

In Baltimore, two photographers were mobbed and their shop wrecked because they were said to have photographs of Booth in their files.

In Poughkeepsie, a woman named Frisby exulted in public over the assassination and found her house surrounded with a roaring mob. A youth named Denton, more to be praised for his gallantry than brains, essayed to drive off the crowd single-handed and, after a quick throttling, was hustled off to jail for his pains.

Common sights in Northern cities on Saturday, Sunday, and Monday were "rebel" sympathizers marching up and down the streets, wretchedly carrying the Stars and Stripes and halting every few feet to let out a compulsory hosanna.

In Troy, New York, a certain D. L. Hunt from Rochester, grew intemperate and declared that Lincoln should have been killed four years before. Only the police saved his life, and they jailed him.

An alderman in Abolitionist New England — Hartford, Connecticut, to be exact — unbosomed himself: "I have been waiting four years for some damned black Republican's bones to make bone-dust to put around my vines, and I don't know but there is a prospect of my getting some now." Others in the town said, "I'm glad Abraham Lincoln was shot and I'd like to go and dance on his coffin." A woman of the town declared her joy and added a wish that Jefferson Davis might take Lincoln's place.

Isolated instances such as these, when snatched up and telegraphed from one end of the stricken sections to another, fanned the loyalists to wilder fury, and as the days brought out the ravings of hot-headed orators and the whiplash editorials of infuriated Republican editors, the North was cast into a fit of hatred such as the war itself had never called down upon the head of the South.

Union County, Illinois — a county with such a name in Lincoln's own State! — was described in the newspapers as having rejoiced *en masse* at the announcement of the assassination, cheering it as something better than a Confederate victory. Young men mounted horses and rode whooping with the news from farmhouse to farmhouse. "My daughter," wrote one correspondent, "out riding on horseback, was met by another young lady who was radiant with joy. She said she had never been so happy in her life. Women went to see their neighbors to speak of the glad tidings. They have an idea that it is a great victory for the South. But some feared that the news was too good to be true."

Across southern Illinois, Indiana, and Ohio, where pro-Southern sentiment had always been strong, were plenty of homes that did not grieve.

Up in Canada among the Confederate refugees who had crouched there either in helplessness or in political schemings, a clergyman, so the papers said, had announced to other hotel guests at breakfast that Lincoln had only gone to hell a little before his time.

As sorrowing people of Wrentham, Massachusetts, on Sunday came out of the church where they had been lamenting Lincoln's death, they saw a horrible sight — a man whipping an effigy that dangled from a tree. Drawing nearer to the fellow as he laid to his work, they saw that he was a fellow townsman, Patrick Travis by name, and that his straw victim bore a placard reading "Abraham Lincoln, the nigger worshiper." With a roar the onlookers made a rush and Travis took to his heels, but they caught him and rode him around town on a rail. Then, inflamed with their powers of retribution, they surged on after another enemy, a certain Patrick Kennedy, farmhand living near by. They rode him on a rail, too, the women reaching up to strike him with whips.

The town of Marietta, in the southern Copperhead section of Indiana, rejoiced wildly at the death news, anvils were fired, and an effigy of Lincoln, clumsily made up to hold a mock bullet-wound in its head, was carried up and down the streets, then tossed into a bonfire.

Reading such inflammatory bulletins as these, the North grew more and more distraught, more deeply and ever more deeply convinced that the South was, as the Radicals said, a land of inhuman traitors.

In Washington, where the military police, both aided and impeded by hordes of professional and amateur detectives who poured in from every part of the North, were arresting suspects by the hundred, the mobs found an outlet for their rage by stoning any man who marched by under military escort. So general did this sport become that cavalrymen had to ride with naked swords, twenty to the prisoner, as they escorted the arrests to jail. Crowds howled around Old Capitol Prison where Confederate prisoners were held, and these would-be lynchers kept up their demonstration so long that the government spirited away most of the military captives to Johnson's Island in Lake Erie near Sandusky for safer keeping.

Miraculously, however, the paroled warriors of Lee were immune. Those who still remained above Mason and Dixon's line were not assailed as they took their peaceful ways about the cities. Somehow, even with its ferment of soul, the North did not blame these "rebels" who had merely obeyed orders in the field. It was the Secession leaders that it was after, and with Lincoln gone, the Radicals might have hanged Southern generals, but for the dogged gallantry of Grant. When it was demanded that Lee and other Confederate generals should have at least a trial for treason in civil courts, Grant broke out in one of the few temper-fits of his lifetime, swearing that unless the terms of surrender were respected, he would resign his commission and take the issue to the people. Before such a threat the Radicals quailed, remembering how Lincoln had worsted them when he had gone over their heads to the masses.

And when President Johnson, in his first yearnings to make Southern leaders suffer, said to Grant, "When can these men be tried?" the man from Appomattox snapped, "Never, unless they violate their paroles."

Grant's friendship, however, was principally for the soldiers among the Southerners. Civilians and politicians he did not understand so well, and in the hurly-burly after the assassination he ordered the arrest of Judge Campbell and other Confederate government officials in Richmond, commanding that they be held in Libby Prison.

"Extreme rigor," he commanded, "will have to be observed whilst assassination remains the order of the day with the rebels."

Unfortunate Grant — the strange world of politics had already begun to bog his footsteps. Better for him if he had owned in that minute his beloved Sherman's cold distrust of politicians and their machinations. Better for him if he, like Lee, had gone straight home after Appomattox Court House. The war was done for Grant, and he had come to unfamiliar ground, seeing not how that little band of Radicals whom he had once helped to fool were now at work, with Lincoln out of the way, to seize the reins and put over, at last, their program of punishing the South.

By Saturday night all chance of a Lincolnian policy of mercy toward the South had gone. From Washington came no word to tell the people that there was no evidence that the murder was anything but the fool exploit of a disgruntled actor performing, as he said, on his own initiative. Papers of Booth's had been seized and found to confess this fact, and they were published, but they meant nothing when it was also published that the military authorities had proof that Jefferson Davis and other Confederate leaders were implicated in the plot. One hundred thousand dollars was soon offered for Davis' arrest.

Lincoln's enemies had seized the government at last. The

Radicals whom he had held at bay so well jumped into the saddle the minute he was gone. With the exception of Sumner, who, for all his belief that Lincoln was bringing chaos on the land, appreciated the President's goodness of heart, the "avengers" made little secret of their joy.

Pointing to dead Lincoln and then to the South, they had scant trouble in persuading most politicians and preachers that the assassination was a godsend to the Republic.

Now the nation's fate was out of the weak, tender hands of a sentimentalist, they said, and safe in the stern, mailed grasp of Andrew Johnson, who had suffered, as a Union man of Tennessee, the contumely and oppression of the proud Secession planters.

To the White House on Monday came the Radicals urging Johnson to have at the blue-grass Ivanhoes who had snubbed him, "poor white" that he was, in peace times, and tried to kill him in war times.

The new President, who had stridently, fearlessly assailed "traitors" in the past, now told the "avengers" that he held treason to be a crime akin to rape. "And crime must be punished. Treason must be made infamous and traitors must be impoverished," he added grimly.

Out of his heart Ben Wade spoke for them all, as he wrung Johnson's hand: "Johnson, we have faith in you. By the gods, we'll have no trouble now in running the government."

With Stanton quivering with vengeance — or was it partly fear? — as he sat in the War Office controlling the news, and with Johnson at the helm, the Radicals knew that luck had played into their hands. The South was to pay and pay and pay. The very thing that the South had once dreaded, then so miraculously escaped, was now, by a freakish accident, hanging over its head again.

Perhaps it was impossible for such men as Stanton and Johnson to see in that first mad delirium after the assassination that the South was as yet not proven guilty of the plot. The military police had uncovered a nest of plotters in Washington, accomplices of Booth, but that they were inspired by Confederate leaders was nothing more than a hasty conclusion. Whatever might have been said to restrain the North from snap judgments in the emergency was not said.

So it was small wonder that Northern crowds should rise to roaring blood-lusts when General Butler, military aide to the civilian Radicals, so to speak, shouted to massed New Yorkers:

"It is said that those who recommend condign punishment for treason are bloodthirsty, but, oh, fellow citizens, could he who has gone before us have foreseen what would have been the end of his policy of clemency and forgiveness, it might not have checked the desire in his heart in that direction but it would have informed his judgment, and we would have been spared his death this day and hour. If he could have foreseen that forgiveness meant assassination, that clemency meant death, if he could have foreseen that the devilish spirit of rebellion would have gone into the sick-room and stricken down the man whom God had spared a little longer, he would have known that mildness and clemency to traitors is cruelty to thousands. It is left for us to review his course and see whether or no we are to be instructed by his death."

Nor was it surprising to find the trustees of Columbia University (then College) passing resolutions which revived all the atrocities which the North had charged up against its adversaries.

The trustees recognized the assassination of Lincoln and mangling of Seward as "only the legitimate manifestations of that spirit of hostility to all law, human and divine, which originally prompted and has since sustained the nefarious attempt upon the life of the nation." Robustly the Columbians called upon all good men and good government everywhere to make common cause against the slaveholders "as scourges of mankind and enemies of the human race."

Characteristic of countless other resolutions passed by civic, educational, commercial, fraternal, political, and religious bodies was the demand of these trustees that all men accept the Christian duty of punishing pro-slavery people to the bitter end.

In the minds of countless Northern children was fixed this Radical view of Southerners, an idea that was to do yeoman service for the next generation, at least, in binding the bulk of Yankee and Middle Western voters to the Republican party, at whose masthead, whenever needed, floated the "bloody shirt."

Nor was it strange, even if it was mistaken, for the Athenaeum Club of New York to resolve that "the claim of the South to represent chivalry has departed. A gentle heart was as necessary to it as was gentle blood. Such a heart beat in the bosom of Abraham Lincoln, and it beat long enough, after humbling the haughty and setting their bondsmen free, to temper his treatment of the vanquished with mercy, and allow his captives to depart in safety, each with the free gift of his charger and his sword. Chivalry had no nobler achievement or more gentle courtesy than this. Contrast it with Libby Prison, and the prison-pens of the remote South, where our brother members have participated in Southern hospitality. They were not arranged after the fashion of chivalric receptions of a fallen foe. . . . It is to the savage teaching of Secession and not of chivalry that we are indebted that we have today a wide house of mourning in our land, and a martyred successor of Washington in our annals. . . ."

The Historical Society of Philadelphia in its resolutions named the assassination as the crowning horror in the long catalogue of crimes committed by the slaveholding power against liberty and humanity for the past fifty years.

In Philadelphia, too, the Baptist ministers adopted resolutions, one of which was: "Resolved, that we recognize in this atrocious deed the ripened fruit of the vile spirit of rebellion, and hereby express our hope that the government will see to it that the full measure of a righteous retribution be meted out to the instigators and accomplices of this deed of blood."

The Union League of San Francisco resolved that the assassination be recognized as the legitimate fruit of the barbarism of slavery, and called for the extinction of slavery and punishment of its leaders.

Citizens of Zanesville, Ohio, resolved "that in these diabolical murders we have but the fuller development of the spirit of the rebellion and its acknowledged cause and the consummation of purpose and plans formed before Mr. Lincoln's first inauguration; and that the teachings and acts of the rebel leaders have all tended to this result; and that they are justly responsible before God and the world for these hellish deeds; and in the name of humanity, as well as that of justice, we demand their punishment."

It did little good in so frenzied a time to inquire how the Southern people took the assassination news. That, from Davis down, the Confederates preferred Lincoln to Johnson as their master, was forgotten in the passions of the hour. Lee might declare that he had surrendered as much to Lincoln's goodness as to Grant's artillery, and say that he, as much as any Northerner, regretted the death of Lincoln, whom he believed to be the epitome of magnanimity and good faith; other generals, Joseph E. Johnston, for instance, might say that the assassination was the worst blow that the South could possibly receive; public mass-meetings in New Orleans, Savannah, Wilmington, N. C., and Huntsville, Ala., might deplore the removal of Lincoln, friend of the South; the Richmond *Whig* might declare the calamity to be worse for the South than any defeat, and all these things might be published in Northern newspapers. It was useless. The damage was done, the South was convicted.

Perhaps the Radicals in Washington, that little band of willful men, really continued to believe, in the weeks that followed the murder, the myth that the Confederacy had plotted Lincoln's death. Possibly Stanton believed all that mass of flimsy and fraudulent evidence that his outlandish detectives brought him to prove that Jefferson Davis, Jacob Thompson (Secretary of the Interior under Buchanan), and Clement Clay (ex-Senator from Alabama) and others had fomented the conspiracy. On May 2 President Johnson officially proclaimed Davis guilty of complicity; it was not until June, 1867, that the absurdity of this evidence was shown to the country at large, and by that time it was too late to bring back reason. The small group of politicians had captured the popular imagination, most ironically, by waving aloft the bloody shirt of the martyr whose death they themselves could not patriotically deplore.

Even so late as the last of May, 1865, when Davis was in prison, the North was in a panic lest the conspiracy which had killed Lincoln should strike again and deliver the ex-President of the Confederacy from his cell, where he had been confined since his capture in Georgia on the tenth of the month.

Sweeping President Johnson with them for a time, the Radicals junked Lincoln's plan for limiting negro suffrage, and even when, coming under more humane counsels of Seward, Welles, and other moderates, Johnson broke with them, they, with Stanton's help, still ruled the country, and lunged on to force through the constitutional amendment giving all negroes the vote.

If they were extreme, so were those Southerners who, having learned nothing of the woes of radicalism from their experience in letting the fire-eaters plunge them into destructive warfare in 1861, made matters worse in 1865 and '66 by trying to nullify many of the acts wherewith the negro was being elevated to his new rights.

Neither North nor South allowed their moderate leaders to adjust the twisted quarrel. The South cried that the North was tossing it to the mercies of savage blacks. The North replied that the South was proving that it was as bellicose and unmoral as before the war; and so the wrangling went, with the split widening.

Into this breach dashed "carpet-baggers," those Northern adventurers who saw a chance to exploit a whole section of the nation. Into it, too, rushed Southerners, to riot and maraud. Sober, sensible men on both sides were drawn into the new inferno, the Northerners to vote for oppression, the Southerners to ride by night in violence.

The man who would have prevented it all was dead in the White House, and the South, from which his parents had come, was made solid indeed, solid for two generations.

☆   ☆   ☆   **8**   ☆   ☆   ☆

"BLACK EASTER"

THE COLD RAIN STOPPED on Sunday morning, April 16, and the Spring sun shone.

Tad Lincoln, looking out of the White House window, saw

the world grow bright. His tears, which had fallen since Friday night, dried on his cheeks. Maybe his father was happy now that the sun was out. He felt comforted.

Something of Abraham Lincoln's mysticism was in that boy —inheritance, perhaps, from generations of woodsmen who had lived under the inscrutable, capricious forces of Nature.

"Do you think my father is in Heaven?" Tad asked one of those solemn, important men who had filled the White House since Saturday morning.

The man said yes, he was sure of it.

"I'm glad he has gone there," said the little boy in that difficult speech of his, "for he wasn't happy here. This wasn't a good place for him."

It was Easter Sunday, 1865, the festival of flowers, but for all the shining of the sun that morning, there was no blooming of the spirit in the United States of America. Unlike little Tad, the citizens of the North could not take the Easter sunshine as a symbol of happiness. The President was dead in the White House, and the victory that he had won seemed lost, with the South looming as vicious and unchastened as ever. So the people thought as they wound their way dolefully to church.

They had wept, wailed, raged, stormed, chased Lincoln's enemies, given vent to their pitiful confusion of soul in extravagant excesses. Now they would go to church on Easter morning, where the preachers would comfort them.

Not since the days of '57 and '58, before the war, when religious revivals had swept the land, had the churches seen such outpourings of people as on this Sunday morning.

"Black Easter," the people called it, for there were no flowers in the choir lofts, nor by the pulpits, nor near the altar—an Easter Sunday without flowers and, instead, with mourning draped from pew to pew.

In some churches where the clergymen had not decorated the house of God with crape, women, entering, took off their veils and spread them upon the pulpits.

All the Easter bonnets and gowns, all the stiff, new suits which the North had bought to celebrate those twin victories, Springtime and Appomattox Court House, could not be worn.

Wintertime and Lee's army were both gone, but little could that mean now. The President was dead in the White House.

To dress in solemn black, veil its face and creep back to the priests who understood God's puzzling ways, was all the North could do. From the pulpit would surely come consolation.

Instead, there came down from the pulpit a clarion call for "vengeance," the old battle-call of the Covenanters to be up and at the sinful aristocrats. It was not of Jesus and the resurrection of love that the dominies talked most this Easter Sunday; it was of the stern and bitter Jehovah who stood in the great gloom waiting for more and ever more "rebel" atonement.

Lincoln, the man, was never so dead as on "Black Easter," his policies drowned in his own blood. Here were the preachers, those vicars of Christ's mercy, as they claimed, calling more loudly than the Radicals of Congress for the doom of the slave-holding South. With almost unanimous accord they held up Lincoln's murder as the one final proof that the Confederacy was not yet dead and that villainous sedition was still afoot — still thriving as unchastened as before the war.

It was a day when clergymen had dazzling power — influence that they were to lose little by little with the years as the cities grew, enabling men to hide themselves in teeming crowds and thus be free from the scrutiny of pastors and neighbors.

Since colonial times the preachers had been leaders in politics as well as in matters of the soul. The North had been settled by religious sects of the Old World seeking freedom of worship in the New. Naturally these first immigrants had grouped themselves about the clergy in the coast villages, and when their sons and grandsons had forged out into the western forests and plains, itinerant circuit-riding preachers had served as teachers and entertainers as well as spiritual guides. Revivals had burned intermittently through the frontiers with glowing success — one of them, perhaps the greatest, having been that of 1858.

The very name "parson" indicated something of the cleric's position — that title having come into use through the alteration of the name, "The Person," which illiterate villagers had given their preachers in the earlier times when a clergyman was the only man in the community who could read or write.

Sermons were weighed well and attended avidly by the pioneers. And although there had always been plenty of hard-headed, free-thinking skeptics among the woodsmen — inheritors of the Thomas Jefferson tradition — exponents of the "rights of man" and shot through with the French republicanism which declared native man to need no supernatural savior, no guiding priest or God-sent king — although the frontiers had such men in numbers to ridicule the preachers and their dogmas, there were greater groups of wood-choppers, merchants, and farmers to ally themselves with the women in revering the clerics as leaders of thought.

The Civil War, with its superior dramatic appeal, had distracted the parishioners and the churches had waned somewhat in power, but with the battles done and Lincoln dead, the people came flocking back to the meeting-houses this Easter morning, seeking whatever explanation there might be for the mysterious actions of God.

Rejoicing at this change of the popular heart, the preachers welcomed the chance to reap a harvest for the Lord.

Their first duty, if they made the most of their opportunity, would be to convince the public that the death of Lincoln was all for the best. It would be a delicate matter, indeed, to persuade the masses that divine justice was behind so unfathomable a horror as this murder of the victorious President, occurring as it had just at the moment when his very existence seemed to be so imperative to the peacefulness and prosperity of the nation. But the iron shepherds were equal to the emergency, and, as they opened their mouths and explained God's purpose in allowing the assassination, it was apparent to most listeners that the Lord God of Hosts had not been on the side of Abraham Lincoln at all in his policy toward the South, but that He had gone over to the party of Stevens and Sumner and Davis and Wade and Andrew Johnson. Lincoln, God knew, was too good and tender a man, too soft and weak to cope with the villainous "rebels," so He had taken him away, that awful justice might be meted to the South.

"May it not be," intoned the Rev. Joel E. Rockwell, pastor of the Central Presbyterian Church of Brooklyn, "that God has permitted this great crime to awaken us to a sense of justice and to a full exaction of God's law upon those who have planned and accomplished the horrible scenes of the past four years?"

"It is the last spasm of the demon," cried the Rev. George Barrell Cheever in the Church of the Puritans, New York City, calling upon his congregation to stiffen their resolutions of vengeance upon the South, and adding that God had caused the assassination to take place toward the end of the week so that Sunday's sermons might the better instruct the nation in the appropriate moral.

"God has a purpose in permitting this great evil," said the Rev. S. D. Brown of the State St. M. E. Church in Troy, New York. "Our late President has nobly acted his part and carried us successfully through the struggle. And his name shall be honored by the latest generations of men. But may not another instrument, a man of different character, be needed at the present moment? It is a singular fact that the two most favorable to leniency to the rebels, Lincoln and Seward, have been stricken. Other members of the Cabinet were embraced in the fiendish plan, but as to them, it failed. May it not be that God is teaching that those guilty of the great crime of treason shall receive condign punishment?"

"Out upon the mawkish sentimentalism which would stay righteous vengeance," cried the powerful John Chase Lord, D.D., one-time ardent enemy of Abolition, addressing the people of his Central Presbyterian Church in Buffalo. "It is neither Christian nor manly. God demands that there should be a vindication by law, by the sword of lawful authority, and Andrew Johnson will see to it that this is done. . . . The South has put away a Son of Consolation and taken in exchange a Son of Thunder."

"Pity for criminals must cease," preached the Rev. J. L. Dudley to his listeners in the South Congregational Church of Middletown, Connecticut. "In the exultant ebullition of our joy, we were becoming willing to connive at wickedness in a universal pardon. We were almost ready a week ago to welcome arch rebels to princely ovations. In this solemn hour, this tearful, heart-broken hour of the nation I seem to see a divine interest to dry up all fountains of false sympathy and to bring the land to a proper sense of duty."

In Boston the Rev. E. N. Kirk seized the opportunity to point out how correct had been Sumner's estimate of the "rebels'" depravity, and by the silent comparison, how wrong had been Lincoln's trust in the South.

To the parishioners of the Mount Vernon Congregational Church, Kirk sent down from the pulpit such denunciations as:

"'For behold, the day cometh that shall burn as an oven; and all the proud, yea, and all that do wickedly, shall be as stubble.'

"What a development have the slaveholders made of their character! Some thought it severe, some untimely, for a Senator to utter that sentence of judgment on them, pronouncing slavery barbarous. But the burning day of judgment has now come, and they are witnesses on the stand to the truth of the indictment — arrogance, treasons, perjury, breach of trust, browbeating, cruelty, assassination; these are the epithets history will apply to their conduct. The great white throne is set, and black appears black before it. Davis and Stephens, Lee, Toombs and Floyd, Mason and Breckenridge, every naval and military officer that left our service; every member of their Congress; every jail-keeper that guarded our soldiers in their prisons; every act of violence to our negro soldiers in their hands; every loyal man of the South that they robbed and murdered, the corpse of Abraham Lincoln, the mangled frame of William Seward, are their witnesses. Truly there is a Nemesis. They have gone like Judas to their own place in history. . . . Look at these conspirators. They have now sealed the verdict of the world; the Confederacy is a conspiracy of assassins. It began with attempted assassination of the chief citizen, the representative man of the nation. It ended in securing his murder. They have murdered their strongest friend and broken down the last bulwark that kept the popular will from being executed upon them. A dark destiny is now before them. And woe to the man who now comes between them and the preparing blow! They have united the loyal citizens more completely in that purpose which will leave in some places no vestige of them but the desolation their wickedness has wrought. . . . Die they or the nation must."

"Ay, woe to Slavery!" roared that Boston pastor, W. S. Studley, "woe to its perjured, bloody-handed champion Jefferson Davis! Woe to its adherents and defenders, its advocates and apologists, whether in Carolina or Massachusetts. Behold, the hour of its destruction is at hand. Nay, this very Easter Sunday is the day of its resurrection. Its resurrection to everlasting shame and contempt, its resurrection to complete and eternal damnation. Its doom is sealed."

Whatever leaning the Northern masses might have had on Friday toward Lincoln's policy of forgiveness, the Boston congregation of the Rev. E. B. Webb could have retained it with difficulty on Sunday as it listened to the clergyman thundering:

"There has been a miserable, morbid, bastard philanthropy which, if it did not make the murderer's couch a bed of flowers and set his table with butter and honey, made him an object of sympathy and, after a while, of executive clemency. . . .

"And so in regard to the leaders of this infernal rebellion. The feeling was gaining ground here to let them off really without penalty. They are our brethren, it is said. Then they have added 'fratricide' to the enormity of their crimes and are unspeakably the more guilty. . . . Let these men go and we have said practically that treason is merely a difference of political opinion. I do not criticize the parole which was granted" (Lee's), "though for the life of me, I cannot see one shadow of reason for expecting it will be kept by men who have broken their most solemn and deliberate oath to the same government. It was not kept by the rebels who gave it at Vicksburg. . . . I considered the manner in which the parole was indorsed and interpreted as practically insuring a pardon; and to pardon them is a violation of my instincts, as it is of the law of the land and of God. . . . Mercy to those leaders is eternal cruelty to this nation; it is an unmitigated, unmeasured curse to unborn generations. . . . Because of this mawkish leniency four years ago, treason stalked in the streets and boasted defiance in the halls of the Capitol; Secession organized unmolested, and captured our neglected forts and starving garrisons."

And as the Rev. Mr. Webb warmed to his theme, he could have been hitting at nobody as much as the dead President when he said, "Because of a driveling, morbid, perverted sense of justice, the enemy of the government has been permitted to go at large, under the shadow of the Capitol, all through the war. God only knows how much we have suffered for the lack of justice. And now to restore these leaders seems like moral insanity. Better than this, give us back the stern, inflexible indignation of the old Puritan, and the *lex talionis* of the Hebrew lawgiver. Our consciences are debauched, our instincts confounded, our laws set aside, by this endorsement of a blind, passionate philanthropy."

Cincinnati crowds in Pike's Opera House yelled their bloodlusts when the firebrand clergyman, M. G. Gaddis, came to the climax of his oration with the words: "The wrongs of liberty culminated in the assassination of Mr. Lincoln and, minister as I am, I feel like saying tonight that these wrongs must be avenged. One of the results of this execrable act is the opening of our eyes to the fact that in the midst of our joy we were about to take to our bosom a half-frozen adder to warm it to life again. Now *the adder must die*. For every drop of blood that flowed from the veins of the great, good man, at least one leading rebel must die or be banished from this country forever."

Where in the Republic was anybody to remember Lincoln saying, "Judge not that ye be not judged!"?

Few of the pastors of the East — their sermons have been better preserved than those of the midlands — asked their congregations to suspend judgment upon the South until its guilt be clearly proven or no. One pastor who did counsel care in fixing the blame, the aged John Todd, speaking in the First Congregational Church of Pittsfield, Massachusetts, qualified his remarks in a manner to strip them of any merciful intent.

"Let us not jump hastily," he said, "to the conclusion that the perpetrators of this vile deed were in the employ or the counsels of the enemy. For one, I do not believe that the Southern leaders are too honorable to stoop to such a deed; I do not believe that they are too shrewd to see that it would injure rather than serve them. But let us not come to conclusions without proof.

"But there is one direction in which the general indignation may be properly turned—always in lawful ways and appropriate channels—and that is against the rebellion, and all who uphold it. . . . It will begin to be found out at last, that the men who are rabid with Secession, the leaders, or rather, the mis-leaders of the South, are not men to be paroled, and let off with political disabilities, and shaken by the hand, and fêted; they are men to be hunted down like wild beasts, and sent to prison and to the gallows; that Secession is not to be vanquished by leniency and kindness, but is to be stamped out with the iron heel."

Phillips Brooks, the scourge of slaveholders, prayed for their doom at the mass-meeting of the Union League in Philadelphia.

"We pray not for vengeance," he cried, "but for justice. Make bare Thine own arm and do the work that must now be done. Leave us not until every vestige of the accursed thing, that has brought us this fearful wrong, be done away with. O God, Thou hast Thy martyr for Thy cause, assert that cause until slavery be rooted out from all the borders of our land."

Universally the clergymen, at least of the East, accepted Stanton's word that Booth had murdered Lincoln as part of a Confederate plot. No Northerner of a clergyman's standing or interest in public affairs could have failed, in that time, to know that the politicians, avid for further punishment of the "rebels," were in Washington interpreting the crime for public consumption. Yet in the hysteria the pastors, as a class, lost their heads as completely as did the slowest-witted of their parishioners, and assumed that the guilt of the South had been proven.

The New England Puritan leaped at this fresh chance to have at his ancient enemy, the Southern cavalier. The intellectual snob had his old foe, the social snob, down at last. The industrious husbandman of the Yankee States had his time-honored enemy, the proud Southern planter, where he wanted him. The democrat was on top of the aristocrat.

All these emotions, deep-rooted through two generations of political wrangling and vented in four years of throat-cutting, had promised to dwindle after Appomattox, with both the brothers, North and South, feeling clearer-headed and kindlier for having fought out their old grudges.

But here the traditional venom had risen again, blacker than ever, at Lincoln's death.

Even so temperate a divine as the Rev. James Freeman Clarke, trustee of Harvard University, told his hearers in the Boston Church of the Disciples:

"The people of the North, always hopeful and good-natured, needed perhaps another example of the spirit of barbarism which had grown up in slavery, in order not to trust again with power any of this existing race of rebels.

"Always audacious, they were just about to come together to tell us how the Union was to be reconstructed. Having been beaten in the field, they were quietly stepping forward to claim the results of victory.

"But this murder has probably defeated their expectations. As Abraham Lincoln saved us, while living, from the open hostility and deadly blows of the slaveholders and Secessionists, so, in dying, he may have saved us from their audacious craft and their poisonous policy. We are reminded again what sort of people they are.

"It is idle to say that the assassination was the work of only one or two. When the whole South applauded Brooks in his attempt to assassinate Charles Sumner" (a reference to the clubbing which Preston Brooks, a hot-headed Congressman from South Carolina, had given Sumner on the floor of the Senate in 1856 as punishment for the devastating and excessive sneers which the Massachusetts statesman had delivered against the South), "when during these four years they constantly offered rewards for the heads of Lincoln and of Butler, and when no eminent Southern man has ever protested against these barbarisms, they made themselves accessories before the fact to this assassination. Throughout the South today there is probably very general exultation. Fools and blind! Throughout the North this murder will arouse a stern purpose not of revenge, we trust, or only such a revenge as will be consistent with the memory of Lincoln. The revenge we shall take for the murder of Lincoln will be to raise the loyal black population of the South not only to the position of free men but of voters, to shut out from power, forever, the leaders of the rebellion; to readmit no Southern State into the union until it has adopted a free State constitution and passed that anti-slavery amendment so dear to Abraham Lincoln's heart. . . . We need guarantees that the substantial results of the war shall not be lost, that the cure of the South shall be radical, that there shall be no more treasons, no more rebellions."

Henry Ward Beecher, that mighty man whose voice was the "bell of his soul," did not hesitate to link the murderer Booth to slavery when he got back to his Brooklyn pulpit after addressing the celebration at Fort Sumter in Charleston, S. C., on the 14th.

"He (Booth) was himself but the long sting with which slavery struck at liberty. . . . And as long as this nation lasts it will never be forgotten that we have had one martyred President — never! Never while time lasts, while heaven lasts, while hell rocks and groans, will it be forgotten that slavery, by its minions, slew him, and in slaying him, made manifest its whole nature and tendency."

Like the Radicals in politics, the Radicals of the pulpit sprang to the conclusion that all the South must be exulting over Lincoln's death.

The Rev. Charles S. Robinson of Brooklyn stormed at his parishioners like a madman: "Southern hearts have been made black by the pride of power engendered by the tyranny over the unprotected black race, and it has betrayed these miserable wretches into the mistake of supposing that they could lord it over the white race. How else will you explain this appalling fact; there are *women,* with babes in their arms, who will declare that this murder in cold blood of a man, in the presence of his wife, is *chivalrous!* Underlying all the ferocity of such a sentiment is found the subtle working of mere pride of caste. Slavery has debased the feminine and human sentiments with which they were born. That code of morals always did tend to barbarism. The young men of the South were corrupt before the war. The women were brutalized in the finer feelings of natural decency. They would send women to be stripped and whipped by men for a price. Passion grows wild with mere indulgence. Hence it is that a deed combining so much of ex-

ecrable meanness with so much hellish cruelty find women un-
sexed enough to applaud it! Home on the diabolical system it
represents, do I soberly urge the responsibility of this murder.
It is high time to have done with it, root and branches."

Like those Union soldiers who had in their first rage cried
out that the war be renewed and fought out to the death, so
did clergymen here and there call upon the North to pick up
its arms again. Perhaps some of the ministerial faction abandoned their bloody program as quickly as did the troops in the
field, but for a time plenty of them had such gory hopes.

"I would give this rebellion war to the knife," cried that
wrathful old divine, Samuel T. Spear, pastor of the South
Presbyterian Church in Brooklyn, as he denounced "conciliation," which he said had been growing. He would next extend a
"generous" amnesty to the masses of Southern people providing
they gave up slavery and reorganized on the basis of absolute
loyalty, holding them meanwhile under military rule. "I would
then divide the responsible leaders and prime authors of the
rebellion into three classes, according to the grade of their
guilt. The first of which and the smallest — of which Jefferson
Davis is a conspicuous example — I would hang by the neck till
they are dead. The second class of which, and a larger class, I
would expel from the country, and send them forth as fugitives
over the face of the earth. And a third and a still larger class I
would dispossess of all political power, denying to them the
right to vote, and making them ineligible to any office of profit
or trust under the government of the United States. I would
visit these penalties upon these men for the enormous crimes
which they have committed. Justice requires it. The future
safety of the nation demands it. Away with the mawkish sympathy that ignores justice and ruins government."

The Rev. George D. Putnam condensed the attitude of many
pastors into this, as he addressed his Boston congregation: "Justice is as divine a principle in God and man as is mercy. An unfit
clemency to guilty individuals is cruelty to innocent millions
and to unborn generations. Not from the kindly lips and tender
heart of Lincoln do we derive these stern counsels of duty; but
from his gaping wound and flowing blood do we take them,
and must heed them."

Many a pastor started his sermon on the note of sorrow and finished it in raging damnations as did the Rev. A. L. Stone in Boston. "Oh, weeping April! Oh, month of tears! Pour down all thy warm showers; from our eyes the rain falls faster yet! Evermore, from henceforth, at thy return, thou and the sorrowing nation shall weep together!" He sang, but as he warmed to his work he soon was roaring: "That black, consummate crime is only the ripe fruit of that system of barbarism which has struck its roots so deep, made shedding of blood like the pouring out of water; the cries of famishing men as whisperings of the idle wind."

Rare indeed was the spirit of tolerance as the Rev. E. J. Goodspeed voiced it to his parishioners in Chicago's Second Baptist Church.

"The idea of vengeance should be carefully excluded from every mind," said he, "and the spirit of revenge from all hearts. We may cry to God for justice, we may appeal to our magistrates for justice, but remembering that we, too, are sinners, that fortuitous events gave us birth in the North and determined our creed that our late lamented President, in the spirit of Jesus, counseled moderation and clemency, let us show the deeds of mercy, and push on the car of civilization to new elevations of humanity and Christ-like love."

Even such humane Boston preachers as Edward Everett Hale and Rufus S. Ellis tiptoed gingerly through those portions of their sermons which implied that the nation should still its cry of vengeance. Hale confined himself to guarded and vague repetitions of the phrase "Peace on Earth; good will to men" and Ellis asked his listeners not to misunderstand him when he suggested that they refrain from extending the death of Lincoln into a reign of terror and blood. And a few months later, when Ellis' sermon was published, he had been sufficiently cowed by the spirit of vengeance to add a footnote which said, "The preacher desires that the paragraph above may not be interpreted as recommending lenity to the authors of privy conspiracy or rebellion."

"Black Easter" was the day well nicknamed.

"Revenge, revenge, revenge" was the chanting refrain that the clergymen sent down from the pulpit as they rushed, wittingly or no, to throw their support to the party of Sumner and Stanton and Henry Winter Davis and Wade.

And by the time this Sabbath sun was down, the Radicals would know that the pulpit was behind them in their wrathful program.

Since Friday night the Republican enemies of Lincoln had owned the War Office and had thus controlled the news; since Saturday they had claimed the White House; on Sunday, they learned that the pulpit was theirs, too. The moral force of the North was arrayed at their backs. God had delivered the South at last into their hands.

Where was Lincoln, now, with all his power?

✿ ✿ ✿ 9 ✿ ✿ ✿

THEY KNEW WHAT GOD WANTED

FROM BOTH THEIR PREACHERS and their politicians the Northern people learned that the blood of Lincoln must henceforth be laid upon the doorsills of the South.

What the people did not yet know, on April 16, 1865, was that the Radicals were, in private, acclaiming the President's murder as a godsend. The "avengers" were not anxious to make public the brusque joy they felt at the turn of events.

But from many pulpits on this "Black Easter" morning, the people caught the same idea, swathed, however, in reverent eloquence and religious mysticism. To thousands of churchgoers, listening in the pews, it was plain from the pastors' words that the miraculous hand of God had passed before their very eyes, lifting Lincoln out of the President's chair for the good of the nation.

It had been God's purpose to remove the President so that the Northern people might move forward, the preachers said. As to what precisely God's purpose might be, various ministers had various understandings, but on one thing they agreed: the President had been taken from life as biblical heroes and prophets had been taken, in drama that was mystic and sacred.

In the explanations of some pastors, the people saw visions of Jehovah's awful power, not unmixed with righteous jealousy and wrath.

"I accept God's action as an indication that Lincoln's work as an instrument of Providence ended here," said the Rev. Martin R. Vincent in the First Presbyterian Church of Troy, New York, "and that the work of retribution belonged to other and doubtless fitter instruments. I will not positively assert that his policy toward traitors was so much too lenient that God replaced him by a man, who, we have good reason to think, will not err in this direction. Yet I say this may be and it looks like it. Lincoln's policy was setting much too strongly in the direction of lenity and conciliation.

" 'Little children, keep yourselves from idols!'

"We are hero worshippers.

" 'Put not your trust in princes!'

"I trembled when I heard men say, 'Grant is left! Sherman is left! Sheridan and Thomas are left!' God wants this nation to trust Him and in Him only. God is left."

From the pulpit of Trinity Church the Rev. Francis Vinton, old Indian fighter, and now Episcopal clergyman of the fashionable New York congregation, warned his listeners:

"A lesson is that there have always been found men, instruments of God, fitted for their offices — one man to organize an army, another to lead it to victory, and, as soon as they have accomplished the work given them to do, they have been removed and other men raised to their places. When we saw the one man, Abraham Lincoln, like Saul head and shoulders taller than the rest, our disposition for hero-worship might have led us to give him more honor than belonged to providential man, and a jealous God has removed him from us to show that the Lord Jesus Christ alone was our President, our King, our Saviour."

And the Rev. J. Wesley Carhart of the Second Street Methodist Episcopal Church in Troy had similar insight into God's motives, saying to his flock:

"His death may serve the purposes of God with reference to the nation better than his life. Not that his life was unimportant, but it may be that we have come to depend too much upon

him, and God suffered him to be taken away to show us that
the salvation of the nation was in His hands, and safe; that we
can carry on His work, though His workmen fall. It is God's
purpose that treason shall be punished. President Lincoln's
position of leniency seemed to be a necessity from which he could
not well recede. He was suffered to be removed from that position by means the best calculated to excite, not a spirit of revenge,
but a desire and determination on the part of the people that
the penalty of the law should be inflicted."

Likewise the Rev. C. B. Crane of the South Baptist Church
of Hartford, Conn., discerned God's way of removing a rival
from the people's heart, and, as he spoke, made this devout
suggestion: "Although we are not aware of it, we have been,
for a considerable time past, placing our confidence in our
lamented President rather than in our God. . . . The destiny
of our country was not suspended upon the life of Abraham
Lincoln. God has smitten him down upon whom our faith was
impiously reposed, in order that He might transfer our faith to
Himself."

From the pulpit of Broadway Tabernacle, the Rev. J. B.
Thompson, head of the Home Missionary Society, suggested,
very piously, that God Himself had shot Lincoln. "An artist
wanted me to hang a painting of Lincoln on the pulpit for the
memorial service today," said he, "but I replied, 'In the pulpit
only God should be exalted. No man is great enough, nor good
enough to share the honors of the House of God.'

"Yet this is just what we are doing as a nation, lifting Abraham Lincoln between ourselves and God. Before his election we
prayed and felt our dependence on God, and afterward said,
'Now all is sure for four years,' and we were trusting Lincoln
in place of God.

"The great irreligion of our times is the exclusion of a living,
personal God from human affairs. The sharp crack of a pistol
lays low the head of a nation and from the unseen comes the
voice, 'Be still and know that I am God.'"

In Detroit's First Presbyterian Church, the Rev. George
Duffield, after suggesting that God had taken Lincoln away
because of his inability to punish treason according to its deserts,

broke out with: "How jealous God has been of us! He has over-turned every human idol which we have set up among our generals and glorified for triumph. . . . In the death of President Lincoln He has pursued the same plan of His gracious providence. We might have put him in place of God and forgotten whose right hand hath gotten us the victory."

In the pulpit of the United Presbyterian Church of Troy stood the Rev. Hugh P. McAdam, on this Sabbath, presenting to his flock this interpretation of events: "God designed, by this dispensation (the assassination) to teach us not to invade the sanctity of the Sabbath. When news of Lee's surrender came on a Sabbath evening, the whole Union in uncontrolled enthusiasm proceeded to such lengths in their rejoicing as ill became the sacredness of the day, which God had set apart as the day of rest to be kept holy to Himself. I trembled then for the consequences.

"I have frequently seen the statement in our papers," he declared, "and I have often heard it remarked, that Lincoln was the idol of the people. I fear this declaration was founded in truth. The people of this country are inclined to hero-worship. There is a tendency in the human heart to exalt the creature to the throne of the Creator and render him that homage which is alone due to God. It may be on this account that our President has been taken from us. God is a jealous God and will not suffer the honor and glory that are due Himself to be ascribed to any creature. God will punish idolatry."

Scores, perhaps hundreds, of clergymen explained that God had removed Lincoln because the good man had been too merciful, too forgiving toward the Southerners, those enemies of the Lord.

"Wherever Lincoln has erred it has been on the side of mercy," said the Rev. Alfred S. Hunt to his Methodist congregation in New York City. "And there are those who listen to me today who think that Providence has permitted this calamity to befall us that a sterner hand might rule in our national affairs."

This belief that Andrew Johnson was a better man than Lincoln for the nation in its present need was a favorite theme

with many clergymen, the Rev. Warren E. Cudworth express-
ing it emphatically as he said to his Boston congregation: "God
may have seen that a sterner hand than his (Lincoln's) was
needed to hold the helm of state during the next four years of
reckoning and reconstruction. We have all marked how gentle
and kind he has been. His death under God will do as much for
the cause he had at heart as did his life. We know that already
several of the leading supporters of his administration had taken
issue with him on Reconstruction in the rebel states."

Aid and comfort for the Radicals in such words!

Also, in the words of the Rev. A. S. Patton of the Tabernacle
Church of Utica, N. Y., "For other service the Almighty has
other instruments and if a less loving and gentle heart is necessary to a proper and final adjustment of our difficulties — if a
heavier hand and a sterner man are needed to inflict impartial
and terrible justice on those who have been seeking the country's life then, though we weep our bereavement, we will accept
the sad event with all its consequences as a thing permitted of
God."

All this approval of "the sterner hand" must have made
churchgoers of that Easter Sunday smile wanly as they remembered it in the years to come, for the hand, without any particular sternness whatsoever, had been plucking at the sheets in a hall
bedroom not far from the theater of John T. Ford at the moment Booth's pistol cracked. This heavy hand which the clergyman and the politicians compared so favorably to the feeble
fingers of Lincoln, belonged, of course, to Andrew Johnson,
and at the moment when the pulpit was hailing him as the "new
Moses" or the "Joshua" whom God had produced for the work
which Lincoln could not accomplish, Johnson had barely re-
covered from a big drunk. Or at least it was so said in Washington by men who had seen him at this hour.

Considering the inestimable damage done to the Republic by
the blindly careening Republican party during the four years of
Johnson's futile Presidency, it was respectfully wondered in
later years if the clergymen had, after all, reported God's plan
so accurately to their listeners that Easter morning.

The South was permanently injured — indeed, wrecked for

two generations — when Johnson's administration collapsed into back-fence wrangling.

To convince listeners on "Black Easter" that Johnson was the man of the hour was a delicate task for any orator, since the Vice-President had performed some comic, loud and impertinent antics at his inauguration ceremonies only six weeks before, speaking in a manner to make his alcoholic condition very clear to all present.

Yet, for the good of the country, it must be done, this job of exalting the new executive, and the clergy went manfully to work, many among them sincerely believing Johnson a better man than Lincoln for Reconstruction days, many others, perhaps, choosing to eulogize him in order to counteract the popular worship of Lincoln.

The aforementioned Rev. C. B. Crane, that sad day, decided not to evade the John Barleycorn phase of Johnson's past.

"I believe that God purposes to bring final deliverance to the Republic," he said, "by the same Andrew Johnson in whom, on the fourth of last March, we lost faith. Not only is the man whom we trusted taken away, but the man whom we distrusted is made captain of our hosts.

"True, Andrew Johnson stumbled fearfully at the start. But there has been wrought a marvelous change in the forty-one days that have elapsed. Do you not remember how our confidence in Abraham Lincoln was shaken when he went from Springfield to Washington making little speeches from the platform of the car all the way?

"Abraham Lincoln's work is done. From the fourteenth of this April his work was done. From that time God had no further use for him in this position which he held. At that time God had use for Andrew Johnson. . . . There was danger that Lincoln would subordinate his executive function to his personal sympathies; . . . that he would even pardon Davis and Stephens and Johnston and Lee if they should come into his power. . . .

"But Andrew Johnson, a man of nerve, has had his heart wrung under the iron heel of rebellion. His sense of justice is paramount to his tender sensibilities. I believe God has raised him up to bring this rebellion to the consummation of just retribution. It is not private revenge that he will wreak, but the vengeance of God whose appointed minister he is.

"The nation will understand ere long that the dark Providence of last Friday night was a merciful Providence. Andrew Johnson is the Joshua whom God has appointed to consummate the work which our dead Moses so nobly commenced."

However, it was not Lincoln but Johnson himself who was "Moses," according to the Rev. A. A. Miner's view as he gave it to his Boston congregation: "And shall we not find a satisfactory leader in our new, let me say, our God-given President? . . . He may be better prepared than Mr. Lincoln himself to estimate the rebels' deep demerit and mete out to them the need of justice as traitors before the law.

"It is narrated of Mr. Johnson that, in October last, on an occasion of addressing some thousands of colored people in the city of Memphis, if I remember correctly, he exhorted them to patience and assured them that God would raise up for them a Moses to lead them out of the wilderness. His auditors shouted, 'You shall be our Moses!'

"Mr. Johnson modestly replied that he was not equal to so important a labor. But they repeated the claim, 'You shall be our Moses, we want none other than you!'

" 'Very well, then,' said Johnson, 'I will be your Moses.'

"Was this incident prophetic?"

Very human, very complex forces were shaping the words of these leading clergymen — and others like them — as they explained to the people why Lincoln had been so mysteriously taken away. Tangled in the preachers' minds were many emotions as they thought of Lincoln — emotions of admiration, distrust, disappointment, jealousy, love.

The man had been a puzzle to them, as he had to most Americans who had received higher education and orthodox ideas as to what constituted culture. He was from out of the West, a region which to educated Easterners was wild, uncouth and coarse, yet, as President, he had used the English language with a classic strength and purity that shamed university-trained minds.

Clergymen had been drawn to Lincoln by his unfeigned love of humanity, yet the more orthodox among them had wondered if he wasn't carrying that faith a little too far. Wasn't this prairie champion of the masses too close to the dangerous "rights of man" theories of those skeptical Americans of an earlier day, Thomas Jefferson and Tom Paine?

Lincoln, the vast symbol of honesty, had helped the preachers in their work of promoting goodness and morality, yet he had gone so far with it as to become the moral leader of the people and, as such, the rival of every pastor in the land. To the average clergyman, keyed to the everlasting battle for the salvage of human souls, it was disquieting to see the Northern masses idolize a non-church member like Lincoln, who had said he would never join a religious body until he saw the Golden Rule standing solitary above its church doors.

Moreover, this strange President had never denied the charge that he was an infidel. Back in 1846 when Lincoln had defeated the Rev. Peter Cartwright for Congress, and in two Presidential campaigns as well, the charge of atheism had been hurled repeatedly at his head. His enemies said that in his youth he had called Jesus a bastard, had dismissed biblical miracles as against God's law, and had written a piece to prove Holy Writ "uninspired."

No President, it was likely, had ever prayed so devoutly or earnestly to God, yet Lincoln had rarely, if ever, spoken of Christ.

He told Rabelaisian stories, they knew, indeed relating them without looking to be sure no clergyman was within earshot. He was a good husband and father, had joined an anti-rum society and spoken for temperance; he had no use for liquor, tobacco or other men's wives, yet he kept firm friendships with free-thinking, bold fellows who got howling drunk and who frolicked with sex.

In 1860 all but three of the twenty-four ministers in Lincoln's home town, Springfield, had opposed him. Much of the ministerial support that he had received in that campaign had only come to him because clergymen as a body detested Stephen A. Douglas, his chief opponent. Douglas, criticized by the clergy in

1854 because of his sudden favoritism to the slaveholding South, had told them to stick to their spiritual sphere. "You have desecrated the pulpit and prostituted the sacred desk to the miserable and corrupting influence of party politics," he said. As between Douglas and Lincoln, the Northern clergy chose the latter. He at least would keep the slave-power from further expansion, while Douglas would turn it free to seize the Northwest Territory.

Up until that moment, 1854, the priest-class North and South had condoned slavery, either by refusing to discuss it or by warmly commending it. Southern clergymen were fond of justifying it on the grounds that it was God's way of bringing the black heathen out of the African jungle, where they were inaccessible to His gospel, and establishing them in the enlightened South where they might be the more easily salvaged for Christianity even if it took the whip on Sunday morn to make them see the light.

The Northern Abolitionists, fanatical, warm-hearted, consecrated to the task of freeing all colored people, knew the churches as their enemies. So long as the professional pulpit refrained from assailing slavery, the common people would remain indifferent to the great moral crusade that the Abolitionists conducted through the printing press. Stephen Foster wrote "The Brotherhood of Thieves," denouncing the churches for their "shoddy association" with the great evil, and the country was blanketed with pamphlets breathing similar scorn. The large denominations, in the '30s split at Mason and Dixon's line, yet the Northern halves still refused to condemn slavery. They wanted the issue hushed for the sake of peace. Not even the Religious Society of Friends, commonly called Quakers, and commonly zealous for Abolition, would go on record against the institution. Their chief poet, John Greenleaf Whittier, spoke his mind, saying, "No power on earth could save slavery if the organized churches would oppose it."

Such pulpits as did attack it were independent of bishops and deacons — churches like those of Theodore Parker, William Ellery Channing and Phillips Brooks, unorthodox, "free" churches. Only such powerful figures could escape the ousting which disciplinary boards gave lesser dominies when they dared protest against the "national curse" of slavery. In the larger cities of the East, wealthy pew-holders did not want slave-holding criticized. Cotton profits were too high for that. Thousands of church-members, growing slowly adamant against "human bondage," left their pews never to return.

So matters stood until Senator Douglas of Illinois in 1854 proposed in his "Kansas-Nebraska Bill," to open up the new territories of the West and Northwest to slavery. He would allow the citizens of these regions to decide the question for themselves. Since this broke the old compromises which said that Southern States might always be "slave" and Northern States must always be "free," the clergymen, flanked by the majority of their followers, began to cry that the South was seeking to rule or ruin, and that the only solution for the nation's sickness was to set all the slaves free.

The suddenness of this "conversion" aroused the Abolitionists to bitter laughter, but the churches forged ahead so rapidly that by 1860 they were far readier for emancipation than was the Republican candidate, Abraham Lincoln. Through his first two years of office, the clergymen pleaded with Lincoln to free the slaves, abused him when he would not, and branded him as a "slave-hound."

When in September, 1862, he did issue his Emancipation Proclamation, liberating slaves in those States which were fighting the Union, the clergymen generally felt that the President had only followed their urging and that he had made a belated response to their leadership.

As a matter of fact, Lincoln had freed the colored man because the political situation needed just such a bold and masterly stroke. The thing would cost him countless votes in the North. Thousands of Union Democrats who had supported him against Secession would desert him the moment he made the war seem to be one against slavery. But against this loss he had much more to gain.

In Europe kings, princes, money-barons, social aristocrats, were making signs as though to recognize the South as an independent nation. Ruling classes of the Old World felt akin to the feudal plantation-owners of the New, and estranged from the democratic, hard-working, money-grubbing North. They wanted the cotton that Lincoln's blockade shut off from the seas.

To prevent their fatal recognition of the Confederacy, Lincoln played his trump card, long held in his sleeve — Emancipation. With it he captured the hearts and imaginations of the European masses, who kindled to Republican doctrines. The laboring-classes of older countries saw in a flash that the American North was for freedom, for human rights, for humanity, and with a cheer they forced their Bourbon leaders to keep hands off New World affairs.

Most of this had taken place behind the scenes, where few in the embattled Republic could see. What the North debated was the question of Lincoln's governmental right to do what he had done, and although it distressed both Abolitionists and clergymen, to see the President thus take unto himself the toga of "The Liberator" and "The Great Emancipator," the tidal wave of adulation for him had begun. The Northern Democrats might desert him for the time being, but he had become the moral leader of the nation.

As against the natural resentment which clergymen felt under these circumstances, was to be set the generous thanks which Lincoln gave the churches for their steady support and their relief-work. In May, '64, he said to a Methodist delegation in the White House:

"Nobly sustained as the government has been by all the churches, I would utter nothing which might in the least appear invidious against any. Yet without this, it may be fairly said, that the Methodist Episcopal Church, not less devoted than the rest, is by its greater numbers the most important of all. It is no fault in others that the Methodist Church sends more soldiers to the field, more nurses to the hospital, and more prayers to Heaven than any. God bless the Methodist Church. Bless all the churches. Blessed be God, who in this our greatest trial, giveth us the churches."

To other delegations he had spoken with similar gratitude. Less pleasant to the clergymen, perhaps, were the memories of those times when Lincoln had seemed a trifle testy in answering the world of advice, counsel, admonition, congratulation, fault-finding which, singly and in delegation, they brought to the White House so freely across his administration.

There was the time that a delegation had taken him strongly to task on some action and had been told by the President to imagine all their wealth in the hands of Blondin, famous tight-rope walker of the day.

"Suppose Blondin held it in a rope over Niagara Falls," he said. "Would you keep shouting, 'Blondin, stand up a little straighter! Stoop a little! Go a little faster! Lean more to the South! No, more to the North.'

"Gentlemen, would you rock the cable? No! You would hold your breath, every one of you, as well as your tongues. This government, gentlemen, is carrying an immense weight. The persons managing the ship of state in this storm are doing the best they can. Don't worry them with needless warnings and complaints. Keep silence, be patient and we'll get you safely across."

There had been an apparent shyness of pastors about the White House for a time after this abrupt piece of advice, but as Ward Hill Lamon, Lincoln's body-guard, told it, the President relented. "The latch-string is out and they have a right to come here and preach to me if they'll go about it with some gentleness and moderation," he said.

At another time, when some frocked visitors assured him that he could accept their urgings as having come from the Lord, Lincoln had answered, "Well, gentlemen, it isn't often one is favored with a delegation direct from the Almighty." And to a dominie who had said that the Lord was on "our" side, he replied, "I'm not at all concerned about that; for I know the Lord is always on the side of the right; but it is my constant anxiety that this nation and I may be on the Lord's side."

So, when Lincoln was dead and funeral sermons were to be preached, there were many complex memories and tangling emotions to guide the preachers' tongues.

THE DYING GOD

Of all the pictures of Lincoln that were painted in words that "Black Easter" morning, one was more lasting than the rest — the mystic picture of Lincoln, the prophet from on high, linked more closely than other men to the Infinite.

Most of the other pictures soon faded. Within a few years nobody would believe any more that the South had prompted the murder, or that God had killed Lincoln in jealous wrath, or that the peaceful man had been removed so that Providence might work through the stronger Andrew Johnson.

But that the Lord had sent Lincoln to earth as His mysterious representative, to die for His people, was a belief that rose from many of the Easter sermons and grew with time to blend into the American faith that the humble backwoodsman had been by some miracle, the savior of the Union.

That the Northern voters should so accept Lincoln, satisfied the Radicals well enough. Those politicians who regarded the people as simpletons and idiots for their admiration of Lincoln, were content that the masses should have Lincoln dramatized for them as a saint, a sweet and helpless creature, incapable of understanding the deep depravity of slaveholders, a man too vague and too good to cope with the intricacies of Reconstruction, too unworldly to manage the political battle that must come with the insidious, treacherous South.

To the "avengers" who knew, all too well, the cunning political resourcefulness of the man who now lay dead, the words of pastors who called the martyr "unworldly" must have seemed ironic in the extreme, but they let them pass, content for Lincoln to have all possible fame so long as the party of Sumner and Stevens and Wade had the earthly power.

Most clergymen who spoke of Lincoln as they spoke of Jesus and Moses did so from devout sincerity. Others, distrusting the President as they had, must have seen that to picture him as a meek and holy dispensation of God, would solve their dilemma.

They could not by any chance directly assail Lincoln in the face of such popular grief, neither could they compromise their own immortal souls and say that Lincoln was the right man to lead the people. What they could say was that Lincoln was something more than a man, a strange, supernatural being whom God had sent to earth to be slaughtered in all his childlike purity so that the North might see to what foul lengths the South would go.

It served the purpose of many ministers — and politicians, too — for the people to believe that Lincoln had been more heart than mind, more of the spirit than of the flesh, a divine, seraphic figure who had appeared for no other purpose than to be sacrificed for the American nation.

God, according to such explanations, had arranged the sacred drama so that Lincoln might be stricken down at the very moment when he was preaching love — "malice toward none, charity for all" — thus making plain to all beholders the full and awful wickedness of the South.

"Moses" was the name most commonly bestowed upon Lincoln in the pulpit on "Black Easter." Like Moses, it was said, he had guided his people miraculously through the desert of war, and like Moses, he had been mysteriously taken away when his work was done, leaving the more earthly and harsher task of reconstructing the nation to hands more mundane and capable.

It was as though a cosmic trade had been accomplished, giving Lincoln the glory of a blind and beautiful god, and giving his enemies the Republican party. He had the crown, the Radicals had the power. He was dead on the mountain, they were loose in the promised land of Dixie, their hands already on throats that they had promised themselves through long years of rankling denial.

"Like Moses he died," cried the Rev. J. D. Fulton of Boston, "not because of disease nor of advanced age; his eye was not dim, nor was his natural force abated. He died because his work was done. He had passed through battle, sorrow and war; had climbed the heights of Pisgah, and had gained a view of the Canaan of peace lying in the distance; and when the Lord had showed him all the land, and had assured him of the promise that the sons of freedom should possess it, by his providence He declared, 'Thou shalt go over thither.' "

To give the pastor his due, it must be said that he might not have known how Lincoln, these many months, had been striving with all his craft to prevent the sons of freedom from possessing the Southern Canaan. Most likely, however, Dr. Fulton did know it, since preachers of his day knew politics inside and out.

From the Rev. John Todd, standing in his pulpit at Pittsfield, Mass., this day came the pious thought that Lincoln's passing had been at the best possible time.

"I do not believe that the safety and prosperity of this country are dependent upon the life of any one man, however great and good; much less can I believe that they are in the hands of an infuriated and probably drunken actor. God is able to raise up other instruments instead of those that he lays down. Moses may lie down to die, on the very borders of the promised land, but a Joshua shall be raised up to lead the people in to possess it. And it is remarkable how often it happens, in the providence of God, that the Moses dies. It is seldom granted to the same man to guide through the desert, and to enter into the land of promise. For President Lincoln himself, perhaps there was no better time to pass away. He fell in the very height of glory."

In the views of Dr. Gaddis of Cincinnati, God had removed both Lincoln and Moses from the world because of their tendencies toward excessive leniency, killing them "in order that mercy should not become a crime."

"O Liberty," he shouted, "here tonight on thy bloody but triumphant altar, we offer thee the Moses of the nineteenth century — the Winkelried of America."

A heavenly brotherhood between Lincoln and Moses and Jesus was pictured in the sermons on that sixteenth of April, 1865.

"Oh, I thank the Lord of heaven and earth," exulted the Rev. George Dana Boardman of Philadelphia's First Baptist Church on "Black Easter," "that He hath so woven the web of nations as to permit the American people to set before the

ages the grandest human illustration the world has ever witnessed of that sublime principle which seems to pervade the uni-
verse and which lies as the very cornerstone of Redemption —
Vicarious Sacrifice."

Not only in the giving of his life did Lincoln seem like Jesus,
the very day of his death touched the superstitions of a great
army of pastors. Said the Rev. Warren E. Cudworth of Boston:
"The week through which we have just passed has not been
unlike that Holy or Passion Week, which, in Judea of old, was
so eventful to the Saviour and his disciples. It began in triumph
and rejoicing. . . . But alas, it ended like the week of sorrows,
in gloom and blood. And is it not strange that Good Friday was
the day, of all days in the year, chosen by the murderer for his
infamous deed? It is one of those remarkable historical coinci-
dences, which, whether we will or not, challenge observation
and cause remark; and, no doubt, could our President have
spoken after he was shot, he would have forgiven the cowardly
perpetrator of this inhuman act, and rounded the parallel with a
final and complete imitation of our Lord's example."

And the Rev. C. B. Crane, aforementioned, was comparing
Lincoln to both Jesus and Moses saying:

"Oh, friends, on the evening of Good Friday, the memorial
day of the crucifixion of our Lord, our good, true-hearted, magnanimous, supremely loyal, great President was smitten down
by the hand of an assassin; and yester morn, at twenty-two
minutes past seven of the clock, his noble and holy soul went up
from its shattered and desecrated tabernacle to its God. It is the
after-type of the tragedy which was accomplished on the first
Good Friday, more than eighteen centuries ago, upon the
eminence of Calvary in Judea.

"Yes, it was meet that the martyrdom should occur on Good
Friday. It is no blasphemy against the Son of God and the
Saviour of men that we declare the fitness of the slaying of the
second Father of our Republic on the anniversary of the day
on which He was slain. Jesus Christ died for the world, Abraham Lincoln died for his country. The consecration of Jesus to
humanity began in the antiquity of eternity and found its

culmination when He cried with white, yet triumphant lips on the cross, 'It is finished.'

"And as the tragedy of the cross has startled tens of thousands of sinners into a recognition of their sins, while it expressed the inflexibility of God's law and authority, so we may hope that the tragedy of last Friday night will startle the multitude of rebels, North as well as South, into a recognition of their crime, stiffen the government, which might otherwise bend, into requisite rigidness, and hasten the consummation of peace for which we devoutly pray.

"The last and costliest offering which God demanded has been taken."

The erudite and learned Dr. Henry W. Bellows, president of the United States Sanitary Commission (Civil War prototype of the Red Cross) spoke to a church audience of "Lincoln, the lost leader, honored in the day of his death, dying on the anniversary of our Lord's greatest sacrifice, a mighty sacrifice himself for the sins of his people." Dr. Francis Vinton, in his Trinity Church sermon, thought it remarkable "that Good Friday should have been solemnized by the murder of one who had tried so much to imitate his Divine Master." The Rev. Dr. John Chase Lord told his churchmen of Buffalo that no such crime as this had taken place in a thousand years, "perhaps not since the day of the murder on Calvary, when the heavens darkened, and the earth staggered, and the dead rose as the God-Man mediator hung upon the cross. Abraham Lincoln's death by murder canonizes his life. His words, his messages, his proclamations are now the American Evangel. God has permitted him to die a martyr because He wished to consecrate the works, the policy and proclamations of our President as the political gospel of our country, sealed in blood."

Likewise the Rev. William Adams likened Lincoln's death to Christ's crucifixion in his New York Madison Avenue Presbyterian Church and added, "God left George Washington childless so that, by a grateful people, he would always be called by the name of Father of the Nation! And now another father of his country has been taken from us, thus rudely the crown of martyrdom his."

On Monday, April 18, the Rev. Sidney Dean, addressing citizens of Providence, Rhode Island, in City Hall, declared: "Judas covenanted with high officials, himself a hireling, for his Master's life. This second Judas, worse than his namesake, went out from the presence of the chief priests and counsellors of treason and himself committed the murder. The first Judas, under the pangs of remorse, cast the price of blood — of which he was the only accessory before the act — at the feet of his employers and hanged himself. The second Judas we trust will be hanged in the sight of the world, whose air he poisons in inhaling, by the hands of a pure justice, and we trust all his bloodstained employers will be hanged with him.

"To worldly vision the nation's earthly Saviour has left us in an important hour. We are not gifted with the prescience of the Great Ruler. . . . Like the sorrowing disciples who, journeying toward Emmaus from Jerusalem after the tragedy of Calvary, talked of the crucified Saviour of the world, extolled his virtues and discussed his character, so we, so the nation, will talk of the virtues of the pure and noble character whom we trusted and who had been given of God for the utter redemption and restoration of the Republic."

The Rev. James Freeman Clarke joined, too, in likening Lincoln to the Man of Galilee.

"Perhaps," said Dr. Clarke, "the crime committed last Friday night in Washington is the worst ever committed on any Good Friday since the crucifixion of Christ. It was not only assassination, it was parricide; for Abraham Lincoln was as a father to the whole nation."

Newspapers that had supported Lincoln frequently echoed the words of those clergymen who dwelt upon the similarity between Jesus and Lincoln, Joseph Medill printing in his Chicago *Tribune* an editorial which began:

"On the sacred anniversary of the day made holy by the crucifixion of Him, we mourn another martyrdom. No temple's veil is rent in twain, the earth does not quake, nor are the rocks rent as when the Lord God finished in bitter agony His appointed work.

"But our hearts instinctively recognize the relation of leader and follower between our martyred Lord and all those who die because the wicked hate righteousness."

At a tremendous mass-meeting in the New York Customs House on Saturday, April 15, James A. Garfield, devoutly religious, a member of Congress as well as general in the Union Army — and later to be the second assassinated President — anticipated the zealous view of the clergymen, when in his emotional eloquence he said: "It may be almost impious to say it, but it does seem that Lincoln's death parallels that of the Son of God who cried out, 'Father, forgive them for they know not what they do.'"

Within a week after the assassination the phrase "savior of his country" was a slogan for orators, editorial writers, and makers of funeral mottoes over the entire North.

How many of these eulogies that went up on the Saturday, Sunday and Monday after the disaster of Friday, were from conviction, and how many from a lip-serving desire to speak well of the dead — and particularly the distinguished dead — became more and more of a question as time and distance gave proportion to the scene. That the great bulk of the common people received the tributes with pathetic sincerity is not to be questioned, but that the professional classes of lawyers, clergymen, politicians and wealthy merchants could so suddenly have abandoned their long-held doubts as to Lincoln's mental distinction is not within reason. Few of the dead man's eulogists indicated that they thought his intellect at all superior. They generally agreed that his soul, his heart, his integrity, were cast in a great mold, but there was very little said of his greatness of mind. Here and there a voice would laud his brain, but it was but a thin piping in a mighty wind — a wind that was blowing up clouds of foggy myth in which to hide the real nature of the man. Even Bishop Simpson, preaching Lincoln's final funeral sermon in Springfield, praised the late lamented's soul at the expense of his intellect. "It was not, however, chiefly by the mental faculties that he gained such control over mankind," said Simpson. "His moral power gave him preëminence. . . . It was this moral power which gave him the greatest hold upon the people and made his utterances almost oracular."

The only Americans who seemed to know the shrewdness, the cunning depths and patient foresight of Lincoln's mind were silent. The Radical politicians who had opposed him understood very well indeed how baffling and adroit was Lincoln, but they said little or nothing, now, about the departed, and Charles Sumner, on June 1, 1865, in giving an address on Lincoln in Boston converted fully half of his eulogy into a "stump" speech advocating the Radicals' policy on Reconstruction. This departure, coupled with the fact that his spectacles kept falling off, caused the speaker to lose his audience — a rare thing for Sumner.

However, like his fellow Radicals, the preachers, he drove home the point that the calamity had been all for the best. As he saw it, God had killed Lincoln to make freedom doubly certain for the slave.

"Who will say that Lincoln's death was not a judgment of the Lord?" he said. "Perhaps it was needed to lift the country to a more perfect justice and to inspire it with a sublime faith. Perhaps it was sent in mercy to set a sacred, irreversible seal upon the good he has done and to put Emancipation beyond all mortal question."

In the West were lawyers and judges, old associates who knew the power and play of Lincoln's brain, which could grind exceeding fine for all its slowness whenever its owner wanted anything that he thought might honestly and properly be his. To these Westerners it was a matter for angry resentment when New York chose, as its orator for the funeral ceremonies, George Bancroft, the historian and Democratic political figure. Bancroft, making scholarly, ringing tributes to Lincoln's character, raised the doubt as to how much of Lincoln's wisdom had come from within and how much from the common people upon whom he leaned.

Sweetly such parsons as the Rev. George C. Chaney of Boston impeached Lincoln's mentality in the fulsomeness with which he dwelt upon his innocence and simplicity — a simplicity that seemed, in Chaney's words, to have dangerously approached stupidity.

"He was kind and forgiving," said the preacher, "forgiving

to a fault, some have thought and said. Our good President never knew, never could know, the wickedness and spite of the enemies of his country."

Similarly the Rev. John McClintock, D.D., LL.D., of New York spoke in St. Paul's Church:

"All over the world men will weep the death of Mr. Lincoln. Why? Because of the grandeur of his intellect? No! No! And yet the speaker has no sympathy with much that was said about his intellect; possibly it might in some degree be lost sight of in the ineffable sublimity of that moral power which overshadowed all, but of intellectual power he had a great deal.

"Yet it was not for the intellect but for the moral qualities of the man that we loved him. It is a wise order of Providence that it is so that men are drawn. We never love cold intellect. We may admire it, we may wonder at it, sometimes we may even worship it, but we never love it. The hearts of men leap out only after the image of God in man and the image of God is love.

"We had no fear about Abraham Lincoln except that he would be too lenient. Oh, what a fear was that. The only fear was that he would be too tender, that he had too much love, in a word was too Christ-like, and how Christ-like was his dying! His death was on Good Friday, and his last official words were in substance, 'Father, forgive them for they know not what they do.' "

Considering that Lincoln, from boyhood, had been one of the most compelling personalities that anybody could have met anywhere, persuasive in his diplomacy and captivatingly droll in his humor, it was natural for those who sought to explain him to think of him as a personality rather than as a thinking organism. Then, too, he had never looked like an intellectual creature to Easterners who had been taught to value formal education, training, manners and culture.

Only a few clergymen seemed to sense the far-reaching cerebral powers behind that melancholy face, with its thick, sallow skin and heavy eyes. The Rev. Richard Storrs described him as a shrewd politician as well as a great statesman; the Rev. A. N. Littlejohn, in Brooklyn's Church of the Holy

Trinity, declared a great man to have passed from our midst, but almost alone of hundreds of preachers whose sermons may be read, the Rev. Theodore Cuyler, pastor of Brooklyn's Lafayette Avenue Presbyterian Church, thought, even momentarily, that Lincoln had died too soon.

Cuyler, rival of Henry Ward Beecher, caught a glimpse of stark reality and visioned the tragedy that there was for the Republic in Lincoln's passing.

"Did Lincoln die too soon?" he asked. "For us and the world he did. . . . It has been too common to speak of Mr. Lincoln as merely a good, honest man whom the 'accidents' of politics made conspicuous — a man who merely drifted on a current of events that he was powerless to control. Such will not be the verdict of posterity. The next generation will acknowledge that the man who rose from a log cabin to the Presidential chair has no superior in the American annals."

But the good cleric could not hold to the facts. His duty called him, visions swarmed back upon him and before he had finished this sermon he was saying that Lincoln had "died at the right time; for his mighty work was done. The time had come when, like Samson, our beloved leader could slay more by his death than by his life. He was slain by the accursed spirit of slavery yet lurking in the North."

In general, the clergy seemed to think that the pouring out of Lincoln's blood was of more value than the continued use of his brain. They called him consecrated, sagacious, honest, good, loving, "embalmed forever in the hearts of his countrymen," but few or none suggested that it would have been better for the United States if he had lived on.

"God has the right to the blood of his servants," preached the Rev. William Ives Buddington, fundamentalist of Brooklyn's Clinton Avenue Congregational Church. "There are times when the death of a good man will do more than his life. Suffering wrong with patient love will sometimes triumph when everything else fails. God needed for his purposes the death of his Son, so imperatively needed it that not even the prayer of that Son, whom his Father had always heard, could avail to make the cup pass from him. God needed the blood of the martyrs in their day to corroborate and sanctify His gospel. God needed likewise the blood of Abraham Lincoln. We can see already that it is doing what his life and best services were powerless to accomplish."

More sonorous than any boomed the voice of Henry Ward Beecher, the critic of '61 and '62, who in April, '65, sang a different tune, saying, "And now the martyr is moving in triumphal march, mightier than when alive. The nation rises up at every stage of his coming. Cities and States are his pall-bearers and the cannon speak the hours with solemn procession. Dead! Dead! Dead! Is Washington dead? Is David dead?

"Disenthralled of flesh, risen to the unobstructed sphere where passion never comes, he begins his illimitable work. His life is now grafted upon the infinite and will be fruitful as no earthly life can be. . . .

"Four years ago, O Illinois, we took from thy midst an untried man and from among the people. We return him to you a mighty conqueror. Not thine any more but the nation's, not ours but the world's.

"Give him place, O ye prairies!

"Ye winds that blow over the mighty places of the West, chant his requiem!"

Under the tongues of his eulogists Lincoln had already begun to lose the very form of man. His human qualities had commenced to fade in the exaltation which was being raised to his heart and his soul.

That he had met his God-sent death in so wretched a place as a theater grieved many clergymen who were picturing him as a prophet from above. The clergy hated the theater, regarding it as the rival of the church, a place of scarlet temptation and carnal license, or, at best, a center for those who valued fleeting pleasure more highly than prayer. To admit that Lincoln could have gone to such a place of his own free will was more than many preachers could do. His presence there must be explained as having been somehow in keeping with the mystic and simple saint whom they sketched so reverently to their listeners.

In Tremont Temple, Boston, the Baptist divine Justin Dewey Fulton said:

"We remember with sorrow the place of Lincoln's death. He did not die on Mount Nebo with his eye full of heaven. He was shot in a theater. We are sorry for that. It was a poor place to die in. It would not be selected by any of you as the spot from which you would desire to proceed to the bar of God. If ever any man had an excuse to attend a theater, he had. The cares of office were heavy upon him. His brain reeled. His frame grew weak. He longed for a change. He desired to get away from the crowds, from the cares and responsibilities of office. Washington's closet would have been preferable. In conversing with a friend he said, 'Some think I do wrong to go to the opera and the theater; but it rests me. I love to be alone and yet to be with the people. I want to get this burden off; to change the current of my thoughts. A hearty laugh relieves me and I seem better able after it to bear my cross.'

"This was his excuse. Upon it we will not pronounce our judgment. This we will say: We are all sorry our best loved died there. . . . His integrity was thorough, all-pervading and all-controlling. He hesitated to put down his foot. There is little doubt but thousands of lives were sacrificed because of his slowness; but when he put down his foot it was as immovable as the rock itself, and his waiting may have saved the nation. . . . The people confided in him, not so much because they believed in his genius, or in the quickness of his perceptions, as because of a sense of safety and security which was begotten by the methods chosen to reach important conclusions."

On similar ground of necessary escape from toil was Lincoln's theater-going explained in the Park Street Church, Boston, by the Rev. A. L. Stone. He said, "We feel, many of us, that we could have wished for him whom we mourn a different scene for the last hour of his health and consciousness on earth, that he could have met the fatal missile on some stage of official duty, or in the retirement of home, or in the circle of religious worship rather than within those festal walls. Yes, it would have been better. But they were scarcely festal walls to him. They were a sort of refuge often for one who had no retirement of home from the incessant calls and wearying importunities of aspirants for place and office."

Of like mind was the raging pastor of Detroit, Dr. Duffield, as he said: "Would that Mr. Lincoln had fallen elsewhere than at the very gates of Hell — in the theater to which, through persuasion, he reluctantly went. How awful and severe the rebuke which God has administered to the nation for pampering such demoralizing places of resort. The blood of Abraham Lincoln can never be effaced from the stage."

And the Rev. L. M. Glover of Jacksonville, Illinois, speaking on April 23 in the town hall, regretted that if Lincoln was to die the event had not occurred elsewhere, "in the street, in the council chamber, in the national museum or even the sanctuary of God." However, Glover drew the line here and declared that he could not share the feeling of many people that Lincoln, "being in a theater, had been out of God's jurisdiction and had forfeited the divine protection."

The Rev. R. H. Neale of Boston's First Baptist Church discounted Lincoln's fondness for the wicked theater. "He was a good man," said Neale, "a truly pious man. He did not wish to go to the theater. The etiquette of public life required him sometimes to sacrifice his individual preferences; besides, as General Grant had been advertised to be there and could not go, he was afraid the people might be disappointed. How much was this like Abraham Lincoln, erring, if at all, always on the side of kindness."

Perhaps the clerics really believed this explanation of why Lincoln went to the theater. However, his delight in theatergoing had been widely reported in the newspapers for four years. His pleasure in any kind of magic-lantern show, play, drama, amateur performance, tent-show or strolling troupe that came within range of his circuit-riding life in Illinois was well known to all the politicians and lawyers who had known him before his election. Often, so they said, Lincoln adjusted his business on the circuit to bring him to a town on the night of a concert, and the only woman about whom his friends ever joshed him after his marriage was Lois Newhall, a soprano of town-hall Lyceum fame in central Illinois.

So concerned about his admiration for Miss Newhall did his lawyer friends become that they talked to him about it, reminding him that he was a married man and warning him that he must uphold the honor of the bar.

Lincoln had waved their worries away.

"Don't trouble yourself, boys," he had said. "There's no danger. She's actually the only woman in the world, outside of my own wife, who ever dared to pay me a compliment, and if the poor thing is attracted to my handsome face and figure it seems to me you homely fellows are the last people on earth who ought to complain."

✵ ✵ ✵ 11 ✵ ✵ ✵

THE MIRRORS WERE DRAPED

FOR THE LONG BODY of Abraham Lincoln, as it lay in that unfamiliar East Room of the White House, attendants brought down a suit of burial clothes as good as new, and handed it to the undertakers. It was the suit the President had bought for his inauguration five weeks before and it was doubtful if he had worn it since.

Dr. Brown was the undertaker, from the firm of Alexander & Bryan, who had worked such seeming miracles with the tiny body of Willie, the Lincoln boy who had died in 1862. Willie had looked so lifelike in his casket that his father had had his body twice disinterred, seeking comfort in another—and then another—long look at the little boy.

But Dr. Brown could not work unimpeded now. Over him brooded the orders, if not the person, of the "Iron Secretary," Edwin M. Stanton himself.

In and out of the White House went the war minister who would rule Lincoln in death as he imagined he had in life. Stanton was mad with fear, detectives prowling near him, watching for assassins whom he expected. In his mind was fixed the notion that everything, even the body of Lincoln, must be used to save the Republic from the terrible "rebels," those cutthroats who were creeping everywhere.

Stanton was, as has been said, too close to a dead man, and his phobia, blazing now, made him do wild things. Not without cunning for all his aberrations, he decided to make the corpse of the martyr an exhibit to the North of Southern perfidy. How he did it can best be judged from the report sent to the New York *Herald* from its accurate if ungrammatical Washington correspondent:

> "The eyes and upper part of the cheeks are still discolored by the effects of the cruel shot which caused his [Lincoln's] death. It was proposed to remove the discoloration from the face by chemical processes, but the Secretary of War insisted that it was a part of the history of the event, and it should be allowed to remain as an evidence to the thousands who would view the body, when it shall be laid in state, of the death which this martyr to his ideas of justice and right suffered."

How complete was the triumph of the Radicals! With the undertakers under their thumbs, the corpse of Lincoln itself could be turned into a weapon against the Lincolnian policy of mercy toward Southerners.

Stanton had his way and Lincoln went to his grave with the marks of assassination upon him.

How and where Lincoln was to be buried was also largely in Stanton's hands. He conferred with Mrs. Lincoln and with her stripling son Robert. The widow was bedfast and distraught, and Robert was young.

From the nation, outside, came a clamor to behold the dead man. New York City, which was always New York, urged that Lincoln be buried there in the great metropolis of the land. The irony of such a suggestion coming from a city where so many had guffawed at Lincoln's looks, his birth, his boyhood, sneering so openly at his slow wisdom, must have been apparent in spite of the somberness of the hour, for the city's claim got nowhere.

Washington had a better claim and it made it, despite all the scoffing its "best people," tinged with feudal chivalry, had done at the boorish manners and plebeian weaknesses of Lincoln in his lifetime. Washington was the nation's capital, it argued, and it had the ideal spot for Lincoln's body, that niche under the Capitol's dome which had been originally made for the corpse of George Washington, but which had remained empty when the first President's family had insisted that he sleep out at Mount Vernon. This was the place for Lincoln, the city said, Mrs. Lincoln half-willing, in her lucid moments, that this should be true.

But from Illinois, among all the law-makers, governors, mayors, politicians, who deluged Washington came a delegation, deadly intent upon bringing Lincoln back to Springfield, Illinois. They said their say plainly and decidedly.

Amid all that chaos of madmen, dreading the South, thousands of detectives grilling assassination-suspects, mobs careening on the streets, pompous politicians publicly lamenting and secretly rejoicing, cities squabbling,—amid all that morbid hysteria, the word from Illinois came with a sane, unanswerable force.

The prairie seemed to have spoken, the black fence-rails to have reached out, like arms wound in crape, the slow bosom of the midlands to have moved achingly, home to have beckoned with an irresistible power—and Illinois brought the dead man back.

So it was decided on Monday, when the Congressional committee appointed by Johnson took charge of the funeral. Six Congressmen and six Senators were to be pallbearers, flanked by ten others from the Army, the Navy, and civil life. Ben Wade was to be a pallbearer, being chosen with the rest on the very day that he told Andrew Johnson that now there would be no nonsense running the government.

The funeral would be a long and stately one, that was soon decided. From all over the North cities were pleading frantically that the cavalcade of death come their way. Telegrams begged, urged, almost demanded. Representatives laid down the law to the committee. The people simply *had* to see the body.

In the end, however, Stanton ruled. The funeral was to be

in the War Department's hands—a war funeral for the man of peace.

Back to Springfield Lincoln would go, but by a long path of grandeur and pomp. His funeral would be a processional whose splendor would dazzle the world. Politics may have decided this; nobody knows for certain. The fortunes of the Republican party were not undermost in Stanton's mind. Quite likely he saw that he would please the people and at the same time sustain their anti-Southern rage by displaying the corpse surrounded by soldiers, those heroic reminders of all that the North had suffered.

Significant it is that the funeral route was mapped to retrace in general the path Lincoln had taken in 1861 when he had come from Springfield to Washington to take the oath of office. Of the cities on that early route only Cincinnati and Pittsburgh were now omitted, and only one city, Chicago, was added to the funeral journey. Thus was the nation dramatically reminded of the assassination-threats that had swarmed about the President-elect four years before.

When Lincoln had gone eastward to Washington to his first inauguration, the whole nation had wondered if he would reach the capital. Prophecies of his murder had been everywhere. Passionate Southerners, preparing for Secession, vowed that he would never take the oath of office. Anti-Republican Northerners had been as emphatic in their prophecies. And by the time Lincoln had reached Philadelphia, detectives had uncovered what they thought to be a plot to assassinate him in Baltimore. So vividly was this sketched to Lincoln by his companions, by the railroad police and by the son of William Seward who arrived with his father's warnings, that the traveler allowed himself to be brought into Washington secretly—and, as he afterward felt, shamefully—in disguise.

True or untrue, this threatened plot in Baltimore was believed in its day, for both the Maryland metropolis and the city of Washington were filled with Southern sympathizers. General Winfield T. Scott, aged head of the army, discussed planting cannon at each end of Pennsylvania Avenue to keep the Maryland and Virginia planters from killing the President upon the inauguration platform. "If any of them show their heads or raise a finger, I'll blow them to hell," swore the ancient hero of two past wars, those of 1812 and Mexico. The inauguration passed peacefully and without the protection of cannon, but in 1865 it helped the vengeful Radicals for the people to remember the assassination-rumors of 1861. If the South had vowed to kill Lincoln only four years ago, it seemed to them that it must have been the South that killed him now.

Lincoln's death, so Stanton and the Radicals ruled, had been an act of war, nobody dissenting — nobody being in a position to dissent, with Stanton assuring the leaders and the reporters that his bureau of military intelligence had proof, full and complete, of Confederate guilt in the conspiracy. It would be a military funeral from first to last.

A military funeral it would be, in charge of Stanton's own man, Major-General David Hunter, hero to every Abolitionist and Radical in the North.

On the surface this selection of Hunter appeared to be one of sentiment for Lincoln. Hunter had, as a major, been sent to Springfield in 1861 to escort Lincoln eastward for his inauguration, and had come as far as Buffalo, guarding the President-elect. There crowds, pressing to see Lincoln, had snapped Hunter's collar-bone, and he had to leave the party. On the strength of this service and of Lincoln's occasional talks with him across the war years, Hunter, promoted to a major-generalship, had become known as an "intimate" of the President, which he was not, since no man was. Now it was regarded as fitting that Hunter, who had brought Lincoln out of the West, should take him back.

In reality, Hunter belonged to the anti-Lincoln philosophy of the war and its conduct. Although of Virginian parentage, Hunter had been, from the outbreak of war, a violent champion not only of the Union but of negro rights. In rash haste he had, as a general, started to free all Southern slaves within the reach of his army, the very thing Lincoln did not want done in those early days of the struggle, lest it make Abolition seem to be the purpose of the war. Lincoln, fighting the war to preserve the Union, not to free the slaves, had been forced to annul Hunter's orders. Later on he allowed Hunter to indulge his zeal for the colored brother rather harmlessly in organizing black regiments, which, though gallant and often heroic, were numerically too few to influence greatly the result of war.

It was for this supposedly heinous crime of arming the blacks that Jefferson Davis had outlawed Hunter under the rules of warfare and ordered that he be imprisoned as a felon if captured. Naturally this had made Hunter a hero to the Abolitionists of the North, a fact of which Stanton must have been aware when he appointed him to stand at the head of Lincoln's bier on its exhibition tour.

Some persons thought this proposed display of Lincoln's body, as the committee announced the route, would be a ghastly profanation, a terrible thing to do to so gentle a corpse.

But the people wanted it, answered the funeral officials truly enough, and it was arranged, the undertakers embalming the body in "extreme rigor" so that it might stand the fourteen days and sixteen hundred miles that would be consumed in the trip.

The funeral would come on Wednesday and the public could "view the remains" the day before. And on Tuesday the White House doors were thrown open. The people crushed in, yet not so wildly as they would in cities outside of Washington. No troops were needed to preserve order here. The masses inched past the coffin, many weeping, some speaking to the corpse. It was a hint of the storm that was to come when Lincoln's body should move out of the officious and stately capital into the nation, but it was only a hint, for the pall of those bureaucrats and politicians who disliked the dead man was over the town. It was plain that to the people Lincoln's death was no godsend; they had trusted him just as he had trusted them. They had been his power, and he theirs. If there were tears for him in Washington, there would be wild transports of emotion awaiting him outside those cold walls.

By night on this Tuesday, when the White House doors were shut, twenty-five thousand persons were estimated to have crowded past the mahogany coffin. Wednesday came. Six hundred tickets were out and the hour set for eleven in the morning.

First to arrive were sixty clergymen, "among them," said the newspapers, "the Rev. Robert Pattison of the Methodist Church," who though of slaveholding people, "yet followed Lincoln to the grave as the apostles did the interred on Calvary." They came to the White House through crowds already beginning to stifle. Inside the East Room they took their places at the far south end and waited.

Came next the heads of government bureaus, governors of States, delegates from the States, from chambers of commerce, from Union Leagues, mayors of cities, Congressmen, Senators, justices of the Supreme Court, the Cabinet members and Andrew Johnson, the new and God-found President, accompanied now by Preston King, the politician who was massing the New York Radicals against the less vengeful Seward, and who had captured the confidence of the new President. Seward, alone of the Cabinet, was missing, lying with his head in a steel frame, recovering from the knifing he had received on the night Lincoln was shot to death.

By the casket stood Grant and his generals, the little hero of Appomattox dressed up properly for once and wearing a white sash across his breast to show that he was head pallbearer. Near him stood Admiral Farragut of garb resplendent, but firm of mouth as when, at the moment of his navy's greatest victory, he had growled, "Damn the torpedoes! Full speed ahead!" Uniforms gleamed and rioted in color, foreign ambassadors brightening the scene.

In the East Room was an honorable and oppressive body. Swords clanked softly as the dignitaries tiptoed in. Awesome military guards towered by the man who had wanted peace.

Lonely and lost in the august assemblage were the family of the deceased, two boys, one Robert, twenty-two, in a stripling captain's uniform, the other Tad, twelve, his face swollen with tears, scarlet with bursting chokes. Near them stood a battery of Mrs. Lincoln's relatives, the Todds and their husbands and wives, the Kentucky and Illinois aristocrats, about whom Lincoln had once made a revealing joke, saying that one "d" was enough for God but not enough for the Todds, who wanted two. The widow was still too distraught to be brought down for the services.

On the walls of this East Room the mirrors were draped in black alpaca and white crape, a touch of superstition that was common in the day.

It was time to begin if the parade was to start on schedule at 2 P.M. A clergyman, the Rev. Hall, opened a little book to the Episcopal burial-service and began: "I am the resurrection and the life, saith the Lord," and spoke the resonant poetry in which man is said to fade away suddenly like the grass. Then he opened his Bible and began the 15th Corinthians at the 20th verse, where it says, "But now is Christ risen from the dead." When he had read the chapter through he stepped back and Matthew Simpson, the Methodist bishop of Philadelphia whose friends said that Lincoln regarded him as "the greatest orator he ever heard" stepped forward and prayed.

Followed him Dr. Gurley, the Presbyterian clergyman of Washington in whose church Lincoln worshiped of Sundays when he worshiped at all, which had been more frequently of late war years. Gurley, who had known the dead man well, spoke in a simple trust that made plain to them all why Lincoln had liked him. Unlike his class, this preacher saw no reason for this "mysterious and most afflicting visitation" but would wait, serene in the faith that somehow, sometime, God would explain. No man, said Gurley, had so gripped the hearts of the people, and no man so well deserved their love.

And when Gurley was done, the Rev. E. H. Gray, a Baptist, prayed, asking God to make Andrew Johnson like Abraham Lincoln and bespeaking His blessing upon all but "treason, that has deluged our land with blood and desolated our country and bereaved our homes, and filled them with widows and orphans; which has at length culminated in the assassination of the nation's chosen ruler. . . . God of justice and Avenger of the nation's wrong, let the work of treason cease and let the guilty perpetrators of this horrible crime be arrested and brought to justice. Through Jesus Christ, our Lord, Amen."

On this the service was done.

Again the Radicals had had the last word.

HALF CIRCUS, HALF HEARTBREAK

THE SERVICES OVER, Abraham Lincoln's trip to mythland began. As the pallbearers came out of the White House door into the Spring sunshine, all the church-bells of Washington and Georgetown and Alexandria, across the river, began to toll. From the fortresses, that ringed the city round, minute-guns began to boom. Stanton, in charge of the ceremonies, was master of clock-like efficiency.

Pennsylvania Avenue stretched away to the Capitol like a river between black banks. Crowds had been standing for hours, packed and squirming, while thrifty boys sold crape badges or arm-bands up and down the lines. For a front-row post on the curb as high as ten dollars was paid. Twenty-five cents might buy an agile man a toe-hold in a tree. The windows and roofs were full.

Troops had been maneuvering into line, marshals were ordering the endless delegations from churches, clubs, fire-companies, States, cities, lodges, that had come from all over the nation to march in the grand procession.

At 2 P.M. a negro regiment, hurrying down the avenue to be placed somewhere back in the line of march, found itself caught in a jam and had to stand where it was; lucky accident, for when the parade began, a few minutes later, the colored soldiers found themselves, by their mishap, placed at the very head of the whole procession. Unable to extricate them, the grand marshals made the best of it and let the black boys lead the parade, while the moving word went out over the North that the freedmen, symbols of Lincoln's greatest deed, had marched ahead of all the rest at his obsequies.

At the door of the White House waited a hearse with six white horses — a large and horrible hearse with black tassels and flounces that twitched and rocked. The coffin was set on a high platform in the case of glass, elevated so that the crowds might see. So immense was the hearse that the long coffin now looked like a child's.

Up and down Pennsylvania Avenue silence hung. Crowds strained forward, speaking, if at all, in whispers.

A roll of muffled drums, like the flutter of black wings, beat with soundless reverberations in the air.

They were coming!

The distant guns were pulsing, the bells heavily clanging, the pop of horses' hoofs on cobblestones began. A mile up the avenue to the dome that floated white against a white sky, the tramp, tramp, tramp of soldiers' shoes, pacing death-march steps—slow roll and rasp of wheels on the pavement—slow fidgeting of black tassels around the casket—slow whine and drone of black music.

Out of line forged hundreds of onlookers as the hearse went by and, like a wall of water coming down a river, they swept along even with it, men, women, children—black and white, some in tears, most of the negroes sobbing.

Further along in the procession a demonstration almost as great met Grant when his carriage rolled by, dense throngs struggling quietly and trampling each other to see him.

At 15th Street, one of the horses hitched to President Johnson's carriage grew fractious with the density of things in general and cavorted so briskly that His Excellency alighted, and with the watchful Preston King was taken into another carriage.

On his bed, Seward, propped up, looked out the window to see the hearse go by.

At 3 P.M. the funeral's head neared the Capitol. Officials there, staggered by the enormity of the crowds bearing so slowly down upon them, put soldiers to tearing up the wooden fences around the building lest weaklings be crushed upon them.

Into the rotunda of the Capitol the pallbearers carried the casket, the dignitaries who had heard the White House ceremony were admitted—a short service was said, and then all went away but the guard of honor, Union soldiers standing around the bier.

At ten the next morning, wounded soldiers from the hospitals — many of them arisen from their beds — filed through, and after them, the deluge. Crowds, three thousand persons to the hour, streamed through all day long, twenty-five thousand in all having passed when the doors were shut at midnight.

It was Washington's farewell. Lincoln was to be taken away tomorrow, in the morning.

Before sun-up on Friday, seven days after Lincoln's death, his coffin was closed, Gurley praying, Grant, the Cabinet, the Illinois delegation and a scattering of officials looking on. Down to the Baltimore and Ohio depot the little procession went through the dawn that shuddered again with those bells and guns.

In the yards the funeral train was ready, eight coaches, swathed in black, six for the mourners, one for the guard of honor, one for the bier. At the foot of the big casket was the little coffin of Willie Lincoln, disinterred again, this time to go back with his father's to Illinois.

The engine that stood ready puffing in all its death-decorations was named the "Edward H. Jones."

Between regiments at present arms — two of them white-gloved colored artillerymen who blubbered openly — the funeral train drew out, Baltimore-bound, a pilot engine scooting ten minutes ahead to make sure the track was clear.

Lincoln was at last escaping the city that had worn him down. To his wife he had said, on his last day, as she was later to remember it:

"We've had a hard time since we came to Washington, but the war is over, and with God's blessings, we may hope for four years of peace and happiness, and then we'll go back to Illinois and pass the rest of our lives in quiet. We have laid by some money, and during this time, we'll save up more, but shall not have enough to support us. We will go back to Illinois. I'll open a law office at Springfield or Chicago and practise law, and at least do enough to help give us a livelihood."

He had not as much money saved up as he thought, for his wife, who could never curb her desires in the way of clothes, had many bills outstanding, bills so large that she kept them secret from him in fear.

As the funeral train crept slowly, traveling at twenty miles an hour, through Maryland, there was nothing to indicate to the politicians and bureaucrats in Washington that there was anything more than a gigantic pageant to come. Everybody knew that the procession across the country was to be a great one, but that it was to throw the whole North into a prolonged convulsion of grief was in nobody's expectations.

Fifty-five per cent. of the Northern voters had supported Lincoln at the November elections; the majority of the people were known to regard him as the wisest political and the best moral leader of their day, but there was no reason for anybody in Washington officialdom to foresee the depth and universality of the popular woe. Most of the fever that had been sweeping the country since Friday night was that of rage, not of personal sorrow, so it was felt in the capital.

Neither did the popular demands for a mighty funeral indicate that the people were inconsolable. People loved funerals in those Victorian days; they loved to weep and mourn. Drama was scant in their lives, and they welcomed the lavish costuming and stately processionals that funerals provided. Puritanism gave them no emotional outlet like that of a burial-service.

While Washington had staged its ceremonies, stiff and splendid, the North had held sympathetic services with processions and speeches, mass-meetings and church ceremonies, hundreds of thousands attending. In New York's observance the statue of George Washington in front of the Belvidere House had been draped in crape, a festoon of it placed in a raised hand, and a sash put around its waist. Mourning covered the land.

Still, all this was but practice for the strenuous events to come.

As the "Edward H. Jones" drew the funeral-train out of Washington, the people waited for the grand and awesome show at which they could honor the good and friendly man who had, as their spokesman, met death. Not yet did the North seem to know how it loved the dead man. It was like a girl who does not know her heart.

Even the extravagance of Baltimore's demonstration, into which the death-train came rolling at ten Friday morning, told nothing of the hysteria that awaited across the country. Baltimore was expected to be effusive and fulsome in its grief, in order that it might atone for all the anti-Lincoln acts of its past.

Strangely, the entrance of Lincoln's corpse into the Maryland city came on the fourth anniversary of the first spilling of Union blood, the mobbing of New England troops by Baltimore hoodlums as the blue-coats marched through on their way to Washington. Baltimore would outdo itself now, just to show that its old contempt for Lincoln was gone. The city was packed at dawn; cataracts of crape fell down the front of buildings, maudlin mottoes dangled on ribbons from buttonholes, rode on placards and adorned wreaths. Bells tolled, guns boomed, one to the minute.

"The ingenuity of grief does everything it can devise," said the newspapers. To the Exchange Building the coffin was carried, the lid removed and the doors thrown open. Between 11 A.M. and 2 P.M. ten thousand persons shoved their way past the dead face, and when the coffin was returned to the station, delegations of "select" ladies walked beside the hearse, their arms heaped high with flowers.

Up into Pennsylvania steamed the "Edward H. Jones," its pilot engine still flitting ahead. From the windows of the train the funeral party began to see faces beside the track, faces that massed thicker and thicker the farther the train went into Union territory. Farmers with their wives and children, hat in hand, stood staring at the sable train that passed. Little towns were packed as the hearse-car rolled slowly through like a black phantom; town bands could be heard playing dirges, the depots were solid masses of staring faces, mourners, anxiously holding up draped flags, crape-bound mottoes, as if for the corpse to see.

With each mile the thing grew more overwhelming. All afternoon the official party kept awakening more and more to the vehemence of the people's grief.

At York, where the train halted momentarily, six ladies boarded the death-car with roses, "and all who saw them wept afresh," as the telegraphers told the country.

Farm dwellings, like those of the cities, were wreathed in crape. All the houses of the land seemed to have been wounded and to have bandaged themselves in black.

Harrisburg loomed through heavy rains at 8.20 in the evening. Soaked, steaming masses of humanity waited to file through the State House, past the coffin. At midnight they were stopped, but armies of farmers, outlying pilgrims who had driven miles with their families, sat up all night to be there when the doors opened at seven the next morning. Myriads were disappointed when the funeral went on at noon. Rural crowds lined the right of way eastward, and at Lancaster, Pennsylvania, old men were sitting in chairs by the track, having been carried out of homes and invalid-beds to see the catafalque go by. On a rock, under a railroad bridge outside Lancaster, stood Thaddeus Stevens, alone, wrapt and brooding. This hearty hater of Lincoln raised his hat solemnly to the train, recognizing none of the familiar Congressional faces at the window.

Lancaster was a black sea around the station. Ex-President Buchanan, who had mistakenly called himself "the last of the Presidents" four years earlier, sat in his carriage on the outskirts of the crowd.

For miles out of Philadelphia the train ran between solid walls of people. Acres of faces surrounded the station; five hundred thousand jammed the streets. Before dawn, queues had formed outside Independence Hall, where the body was to lie, and at 5.20 P.M., when the ponderous parade in eleven divisions started down Chestnut Street toward the cradle of Liberty, the ribbons of waiting mourners ran from the Delaware River to the Schuylkill, three miles and more. Since ten in the morning boys had been selling places in line. Women had been fainting in droves all afternoon. Now, as the air sobbed with those everlasting guns and bells, the mobs began inching past the casket whose head almost touched the Liberty Bell. Wreaths swamped those who received them at the door. At midnight three ladies were admitted bearing a white cross with biblical lamentations. Evergreens banked the casket and tapers burned at its feet.

Thousands of persons kept their places all night, after the doors swung shut on the stroke of twelve, and at three Sunday morning the crowds were greater than the day before. To enter the creeping lines at sun-up meant reaching the coffin five hours later. The crush trembled always on the edge of riot. Hundreds were injured. One hundred and fifty soldiers, veterans of battles, collapsed up and down ranks as they tried to maintain order. Nor had the crowds lessened at 2 A.M. that night, when the hearse journeyed to the railroad amid the resuming clangor of the bells and cannon.

The country had gone wild. Newspapers were stunned, groping for words to describe what was happening.

All New Jersey seemed to have come to the tracks in the ghostly dawn. Twenty thousand persons had gathered in Trenton just to see the train go through. A great choir of Germans filled the ferry-station at Jersey City with hymns as the casket was carried to the boat, and their voices floated across the water as Lincoln passed to that mad celebration in New York.

What had gone before was nothing to what was now to come. New York, where there had been rioting when Lincoln had demanded the draft and where in '61 men had talked of seceding from both North and South, now put on the biggest show of its career, a hippodrome of sorrow, much of it pure ostentation. For hours the streets had been immovable, the police and the military fighting desperately to keep lanes open. A giant new hearse, surmounted by a dismantled Temple of Liberty, lifted the casket six feet from the ground and dangled above it a massive silver eagle amid waving plumes. Minute-guns crashed and the chimes of Trinity Church thundered "Old Hundred." Windows and roofs were black with people, women straddled ridge-poles, men and boys clung in trees and lampposts. Now and then trucks and wagons broke under the load of standing spectators. Forty dollars was paid for a single window commanding the street. Most window-sashes had been removed so that additional heads might protrude.

Into Broadway the hearse turned, its sixteen white horses tossing their black coverlets and chafing at the hands of their black grooms. At the sight of Broadway, loaded beyond endurance with human flesh, the funeral party gasped. People seemed to hide the city.

From the masses came no sound except when, between the

inevitable, incessant pounding of the guns and bells, there were heard exhalations of emotion, sighs as fainting watchers slumped in that jungle of human bodies — such whispers as run through the corn when prairie breezes blow.

Toward City Hall, where it was to be shown, went the body, lines already formed for that exhibition, queues reaching to the Bowery, urchins selling their places in line for ten dollars and more.

It was the greatest sight New York had even seen: one hundred and sixty thousand persons, most of them in organized groups, marched in the parade, each group vying with the others for the happiest manifestation of woe. Cleverness collaborated with invention to devise spectacular floats, impressive mottoes, lavish effects. Lodges, labor unions, commercial bodies, sought to outdo each other like so many Mardi Gras clubs or "mummers" societies.

The New York Caulkers Association, one thousand strong, bore an obelisk with the motto "The Darkest Hour in History." Longshoreman's Union No. 2 carried a mammoth sign "In Memory of Departed Worth," the New York and Brooklyn Sawyers displayed a banner reading "We Mourn Our Loss." The Henry Clay Debating Society, the German Bakers, the Turner Sharpshooters, the German Carvers, Hose Companies galore, Temperance Cadets, women's clubs, all were in line hoisting mottoes. The children of Brooklyn's Fifth Ward waved the legend "The hand of the assassin has entwined the name of Abraham Lincoln in a wreath of immortality."

Celtic societies bore floral monuments with clocks inset, their hands stopped at 7.20, the hour when Lincoln died. Quotations from the Bible, from Shakespeare, of home-made composition, from here, there, everywhere, danced slowly above the parade on banners; they cried from hatbands, lapels, armlets.

Dazzled onlookers remembered some of the signs next day.

> *"Only the actions of the just,*
> *Smell sweet and blossom in the dust."*

> *"Oh, the pity of it, Iago — the pity of it."*

"Oh, why should the spirit of mortal be proud?"

"Barbarism of slavery — Can barbarism further go?"

"Be still and know that I am God!"

"A nation's heart was struck!"

"In sorrowing tears the nation's grief is spent,
Mankind has lost a friend and we a President."

"He was a man, take him all in all,
We shall not look upon his like again."

"We deeply mourn the loss; but God doeth all well.
He deemeth what is best for us.
A friend sticketh closer than a brother."

The National Hook and Ladder Company bore a sign "The assassin's stroke but makes the fraternal bond the stronger." No. 159 Chatham Street was plastered with a banner reading: "Let me die the death of the righteous; may my last end be like this." Small tombs were common sights, borne like Russian ikons on poles or platforms. A great urn, smoking with incense, reared itself in front of Barnum's Museum.

As the catafalque passed Chambers Street, a large St. Bernard dog bounded out of the crowd and trotted for a time beneath the hearse, a certain Ed Morton proudly announcing himself, to the surrounding thicket of watchers, as its owner. Morton elaborated, saying that not long before he had taken the dog to Washington with him on a trip and had introduced it to Lincoln, who had patted the good dog on the head. Reporters, listening to Ed Morton, gasped and noted for their papers "the peculiar instinct of the dog in recognizing Lincoln's hearse."

Delirium was on the city and the North.

Choirs sang from street platforms in those moments when the muted death-marches of the military bands were still.

Crape blackened the whole façade of the city. In poorer districts women hung their shawls and skirts out of windows in pathetic semblances of draped festoons.

Over one hundred thousand strangers had come to town, the hotels were overloaded, private residences were thrown open to care for the transients.

In City Hall, one hundred and fifty thousand looked at the dead face, the military guard working hard to keep people from touching it. Many women tried to kiss it. One did, but no more. General Hunter, standing at the head of the casket, as he had from the first, put a stop to that.

On Monday night the embalmers brushed the heavy dust off Lincoln's face, beard, and clothes, and rearranged the features, which had become unlifelike through exposure. It had worried some people that Lincoln looked unlike himself in his casket under the gas-lights of New York's City Hall, but in the light of the next morning the repairs were satisfactory.

A photographer, Gurney, made pictures of the dead man some time on Monday and sent proofs to the widow in Washington. Back came orders from Stanton to break the plates. Mrs. Lincoln had been shocked "at the shrunken and unnatural expression."

Light-minded men became confused with the hysterical praise of Lincoln and labored to prove that he had descended from an ancient and noble British line. Henry Hays, a merchant at 651 Broadway, attracted wide acclaim by displaying in his window the coat of arms of the old Lincoln family, which he described in heraldic technology as "argent on a cross vert, an estoile pierced with a gold crest; a lion rampant sable, ducally gorged." Its motto was "To live with a wish concealed," a phrase that, according to the beaming Mr. Hays, "coincides curiously and happily enough with the frank, avowed, and undisguised character of the late Magistrate."

Republican editors, however, roasted Mr. Hays, asking their readers what Mr. Lincoln would have thought of the attempts that his post-mortem eulogists were making to trace his lineage from the Lincolns and Ledfords of "an exploded aristocracy." Surely he would have scorned the intended sycophancy.

For twenty-four hours the crowds poured through City Hall in double file, and when at noon on Tuesday the casket was closed, three hundred thousand people had been disappointed.

Mad things happened. An Arctic explorer, Capt. Parker Snow, brought to the casket a leaf from a prayer-book that he had found in Polar ices by the skeleton of a victim in the ill-fated expedition of Sir John Franklin. The only legible word on the page was "martyr," and Capt. Snow wanted the relic put in the coffin with Lincoln's corpse. It was done.

Consuls of Great Britain, Russia and France arrived in their elegant trappings too late to see the body, and went away depressed.

At 12.30 in the afternoon the parade wound from City Hall, one hundred thousand marching, five hundred thousand looking on, among them General Winfield Scott, commander emeritus of the Federal armies, in his eighties and his pathetic uniform. Bands wailed dirges, and guns and bells boomed as before.

On the tail of the long procession came a little cloud of ne-groes, two hundred and fifty brave souls, escorted by platoons of police. For days the colored people had been planning a monster turn-out, but Tammany Hall, echoing the pro-slavery instincts of the Democratic party, had refused the ex-slaves the right to parade, warning them to stay away if they didn't want a repetition of the mobbing and burning of their orphanages that they had suffered in the draft-riots of past memory.

In Washington Stanton, hearing of this warning, had issued one of his own. Let the negroes parade or Union troops will escort them with fixed bayonets, he had told New York. But no more than a fragment had dared the hostile city. Republicans in the crowds applauded as they passed.

At the station waited the locomotive "Union," the same that had brought Lincoln into New York in 1861 on his inauguration journey. Fifteen minutes after four the funeral train set out for Albany, and as it did so, hundreds of persons who had been unable to view the remains entrained for Chicago or other Western stops where the funeral services would be tremendous.

Just at sundown the mourners from their funeral coaches saw a strange sight on the opposite bank of the Hudson River. Masses of country people were staging a weird tableau on a hillside around a newly made grave. Bands were playing sad music and a beautiful lady, made up as the Goddess of Liberty, was dipping a flag into the hole.

All night the train passed flambeaus, torches and bonfires, with white faces watching. At Albany sixty thousand were on the streets that had gone black with crape. Four thousand an hour went by the open coffin all afternoon of the twenty-fifth and all that night. There was to be no more closing of doors at midnight; day and night now the body lay exposed. The newspapers chronicled how "the first young ladies of Albany, dressed all alike in black skirts and white bodices, with heavy black rosettes on the left shoulder, waited on the table of the funeral party at St. Johnsville, a suburb, where a dining-car was put on the train."

At Albany the funeral party seemed to come out of the daze into which the stunning crowds had cast it. The Illinois delegation took fright at the monstrousness of the thing, and sent a member scurrying to Springfield to tell the home folks to get ready.

News of the extravagance with which the funeral was being received whipped expectant cities into a frenzy. Each must now be outdoing anything that any other city had done. Decorations must be larger, crowds bigger, ceremonies finer, orations more idolatrous. Speakers must exalt the dead man with wilder phrases, likening him to higher prophets than had any orators before.

The thing had become half circus, half heartbreak.

Now the train ran under arches of evergreens and flowers. Now committees of ladies watched the blossoms on the casket to snatch them away at the first sign of wilting and to replace them with fresh bouquets from the tumbling piles of flowers which showered into the rooms and the train. At every stop now delegations of thirty-six town belles in white, with black scarfs over the left shoulder, bore onto the train flowers and flags, spoke, sang, wept, recited tributes, enacted little dialogues and departed leaving morbid mottoes; the thirty-six girls representing the thirty-six States of the Union. When the train could not stop, the thirty-six belles could be seen kneeling in the station under torchlights. Hills were studded with arches, signs, mock graves, tableaus. In the dawn, country children waved flags at the train. At the coffin mothers twisted babies downward so that their eyes might focus on the dead face. Under the flambeaus late at night children could be seen opening sleepy eyes as parents shook them, anxious that they should remember always the sight of the funeral train.

At 4 P.M. Palatine Bridge was passed, and from the windows the party saw a white cross on a green mound, banked in evergreens and on each side a woman, apparently weeping. On the cross was inscribed "We have prayed for you; now we can only weep." Coming into Syracuse, the cortège ran between rows of transplanted evergreens, and the station was ringing with choirs. All night the train was illumined by bonfires along the right of way.

Rarely after it left New York was the coffin outside the sound of booming guns.

The engine "Dean Richmond" pulled the train into Buffalo Thursday morning, two flags over its headlight and above the cow-catcher two large portraits of Lincoln. It was seven in the morning when the brakes ground to a standstill; Buffalo was jammed. In the reception committee was ex-President Fillmore, who had been jeered twelve days before because he had not decorated his home with mourning. Under a great tent in the town hall the coffin was laid, a gigantic chandelier lighting the dead man's face. Ladies entered by one door, gentlemen by another and the sexes filed by with the coffin between.

Cleveland had girded its loins, for all the world like a "booster" city of later date, to take first prize in the competition. It would honor Lincoln more elaborately than any of the cities that had gone before. Vast crowds waited on green hills as the train came up, grouped around white arches that bore inscriptions, and guarded by white-togaed ladies who impersonated the Goddess of Liberty.

In a city park Cleveland had erected a special Chinese pagoda, a temple whose ceiling was black velvet studded with silver stars, greatest sensation of the trip thus far. From early morning until ten at night throngs came through the rain, one hundred thousand looking into the casket, some say, others, fifty thousand. At least it was overwhelming.

Columbus outdid Cleveland with a queer kind of Oriental

temple for a hearse, and with roses under the wheels. Its parade resembled a later flower festival of California, fire-engines shrouded in evergreens, carriages bearing beautiful young ladies, clad in white with scarfs of black and singing "hymns in praise of the martyr; their sad, sweet voices full of electric sympathy."

Milford, Ohio, was a lake of slow-waving handkerchiefs, and Woodstock sent young ladies into the funeral car to strew flowers while the Woodstock cornet band outside played a dirge. At Urbana three thousand people surrounded a great floral cross from whose arms hung colored transparencies, while forty ladies and gentlemen beneath it sang "Go to Thy Rest" with pathetic sweetness. Ten ladies entered the car and strewed the coffin with flowers, one of them weeping in loud anguish.

Slowing up at Conners, Ohio, the funeral party saw three young ladies elevated above a crowd singing a patriotic song to a sad and mournful air while the people below slowly waved little flags. At Piqua, the Piqua and Troy bands joined forces and played while young women dropped flowers and tears on the hearse-car floor.

Richmond, the first Hoosier stop, had been waiting eagerly to show that Indiana would shame Ohio. By arrangements the church-bells of the town rang an hour before train time and in the dismal false dawn of 3 A.M. fifteen thousand people, far more than Richmond's total population, received the funeral with pantomimes, tableaus, stage-effects that must have looked like ghastly caricatures of grief to the officials who peeped out of their berth-windows. All the engines in the railroad yards had been run out and with steam up, bells tolling and lamps revolving, illumined the scene. Wreaths showered in upon the coffin, one being noted as directed to little Willie with the additional sentiment "Like the early morning flower he was taken from our midst."

Morning light showed Indiana, indeed, to eclipse its sister States on the path. The tracks were thickly lined with faces, signs, dumbshow. Little villages had exhausted themselves with arches and pantomimes.

Indianapolis was agreed by newspaper correspondents to have

"the most faultless display of elegance that has yet contained the remains." In the State House the casket lay under a black-velvet canopy sprinkled with golden stars and laced with white cords. Friezes of the world's great in portraiture bordered the walls. Reporters thought it a mysterious cavern, eerie and strange. It reminded them of Mammoth Cave. In proportion to population, the crowds increased as the train had come West and Indiana out-mourned Ohio, just as Ohio had out-mourned New York and New York Pennsylvania.

Illinois, Lincoln's State, was next. Michigan City, close to the line, had a triple arch over the tracks; sixteen ladies in white with black sashes singing and thirty-six little girls with rosettes of trailing arbutus to lay a floral cross on the coffin while "Miss Hatty Gustine represented my (sic) Goddess of Liberty in whose left hand was the wand of justice and in the right hand the Constitution of the U.S.A. She was robed in spotless white and the features very poetically enshrined in majestic folds of the finest black veiling."

Across the State-line came the train in the morning, both the engine and the pilot engine adorned more profusely than ever before, portraits of Lincoln pasted upon their searchlights and black blankets trimmed with silver stars thrown across them as though they were hearse-horses.

On pilings at the lake's edge the track lay, and as the train slowly came to a stop at 12th and Michigan, in Chicago, a mystic thing happened, according to the Chicago *Tribune:* "The waters of Lake Michigan, long ruffled by the storm, suddenly calmed from their angry roar into solemn silence as if they, too, felt that silence was an imperative necessity of the mournful occasion."

Under a tremendous arch surmounted by Lincoln's bust, the casket was carried, thirty-six high-school girls strewing flowers upon it and walking beside it. For twenty-four hours all trains to Chicago had been groaning with excursionists, and now one hundred thousand people were bogging the muddy streets of the city to see the parade go by in its wilderness of banners and mottoes that waved over the heads of thirty-seven thousand marchers, ten thousand of them schoolchildren.

It was May Day, the first of the month, and a drizzling rain fell, bogging the streets hideously. Workmen rushed ahead of the parade trying to scoop the mud into the gutters. Crowds stood in puddles, not minding.

Arches swung across the streets, bunting running in solar rays from Lincoln's busts. No city had been so black. Private homes were spectacular with devices and crape, busts of the dead man stood in windows or on ledges near roofs, surrounded by black velvet and the ubiquitous thirty-six silver stars. A favorite placard that hung out was:

> *"In sorrow by thy bier we stand,*
> *Amid the awe that hushes all,*
> *And speak the anguish of the land,*
> *That shook with horror at thy fall."*

Also, this motto:

> *"O'er Lincoln's form in silent grief,*
> *Oppressed Columbia mourns her hero now at last,*
> *But those bright laurels ne'er shall fade with years,*
> *These leaves are watered with a nation's tears."*

In the procession were the city notables, the Union League, the reform-school boys, the Masons, the Fenian Brotherhood, college students, benevolent societies, Catholic societies, delegations of Germans, Swedes, Swiss, the Druids, the Hebrews, the bricklayers, masons, journeymen stone-cutters in black with arm and mallet on their sleeves, and the Butchers' Association marching in their white aprons. Among the troops was a regiment of Confederate prisoners of war who had taken the oath of allegiance and had been recruited into the Union service.

To the Court House came Lincoln's body, to lie in state. Over one door was written, "Illinois clasps to her bosom her slain and glorified son"; over the other, "The beauty of Israel is slain upon her high places." Queues leading to the Court House moved forward one foot an hour. Carriages in and out of the parade had their wheels entwined with crape, black bows on the whips. Black bunting was strung from tree to tree. The policemen had black gloves and children had black ribbons around their hats, their waists, their throats. Even the marble eagle that hung above the corpse in the Court House had a strip of crape around its neck.

Between 6 P.M. Monday and Tuesday night one hundred and twenty-five thousand viewed the body. Then, when the caravan set out for Springfield, the throngs were so enormous that the wooden sidewalks gave way, throwing hundreds into the mud. Souvenir-hunters fell on the hearse as soon as it was empty, and stripped away the draperies till the soldiers bayoneted them back. Denied these relics, women fell to searching on the ground for flowers that had fallen from the coffin.

All day trains had been disgorging fresh loads of mourners into the city. Pickpockets were overworked, and the police were exhausted holding back the crowds in that slippery mud and sending for ambulances to bear away fainted women.

Chicago's funeral for Lincoln had been a strange blend of the ridiculous and the sublime, but in no other city had there been heard such sobbing, such uncontrolled wailing. No other city had brought proportionately so many people to the streets. On the morning after the funeral had gone, the Chicago *Tribune* declared that New York, with eight times the population of Chicago to draw from, had turned out only one-fourth as well as had the city by Lake Michigan.

Toward Springfield through the night of May 2 crept the train, passing under arches illumined by bonfires and carrying the words "Come Home." The thing was growing simpler and more terrible.

For fourteen days the train had been crawling westward. It had passed through the greatest crowds that had ever assembled in Christendom, and long after its passing the States continued to rock in grief. The paroxysm did not wane. Reporters followed the train, telegraphing the details to their papers, which relayed the news to towns and villages that pressed to read and hear more of the dark details.

Some people took to their beds, sick with nervous woe, and here and there a weak mind gave way under the strain. While the funeral was drawing out of Chicago, a youth by the name of Charles Johnson was cutting his throat in New York City, having been for days despondent over Lincoln's death. The incident was telegraphed over the land: "Saying, 'I am going to join Abraham Lincoln,' he killed himself with a razor. Before his mother could secure help he had severed his carotid artery and was a corpse." Seven million Northerners had looked upon the hearse or the coffin, one million, five hundred thousand having looked upon the dead face. Ninety funeral marches had been composed and played.

So with the national frenzy at its peak Lincoln came to his old home town of Springfield. To the people of Illinois were added Easterners who had followed, in their morbid excitement, to see the end of the stupendous cavalcade.

The casket was opened in the House of Representatives where Lincoln, long before, had pronounced doom upon slavery. There, for twenty-four hours, was heard the steady tramp of feet — the feet of prairie people, farmers, atheist lawyers, fanatic circuit-preachers, rail-splitters, crippled soldiers, shysters Lincoln had tricked, mothers he had protected, politicians he had disappointed, bullies he had whipped, girls to whom he had sold sugar, loafers who had laughed at his stories — the feet of prairie people.

Ten o'clock of May 4, and the last service began. Eleven o'clock — the last parade. A general of the army, "Fighting Joe" Hooker, rode ahead of the hearse and "Old Bob," the aging bay that had borne Lincoln over the circuit, was led riderless behind. A long parade, bannered, mottoed, costumed like the rest, but with some new and terrible woe, as of family grief in it, wound out two miles to Oak Ridge Cemetery. Prayers, oratory, religious hymns, boys falling with breaking boughs, apple blossoms in the wind — and the black journey was over.

By the time they got "Old Bob" back to the stable his blanket, a red, white, and blue blanket, embroidered with the words "Old Abe's Horse," was gone. Souvenir-hunters had stripped him clean.

PART TWO

THE AMERICAN
JUDAS

✫ ✫ ✫ 13 ✫ ✫ ✫

PORTRAIT OF AN ASSASSIN'S FATHER

JOHN WILKES BOOTH'S FATHER taught him never to kill a living thing, not even a rattlesnake. The boy, however, wouldn't listen, took to shooting tom-cats around the farm, then a dog or two and finally an old sow that had come over from a neighbor's field to grunt and root innocently in Booth's front yard. This climax impressed the neighbors, who remembered it years later when they heard that J. Wilkes had shot the President of the United States.

As the unbelievable news of Abraham Lincoln's assassination crashed down upon these neighbors, in 1865, they thought how lucky it was that Old Man Booth was dead; it would have been torture for him to have learned that his favorite son had turned out to be a killer. The neighbors had liked Junius Brutus Booth, for although he had been a worry to them sometimes with his "spells," his tenderness of heart had ingratiated him to the farmers of his Maryland community.

Most people who knew Junius Brutus liked him — and most people east of the Mississippi River felt that they knew him. Thousands of persons who had never seen him felt intimate with him. It has always been that way with the public and a great stage-star; and Junius Brutus Booth was a great stage-star, no doubt about it. For a generation he was the Republic's chief

Shakespearean player, and when he died Rufus Choate, scholar, lawyer, statesman, said, "Then there are no more actors." Across thirty years he kept the United States agog with his temperament — and, before that, England. By his twenty-first year he had Londoners rioting over him in theater pits.

The stage, to this day, has never had anybody like him for excitement. Endless anecdotes of his heroic eccentricities coursed the country during his lifetime; the very mention of his name tickled people, and the sight of him in any one of his tragedian rôles sent delightful shiver-trembles up and down the spines of his audience.

Genius and liquor burned in him so incessantly that by the time he was fifty-six his sinews were ashes and he died. Since his hold on the public had been one of personal magnetism and vitality, he might soon have been forgotten had not his favorite son murdered the President of the United States. After John Wilkes had committed his crime, the whole Booth family came under public scrutiny and everybody was soon remembering, with relish, all those rich and fantastic stories of the elder Booth, such as the tale of Junius Brutus, the preacher and the dead pigeon, the yarn of how old Booth made his wife kiss the horse, of how he had chased the actor into the livery stable and of how he had jumped into the Atlantic Ocean after a ghost — stories galore.

As time went on into the 1870s, '80s and '90s lifting his son, J. Wilkes, into ever vaguer and blacker heights of myth, another son Edwin became loftier and loftier in the American mind, acquiring a stage premiership even more commanding than the father had ever achieved. Edwin's fame brought back memories of his parent. But no matter how much of Junius Brutus' position in the background of American folk-lore is due to the fame of his two sons, it must be said that, in his day, "he went under his own steam" if any man ever did.

From his father, Richard Booth, he inherited a wild streak of independence. Richard, as a youth, had run away from his English home to help George Washington in the American Revolution. Caught in mid-ocean and brought back to London, Richard resigned himself to a lawyer's desk, privately nursing, however, rebellious sentiments, and indeed compelling all guests to kow-tow deep and low to a portrait of Washington that hung in his home. Like his mother's relative John Wilkes, democratic firebrand of British politics, Richard Booth hated tyrants so incessantly that he named his son after that Roman liberator, Junius Brutus, ouster of the Tarquins.

This son, who was born in 1796, was intended for a gentleman's career. However, as he grew up, he resisted; flaring with temperament, he tackled, in rapid succession, printing, poetry, the navy, painting, the law, sculpture and eventually the stage, upon which, after a short apprenticeship in the provinces, he got his chance, at the age of twenty, in London's Covent Garden Theatre.

For all his youth, the boy resembled, most strikingly, Edmund Kean, established czar of actors, and one night when Kean was ill, young Booth went on as his substitute. Although the Londoners were chilly at first toward the presumptuous youngster, they were cheering and shrieking hosannas at him by the time he had finished his *Richard III* that evening, and next day his fame was fixed. Within a year he had become Kean's rival, holding sway at Covent Garden while the older star reigned at the Drury Lane Theatre. Kean tried to cut off competition by trapping his young opponent into a co-starring partnership, but after one day's alliance, Junius Brutus discovered that he was to be merely one of Kean's supporting cast and, in rage, departed. Back in Covent Garden he reopened in *Richard III* while lawsuits filled the air.

London divided into two camps. Kean's followers declared Booth an interloper, a pretender to the throne, and added that they intended to break up Booth's opening performance. Junius Brutus had plenty of friends to tell the "Keanites" to come on and try it.

"The Keanites" came on and *did* it.

What a joyful occasion it was, that evening of the twenty-fifth of February, 1817. Mobs packed the streets long before and after the theater was full. Inside the house two hostile gangs yowled and jeered at each other. Upon Booth's first entrance as "Richard," the partisans of Kean hissed deafeningly. The

"Boothites" replied with splitting applause and the legs of chairs.

Up and down the stage the actor went, wretchedly trying to make his lines heard above the roar of the audience. Whenever his enemies showed the least sign of tiring themselves out, his friends set up such tumult of triumph that nothing was gained. He was as helpless before "Boothites" as before "Keanites."

After a time he gave up the brave acting with which he had hoped eventually to quiet the house, and retired to the wings. The rumpus went on as before, both factions seeming to have forgotten him entirely.

He was not, however, defeated, and tried everything he could think of to capture his house. He began acting again, necessarily in pantomime; he addressed the audience; he hid; he reappeared pleading, and then went back to acting again as though nothing was wrong. The shrieking fighters refused to be wooed away from their fun. At length Booth tried big, printed signs on them. First he came down to the footlights with a placard bearing the words "Grant silence to explain." At the sight of this the racket increased. Next he appeared with a sign reading "Mr. Booth wishes to apologize." The fights and catcalls redoubled.

Once more he sallied out and promenaded the stage with a painted legend "Can Englishmen condemn unheard?" and was answered by both camps in the affirmative. Finally he gave up, finished out the play in dumbshow amid the infernal din and went home, leaving his manager to scream this rebuking news through the house.

"Bring him back," howled the "Keanites," angry at having their game spoiled. The "Boothites" shamed their adversaries and sought revenge with fists and teeth. So the opponents kept it up until after midnight when, worn out with pleasure, everybody went home.

Similar revelry was held at every Booth performance for nights thereafter, all London seeming to have joined in the sport. Heads were cracked and passions boiled, but Junius Brutus had a powerful frame, and a tireless voice and in time he wore out his enemies.

By 1821, when he prepared to emigrate to America, Booth

was admitted to be a great actor by all Londoners save a few of Kean's die-hard partisans. Shortly before he departed, Booth co-starred with Kean in amity. His departure was either to achieve further theatrical conquest or to escape serious marital complications. His amorous career was a lively one, starting as early as his 17th year when he was haled into court on a bastardy suit filed by one of his father's housemaids. At 18 he had eloped with his landlady's daughter, four years older than himself, and had cavorted around Belgium with her until his father, a year later, made him marry her. At 24 he had strayed far enough from his wife and infant son, Richard, to start philandering with Mary Ann Holmes, an alluring flower girl of London's theatrical district, and was soon taking her on gay trips to the continent and then, in 1821, to America where her pregnancy could escape the eyes of friends and relatives.

With Mary Ann on the honeymoon ship, Booth brought Peacock, a pet pony of which he was extremely fond, the three of them alighting at Norfolk, Virginia, in June. Booth wrote his wife that he had fled to America to escape difficulties created by his managers, and from time to time in the years that followed, he sent her money and promises of reunion. Whatever ideas he may have had of taking up life again with his wife apparently vanished when his flower girl bore him a son, six months after arriving in America, a boy named Junius Brutus Booth, Jr. Although he called Mary Ann his wife, he hid her from the eyes of British visitors by buying a log house in the deep forest twenty-three miles from Baltimore and keeping her there forever after, except for occasional trips to market, where they sold vegetables. Additional rooms, orchards, negro slaves and nine more children came with the years. Twice, in spasms of recklessness, Booth took Mary Ann, several of the children and a rented negro slave with him on acting visits to London, and was successful, as his most searching biographer, Stanley Kimmel discovered, in keeping all knowledge of his illegal family from his wife. On one trip Mrs. Booth welcomed him and sat with him and their six-year-old son, Richard, while a portrait of the happy group was painted.

But each time Booth sped back to America to live in his woodland retreat except when he was charging around the New World astonishing the natives with his dramatic talent. There seemed no telling how long this double marital predicament might have lasted had not his son Richard, at 22, come to America to join his father. For a time Booth employed him as his valet on tour, keeping him ignorant of all those half-brothers and -sisters in the Maryland thickets. But eventually gossiping tongues around the theaters enlightened poor Richard and he quit his father, wrote his mother the bad news and begged her to come over and help him out. She came, raised the very devil for a time around Baltimore, then settled down with Richard supporting her and himself by teaching school. She died in 1858, after having divorced Booth in April, 1851, for desertion and adultery.

Three weeks after divorce freed him, Booth married Mary Ann and gave their houseful of children a legal name. Poor Richard, according to Kimmel, disappeared, although in the late '60s there were rumors that he had been a Confederate soldier.

Gaudy versions of these adulteries and desertions broke out in the American press in 1865 after J. Wilkes had made any Booth scandal good copy. One of the commonest tales was that Booth's wife had haunted the streets and markets of Baltimore, drunken and blasphemous, abusing Junius and Mary Ann most spiritedly. But pamphleteers of 1865 did not describe poor Richard as having fallen so low as to have become a Confederate. They only said he had grown up to be a Philadelphia lawyer.

The arrival of Junius Brutus, Mary Ann and Peacock at Norfolk in 1821 was a quiet one for such a tempestuous man and so renowned an actor. Ready as the Southerners were to receive thundering London favorites, they could not believe, at first, that this simple, modest little man, could be the great Shakespearean star. The fellow was apparently an impostor and it was with dubious reluctance that a Richmond manager, at length, agreed to try him out. For two acts the audience shook its head. This could not be Booth. Then suddenly in the third act, the player cut loose with such a shock of electric dramatics that the Virginians whooped themselves hoarse. It was Booth indeed, and no more proof was needed.

In the years that followed, New York, Baltimore, Petersburgh, Charleston, Savannah and New Orleans acclaimed him as the brightest of all stars. Booth, however, received this success without emotion and began, calmly, to negotiate with the government for a post as lighthouse keeper on lonely Cape Hatteras. He was serious. The roar of the surf and the cries of the sea-gulls were all he wanted, then. America, just beginning its worship of money and of popularity, could not understand the man. Such a fellow must be more than a fool, he must be crazy. Horrified managers came flocking, with contracts dangling, and in the end Booth gave up and came back to the stage, having installed his family in the forest home. There were born to him Rosalie Ann, Henry Byron, Mary, Frederick, Elizabeth, Edwin, Asia, John Wilkes and Joseph Edward, the first five of these dying in infancy.

From this retreat, where he was happy, Booth went on money-making tours, each trip increasing his fame and fixing him in the American mind of that time as the most sensational figure on the stage. His Shakespearean performances beggared the critics of ecstatic adjectives and he ranged far and wide into French, German, Hebrew and Greek translations for his rôles. He was equally successful in all kinds of drama and once, at least, acted in Hebrew.

Although short and thick of stature, he could, under the expanding power of his own imagination, give the illusion of herculean size. When he was warmed to his work, glowering, smiting his chest and making the rafters ring, he could, at one swoop, ravish the scholars and frighten the yokels. Actors, too, were often terrified by his abandon. Some of them wilted before his realistic rages, forgot their lines and spluttered like children; one member of his cast, indeed, lay right down on the floor, scared nearly to death by the ferocity of the star's impersonation. James E. Murdock, who used to play with Booth, said his eyes were terrible, with green and red flashes in them as he fixed his fellow actors spellbound to the spot.

Audiences loved all this. They loved Booth more than ever when, at the slightest interruption from the spectators, he would halt the play, and striding to the footlights, denounce the offenders in grandiose epithet. They joyously forgave him such non-sense as when, offended by what he thought was inattention from his patrons, he stopped *Richelieu* in a deadly scene and be-gan waltzing merrily around the stage with an amazed actor, in priest's cassock, upon his arm.

To his dying day he acted with prodigious energy. Even after he was shattered in health he could manage to bring the house to its feet with his frenzied sword-fights. In such scenes he ap-peared to the critics to be a demon, laying on with such ferocity that his opponents had to fight for their very lives. Actors were afraid to play "Richmond" to his "Richard," so intent would he become on killing his stage enemy.

In Richmond, Virginia, E. V. Valentine, the distinguished sculptor and intimate friend of Edwin Booth, recalled, in 1928, the occasion when the town was telling it that Junius Brutus, in a stage duel, had backed his adversary clear off the boards with his desperate sword-play. Around behind the scenery they fought, among scampering carpenters, up and down, until Booth forced the wretched fellow out the stage-door, through the alley into the main street and downtown, block after block, until the affair wound up in a hotel lobby.

Another tale is that Booth as "Richard" fought his "Rich-mond" out of the stage door, across the alley into a livery stable, where astonished hostlers eventually disarmed him.

It was in a too realistic bar-room rehearsal of *Othello* that Booth was maimed for life. In a condition best described as "howling drunk," Booth was warning a friend, "Villain, be sure thou prove my love a wanton," when the situation became so real that he laid wild hands on his imaginary Iago and caught, in return, a wallop across the nose from a poker, and, as a re-sult carried a flattened face the rest of his life.

How much of his goings-on were due to liquor, how much to insanity, and how much to his general desire to have fun with himself can never, now, be accurately determined. American his-tory calls him a madman, but then American history has taken its view of him from the days when it was easiest to explain J. Wilkes Booth's notorious crime on the grounds of congenital insanity.

Junius Brutus, judged on the evidence to be found, was a simple, religious soul, artistic and sensitive, bored with rude Americans, seeking relief in drink and in eccentric whims. He was drunk, pretty much, for thirty years, and towards the end of his life would fall into spells of melancholy, followed by nervous prostration. He was his own best company, one day with another, and achieved the ideal state of being able to do whatever sprang into his head.

He liked to go to fires and help man the hand-pumps while his audiences waited and theater-managers searched their souls for appropriate "cuss" words. On a certain trip to New York, he pawned himself to a loan-broker for the price of a drink, coming back, honestly, after he had consumed the amount of the loan, to stand in the pawn-shop window, wearing a ticket like the guitars and family crockery that shared his place of display. There friends found him and "redeemed" him.

Once, shipping down the Atlantic coast for a Southern tour, he suddenly popped overboard with the strange cry that he had a message for "Conway." Duly fished out and dried, he explained that an actor friend, William Conway, had committed suicide at this point in the Atlantic.

Driven desperate by Booth's drunkenness, one of his managers tried locking him up of afternoons to make sure he would be sober for evening performances. In Philadelphia Booth worked out a way to get round this new barrier. He bribed a bell-boy to stand outside his door holding a saucerful of brandy at the keyhole. Through the aperture — keyholes were big in those old doors — Booth thrust a little clay pipe and, inverting the bowl, sucked himself full. When twilight came — and the manager — the star was dead drunk.

Being sentimental, Booth was pleased to help sufferers. Fontaine, alias Lovett, a notorious horse-thief who was awaiting the noose of obvious justice in a Louisville, Kentucky, jail, came to Booth's attention, and with bleeding heart the actor poured out funds for the scoundrel's counsel, paying all court costs and accepting in return the executed man's skull, which the fellow had wished to be used in his benefactor's performances of *Hamlet.* Mrs. Booth, receiving it while her husband was away, sent the horrible thing to her doctor, who kept it until 1857, when he gave it to Edwin, who in turn employed it sometimes when speaking the "Alas, poor Yorick" passage.

It was to dumb animals, however, that Booth gave most of his curious sympathy. He forbade his boys to hunt and warned them not to kill even the opossums or the poisonous snakes with which the farm abounded. A letter survives in which he advises his sons that "a robber of life can never give back what he has wantonly and sacrilegiously taken from beings perhaps innocent and equally capable of enjoying pleasure or suffering torture with himself. The ideas of Pythagoras I have adopted, and as respects our accountability to animals hereafter, nothing that man can preach can make me turn to the contrary. 'Every death its own avenger breeds.'"

Because branding animals meant burning them with hot irons, Booth forbade the custom on his premises, relenting only when the disappearance of so many hogs and sheep made it imperative. No meat was ever eaten at "The Farm." The order of "no killing" was evidently obeyed by the older boys, Edwin and Junius Brutus, Jr., who were serious, toiling fellows, getting along without much schooling and perfecting themselves as soon as possible in their father's profession. But around 1836, when Henry Byron, an infant son, died, the groundwork was laid for the advent of that wild son who was to begin by killing tom-cats and end by murdering a President.

Little Henry Byron had been his father's favorite, "*so* proud was I of him above all others," the grieving parent wrote to his own father. And when the next child was a boy, two years later, Junius Brutus welcomed it with pathetic eagerness. He gave the baby the prize name of the family, "John Wilkes," calling him after that tinder-headed ancestral demagogue of England.

The baby grew up an old man's darling, hopelessly spoiled, an extraordinarily naughty little boy who was allowed to do whatever he pleased. His father had hoped to give his son a better education than he had been able to provide for the two older boys, Edwin and Junius Brutus, Jr., but when young J. Wilkes objected on the ground that he preferred to ride and roam the woods, Junius Brutus weakened.

Edwin, who never had much use for John, even in those days, recalled him rather vaguely, in after years, as a good-hearted, harmless though "wild-brained" boy, a sort of amateur Don Quixote, "who would charge on horseback through the woods on the Maryland farm, spouting heroic speeches, holding in his hand a lance, a relic of the Mexican War." Although he was only five years older than this windy brother, Edwin had begun so early in life to accompany his father on tours that in all probability he never knew John Wilkes very well. Like his brother Junius Brutus, Jr., Edwin was closer to his father than to his mother, adored the old gentleman — who had seemed like an old man at forty — and went away with him at every opportunity, although, even as late as 1852, his father thought him nothing more than a good banjo-player. John Wilkes loved his mother best and was idolized by her in return. That he loved his father, too, is not to be doubted, but Junius Brutus, Sr. had begun to go to pieces like a wreck in the sea by the time John Wilkes' character had begun to form, and, while the boy had an unquestioned ambition to be as noted a man as his father, he had less filial respect than did his older brothers.

Under such circumstances it was natural for a growing boy of John Wilkes' disposition to want to kill animals if for no other reason than that this was the most sacred of all family taboos. Securing a rifle, he began, very early, banging away at his mother's cats and the slaves' hound-dogs, progressing from that point to the catastrophe wherein he killed the neighbor's sow. A good spanking administered to the boy at almost any point in this line of shootings might have been the means of saving the life of Abraham Lincoln in 1865. But no reproof was forthcoming.

Junius Brutus Booth was not always so considerate of his wife, Mary Ann. Sweet and tender toward his whole family, he nevertheless made things miserable for them when a drunken "spell" came on him and particularly did the burden then fall upon his wife. When Peacock, the pet pony that had shared their honeymoon voyage, came upon his last illness, Booth had featherbeds brought out from the house for the horse to lie upon. He brought out Mary Ann and had her kiss Peacock. When the animal died, neighbors were sent for and arrived to see the corpse wrapped in a sheet and poor, terrorized Mrs. Booth sitting on it while her husband paraded up and down with a musket over his shoulder, preaching a funeral sermon to gaping slaves.

A little neighbor girl, Ella V. Mahoney, remembered how the neighbors grappled with Booth, disarming him, and how, when he saw they had him, he gave up and politely asked everybody to come in the house and have a drink. Afterwards he was very ill.

On one tour Booth came upon some wild pigeons dead from hunters' bullets and, gathering them up, carried them to his hotel bedroom, where he summoned a preacher. When the flustered cleric refused to preach the funeral sermon, Booth did the speaking himself, burying the birds in the town cemetery.

Religion played strangely through this strange man. He worshiped at all shrines alike, doffed his hat at every church he passed, and knew the intricacies of every faith so well that all denominations claimed him. His family were Episcopalians, the Masons buried him in a Baptist vault, and away back in his ancestry there was Jewish blood. Yet after he died, there were Catholic priests who believed that Booth was of their faith, so deeply grounded was he in the finer details of their church organization. Rabbis believed that he was a Jew, pointing out the many times he had joined in their synagogue services, speaking fluently their Hebraic tongue. The Koran he knew well, and observed some of its sacred days. Best of all churches he liked a certain floating "Bethel" where sailors were saved, and there, his daughter Asia recalled, his face was "so earnestly inspired with devotion" that she, too, fell in love with the place, seeing it through his simple eyes.

In the last decade of his life he acted with less frequency, going out more often to village theaters than to the large cities where packed houses and high praise always waited. The death of two infant children had shaken him even more than liquor or depressing illness. When the word had come that those two youngsters were ill, he had abandoned his engagements and had ridden home, whipping his horse with his hilted sword. He loved life and broke when he saw it go.

Nevertheless, in those last ten years he would flame out now and then, and in 1852 he went to California with his two older boys. Upon Edwin, then a frail boy of nineteen in whom a tremendous fire was already alight, fell the task of keeping the old man from going to pieces altogether. To play rôles in the family company by night, rehearse and travel by day, and guard his father from accident by both night and day taxed young Edwin heavily. Luckily for the boy, his father, not long after they arrived on the west coast, took a whim to go back home and Edwin, remaining, found success as a star in his own right while Junius Brutus, Jr., less of an actor, began to show his talent at managing.

Homeward the tottering old actor came. He stopped for a few nights in New Orleans to play before those audiences which he loved better than any. Growing restless, he started on home, boarding a steamboat for Cincinnati. The Mississippi River water gave him fever and he kept to his cabin, trying to cool his blood with more Mississippi River water. There was no physician aboard, and rather than worry the captain with requests that the boat halt for one, the old man, grown sweeter with his years, kept his silence and suffered alone. He didn't want to be a bother to the crew or the passengers, so he died, being too far gone for medical aid when his condition was discovered. The steward, reporting the event as of Tuesday, November 30, 1852, at 2 p.m., said he just could make out the shadow of that great voice murmuring its last words, "Pray! Pray! Pray!"

Mary Ann came to Cincinnati for the body, which had been placed in a temporary vault in a Baptist cemetery, and took it home to Baltimore, where it lies today by the family shaft in Greenmount Cemetery. Mary Ann lies in the same grave now, with Junius Brutus, and near by sleep six of the old actor's ten children, among them John Wilkes, his "bad boy Absalom."

WOMEN "SPOILED" HIM

J. WILKES BOOTH HAD TURNED FOURTEEN when his father died in the year 1852, and surveying himself in the light of that tragedy, the boy felt that the time was near when he should take up the family destiny — acting. He had been raised to believe that the Booths were all great actors and that he was certain to be the greatest of them all.

To inflame him the more, his two brothers had already gone from the home-nest, soaring in the theater world, Edwin as an actor, Junius Brutus, Jr., as a player-manager. Thinking of them, J. Wilkes could hardly wait to try the wings that God had most surely given him.

In his mind Fame was a woman, a being something like his mother. Mary Ann Holmes had indeed spoiled this, her favorite of ten children. To her, as she sat in the Maryland farmhouse watching him ripen, it was perfectly apparent that here was the flower of her flock, the most beautiful, the most spirited, the most winning. Besides, he was the most loving.

So she had always excused him for that headlong, captivating way he had of disobeying her commands, reconciling herself with the thought that genius was privileged to scorn discipline. If he wouldn't study, or remain in school for long at a time, that was only the sign of his destiny. If he chose to spend his wild, strong youth in uncurbed horseback rides and hunting trips rather than in the long drudgery by which his father and brothers had mastered their craft, no need to worry; the boy would conquer the stage, when he came to it, at one bound.

Still, for all his impatience to be away, his mother held J. Wilkes on the farm until he was seventeen. Once, it was true, he had run away to join the oyster pirates on the neighboring waters of Chesapeake Bay, but he had soon come home. That kind of action did not satisfy him. It was his father's fame that he wanted — the roar of applause, the fascinated eyes of crowds following him.

In 1855 the year that he was seventeen, J. Wilkes began haunting the St. Charles Theater in Baltimore, begging the manager for a chance to act. For his father's sake the manager was kindly, but saw no chance for the boy, since he was wholly untrained. One day, however, a member of the stock-company fell suddenly ill and the manager thrust young Booth into the vacant place so that the performance of *Richard III* might go on. The curtain went up; J. Wilkes stepped out. His rôle was small, but still too much for a boy who had never been taught to study anything, and J. Wilkes floundered piteously. Hisses rang in his ears and he fled for home and mother.

It was two years before he tried the stage again. This time he went about it differently. His sister Asia had a beau, John Sleeper Clarke the comedian, and upon this young man's coattails J. Wilkes hung, teasing for a job. Finally Asia's suitor took him to the manager of Philadelphia's Arch Street Theater and persuaded that official to place the boy in the resident stock-company at eight dollars weekly.

Booth was now nineteen, old enough to have mastered the four tiny speeches with which he made his début in Sheridan Knowles' *The Wife* — all he had to do was to come on as a courier and say little things like "Here comes the Duke" — but he had not prepared himself for even such simple lines, and botched his performance badly. A little later, he bungled still another small rôle, that of an incidental character in Hugo's *Lucrezia Borgia,* stammering and spluttering until the theater rang with laughter that was infinitely more terrible than the hisses of Baltimore. All at once, J. Wilkes was the town joke, and when he made his appearance the following night, crowds howled with glee at the mere memory of his former awkwardness, thundering in mock applause and imitating his stammerings in derisive choruses so loud that the manager cut out his rôle for the rest of the evening.

Philadelphia's critics, who went easy on him for the sake of his family, could give him nothing warmer than the faint word "promising," and when new stars joined the stock-company later in the season young Booth was dropped. Perhaps it was then that he began hating the Northern people.

As though by instinct, he headed southward for his next assault upon the fame that he wanted so desperately. In Richmond, Virginia, where his father had made his American début in 1821, and where his brother Edwin was lionized, J. Wilkes appeared in 1859, finding employment at twenty dollars a week in the stock-company of George Kunkel.

Here social if not artistic success met him. Richmond's critics might pointedly ignore him, but Richmond crowds did not hiss him. Southern people liked actors generally. It was a legacy from old days in England.

The Cavaliers, who had settled the South, had liked actors since the days when the Stuart kings made the London theater a thing of social prominence, whereas the Puritans, who had colonized the Northern States, had despised "play actors" from the time that Cromwell's "Roundheads" shut up theaters as "devils' dens" and whipped players at cart-tails. To the swaggering dandies of Charles II's court, theater folk were lions to be wined and dined, while to their enemies, the grim Puritans, actors were godless vagabonds, painted tools of Satan.

Children of the "Roundheads" transplanted these prejudices to the Northern settlements of the New World and in the time when Booth's character was plastic no actor could find in "Yankee" States the social recognition which the South was eager to lavish upon him. After the theater of nights, up North, actors found society in barrooms; down South, in drawing-rooms. The first playhouses in America had been Southern, and although theaters soon became the more numerous in the North, thanks to the favor which wider popular education brought the drama as a form of literature, the players themselves preferred touring Dixieland to Yankeeland. Into the civilization of the Cavaliers the gallant manners and fashionable attire of the actors fit snugly.

J. Wilkes Booth, in his winning way, loved those who loved him. He wanted to be noticed, to be a devil of a fellow. Around him in Richmond blazed the Secession fire of a loud, hot-headed minority that was for fighting the "black Abolitionists" and "nigger-loving Republicans" of the North who were storming against slavery. J. Wilkes himself caught the fever, when on October 18, 1859, a few months after his arrival in Richmond, the word came that John Brown and his Abolitionists had fallen upon the arsenal at Harpers Ferry and were passing out rifles to the blacks. Rage swept Virginia — the whole South — still, angry as were the citizens of Richmond, they found amusement and relief in the outlandish oaths of the new actor of the town, Booth, who dashed about crying that he would "shoot every Abolitionist who might desecrate the sacred soil of the Old Dominion."

Militia companies assembled and set out for Harpers Ferry but, long before they could reach the scene of the fighting, word came that the United States Marines under Col. Robert E. Lee had the insurrectionists in chains. Richmond's crack company, The Grays, heard this news when it arrived in Washington on its dash, and back home it came to remain until December, when it journeyed to Charlestown, Virginia, to guard John Brown from possible rescue on his hanging day.

That day was December 2, 1859, and the scene is one at which it pays to look. Old John Brown jolted in a wagon to the gallows. He looked at the sleepy town, awake now with bustling crowds; he looked at the soldiers, the sun, the sky and the blue Virginia hills — hazy blue with the smoke of dying Autumn.

"This is a beautiful country," he said to his jailer, who rode with him on his last journey.

Up the scaffold steps John Brown walked with a free, firm tread, then turned to the crowd, smiling. Officials blindfolded his bright hawk-eyes and left him waiting while they fussed with arrangements, like women at a wedding. Motionless as a statue, John Brown stood there — stone statue of an American Jeremiah, pointing to the gloom and destruction to come.

"There is an eternity behind and an eternity before, and this little speck in the center, however long, is but comparatively a minute," he had said two months before when the soldiers had quizzed him as he lay, bleeding and bound, on the floor of the arsenal where his last stand had been made. Death seemed to him hardly worth noticing. His soul was already marching on.

On the gallows, now, he stood alone. No clergyman was with

him. "These ministers who profess to be Christian and hold slaves or advocate slavery, I cannot abide them," he said. "My knees will not bend in prayer with them, while their hands are stained with the blood of souls."

No friends looked up at him from the throng below. He had expected none, understanding well why the South should have poured in its burning militiamen to help the law of the land fulfill its judgments; understanding perfectly why the owners of slaves should want to kill the man who had attempted to lead their slaves back to the North and freedom.

In his prophet's vision he had seen gulfs of blood rising to drown his country, and in his fanatic's brain he had dreamed that by dipping out a handful of this red water he could keep the sea from overflowing the land. One sharp stroke from him, he believed, would solve once and for all the tremendous issue of slavery upon which the Republic was splitting.

The slaves, however, had not risen to his call. Their masters had caught him and now he was at rope's end, no friends with him except those blue Virginia hills and history. Up North, where friends might now be numbered by the hundreds of thousands, rescues had been plotted, though none had been attempted, for John Brown had shaken his head "No," preferring the martyrdom that so obviously awaited him.

Hemp around his throat and hands, he waited on the gallows fifteen minutes more while four companies of United States Marines and fifteen hundred militiamen went through extravagant evolutions in the square around the scaffold. Perhaps these strutting displays were unavoidable. The colonel of those marines was known, before and afterward, as a merciful man — indeed as a Christ-like man even in those years to come when he would be leading Confederate armies through slaughter. He was Robert E. Lee.

At length the troops were ready; the drop banged down and the gray beard of Osawatomie rested at a tragic angle on his breast. In the hollow square of infantry a militiaman went fishbelly white and begged for a drink of liquor. He was John Wilkes Booth — a popinjay come to watch an eagle die.

Great matrix for American myths that scene — two of the Republic's strangest characters together there, as though by destiny, at the gallows; one dying, one looking on, both on their way at that moment to immortality.

Never again, after that day's work, was John Brown to be clearly a man any more in anybody's memory; thereafter he was to the South a gathering thunderhead on the Northern sky, promise of the hurricane to come. Thereafter he was to the North a song. All too soon armies of Union men would be marching and killing to the remorseless rhythm of "John Brown's body lies a-moldering in the grave; his soul is marching on," greatest of the world's war songs.

From that day, too, dated J. Wilkes Booth's reputation as a Southerner. Forever after, he was boasting that he had helped both to capture and to hang John Brown. Most likely half of this story was untrue, for, as has been seen, the Richmond Grays were not present at the capture, and the records in Richmond declare that Booth joined the militia company "shortly before" the regiment marched off to see John Brown swing in the Blue Ridge winds. Always there must be the suspicion that the actor had enlisted after the danger of fighting was past.

It was at the drama of John Brown's hanging that Booth made his first and last appearance in an adult military uniform. Tights fit him better, and as soon as the Richmond season was over he was off for a tour of Southern capitals appearing as a visiting star with local stock-companies, and capturing quickly the status of a matinée idol. Dressed to kill, and killing hearts right and left, he became a social lion among gay blades in barrooms and ladies in parlors. He had the voice, the eye, the vocabulary to gasconade with the fieriest of the fire-eaters when the iniquities of the plebeian and "nigger-loving" North were up for haranguing. It was the year when the hot-heads of the cotton kingdom decided that the election of the Northerner Lincoln, as Republican candidate for President, would justify Secession, and Booth added his mite to the tide of passion that, by the early Winter of 1860, had drowned out so many minor excitements that the Southern theater, itself, was dead.

His occupation gone in the region of his choice, himself unwed, athletic, a good horseman, a fine pistol shot, and still versed in the manuals of the Baltimore military school he had attended in his 'teens, Booth had every apparent reason for springing forward to fight for the cause he had championed so loudly. But, instead, he scurried north to Baltimore, one explanation having it, five years later, that he had explained to his Southern friends that a pistol had exploded accidentally, wounded him in the foot, and he must go home for healing. Probably this tale was only a twisted version of an actual occurrence unearthed eighty years later by J. Wilkes' most painstaking biographer, Stanley Kimmel. During a spasm of fun with a pistol in the dressing-room of a theater in Columbus, Georgia, sometime in late 1859 or 1860, Booth had been accidentally shot in the buttocks by his manager and, as late as the Winter of 1860–61, the bullet was still paining him.

Whatever might be the true reason for his evasion of service in the Confederate army, it was clear that Booth did nothing more audacious in the early days of the war than talk furiously about "rebel heroism," join the Baltimore chapter of the Northern anti-war secret society, the Knights of the Golden Circle, and brag about a Paul Revere-kind of horseback ride he proposed making. When the Federals in the Spring of 1861 moved on Maryland, Booth plotted a piece of histrionics which could take him, on a lathering horse, through certain rural parts of the State, calling the farmers to arms and then leading them all aflame with revolutionary ardor, down to join the Confederate army which was forming. However, the sight of bluecoated soldiers moving about the State put all thoughts of the thrilling ride out of his mind if, indeed, they had ever really been there. Another tale was that he refused to help old school friends form a Confederate company in Baltimore.

In the North, as Booth returned to it, the theaters were still open, so many were the Yankees who could not yet read the bloody stars a-right and who believed the civilization of the slavery barons was only a hollow shell which must collapse within ninety days. Up North, John Wilkes' brother Edwin was coming into the fullness of his fame, coining wealth and reaping critical tributes. Always jealous of Edwin, yet never willing to master their common art by Edwin's diligence and study, J.

Wilkes decided to storm the Northern cities as a star, a dazzling star. He would conquer the Yankees in their theatrical capital, and make them eat the hisses which they had once hurled at him.

A woman helped him in his début — just as women always helped him — Miss Mary Provost, manageress of Wallack's, backing him in his opening engagement, for which he chose his father's favorite *Richard III*.

Failure again, prompt and unanimous. "Youth may be an excuse for his errors," sneered the New York *Herald*, "but it is no excuse for presenting them to a metropolitan audience." William Winter, soon to become dean of American critics, thought the young star's acting "raw, crude and much given to boisterous declamation."

As Richard the wretched young actor stuck it out for three nights, then switched to Shylock with like disaster. He fled to Boston, where his *Robbers* was better liked, then after a little he passed, like so many before and after, to "the road," where except for infrequent returns to the larger cities of the East, he was sentenced to spend his career. New York and Philadelphia were always too critical of him. Even in Boston, which alone of Eastern capitals gave him prosperous engagements, his audiences were mainly women, a situation that an actor of the '60s felt belittling to his reputation. Women of that day were denied higher education and were currently supposed to lack inherent critical appreciation for the fine points of classical acting. Gushing floods of girls jammed Booth's stage-door in smaller towns as well as in Boston. Perfumed notes rained upon him. Clara Morris, as emotional by nature as in her art, used to grow ecstatic in remembering his beauty in the days when they played together.

"He had an ivory pallor that contrasted with his raven hair," she said. "And his eyes had heavy lids which gave him an Oriental touch of mystery. Girls in restaurants always gave him extra food; women naturally loved him."

Miss Morris, having seen him shear away the signatures from his "mash" notes before reading them, thought him pure. Popular legend of the time, however, had it that Booth was a great libertine, accepting gayly the women, high and low, who threw themselves in his way. In 1861 Henrietta Irving, an actress, knifed Booth and then herself in a hotel-room, both attempts proving trivial. And in 1865 it is known that Booth was maintaining a scarlet sweetheart, Ella Turner by name, in a Washington "parlor-house." On the morning of April 15, when she heard that her lover had become a murderer, Ella took chloroform, put his picture under her pillow and lay down upon it to die. Her sister Molly and some of the other girls revived her, but she never thanked them.

In the arms of women Booth could forget the failures of his ambition, for after that opening *débâcle* in New York, the young actor was in his own eyes a failure indeed. That he won the plaudits and dollars of the "road" audiences through the East and Middle West could never atone for his inability to capture the metropolitan critics. It was no comfort to him to know that his popularity in the smaller cities was remarkable — in one season he pocketed twenty-two thousand dollars, and this in spite of the hard times that were on the land in 1861 and 1862, with the theater ebbing as the North grew sadder and sadder over its mounting death-lists and taxes. It was no time for gayety as the Union saw its armies one after another cross the Potomac to be smashed either by Lee's genius or by their own futile leadership. Yet even in such years Booth found popular success, becoming a great favorite in the "provinces," as New Yorkers called the territory outside Manhattan. His most popular rôle was Romeo.

It was a colored woman, Mary Jane Anderson, who most simply and surely hit off the attitude of so large a section of her sex toward Booth. Mary Jane lived on the alley behind Ford's Theater in Washington, and at the trial of Booth's fellow-conspirators after the assassination, the government called her to the witness-stand to prove that the actor had been seen around the fatal theater the day of the killing. Mary Jane said she had seen him there.

"I saw him talking to a lady," she declared. "I stood in my gate and I looked right wishful at him."

In liquor, as well as in the arms of women, Booth could forget the metropolitan critics. Often, said the actors who played in his companies, he was so drunk that his negro servant had to lift him from dressing-room to stage, and in barrooms he liked to loosen his fiery eloquence and magnetic gestures in defense of the Confederacy, which, down below the dead-line, was fighting its heart out.

Drunk or sober, Booth liked to recite pieces of poetry that he had clipped from newspapers; best of all one called "Beautiful Snow," which, said his friends, he spoke "exquisitely and never without tears."

For all his disappointment at failing to capture the fame of which he had dreamed, Booth could never bring himself to learn the secret of good acting. His hatred of reading extended to prompt-books, and he was notorious for forgetting his lines. When these lapses came, he imagined that he could cover them up with violent bellows and sword-wavings. In such moments he would prance and jump about the stage in picturesque displays. When dramatics failed, he would fall back upon athletics. Poor man, he made the mistake of training in the gymnasium instead of in the study!

Pathetically believing that it was more wonderful to stun audiences with a brilliant personality than to capture them with art, he was forever rearranging Shakespeare and Schiller so that his entrances might be made in staggering leaps off precipices and battlements. Theater men like John T. Ford, whose house Booth ruined with his crime, thought these jumps "extraordinary and outrageous." The Baltimore *Sun* nicknamed him "the gymnastic actor."

Booth was all motion. If he couldn't jump, he wouldn't play. Time and again he would doze off if compelled to sit for any length of time on the stage awaiting his turn. Particularly was this apt to be true when he had been drinking — and he usually had. Then there would be the devil to pay, with actors bawling their cue-lines louder and louder, coughing in his ear, twitching at his sleeve; stage-hands on their stomachs poking braces at him from under the back-drop — and, out in front, the critics reaching down for their hats. Mrs. McKee Rankin, the actress, saw him in such a moment, prodded into wakefulness by a scene-shifter, open his eyes slowly, focus dimly on the waiting cast and then, after bawling out, "What's the matter? Don't you know your lines yet?" topple back into sleep.

It was troublesome, too, for an actor to fight him in stage duels. Once as Richard III he knocked his Richmond, E. J. Tilton, into the orchestra-pit, and the number of adversaries he had cut in mock duels was often a boast upon his lips, for although he was by no means cruel, he was vain of his skill in athletics. The temptation to show off his fencing-skill at the expense of his brother players was too much for his naturally affectionate attitude toward them. When an adversary would tartly warn him to be careful unless he wanted to start a genuine fight, he would obey, some actors thinking that he did so from timidity, others that the warning only called him to himself.

On the whole, actors of his time liked J. Wilkes Booth, rating him as good-hearted and merely "frothy" in his talk of violence. None of his friends took seriously his claims to a reckless love of the South. Now and then, when one of them would slyly ask him why he didn't fight for the Secessionists if he loved them so deeply, he would reply, "I promised my mother I wouldn't." Two explanations for this habitual reply were made by people who knew Booth; one that he was hiding behind the skirts of a mother whom he had never before obeyed so conscientiously; the other that his adoring mother had really drawn such a promise from him. One explanation is as good as the other.

When it was that he began to think of seeking fame in political action rather than on the stage, cannot be exactly placed. Probably it was in 1863. In May of that year the war was at its crisis. In the East, Lee, confident that the spell of victory would hold to the end, was planning his Northern invasion, which would end, in July, at Gettysburg. In the West, Grant was strangling Vicksburg, hoping that the citadel would surrender before help should come to it from the South. In July, Grant would win in the West, while Lee lost in the East, but in May two such victories for the North seemed dubious.

It was in that month that Booth, discussing the situation with acquaintances in Chicago, where he was filling an engagement at McVickers Theater, let fall a remark that, two years later, was recalled as having been fatefully significant. "What a glorious opportunity there is," he said, "for a man to immortalize himself by killing Lincoln!"

Then, as the incident was reported by the Chicago *Journal* of April 15, 1865, Booth had elaborated on the theme to his listeners, mentioning how bold destroyers sometimes won immortality, and quoting the couplet:

> *"The ambitious youth who fired the Ephesian dome,*
> *Outlives in fame the pious fool who reared it."*

Among those whom Booth was addressing was one literal soul who spoke up at this, asking the actor to give the name of the ambitious youth whose name had been so imperishable. J. Wilkes was stumped. He had never thought of that. The incident passed off as a joke, for as the *Journal* went on to say, "No one thought Booth would ever do anything to back up his blustering talk. He was regarded everywhere as a coward."

Later in the year, while making what was to be the final appearance of his career in Cleveland, Booth remarked to an acquaintance that the man who would kill Lincoln would occupy a higher niche in fame than George Washington. Many times, according to the memory people had of him in 1865, Booth had said such things, nobody objecting.

The North let actors air their Secession sympathies throughout the war time without restraint, considering players too trivial a class to be of any consequence. Booth's own family thought his Southern talk funny. They were all for the Union, and both Edwin and Junius Brutus, Jr., laughed at their younger brother's rantings. Edwin, according to a tale that went the rounds of the newspapers in 1865, had once turned J. Wilkes out of his house for having voiced "treasonable utterances."

With J. Wilkes, however, the idea of killing Lincoln was more serious than any of his friends could have imagined. Gone now was his first great dream of bounding onto the stage a full-grown star whom the world would acclaim. What good were the "mash-notes" of silly girls or the dollars of small-town theatergoers, when the critics of New York doomed him to mediocrity? If ever he was to become the great man that he had pictured as a little boy on the farm, long ago, he must have a new theater. Affairs of state might well furnish the new stage. Statesmen, generals were the popular heroes now, not actors. Why should not the descendant of that flaming agitator, John Wilkes of England, be somebody in this vivid new American field?

All his life Booth had stressed the "Wilkes" in his name, making his début as "J. Wilkes" only; billing himself in Richmond as "J. B. Wilkes"; signing himself "J. Wilkes Booth," and having his friends call him "Wilkes" more often than "John."

To such a man as Booth, having come to the age of twenty-six so spoiled, so willful, so vain, so disappointed in his hopes of great destiny, the idea of killing Lincoln could have come naturally. And, considering the volume and intensity of the popular discussions over the probability of Lincoln's assassination, such an idea could have come reasonably enough. The idea that only a madman could have dreamed of murdering the President was a development of souls who in the days after his death came to look upon Lincoln as a saint.

No, Booth was sane enough, and very sensible, too, in matters touching his own safety. He was methodical and accurate in keeping his personal accounts, a successful business man in both the theater and land speculation. The theory that he was a lunatic was spread by his fellow actors to save themselves from the tar and feathers which raging mobs threatened to give the whole acting-profession in the turmoil that arose after the assassination.

And, even so, it was first voiced by a player, himself madder than any of the Booths. Edwin Forrest was the man. The tragedian was asleep in his New York hotel — the Metropolitan — on the night of April 14, 1865, when his co-star John McCullough came bursting into the room with the news that their friend, J. Wilkes Booth, had shot Abraham Lincoln.

"But I don't believe it," McCullough added.

"I do," snapped the leonine Forrest from his pillow. "All the —— —— Booths are crazy."

Theatrical people, however, at the first impact of the news, sided with McCullough rather than with Forrest, claiming that Booth couldn't possibly be the assassin as reported. Then, swiftly, came the turn of events that forced them to change their tune. Out across the North the hideous story of the assassination was traveling like a blight, turning the country black with mourning. Following it from Washington came the explanation of the calamity as dictated by Stanton, Secretary of War: The Confederacy, beaten on the battlefield, had switched to wholesale murder in an attempt to paralyze the Union government. Booth had been the tool of countless conspirators.

Fantastic as this explanation was later seen to be, it fell like the truth upon the distraught North in April, 1865, and mobs began riding Southern sympathizers on fence-rails. As notorious friends of Secession, theatrical folk were in peril. One of their number had committed the crime; the murder had been done in a theater. Rumor implicated great groups of actors. Edwin Booth was in hiding and that other brother, Junius Brutus, Jr., was legging it up Cincinnati alleys lickety-split with a Republican posse at his heels. Laura Keane and her company were jailed for no other reason than that they had had the misfortune to be interrupted in their performance at Ford's Theater by the assassin, as he had come sprawling down out of the bloody box.

To clear their skirts, theater people abandoned the belief that Booth could have been innocent, and began declaring that he was a madman, had always been a madman and that, moreover, he was the son of a madman. They raked up all of the picturesque whimsies of J. Wilkes and his father, recalled the assassin's tipsy adventures of the past and interpreted them as lunacies. Luckily for their propaganda, they had the ear of the newspapers, since reporters were at their doors begging them, grilling them for descriptions of J. Wilkes whom they had known so well. The actors could explain everything in Forrest's sweeping epitaph, "All the —— —— Booths are crazy."

Even John McCullough soon forgot his initial refusal to believe Booth guilty and was remembering all manner of instances of his friend's obvious criminal insanity.

As Lincoln's saintliness became more and more apparent with each day's passing, so did it become clear to many Americans that no one but a madman could have killed him. It became easier and easier to dismiss J. Wilkes Booth with a shake of the head and a sighing explanation, "He was crazy, that was all."

But it is not so easy to explain Booth as he was in the year 1863 — a young man wondering to himself how best he could win that thing to which he was destined — immortality!

☆ ☆ ☆ 15 ☆ ☆ ☆

CARTOON ASSASSINS

IN 1863 IT WAS PLAIN to many people that the man who would take Abraham Lincoln out of the White House would win the huzzas of not only the South but much of the North as well. For three years and over J. Wilkes Booth had heard Lincoln's murder discussed by loyalists who dreaded it and Secession sympathizers who hoped for it. He had read newspapers that described its peril and newspapers that enumerated the blessings that might follow it. Loose and wild offers of rewards for Lincoln's assassination had appeared once or twice in Southern newspapers, and there had been occasional calls for his slaughter in Northern papers such as the La Crosse, Wisconsin, *Democrat,* which said, "And if he is selected to misgovern for another four years, we trust some bold hand will pierce his heart with a dagger for the public good."

Among the Secession sympathizers above Mason and Dixon's Line there were always plenty to say that the "foul-mouthed, bloody-minded old butcher" was criminal in the way he aborted all plans for peace. They wished that he would die, the bolder ones wishing that some one would kill him. Most of this talk was not serious, but it was heard everywhere. True it was that Lincoln discouraged peace, rock-firm in his belief that no peace could be permanent until the "rebellious" people had given up their doctrines of extreme States' rights and had, without compromise, returned to the acceptance of national authority. He had evidence before him that the South would never submit to the doctrine of Federal supremacy so long as it could hold a gun. Therefore, the war must go on.

Furthermore, Lincoln was commander in chief of the Union armies, directing campaigns from his desk, frequently telling his generals when to attack and where to march. To kill him would be hardly less fair than killing McClellan or Hooker or Meade, any of his captains. Nor could it be said that his soldiers held the life of Davis, the Confederate President, in any particular sacredness when they sang, "We'll hang Jeff Davis to a sour apple tree, as we go marching on."

In answer, the "Johnny-Rebs" substituted "Abe Lincoln" for "Jeff Davis" and sang the song back at the "Yanks."

Death was in the air.

Every so often, a wave of weary nausea would sweep the North, men saying that if Lincoln were out of the way, dead or defeated for the Presidency, the political forces that cried for a compromise peace would sweep the country and stop the suicidal war.

Gradually the boiling frustrations in the life of J. Wilkes Booth congealed upon this common theme. He would kill Lincoln. Surely that would make the world take him seriously. His stage appearances became fewer and fewer. To friends who wanted to know why he should be giving up his profession just at the time when the theater world was teeming again with prosperity — new play-houses were opening everywhere in the North through '64 — Booth replied that he was going in for oil and land speculation. Often he hinted of vague, nebulous, and brilliant plans.

Secretly he was building, in his mind, a new play for himself — a grandiose political melodrama with himself as hero — an idea that was to start in romance, veer awkwardly into comedy and then, ironically, to soar into tragedy. For six months he toiled over it, tinkering with the plot, assembling his cast. In September, 1864, he revealed it to the first of his supporting conspirators, a little band that he had begun to recruit from the backwash of Southern sympathizers in Baltimore and Washington. From such a group Booth, with his fame, had little trouble in accumulating followers.

"Booth was a peculiarly fascinating man," said John T. Ford, the theater-owner, "and controlled the lower class of people, more, I suppose, than ordinary men would."

J. Wilkes fascinated first Sam Arnold and Michael O'Laughlin; Arnold, a desultory farm-hand of Hookstown, Maryland, loafing, lazy, a deserter from the Confederate army; O'Laughlin, a hard-drinking and haphazard livery-stable worker of Baltimore, also a Confederate deserter. Both had at one time gone to school with Booth, and now their light brains kindled at the chance to be intimate again with so great a fellow.

Once J. Wilkes had reëstablished himself with these two empty-heads, he began, in hot whispers, to sketch the gaudy triumphs which they would all achieve. As he told the plot, the melodrama had changed somewhat from those first crude drafts that he had made in barrooms. Now, it was not to kill Lincoln but to kidnap him. Some night J. Wilkes would follow Lincoln to the theater, rope him and tie him in the Presidential box — single handed — then lower him down over the rail to Arnold, O'Laughlin and such other assistants as would be admitted to the little band. Together they all would take Lincoln to a deserted house, to be hidden until opportunity came to hustle him across the battle-line into the hands of the Confederacy. Richmond would then exchange its great captive for that army of Southern soldiers who were languishing in Yankee prison-camps, an army that grew each day as Grant's fresh captures came in.

What the Confederacy needed most was men. Conscription had exhausted the loyal population, "robbing the cradle and the grave" as Grant grimly observed while he watched gray-clad prisoners file past him. Desertions were growing even in the army of the idolized Lee. In the mountains, notably of North Carolina, thousands of deserters, or Southern opponents of the war, lived in defiance of all exhortations or threats; some of them farming their crops in the hills, seceders from Secession.

Now, when a Confederate soldier dropped in battle or was captured by the Yankees, there was no recruit to take his place.

Lincoln and Grant, foreseeing this in the summer of '64, had put an end to the custom of exchanging prisoners, since the North with its superior man-power had reserves to fill all gaps, whereas the South, bled white, had none. To keep on trading prisoners was to help the Confederacy far more than the Union, so it was stopped, even though Lincoln and Grant had to harden their hearts to the thought of Federal soldiers starving in the wretched Southern prison-camps of Andersonville, in Libby Prison or Belle Isle.

If the Southern prisoners could be delivered out of the North into Lee's ranks once more, the Confederacy would have a strong, new army, one that would revive the waning cause and allow the Army of Northern Virginia to smash Grant once and for all. So Booth dreamed. Lee with his fresh divisions would end the war, then there would be eternal fame for the bold brain that had planned it all and made success possible. Then the South would worship no one so much as J. Wilkes Booth, and the whole world would be ringing with the name of the hero who had stolen Lincoln, given Lee back his legions, and closed the Civil War in a climax of dazzling genius.

But, as in all his plays, Booth had failed to study his part. There is no evidence that he ever consulted Confederate authorities to see how they would welcome such a problem as he proposed to present them, and it is clear that the playwright did not know his villain, Lincoln. Booth imagined himself, the slender fencer, able to outwrestle the President, but lately crack wrestler of the frontier, and who was still, at fifty-six, one of the most powerful of living men despite the harrowing drain of war worries and chronic indigestion. It was easy for Booth, the fop of superficial mind, to mistake Lincoln's shambling repose for debility.

Soon Booth added a third recruit — John H. Surratt, a fifty-dollar-a-month clerk for the Adams Express Company, and occasionally a blockade-runner for the Confederacy. Booth met him through Dr. Samuel Mudd, a well-educated and gentlemanly physician from the environs of Washington, whose chief connection with the conspiracy seemed to be a general desire to avoid Booth without violating normal rules of courtesy.

Surratt was a strutting nincompoop who quickly tumbled into the plot, and walked about as though on air, his low forehead brushing the stars. He himself was of no use, as the thing turned out, but he did one thing that was unwittingly important. He introduced the dashing actor to a woman — his mother, Mary E. Surratt, a pious, hard-faced widow of forty-five, whose white arms could have had no enticements for Booth, but whose home, a cheap boarding-house, gave him the necessary rendezvous for his criminal rehearsals.

Life had been hard on Mrs. Surratt. Romance had disappointed her. As a girl, Mary Jenkins had been hailed as the belle of Prince George County in Maryland, and love had been gay when John H. Surratt, Sr., had taken her as his bride to live outside Washington on the estate which he had inherited. Then a negro slave, driven to fury by cruel treatment, it was said, had burned the house, her husband failed in business, and they moved into a tavern which he bought thirteen miles outside the capital.

The drift was all downhill. Money was scarce. The tavern's profits were eked out with a tiny postmastership which her husband acquired. The war came, and since they both were pro-Southern, their roadhouse degenerated into a nest of spies and blockade-runners. In '63 Surratt, Sr., died, leaving her with three children, Annie, away at a convent school, John, wheel-headed and frothy, and Isaac, who had joined the Confederate army. She leased the tavern and, growing grimmer, moved into Washington to open a lodging-house on H Street. Annie came home from school. John got clerk's jobs and, now and then, carried military secrets for the authorities in Richmond. Now that he had found his fine friend, Booth, young Surratt quit the Adams Express Company and devoted his time to the wonderful plot.

Mrs. Surratt knew of the plot and approved. She had always been for the South in her brooding, religious way, much given to hopes and prayers that the Lord God would punish the sinful pride with which the Northerners celebrated their victories. But, more to the point, she was fascinated by the actor whose moustache was so bold and whose manners were so grand.

He was gallant and handsome, always entertaining the young lady-boarders in the parlor when John brought him home for a call. She had his picture up beside those of Lee and Jefferson Davis. She was charmed, and probably in love — poor woman, at the dangerous age in her sex, probably reveling in amorous fancies with this Apollo, twenty years her junior.

To the house on H Street Booth brought his recruits as he gathered them in. David E. Herold, who, according to his apologists, was a moron, less than twelve years old in mind and in his early twenties otherwise, was one.

"I have known Herold for the last six years," said a Washington physician, Dr. Samuel McKim, testifying in his behalf on the witness-stand, a few months later, "and I consider him a very light, trivial, unreliable boy; so much so that I would never let him put up a prescription of mine if I could prevent it, feeling confident that he would tamper with it if he thought he could play a joke on anybody. In mind I consider him about eleven years of age."

Just as Booth had been a failure at acting, so had this silliest of his followers been a failure at his chosen profession, pharmacy. Druggists had "fired" him so often that when Booth snared him he was doing nothing more serious than roam the thickets outside the city on happy little hunting-trips.

A trifling lout was Herold, too shiftless to work for his widowed mother and seven sisters, all of whom adored him and kept him in spending-money. Livery stables knew him well. There he loafed, talking horses and hounds, and there Booth, out recruiting, found him. Herold was so thrilled by his nearness to the "play actor" that he followed him henceforth like a faithful pup-dog that had been gifted with the human talent of giggling. In Booth's melodrama Herold was to have the part of guide when they took the trussed President down through Maryland and over the river into the Southern lines.

To ferry the plotters and their captive across, Booth must have a trusted man, and around Washington he soon found him, George A. Atzerodt, a cartoon of an assassin, humped, simian, fawning, with hair that hung and whiskers that straggled. Booth won him to the plot with promises of gold. Most likely it was Surratt who suggested Atzerodt, for the simian's business was making carriages at Port Tobacco, a cesspool of a town on the Rappahannock, where, between jobs, he ferried spies and informants such as John Surratt across the river. In Port Tobacco he was known as "a great coward" and Mrs. Surratt, when he was brought to the lodging-house, labeled him a "poor stick."

Booth himself attached Edward Spangler to his troupe of comedians, finding him in the theater world that he knew so well. Spangler, who so far as is known, never came to the rendezvous on H Street, may have counted for little in the kidnaping plot, but he was useful later.

Spangler was the lowest in the entourage of J. Wilkes Booth, being a drunken scene-shifter at Ford's Theater in Washington, a sullen and surly hater of the Union, and champion crab-fisherman of the Potomac. He slept in a stable on the theater alley with Booth's horse, which he curried.

It was exactly the kind of a cast that an actor of Booth's stripe would have assembled. Flamboyant stars of that day, as well as later, never chose to surround themselves with players who might by any chance become their rivals, and Booth, as author and manager of this desperate new drama, was to keep his stardom unquestioned. Still, he needed a "heavy," some one who could be powerful when the climax came. His cast, so far, was too light, too farcical. Even he must have seen that.

One of the first days in March, 1865, brought him his man, Lewis Powell, alias "Payne," the only one of Booth's co-plotters worth noticing twice, a gigantic savage, born with a slanting brow, a protruding jaw and dumb courage. Under-worlds of great cities have had Powells in plenty, stupid youths who were amiable jaguars in dull hours, insensate killers when the right leader came along.

Lewis Thornton Powell he was christened on April 22, 1844, by his father, George C. Powell, the backwoods Baptist preacher of Alabama. Across this State and into Georgia, then into Florida, went the Rev. Mr. Powell, saving souls and accumulat-ing children, six daughters and three sons — Lewis the third — having blessed him and his wife on their missions. In his twelfth year young Lewis professed religion and lived thereafter a pure life, as his father said in 1865.

When the call to chasten the Northerners came in '61 the Rev. Mr. Powell saw his boys begin to go,—the two oldest joining the Confederacy at the first summons, and Lewis, after a few months as manager of the home farm and its slaves, leaving for Richmond with the 2nd Florida Infantry.

It was early Spring when young Powell came to the Confederate capital, and its streets were noisy with young men in uniform crying to each other that the white-livered Yankee tradesmen would soon be all a-running. Thrills were in the air and, in addition, Richmond was Powell's first big city.

Fascinated by the dazzling spectacle, the boy walked the streets, coming in time to his first theater. On its stage he beheld the most entrancing sight of his life—a bounding, thrilling, roaring god whose flashing eye and strutting histrionics bound the boy in a spell. It was John Wilkes Booth, making one of his last Southern appearances before the war shut him off together from the population that he loved.

After the show Powell hung about the stage-door, hoping for a glimpse of his new deity. Booth came out, noticed the boy, and, always gratified at admiration, stopped and spoke. Finding the fellow agreeably worshipful, the actor took him to a near-by oyster-bar, where he was soon filling him with liquor, bivalves and dizzy tales of life back-stage. In a few days Powell had marched away to war, but never did he forget that night—or that prince of enchantment.

Through the gory Peninsular campaign, through Chancellorsville and Antietam the boy went without a scratch, hearing, however, that both brothers had been killed at Murfreesboro. His turn came at Gettysburg, and when Lee drew his riddled columns back from the field on July 3, Powell was lying wounded where he had fallen. Yankee stretcher-bearers picked him up and he was soon recovering. So good-natured and tame was he that the Union surgeons made a nurse of him in the Pennsylvania College Hospital near by, later transferring him to similar work in the West Building Hospital at Baltimore. He was a warrior, however, not a nurse, and in October of that year, '63, escaped, fleeing southward to hunt his old regiment.

Whether he was unable to find it or whether the charm of irregularity had caught him is not certain, but something kept him circulating for the next year and a half through those Confederate cavalry-bands whose depredations kept military organizers both South and North undecided as to whether they were detached raiders or just plain guerrillas. Under Harry Gilmore and Mosby, the Terror, he served until January, 1865, when, like so many other Confederates who saw the hopelessness of their cause, he deserted. Killing had lost its zest for him, and shortly before his departure he saved the lives of two Union prisoners from his fellow-raiders.

On his horse he rode into the Union lines at Alexandria, took the oath of allegiance under the alias "Payne," sold his horse, and went on to Baltimore to hunt up a certain Mrs. Margaret Branson, who had nursed him at Gettysburg. In her lodging-house he hid until scandal drove him out. One morning a negro maid "sassed" him while cleaning his room, and, accustomed as he was to the harsher "far-South" method of handling negroes, he turned into a beast, knocking the colored girl to the floor, stamping upon her with wild cries that he would have her life. Other lodgers pulled him away, the girl sent for the police and Powell hastily departed.

It was March and chilly as he dragged his feet out through the town. Homeless, penniless, enemy of both North and South, he was plodding dumbly ahead when a voice called from the steps of Barnum's hotel, "Powell." He looked up. There stood his god of the Richmond theater and the oyster-bar. J. Wilkes Booth, who could never remember his lines very well on the stage, remembered names and faces well indeed. Golden days now came for the young anthropoid Payne, fat, lazy days in grand Washington hotels, breakfast in bed, new clothes with money jingling in the pockets thereof, long, intimate hours with his idol, thrilling to the secrets and dramatic plots breathed into his ear by a great actor.

A wild young Visigoth was Powell, feasting in Rome until the emperor should have need of him in the arena. But he was no mercenary, merely an eager slave. Unquestioningly he marched through every rôle Booth told him to play. At times he pretended to be a sickly aristocrat confined to his hotel bedroom, at others he was a clergyman, and it was as a doctor's messenger, medicine in hand, that he was to pose when the play called for final action.

To the Surratt lodging-house Booth took his gladiator, introducing him that first evening as "The Rev. Mr. Wood," Mrs. Surratt observing drily that he was "a great-looking Baptist preacher." Madame, herself familiar with religion and its followers, did not swallow the ruse. But she accepted him later when Booth explained who he was. Well dressed and quiet, the Rev. Mr. Wood passed muster with the lady-boarders, asking Annie Surratt to play the piano, raising the cover and turning the music for her like any visiting pastor.

With his troupe assembled, Booth must have been joyous. At last he had an audience that understood how great a man he was. To the lodging-house he could come of evenings and entertain the parlor-guests with his manners, while all the time he could keep saying to himself that immortality was winging its way every hour nearer and nearer to him. By day he could sit with his morons on beds behind locked doors, snapping empty pistols, brandishing bowie-knives, fiddling with false moustaches, like so many Tom Sawyers in haymows across the world, generations on end.

John H. Surratt now sought clerkships no more; Atzerodt mended no more carriage wheels; Herold thought not at all of the need for hunting up another pharmacist's post; Powell, alias Payne, alias The Rev. Mr. Wood, was not planning to desert this glorious ease. Great days for the lodging-house on H Street, with everybody loafing but Madame and she listening to the whispers about kidnaping, and hurrying, almost daily, to church to pray.

Delightful as it must have been to dream bold, brave dreams, some action had to be taken sooner or later, and toward mid-March things began to move. Something, no one knows exactly what, prevented Booth from attempting the capture of Lincoln in a theater. Perhaps his followers, humorless though they were, saw that it might end in burlesque. One story, not well established, has it that Booth summoned his cast to meet him one night at Ford's Theater, where it had been announced Lincoln would attend, but that not one of the principals came to meet Booth — not even Lincoln.

Another tale, more credible, is that Booth attended the second inaugural ball of Lincoln on August 4, 1865, and that he glowered across the ballroom floor at the tall President, muttering threats and clinching his fists so savagely that his friends persuaded him to leave before he could make trouble. That Booth could have been at the ball is likely, since he was at the time dancing attendance upon a girl who would logically have attended the social function — Bessie Hale, daughter of the Union Senator from New Hampshire and high enough in society to be also wooed, as legend has it, by Captain Robert Lincoln, son of the President. Whether "Bob" Lincoln was enamored of the girl or no, Booth was most certainly courting her, for in April his brother Junius was expecting them to announce their engagement.

Certain it is that in March of 1865 Booth had abandoned the notion of roping Lincoln in a theater, and had decided to waylay the President as he rode down some deserted road. One night the conspirators did crouch in the shadows, to snatch their prey as he would come driving back to town from the Soldiers' Home, but when the vehicle rolled by it was as good as empty — in place of Lincoln there sat Salmon P. Chase, Chief Justice of the Supreme Court, game too small for the bagging. They rode back to the lodging-house where Booth, Surratt and Powell stamped about, whipping their boots and cursing their blasted "prospects." The melodrama had turned farce.

At a meeting at the Lichau Hotel on Pennsylvania Avenue, Booth's temper was seen to be mastering him. He quarreled with Arnold, and said that he ought to shoot him, whereupon Arnold snapped back that two could play at such a game, and when Booth backed down, Sam went back to the superior excitements of Hookstown agriculture. O'Laughlin smelled Spring and wandered off to his old job in the Baltimore feed-barn, Surratt thought of finding another clerkship, and finally took to carrying dispatches again for the contriving and devious Benjamin, Confederate Secretary of State. Booth was left alone with the simian Atzerodt, the Neanderthal Powell and the giggling Herold. Everything was black once more.

J. Wilkes saw his chance for immortality slipping, slipping away. Each morning the newsboys cried Union victories. Grant was hammering the life out of Lee with his rain of short body-blows; Sherman, having conquered Georgia and South Carolina, was slashing northward, burning as he came. As Lincoln said, "Grant has the bear by the leg while Sherman is taking its hide off." Soon there would be no Confederacy to receive a trussed Lincoln, even if Booth were to deliver him.

It is apparent that when Booth realized this, he decided that his one remaining way to command the public eye was to murder Lincoln and to explain the deed as an act of a Brutus liberating his people from a Tarquin's oppressions. This, by all the evidence that time has amassed, was the motive for the assassination of Lincoln.

However, in Washington and Virginia there sleeps a legend which denies all this — a legend that says J. Wilkes Booth killed Abraham Lincoln not over war, not over ambition either, but for the one reason that myth might most logically ascribe to so handsome an actor — a woman. It was for Lily Beall that the murder was done, as this story runs. Booth, in school, had roomed with John Y. Beall, of a proud Virginian family, and when in 1864 his friend, now Captain Beall of the Confederacy, was caught in civilian clothes derailing passenger trains in New York State, and condemned to be hanged as a spy, Booth moved to save his life. No one, today, can tell this story as John P. Simonton of Washington tells it — Simonton for forty-three years a clerk in the Judge-Advocate's office of the War Department and tireless student of Booth's history:

"Here in Washington, people said that Booth was engaged to marry Lily Beall, and that when her brother John was sentenced to be hanged Booth promised her to try and prevent his death. Booth went up to the prison in New York harbor where Beall awaited his hanging and promised the condemned man that he'd go and see President Lincoln.

"He went. I got the story of his visit from two doctors in Washington whom Lincoln liked. They said that the President had told them to come and ask him for any favors any time, day or night. Booth knew these doctors, and asked them to get him into the White House. He said that, being a trained actor, he was sure he would move Lincoln to mercy. So the doctors took Booth over to the White House in the night.

"Lincoln got up, dressed and came out. Booth began pleading. And one of these doctors told me that he'd never heard such an eloquent plea in his life; he said that when Booth finished he was on his knees before Lincoln, begging in a whisper that could be heard clear across the room. Booth put his arms around Lincoln's legs and all of them cried, Booth, the two doctors — and Lincoln. At last Lincoln put his hands on Booth's shoulders and said, 'You've made a noble plea; your friend shall be saved.' And he went to a desk and signed a paper.

"'Now,' he said, 'this has to go to the State Department, but you need worry no more. I'll see that your friend's life is saved.'

"Booth threw his arms around Lincoln again and said, 'You are the grandest man in the world!' Then he told Lincoln all about the plot to kidnap him, confessed it all.

"The next day the Secretary of State, Seward, came in with the reprieve for Beall and laid it down, saying that if it went through, he'd resign. He was a profane man and he swore he wouldn't represent a country that didn't punish traitors such as Beall. So Lincoln didn't send the telegram, and Beall was hanged on February 24, 1865.

"That happened to be the day that Booth, proud of his success, went to the prison in New York to tell Beall that he was to be spared. As Booth went inside the gate, he saw a crowd coming out and asked what the excitement was about. He was told that Beall had just been hanged. So he came home and killed Lincoln in revenge."

An unbelievable tale, this one of Booth, Lincoln and Lily Beall, and its existence illustrates how ready many people have been to credit anything that entangled Booth with a woman. Isaac Markens, the scholar, pursuing the story to its sources, found that in several versions it named the two mythical friends who took Booth to Lincoln in the dead of night. These individuals were usually described as having been Senator John P. Hale of New Hampshire and Washington McLean, Democratic editor of Ohio. Sometimes John W. Forney, the Republican editor of Philadelphia, was said to have been in the party. Forney in 1876, declaring that he had never known Booth, publicly branded the story as a fabrication by that same "Brick" Pomeroy whose La Crosse, Wisconsin, *Democrat* had so vilified Lincoln in his lifetime. Markens discovered that the Virginia Historical Society had incorporated the Beall-Booth tale in its official publications, but he dismissed it as fictitious, since there could be no question that Booth had begun to plot against Lincoln long before Beall was sentenced to death.

In his overmastering conceit, Booth spread myths about himself in his day. When a tumor appeared upon his neck, he enjoined the Washington surgeon, Dr. Frederick May, who removed it, to say, if questioned, that the operation was for the removal of a bullet. Later when fellow players asked him what was the matter with his neck, he explained that a pistol ball which he had received in desperate gun-play down South before the war, had just now worked its way out.

Conceit made life unendurable to the tragedian when in April, '65, Lee surrendered. His last chance to perform the kidnaping melodrama was definitely gone. The North celebrated victory all about him, and, in one of the torchlit mass-meetings at the White House, Booth heard the President address the crowd in that deathless speech of April 11. From the steps Lincoln's voice, thin and worn, came down to the people, pleading for conciliation and mercy.

His words were soothing news to the "rebels," informing them that the President would protect the South from the small but powerful band of Northern "avengers." He would not do as some people suggested, doom the ex-slave-owners to the whims of their former chattels. He would not even go so far as to let all negroes vote, he hinted. Only a slender fraction of the colored folk should have the ballot.

As these words, so dramatic in that hour, came down from

the White House steps, any sincere lover of the South within earshot must have known the giant midlander as the one hope of the shattered people down in Dixie. But J. Wilkes Booth, down in the crowd, whispered to Herold, "Shoot him on the spot." Herold refused on the ground that the spot was too dangerous, although he might reasonably have excused himself on the ground that Booth as author of the idea should do the thing himself. Booth stood glowering as Lincoln talked on about his mild policy of Reconstruction.

"That means nigger citizenship," muttered the actor. "Now, by God, I'll put him through!"

Three nights later Booth "put him through" indeed, although it took many buoying gulps of liquor to bring him enough courage for the act. Characteristically, Booth selected a crowded theater for the event which he intended should make him immortal.

To have assassinated the President on one of his many unguarded trips from the White House across the street by night to the War Department, would have been far simpler and safer for Booth, but it would have been unseen, undramatic—no exhibition at all. So Booth chose the night of April 14 when, as the newspapers announced, the President would attend the performance of *Our American Cousin* at Ford's Theater. The play was popular, and with the victorious Lincoln and his guest, the warrior-hero Grant, both present, a crowded house was certain.

On the morning of the great day he walked Pennsylvania Avenue silently rehearsing his coming première as an assassin, learning lines for the new rôle of patriotic tragedian.

Even in such an hour he could not be free from women. A schoolgirl who had been secretly fascinated by him at casual meetings stopped him and began to make fluttering conversation, saying among other things that she had come out to buy some candy. Listening to her prattle, Booth understood her to say "candles," and thinking that she wanted to illuminate her windows in honor of Grant's victory, he flew into a rage.

"What do you want with more candles?" he asked wildly. "The windows are full of them and when they are lighted I

wish they could burn every house to the ground. I would rejoice
at the sight. I guess I'm a little desperate this morning, and,
do you know, I feel like mounting my horse and tearing up and
down the streets waving a Rebel flag in each hand, till I have
driven the animal to death."

Startled by the outburst, the girl tried to turn the talk on to
other things, but Booth cut her short with "Don't you study
Latin at school?"

"Yes," she answered.

"Then tell me this," he commanded, "is *tyrannis* spelled with
two *n*'s or two *r*'s?"

By the next morning the girl would know why he had asked
so strange a question.

In the afternoon Booth saw to it that the Presidential box
in the theater should be made easy for his entrance, once Lincoln should be in his place. Perhaps Spangler aided in this.
No one can be certain whether he did or not, although he was
damning Lincoln all the time he helped trim the box with flags
that afternoon. Somebody crept into the box before theater time,
bored a hole in the door through which a bullet might be fired
from the passage-way, and chipped the plaster by the door-
frame inside the box, so that a stout bar might be inserted to
prevent entrance from without. Evidently Booth planned to
be free from interruption if it took any considerable length of
time to get the killing done.

At eight o'clock that night he assembled the remnants of
his cast in the Herndon House, where he was keeping Powell.
The "star" would kill Lincoln. Powell would murder Seward
in his bed, Herold accompanying, although assigned to nothing
in particular; Atzerodt would work his way into Vice-President
Johnson's room at the Kirkwood Hotel and finish him. Powell,
schooled to killing by four red years, was ready and drew on
his boots. Atzerodt began to whine that he had enlisted to
capture, not to kill, Booth cursing him for a coward and a fool
and telling him to go ahead since, if caught, he'd be hanged
anyway.

So they parted, hurrying for their horses. Booth led his into
the alley behind the theater and gave it to a half-wit stage-

door boy "Peanuts" to hold. Then he continued the task of fortifying himself with liquor, necessary work that he had begun earlier in the evening. A little after ten o'clock he strolled into the theater, passing the ticket-taker, who knew him for a privileged actor, wandered around to the back of the box, opened the door, stepped in, drew a derringer, shot the President in the back of the head, dropped the firearm, whipped out his knife, cut down the military aide who came scrambling at him, and, frantic to be down in front of the audience with his claim to fame, poised on the box-rail for the "most extraordinary and outrageous" jump of his grasshopper career.

The distance down to the stage was as nothing to what he had made so grandly and so easily many times in *Macbeth*, but never in his whole life had Booth made himself wholly ready for the stage and could not now, at twenty-six years of age, be expected to change. Just as he bungled his first stage appearance long ago, so he bungled his last, catching his spur in a draped flag and hitting the floor, ignominiously, on all fours. It was a very funny fall, yet the audience did not laugh. He had come out of the Presidential box, and although scarcely any of the spectators heard the bark of the little derringer, they knew in one awful moment that the emergence of a frenzied figure from that curtained box meant horror, somehow.

J. Wilkes was up in a second, striking extravagant poses with his bloody knife, and taking time to address the crowd with such heroics as "The South is avenged" and "Sic semper tyrannis," the State motto of Virginia, which he had borrowed for the occasion. Dragging his left leg — broken in the tumble — he gestured across the stage, halting only to slit the coat-tails of the orchestra leader who, running wild, blundered into his way.

Out the stage-door he flew, clambered into the saddle, swung down with knife or pistol-butt, clipping poor "Peanuts" a felling blow on the head, kicked home with his heels, and was off in a clatter of hoofs for the Navy Yard bridge and the shadows of Maryland.

"HAM ACTOR"

THE MOON WAS RISING as Booth's horse came onto the Navy Yard bridge with a clatter of hoofs that brought the Union sentries out with fixed bayonets. Across his rifle their commander, Sergeant Silas Cobb, challenged, "Who are you?"

"My name is Booth," came the nonchalant answer. "I'm going home. I live close to Beantown, in Charles County."

The sergeant quizzed him further. Why was he out so late? Didn't he know the rule forbidding any one to pass after nine o'clock? Booth replied casually enough — he was a better actor then than ever before — saying that he had been in town on business, and had waited for the moon to rise to light him home. The story sounded plausible enough, and, as discipline was easing with the end of the war, Sergeant Cobb stepped aside. "I thought he was a proper person to pass," he said afterward, "and I let him pass."

Booth spurred on into the shadows of the Maryland road and was gone. Ten minutes later another horseman rode onto the bridge, sheepishly explaining himself as a Mr. Smith who had overstayed himself with too congenial company in town, and who now wanted to get home to White Plains. Good humoredly, Cobb let him pass, too, and David Herold went down into the Maryland shadows after his chief, thrusting his head into the noose.

He had been gone perhaps half an hour when a third horse sounded on the planking. But the rider was no avenger of the dead President. It was only John Fletcher, the livery-stable man, hunting the roan that he had rented Herold earlier in the evening. Not long after the boy had taken the horse, Fletcher had seen the fellow gallop past the stable in a lather of whip and spur.

"You get off that horse now, you've had it long enough," he had yelled, but the boy had only ridden the faster and Fletcher, mounting another animal, had set out in angry pursuit, dreaming not at all of the tragedy from which his customer was fleeing. Sergeant Cobb answered up as Fletcher questioned him now. Yes, such a horse and such a rider had gone over the bridge. Yes, Fletcher could follow him over, but he could not come back. So Fletcher turned and rode slowly back to his stable, to find the city stark mad with horror, the streets a black mêlée of wild-eyed citizens, soldiers and rushing detectives.

Davy Herold, having done nothing but course the streets in futile excitement, had at last decided to make the rendezvous across the river and accompany his leader to the South, where awaited that fame which Booth had promised. How long the two men waited for Powell and Atzerodt in the shadows no one knows. Whatever it was, it was too long, for they never came. Back in the city each of the morons was wheeling and circling stupidly, helpless without his leader.

Atzerodt had felt his courage ooze out at his finger-tips the moment Booth left him at the Herndon House. Slowly he forced his feet to the Kirkwood Hotel, where his victim, Vice-President Johnson, that man of destiny, was supposedly sleeping, but he got no further than the bar. Liquor could not bring back his heart and he stumbled out to his horse and rode aimlessly about the town, hearing the hue and cry arise around Ford's Theater. Cringing and trembling, he turned his horse in at the livery stable, and went bumping through the streets like a blind rat, vainly begging shelter of an acquaintance, whimpering and shaking as the city went madder and madder around him, pawning his revolver and finally striking off on foot for his childhood home, twenty-two miles north of Washington. There the detectives found him four days later, moping because a neighbor girl had discouraged his awkward love-advances.

Powell, the killer, at least tried to enact the rôle to which he had been assigned. He was to go to the Seward home, where the Secretary of State lay convalescing from a broken jaw, and work his way to the bedside by pretending to be a messenger from Dr. Verdi, the physician in charge.

Powell, tying his horse at the door, rang the bell and told

the colored boy his story, displaying a package of medicine and insisting that he give the accompanying directions to the nurse in the bedroom. William Bell, the negro doorman, objected, saying that no one could go up, and for some minutes they argued in the hall, Powell slowly edging forward as he talked. Finally, since the man was so insistent and "had a very fine voice," Bell thought better of it, apologized for having been rough in his refusals, and let the messenger follow him upstairs, whispering "Doan' walk so heavy."

At the top of the stair Frederick, the Secretary's eldest son, appeared, telling the stranger that he could not enter the sick-room. For five minutes they wrangled quietly, then Powell turned to go, with Bell cautioning him again "Doan' walk so heavy." Suddenly Powell wheeled, clubbed young Seward across the head with his pistol, grappled fiercely with him, and, swinging again, knocked his adversary senseless through an open bed-room door.

At that minute the door of the sick-room opened and George Robinson, a soldier-nurse, thrust out his head. A knife-slash across the forehead sent this guard out of Powell's way, another blow cut down a second nurse, Emerick Hansell, and in a flash he was crawling across Seward's bed, feeling in the dim light for the invalid's throat. Powell, like all of Booth's helpers, was an incompetent, botching his assignment badly. The steel framework that had been set on Seward's head to hold in place the broken jaw bothered the assassin as he struck again and again at the jugular.

In the half-light he worked silently, like a jaguar on a bogged buffalo. Seward, squirming as the thrusts kept glancing off his steel harness, rolled off the bed onto the floor — and although he was badly cut, his life was saved, for the soldier-nurse, reviving, had come crawling on top of Powell and a second later another of Seward's sons, Major Augustus, joined in the fight.

Augustus, thinking that the soldier-nurse, in a fit of insanity, was wrestling with his father, seized the first figure he could reach and pulled him to his feet. It was Powell, who, too strong for both his opponents, cut the major down, toppled the soldier-nurse over with his fist and sprang out into the hallway crying, "I am mad! I am mad!"

His hat and revolver lay on the floor of the hallway, but he did not stop for them and walked down the stair and out into the street without haste. Mounting his horse, he rode slowly down the street while William Bell, who had fled the house at the first sign of trouble intending to get soldiers, trotted along twenty feet behind squalling to the world, "There he is!" For two blocks or more the strange little procession ambled along, until at last Powell, as if awakening to his danger, clapped spurs to his horse and disappeared.

Without his master Powell was a child again — a mentally undeveloped dullard — wandering off into the woods outside the city limits, missing the rendezvous entirely, spurring frantically around and around until his horse gave out, then sleeping in ditches until Monday night, when he came blundering back to the one friendly place he knew, the Surratt boarding-house, and thus into the hands of secret-service men who were watching for suspicious characters, but who did not know that any such man as Powell was on top of the earth.

On Friday night the military police, learning from Laura Keane and other players on the stage of Ford's Theater that Lincoln's assassin had been Booth, the actor, began an investigation that soon established Herold as his companion in flight, Atzerodt as a suspicious accomplice, and John H. Surratt as the assailant of Seward. They had missed Powell altogether, thanks to the secrecy with which Booth had kept his trained tiger disguised around the hotels.

Late in the night, they had raided the Surratt lodging-house, hunting John, whose description vaguely fitted that of Seward's attacker as given by the excited and bleeding occupants of the Secretary's home. Not finding John Surratt, detectives searched for him in the following days through Canada.

In the War Department, Stanton, Secretary of War, was striving desperately to link the assassination-plot to those Confederate representatives of Jefferson Davis who had spent the period of the war in Canada, plotting for British intervention and organizing train wrecks and midnight fires for the North. John Surratt had fled to Canada, Stanton's detectives told him; consequently the plot must have been organized by the "rebel" leaders. The idea swelled and grew in Stanton's brain, and on Monday night the military police swooped down upon Mrs. Surratt's home to arrest all its occupants, and to compel the woman, if possible, to reveal her son's whereabouts.

At the moment that Powell stepped up on the Surratt stoop and rapped at the door, Mrs. Surratt and her lodgers were dressing to go down to headquarters with the detectives who waited in the hallway. An officer answered the knock and saw a muddy giant, pick in hand, a leg of torn underdrawers pulled over his head like a stocking-cap. The fellow mumbled something about having come to the wrong place and turned to go, but the detectives seized him, and drew him in for questioning.

Cornered and confused, Powell stammered that he had been hired by Mrs. Surratt to fix a gutter, and that he had called to find out what time she was expecting him in the morning. As it was then close to midnight, the detectives reasoned that the fellow must be lying. Also, his hands were soft and his clothes expensively made — Booth had dressed him well. So they stood him up under a hall gas-light for Mrs. Surratt to see.

"Do you know him?" they asked the woman.

"Before God, I never saw him before," she said.

The lie went far to hang her.

With that the detectives took the woman and the strange gutter-man to headquarters, where at three o'clock in the morning they brought down the terrified door-boy, William Bell, from the Seward home to identify him. They hid William Bell behind a desk and darkened the room in imitation of the Seward hallway. They then led through the gloom some twenty suspects, among them Powell. Without a moment's wavering the colored boy went up to the guilty man, and touched his lip, crying in terror, "It's him! I know him by his lip." Powell's sulky lip and jutting jaw had stuck in the boy's mind.

Next day the identification was made complete. Powell had

been carried in the night to the *Saugus,* an ironclad monitor, riding its anchor in the Potomac, and had been chained in its bowels. When day came, Major Augustus Seward, the maimed Secretary's second son, was brought on board to examine the suspect, who was led up on deck. Since his view of his father's assailant had been obtained only in a wrestling struggle, the Major stepped up to the chained Powell, now, and put his arms about him as he recalled having gripped him in the fight. Posing thus, while the detectives and sailors crowded around, young Seward recognized the man. To make matters sure, the officers compelled Powell to repeat, "I am mad! I am mad!" several times in order that the Major might identify the voice.

To Powell's cell, in the days that followed, the news came seeping down that Seward was recovering and that Mrs. Surratt was in chains. Dimly the Apache understood that his return had linked her to the crime. Remorse churned inside him, and one day he tried to butt out his brains against the iron door of his cell. A hood of quilted canvas was fastened upon his head to prevent suicide. Thereafter the conspirators, as fast as they were brought in, were hooded in these padded bags and ironed hideously, the War Department being determined that they should not cheat the gallows or communicate with each other. Through the horrible heat of April and May they sweltered in the floating dungeons, shrouded, weighted down with iron bars and balls and chains.

Later on, physicians appealed to the powers that were, saying that the prisoners were going crazy in their hoods, which allowed only a slit for eating, and the bags came off.

Hood or no hood, Powell was silent and contemptuous toward the other conspirators—Arnold, O'Laughlin, Spangler and Dr. Mudd, as though he, the gunman, the bad man, the killer, were above such weaklings. With his guards he was as playful, as luxuriously good-natured as a well-fed leopard in a zoo. His jailers liked him, and played practical jokes upon him —and he upon them.

Sympathy, however, he scorned. Once an aged negress came to the prison, asking to see him, and when they opened the cell-door, ran to him, calling baby names. He pushed her away, saying, "Go away, woman, I don't know you!" She was the only human being to come to him from out of his past.

Physicians and alienists studied Powell in his cell. The coolness of the fellow baffled them. Where Atzerodt gibbered and pleaded and Mrs. Surratt wept, Powell stared them in the eye, cool as a cucumber, as people phrased it in 1865.

They felt his head and found one side of it to be much larger than the other; they observed him and found that he slept well — much better than the other prisoners; that he ate spasmodically, sometimes with gusto, sometimes indifferently, and that he went an incredible length of time, once thirty-four days, without eliminating. In spite of everything, he was the picture of health, they said.

As he lay in the ironclad with the other accused — O'Laughlin, Arnold and Spangler were soon added to the number, as well as a score of suspects subsequently discharged — Powell became the center for a myth that spread from mouth to mouth and thus into the newspapers. So herculean was he and such a super-villain, to have slashed four men to pieces, that the word went around that he was either a nephew of Robert E. Lee, or the base-born son of Jefferson Davis. If he was not the devil he must be closely linked to either of the two Confederates who were in many eyes the Satans of the "rebel" cause.

That he was the illegitimate son of the Southern President soon became a lively, if entirely baseless story. Jefferson Davis, the myth had it, had begotten this evil son in his old army-days at Fort Snelling in the West. As a young officer, Davis had fallen in love with "a rose in the wilderness," and when he had been recalled East, the girl had followed him as far as St. Louis with their baby. The Mexican War took him away, and on his return he was stationed in Washington, where he kept the affair hidden, supplying his former mistress with money and never owning this beast-like son.

Powell's silence regarding his relatives or birthplace added to the mystery and gave impetus to so impossible a concoction as the Davis-parentage myth. It was only when the government appointed a lawyer for him that he told anybody who he was. Meanwhile Booth and Herold skulked through Maryland.

Across the Navy Yard bridge after them poured squad after squad of cavalry the morning after the killing, detectives accompanying. At the tavern owned by Mrs. Surratt they learned from her hard-drinking tenant, John Lloyd, that the fugitives had halted there at midnight on Friday, Herold dismounting and asking for carbines that had been stored there a few days before, also for Booth's field-glasses, which Mrs. Surratt had left there Friday afternoon. A few drinks of whisky, a boast or two about being "pretty sure that we have assassinated the President and Secretary Seward," and they were off for the South. At dawn they came to the home of Dr. Samuel Mudd, to whom Booth had been introduced the Autumn before and who had once been a "rebel" sympathizer, although he had voted for Lincoln at the November elections.

Booth must have a doctor for his broken left leg and Dr. Mudd, stretching the crippled man on a sofa, cut off his boot, patched it in pasteboard splints and gave him a shoe so that he might ride on. Borrowing the doctor's razor, Booth shaved off his moustache and slept until evening was drawing on, when with Herold he galloped away. That constituted Dr. Mudd's part in the great conspiracy so far as any evidence went, but the physician, badly rattled, sought to keep the visit secret, denied it to detectives until he broke down and was, for his little lies, rushed to prison and the hooded bags.

For twelve days more Booth and his pup-like Herold wandered on, sleeping by day, traveling by night, unable, even in so desperate a plight, to keep from boasting of their deed whenever opportunity presented itself. Fiendish as was the pain of his shin-bone, cracked across, Booth's principal torture on this dragging flight was of the spirit and not of the flesh. In canebrakes he read newspapers feverishly, to see what the critics had to say about his greatest performance. Of one thing he had been sure: the South would hail him as "Brutus." Now he found the South cold, scarcely less damning in its contempt than was the North in its rage. To Southerners who refused him shelter he wrote bitter notes and sent sarcastic messages.

The critics were at it again, only worse, with maledictions and execrations. He was no longer even "promising" to any of them.

They put him down variously as a fool, a cut-throat, a "Cain," a hireling thug, or at best a weak tool of Confederate desperado-rulers. They left him no shred of dignity or of political position. It was not until too late to comfort him that the myth of his Southern patriotism and sacrificial purpose was to arise.

It must have seemed to him, fugitive and forlorn, that the whole world was hissing him now. Into his diary he poured all the hatred that any bad actor can feel for the critics who have skinned him alive. Furiously he wrote down his scalding disappointments in tragic bombast, protesting his sincere love of country, straining to establish his sincerity, as anxious as Hamlet to have himself cried aright to posterity. He could no longer hope to escape. His wound made capture certain. All that remained for him to do was to leave such papers as might palm off his personal ambition as patriotism.

For the public which had failed to appreciate this last great appearance he had vicious spite, and this he scribbled down, denouncing the people for having become "too degenerate" to see that he had freed them from a greater tyranny than that which either Brutus or William Tell had taken from their countries' necks. In transparent pretense he concluded: "If the world knew my heart, that one blow would have made me great, though I did not desire greatness. . . . I have too great a soul to die like a criminal."

The end came in the early morning hours of April 26. Two days before, at Port Royal on the Rappahannock River, the fugitives had been ferried across with three Confederate soldiers who were returning from the war. Booth and Herold were on foot, having shot their horses in a jungle a day or two before lest their nickering betray their riders to the Union troopers who were scouring the country.

One pitying Southerner had given them a lift in his wagon to the river. The three soldiers on the ferry were Capt. Willie Jett, Major M. B. Ruggles and Lieut. A. R. Bainbridge, all from Mosby's band that had sourly surrendered on April 21, twelve days after Lee's capitulation. To these paroled men Herold made overtures, claiming that he and his wounded brother, by the name of Boyd, were from A. P. Hill's corps and, as brother Confederates, asked for help. Later on, vanity was too much for his light head and he proclaimed that they were "the assassinators of the President." As speedily as possible the ex-Confederates palmed Booth off upon a farmer, Richard Garrett by name, who lived some four miles from the river on the road to Bowling Green. Then they rode on with Herold, who wanted to arrange transportation southward.

Any returning soldier, particularly a wounded one, was welcome in the Garrett home, and the old farmer gave the newcomer quarters upstairs with his own sons, the eldest of whom was but shortly returned from the Southern army, too. Booth was a quiet guest, lying all day in his room or on the lawn, suffering from his "wound," saying little. At noon the eldest Garrett boy, John, came back from the shoemaker's, down the road, with the story of having seen there a newspaper naming J. Wilkes Booth, the actor, as Lincoln's assassin, and offering a tremendous reward for his capture.

Since "Boyd," their guest, had said he hailed from Maryland, old man Garrett asked him if he had ever seen this assassin Booth. Yes, said Boyd, he had seen him once in Richmond about the time of the John Brown raid.

"I never heard of but one Booth," Garrett rambled on, "and thought it was Edwin."

How that must have seared Booth's soul!

Up from the table spoke one of the little Garrett boys, saying, "I wish that man Booth would come this way, so that I might catch him and get the reward."

To the boy, as the elder Garrett told the incident later, the visitor turned and said, "If he were to come out would you inform against him?"

The boy laughed and said that he would like the money. At this Booth was cool, showing no emotion. Too late he was learning how to be an actor.

Soon after noon Herold came to the farmhouse, was introduced by Booth as his cousin "Mr. Boyd," and while the two men were reclining on the lawn, Major Ruggles rode up, crying, "The Yankees are crossing the river at Port Royal. Take care of yourselves as best you can," and galloped away.

On his crutch, which he had rudely fashioned during his flight, Booth, with Herold helping, hobbled away to the woods near the Garrett farmhouse as the blue-coated troops went by. Then they stole back.

But suspicion had come into the Garretts' minds, not the suspicion that these "Boyds" could be linked with Lincoln's murder, but that they were "wanted" for something or other. Quickly the fugitives tried to laugh it off, saying that the Federals were after some horses that had been stolen. The explanation was an unlucky one, for a little later when the "Boyds" broached the subject of buying a couple of horses from the Garretts, the fat was in the fire. Their hosts now took them for horse-thieves, and began scheming to be shut of such guests by nightfall.

That April evening Booth, sitting in the lamplight that shone on the supper table, listened to Garrett's daughter rattling on and on about the assassination, asking herself and every one else who had done it anyway and why.

"He must have been paid a lot," she guessed.

"In my opinion," Booth suddenly said, "he wasn't paid a cent for it, but did it for notoriety's sake." And with that remark, if the Garretts have handed it down correctly, Booth disposed of the subject.

The meal done, the eldest Garrett boy, Jack, relenting a little, allowed the two fugitives to stay on the premises that night, providing they went on in the morning. They could not sleep in the house, he said, neither could they sleep under the porch as they asked — the Garrett dogs were bad and might attack them. They could sleep in the tobacco barn on the hay.

In they went, Jack Garrett tiptoeing after them to turn the lock on the door. The crowning humiliation of all had come to J. Wilkes Booth. Locked in an outhouse because he looked and acted like an ordinary horse-thief! Jack Garrett and his next brother William were not content with these precautions and, taking blankets, slept in a corncrib near by, to see that no horses were taken away in the night.

At that moment thirteen miles away in Bowling Green the Union troops, who had passed in the afternoon, were hauling

Capt. Willie Jett, one of the three Confederate cavalrymen, out of bed. Captain Willie had gone to the tavern of a certain Goldman, father of his fiancée, for the night, and he awakened to see a rope dangling in his face and to feel a pistol in his ribs. Threats were unnecessary. Out from under the obligations of his hospitality on which the fugitives had thrown themselves, Captain Willie felt free to tell everything and very shortly he was guiding the Union troopers back over the road to the Garrett farm.

It was two o'clock when the squad — some twenty-six men in all, surrounded the farmhouse at the gallop. Quickly the Union leader's pistol-butt was banging on the door. After a shuffling inside, old man Garrett appeared, candle in hand, the night-wind whipping his shirt-tails about his bare shins. To the volleying demands Garrett was silent, tongue-tied with fright. The blue-coated inquisitor brought out a rope, and the old man might have been hanged if his son had not come up from the corncrib into the circle of soldiers, saying, "The men you want are locked in the warehouse."

With a swoop the troopers circled the tobacco barn, and dismounting, sat or lay on the grass, weary from a day and two nights of steady riding. With the Federals at his back, Jack Garrett unlocked the door and was thrust inside to demand surrender. Almost instantly he was out again, followed by accusations of treachery and threats of death if he entered again.

A long parley followed, the Northerners urging their "treed" quarry to give up, Booth answering in high-flown heroics. Herold, however, wanted to surrender, and unmindful of Booth's reproaches came out, fawning and smirking. "He acted silly," said the soldiers afterward.

"I always liked Mr. Lincoln's jokes," said Herold ingratiatingly to the Union lieutenant who held him.

Booth, within, would not surrender, and remained to parley some minutes longer, shouting tragedian's speeches, warning his pursuers to prepare a stretcher for him, offering to come out and fight them all on his crutch, waving his pistol and carbine — but never appearing, never approaching the door where the officers waited.

To catch the fellow alive was the purpose of the blue-coats, and despairing of his surrender, they decided to smoke him out. Reaching through a wide crack in the rear of the barn, they set fire to the hay on the floor and in a few moments they could see him between the wide spacings in the weatherboarding, striking at the flames, a dark actor in the limelight for the last time.

Then a revolver cracked — a crazy sergeant, who always heard God whispering to him, had fired without orders, and J. Wilkes was down with a bullet, curiously enough through his skull at almost the same spot where his own had crashed into Lincoln's head — shot from behind. Blue-coats dragged him out, thinking that he had shot himself, and laid him on the farmhouse porch with a pillow under his head and farm women to hold the pillow in their laps.

A few jumbled mutterings, some fleeting dawns of intelligence, many spasms of naked pain and Booth was dead at seven o'clock by the morning sun.

The instinct of the pretender was the last thing to die in him. Even in death he was a "ham" actor "letting on." His last intelligible words were, "Tell mother I died for my country." And the bloody pillow-slip was carried away by the spinster of the farmhouse, cherished and preserved, with perhaps a sigh, until poverty at last compelled her to trade half of it, in after years, for a barrel of flour.

✰ ✰ ✰ 17 ✰ ✰ ✰

RED SUNDOWN

THE MAN-HUNT for Booth and for Herold, which had ended in Garrett's barn, had begun in wrangling and confusion.

Stanton, almost hysterical with fear for the Union and for himself, had allowed the regular army and the secret service to start the search in a rivalry that wasted time. Then to add to the delirium of the hour, the war minister gave over the chase to Col. Lafayette C. Baker, chief of the Secret Service and melodramatist of the first order. Baker prompted Stanton to post $50,000 in reward for Booth, $25,000 for Herold and $25,000 for John H. Surratt, supposedly the assailant of Seward. To win this gold became the passion of every detective, official and private, in the land. Sleuths crawled everywhere, grilling endlessly the hooded and manacled dullards whom the military had seized as Booth's accomplices.

Fortune-tellers sent information to Stanton. Spiritualists gave "tips." People read the stars and sent solutions. Fanatics sent clues that had come to them in their dreams. Booth was arrested in Toronto, Massachusetts, in Pennsylvania, in Chicago and in Washington. He was seen on trains, in women's clothing, in burnt-cork. Any handsome man with a black moustache and a snow-white brow was likely to be seized and rushed off to jail to sit beside other unfortunately romantic-looking gentlemen — little Booths all in a row. In Pittsfield, Massachusetts, a sober citizen by the name of J. L. Chapman, was arrested so often for Booth that he finally quit trying to go out on the streets at all, and stayed home for days. Police soldiers and detectives trod on each other's toes.

The man-hunt became more and more fantastic as the funeral of Lincoln, working slowly westward home, brought the public to distraction. As the North stared and wailed at the corpse of Lincoln, suddenly realizing as it did how like a god of mercy he had been, so the fury for the punishment of his murderer mounted.

As the days died, one after another, on Stanton's desk, with Booth still free, the secretary grew panicky. He feared that once the assassin got into the heart of the South, the defeated Confederates would rally around him, spring to arms and begin the war all over again. The best Stanton could do was to keep pouring troops and detectives into the Eastern Shore of Maryland, where Booth and Herold had disappeared, and to keep the reward before the noses of its disloyal inhabitants — $75,000 for the two men, dead or alive.

The army and the secret service were in a desperate race for the blood-money, adding jealousy to hysteria; and it was the detective force that won as Stanton discovered at 5 P.M. on the afternoon of April 26, when Colonel Baker, with his assistant Col. Everton J. Conger, came with the news that Booth was dead, Herold captured and both that minute coming under guard to town. Out of Conger's pockets came a diary that was unmistakably Booth's, a knife, a compass and other trinkets that the detective had taken, he said, from the dying fugitive's pockets.

In and out of Stanton's mind darted weird dreams. The need of secrecy was now keener than ever. Booth, dead, might be a greater menace than Booth alive. What if the "rebels" should capture Booth's body and use it as a sacred relic with which to fire the South to arms once more, this time to a holy war as terrible as that which had just ended?

As the three men bent across Stanton's desk with their brooding terrors, the corpse over which they shuddered was jogging and bouncing along a Virginia country road, nearer and nearer to the city, guarded by a detective, Lieut. L. B. Baker, cousin of the secret-service chief. Three days before, this lieutenant, with Colonel Conger, another operative, had been awarded the choicest assignment in the power of Colonel Baker. Into headquarters had come other detectives on the morning of Monday, April 24, with a negro who had seen two suspicious men fleeing through Virginia. And when the colored man, examining photographs, had recognized one of the fugitives as Booth, the secret-service head knew that the scent was warm. His kinsman, with one other detective, should have this most promising chance at the reward, and that same afternoon the lieutenant with Conger and an escort of twenty-five cavalrymen set out on the trail that ended so richly for them at Garrett's barn.

Rivalry between the detectives and the commander of the army escort, Lieut. Edward P. Doherty, had been keen from the first, the secret-service operatives later charging that the soldier had hidden under a corncrib during the fracas at the burning shed, and Doherty countering with the story that he himself had unearthed the chief clues during the pursuit while Conger slept in a farmhouse by the road.

There had been scrambling haste from the moment that Booth had been shot down. While the dying man lay on Garrett's front porch, Conger had rifled his pockets and then, eager to tell Washington the news, had galloped away. Lieutenant Baker, reward-hungry too, had kept the body out of Doherty's hands, indeed scarcely waiting for a country doctor to pronounce it lifeless, before he rolled it into a blanket, loaded it into a neighborhood negro's cart, and was off posthaste for the Potomac River where a steamer awaited the party.

Doherty, chagrined, was thus left behind to fume and fret while he made lavish efforts to marshal his sleepy men and, at the same time, to load three men on one horse — Herold and two of Garrett's sons who must go along as material witnesses.

The speed with which Lieutenant Baker rushed the death-cart was too much for the rickety old contraption, and all at once its king-bolt snapped, letting the front end fall, sending the dead man's body, in its red-soaked blanket, lurching forward as if in a last effort to escape. The officer ordered the white-eyed negro driver, Ned Freeman, under to mend the break, and as the shivering fellow obeyed, blood, which had been dripping down onto the axle and splashing off into the dust for miles behind, fell on his black hands. With a screech that might have awakened the dead man, the negro came scuttling out backward like a crawfish and tumbled in the side-ditch, squalling, as Baker told it later, "It's the blood of a murderer — it will never wash off."

No time to wait. The detective appropriated another wagon from the neighborhood and pushed on, leaving the colored man to wander off home with his horse and two dollars, while the bloody wagon stood derelict by the roadside until rain, rust, and time brought it merciful decay.

At the river Baker was forced to wait for the steamer, and by the time it had arrived Lieutenant Doherty and his cavalry-men had caught up. So in the late evening they all came up the Potomac together, headed for the comic-operatics with which Stanton and Colonel Baker were awaiting them.

At 10.40 that night the play began. As the steamer reached Alexandria, a tug drew alongside, and on board came the secret-service chief himself, posturing as ever. To this tug he transferred the captive Herold and the corpse, then chugged away, $75,000 worth of booty safe out of the army's hands.

At 1.45 in the morning the tug tied up to the ironclad *Montauk*, which lay off Washington with the Lincoln conspirators sweltering in its hold. Among these wretches Herold was chained, while on the deck was laid the body which Baker announced was Booth's. There it lay till the next sundown.

The word went out over Washington, and thence to the nation, that Booth's body had arrived, yet no one save the secret-service chief, unpopular in Washington and distrusted as a *poseur*, could have been said to have seen it. Brought up in the night and secreted on an ironclad in midstream, it begot suspicion by the very stealth which surrounded it. Soon the whisper was all over the capital, "They haven't got him. That body's not Booth." Not long was it before this muttering had grown into an open declaration heard on the streets, and Stanton, even in his ferment of soul, realized that some sort of identification must be made. In the afternoon he sent an autopsy-committee, handpicked from his department, on board the *Montauk*. Two civilians were added, one Charles Dawson, clerk in the National Hotel where Booth had stopped, and the other, Dr. John Frederick May, the surgeon who had cut the tumor from Booth's neck and who now would be asked to identify his mark.

It was no jury worth the name. None of the assassin's friends were asked to identify him; none of the theater folk who had known him for years were called. The autopsy was not recorded, nor its findings made public, other than the bare official word that the body had been identified as Booth's. Over the town suspicion winged its way, faster than ever.

In the afternoon Colonel Baker came to Stanton with the report that he had caught a group of Washington people on board the *Montauk* — admitted on deck somehow against orders — and that they had opened the shroud. One lady had been halted just as she cut off a lock of the dead man's hair — hair through which, if it was Booth's, many women had wanted to run their hands. Baker had twisted the souvenir from her and had shooed the civilians back into their skiffs.

Stanton listened in alarm. "Every hair of Booth's head will be a valued relic to sympathizers with the South in Washington," he said, and decided to hide the body quickly. Baker was assigned to secrete the corpse and he obeyed orders with excessive zeal, but he went further, preposterous dramatist that he was, and set out to hoax the phantom Confederacy as well.

Evening came with a red sundown on this twenty-seventh of April, and all was quiet along the Potomac as Baker and his cousin, the lieutenant, went down to the wharf. Dense crowds stood along the Northern bank staring out at the *Montauk* as it rode its anchor. They muttered their morbid doubts and beliefs about J. Wilkes Booth as the color died in the west and dusk came up the river. Into a row-boat the Bakers climbed, and pulled to the ironclad. Over the side of the warship and down into their skiff they lowered the dead man in his new coffin, a gun-box, and after it, brought down in plain view of the gaping crowds, a ball and chain. Then they shoved off and drifted downstream while the throng swept even with the boat, alongshore, splashing through the shallows, jostling, shoving, racing to keep up.

Clouds which had let the sun go down in melodramatic fire now hid the stars, and it took sharp eyes to follow the skiff in mid-stream. For two miles the watchers kept even with the drifting detectives, then lost them as the boat turned into the great swamp behind Geeseborough Point. Even the hardiest of the followers could go no further in the muck. Furthermore, few human beings dared to penetrate that ghastly slough by day, let alone by night. White men, no less than black men, dreaded it, for in its shallows the Federals had been accustomed to throw their worn-out horses and army mules.

Alone in the silence of this dread morass, the two detectives lay on their oars and waited for midnight. When the hour came they muffled their oarlocks and rowing stealthily, crept upstream to the old penitentiary building, where a hole had been chopped in the masonry for their entrance. Inside the grounds, which were used as a government arsenal and where, a little later, the four Lincoln conspirators were to be hanged, they carried the coffin, handing it to a grim little party that waited. Dr. G. L. Porter, physician of the post, and four private soldiers took the casket, a white-pine affair across whose lid was printed the words "John Wilkes Booth," and buried it under a warehouse floor. The door was locked, the four soldiers swore by sacred oaths never to disclose what they had seen or done, and the key to the room was given to Stanton.

Next day it was seen that the ruse had been successful. On every hand the plotters heard the public spreading the news: the government had sunk the body among the carcasses of mules, a terrible revenge. Who can doubt that Stanton and Baker chuckled to themselves, too, at the word that scores of persons could be seen wading and rowing in the morass behind Geeseborough Point, raking, dragging, feeling for the corpse? There were other grisly fishermen on the Potomac outside the point, for another wind-whisper had been blown up in the night, saying that the disputed body had been dissected and its pieces, heavily shotted, dropped overboard from a small vessel which had circled on the river at midnight.

The fishermen never found what they were dredging for, but the sight of them feeling, feeling on the bottom with their hooks so confidently, set curiosity burning in Washington more feverishly than before.

"What have they done with the body?" neighbor asked neighbor. "What have *you* done with the body?" bluntly demanded newspaper men of Colonel Baker, soon to become General Baker as Stanton's reward. Baker replied in dark, pompous enigmas: "That is known," he countered, "to only one man beside myself. It is gone; I will not tell where; the only man who knows is sworn to silence; never till the great trumpeter comes shall the grave of Booth be discovered."

As a result, next day the public read mysterious things like this in its newspapers: "Out of the darkness Booth's body will never return. In the darkness like his great crime, may it remain forever; impassable, invisible, nondescript, condemned to that worse than damnation—annihilation. The river-bottom may ooze about it, laden with great shot and drowning manacles. The fishes may swim around it or the daisies grow white above it; but we shall never know."

And in these first mad days of May, Baker kept at his strange game, inspiring a welter of conflicting rumors which would, he thought, muddy the waters so thoroughly that none of Booth's admirers, real or imaginary, might find the corpse. The newspapers, which had not questioned that the body was Booth's, took his hints with alacrity. Weekly magazines were soon out with "eye-witness" sketches of two men sinking the cadaver into the midnight Potomac, but on May 2, the Boston *Advertiser* was declaring that Booth's head and heart had been deposited in the army medical museum at Washington, while his body had been buried close to the penitentiary. Other papers spread the rumor that it had been burned or sunk in the sea. The hoax had done its work; the nation did not know what to believe.

However, it had done its work too well; the elaborate secrecy boomeranged on Stanton and Baker. Soon people in all parts of the country were saying the things that Washingtonians had said from the first: that dead man wasn't the assassin, Booth had got away and all the mysterious actions could mean but one thing — the Secret Service had shot the wrong man, and had destroyed the body to hide its mistake, also to collect the reward. Sometimes this whisper insinuated that Stanton had known of the error and had been forced to conceal it to keep from making the government ridiculous; sometimes it said that Stanton had been tricked by Baker and his detectives into believing that the body was really Booth's.

Rumor piled on top of rumor. One whisper in particular fattened in the feverish mood of the moment; the whisper that charged something sinister in the ease with which Booth and Herold had escaped across the Navy Yard bridge that night of the murder. How was it that the sentries had allowed the two guilty men to pass and had held up the good man Fletcher who had followed? Surely the sentries must be hiding something! Surely Booth and Herold must have had the password of the day!

From wondering and guessing, the gossipers of Washington proceeded to conviction, and soon were saying that the fugitive had been supplied with the password by some fellow plotter close to the seat of the mighty. The conspiracy had originated higher-up in the Union government. Who could this "higher-up" be? Could he be the Vice-President? People asked each other that when it became known that Booth had tried to see Johnson on the fatal Friday afternoon and, failing, had left his calling-card in Johnson's hotel mail-box.

Perhaps it was the Secession sympathizers in the half-Southern city of Washington who launched this attack upon the Vice-President. They hated Johnson as a "white trash" renegade, a Tennessee man who had committed the political heresy and social blunder of siding with the plebeian North instead of with the proud Southern civilization. Poor Andy Johnson, drunk too often, talking always too much, was nevertheless the last of men to have wished for the death of Lincoln, who had, single-handed, lifted him, poor mountain white that he was, to the second highest of all American offices.

The wretched sentries had their apologists who said that their mistake had been a natural one. They had merely failed to enforce a rule that had already grown slack with the dawn of peace. The war was over and military law was relaxing. Booth and Herold had told humanly plausible stories, and had been allowed to pass. Fletcher, the third man, had come thundering up with a tale of chasing somebody. His excitement had aroused the sentries' suspicions and they had evidently decided to check his comings and goings lest trouble come and they be blamed.

Wild talk flew as the days wore on toward the trial of Booth's followers who waited in prison — Mary E. Surratt, Lewis Thornton Powell, George A. Atzerodt, David E. Herold, Samuel Arnold, Michael O'Laughlin, Dr. Samuel Mudd and George Spangler.

Back from Springfield was hurrying Major General David Hunter to act as President of the Military Commission that would try the cartoon-assassins — Hunter, the Radical, returning from fourteen days spent on guard at the head of Abraham Lincoln's casket in big towns and small as the funeral crushed its way from Washington to Illinois.

Just as the funeral had been a military affair, so was the trial of the conspirators. With the long, strong hands of the army, Stanton would rule.

18

"THE WIDOW-WOMAN"

TEN O'CLOCK in the morning of May 11, 1865 —

A little room, with small barred windows, on the third floor of the old penitentiary building in Washington —

Nine men in blue uniforms and glittering brass buttons, one colonel and one lieutenant colonel, three major generals, four brigadiers, sitting on the case of persons who had combined, conspired, and confederated together to murder the President of the United States —

A military trial, in spite of all the arguments by defense counsel that the case was one for civil courts — Stanton had seen to that. Early in the game he had served notice that the conspirators, when caught, would be tried by his army, and now Attorney-General James Speed came forward with an opinion that the crime had been committed against the person of the commander in chief of the army and navy, that it had taken place in a city which was under military rule and that the trial was not in the jurisdiction of civil judges and juries.

Close by the court-room were the prisoners' cells, all the accused having been brought to the penitentiary from the ironclads two weeks before, and kept there with light flannel bags over their heads.

As trial-time came, guards slipped off these bags and led the seven men and the one woman before the court, chains clanking on all but the woman, and spectators imagining that they heard iron scratching on her, too, under her skirts. The seven men sat in a row, handcuffed with "stiff shackles" — a method which linked each cuff to a bar of iron. On the left ankle of each dragged a cone-shaped weight, seventy pounds of iron.

The woman was veiled, the men staring curiously at their enemies, Powell calm and easy, Herold twittering and grinning, Atzerodt gibbering, Mudd, Arnold and O'Laughlin sad and forlorn, Spangler wondering what it all meant. Armed soldiers sat between them, separating each from his fellows. Guards were everywhere, rifles in hand.

Above the eleven military judges sat Joseph Holt, Brigadier-General and Judge-Advocate of the army. Since 1862 Holt had ruled the legal affairs of the War Department; Stanton's own man, a Kentuckian who had made a great name for himself as a lawyer and orator through the South before the war, but who had trained with the Union when the break came in '61; Holt a Radical through and through, like Chase and Wade and Stevens a battler for negro rights, and like Hunter and Stanton ardent for the arming of the blacks in war regiments. Red-hot burned Holt's soul against "rebels" and in particular against the fiery ladies of the South who had spoken so freely against Union invaders. "There have not been enough Southern women hanged in this war," he had been reported to say, a fact that argued badly for Mrs. Surratt now.

Wrangling developed at the very outset, the newspapers of the North ranting against the high-handed manner in which their reporters were to be excluded from this secret military hearing. This difficulty disappeared when the War Department gave in and allowed the reporters to view the proceedings. Immediately the nation was flooded with wild descriptions of the accused, and photographs were broadcast, showing the comic and frustrated nincompoops, grimy from confinement, as hideous desperadoes. "Monstrum horrendum," the Chicago *Tribune* called Powell, and chronicled how he had laughed when the prosecutor placed upon his head the hat that had been dropped in the Seward home the night of the attack. Women clamored at the doors to see him.

For Powell and Herold no good defense could be made. They were doomed. Skilled attorneys might argue that the former had been brutalized by war and had struck under what he considered to be the rules of the game. They might claim that Herold was nothing but a feeble-minded tool of Booth's. It was useless. Death by hanging was their verdict. For Atzerodt, Arnold, and O'Laughlin it was said that they had conspired to kidnap and nothing more, but Atzerodt drew a death-pronouncement, Arnold and O'Laughlin life-imprisonment. Dr. Mudd also received "life"; Spangler was given six years.

The heart of the fight was reached when the commission came to hear the government's case against Mrs. Surratt. She was a "widow-woman," a mother and a devout churchgoer, as witnesses proved, and these facts could not but tell heavily in her favor, since her judges were of a civilization that gave women unusual reverence. The Civil War had been singularly free from sex-crimes, the fighters both North and South having come from a social structure that gave the rearing of boys, at home and at school, chiefly into the hands of women. This idea of feminine sanctity was carried into the war by the citizen-soldiers of both armies and, characteristically, invading forces permitted women of the raided sections to jeer, snub, and defy them with impunity.

Except for two witnesses there was no case against Mrs. Surratt, but those two hanged her. One was John M. Lloyd, her bibulous tenant at the Surrattsville tavern, the other was a boarder in her own home, Louis J. Weichmann.

Weichmann, at twenty-three years of age, was the storm-center of the trial, just as he was to be for a generation of argument and abuse thereafter. A strange boy setting out now, as he mounted the witness stand, upon a career of tragedy that was to wind into the mass of Lincoln-myths later on. Now he held up his hand and swore to tell only the truth and all of it, his bright young face agitated. How he had come to this dramatic pass, testifying against his lodging-house keeper, is a story in itself.

"Lou was just a boy when he went to live with Mrs. Surratt," said his sisters, sixty years after, in telling about the tragedy as they sat in their home at Anderson, Indiana, far away in distance and time from the Washington, D. C., of 1865.

"He was only twenty-three years old, and young for his age, too; just a simple, good-hearted, thoughtless kind of a boy. Father had a tailor-shop in Philadelphia before the war, and when Lou was through high school, father sent him down to St. Charles Academy near Baltimore to study for the priesthood. He intended to finish up his work in Richmond, Virginia, but the war stopped that, and he took a job teaching school in Washington. Lou had a wonderful education and could read and write eight languages and do shorthand, but he wrote home that he could make more money, eighty dollars a month, clerking in the War Department, and was going to take up that work.

"One day in Washington an old school friend from St. Charles, a boy named John Surratt, met him and asked him to come and live up at his mother's boarding-house there in town. Lou had been to visit John several times at Surrattsville, where his mother, the widow-woman, was trying to keep a tavern. The boarding-house business was better in Washington, so they had moved to the city.

"Lou went to live with them. His letters home said that Mrs. Surratt was the nicest kind of a woman, a great churchgoer, and Lou used to go with her to mass lots of the time. She gave him room and board for thirty-five dollars a month, and treated him like a son. Lou was the last person in the world to suspect anybody, though."

On the stand in the hot, clanking court-room Weichmann was a puzzle. He talked readily and well, "too well," insinuated counsel for the defense repeatedly, as his testimony could be seen to settle the noose tighter and tighter about the woman's neck. He was too glib, Mrs. Surratt's lawyers said, too ready to hang his former friends. Could it be that he had been one of the conspirators in the kidnaping plot and was now turning state's evidence to save his own neck? They hinted at this over and over, but the prosecutors fought back stoutly, maintaining that the witness was plainly just a nervous, patriotic boy, eager to clear up the crime and tell the truth no matter who it hit.

His testimony stood. Mrs. Surratt, the boy explained, was a lady of exemplary character in every particular, kind and good to him. But as he talked on, a mass of straightforward and convincing detail began to gather about the woman. Life in the Surratt lodging-house was made very real to the listening judges, as Weichmann talked. All the lodgers had fun in the parlor, he said. Annie, the daughter of the house, played the piano and the girl-roomers sang. John Surratt, the son, for all his vague talk of oil and cotton speculations, and all his unexplained absences, was still Weichmann's closest friend. Furthermore John *did* bring home interesting friends.

For instance, John Wilkes Booth, one of the most thundering of stage idols in that day. Booth came and went in the Surratt household, flashing smiles at the roomers, but spending most of his time in conferences with John Surratt and his mother. Many an errand did young Weichmann run between Mrs. Surratt and Booth, he said, carrying messages down to the National Hotel, where the actor lived.

Then there was a Mr. Spencer Howell, who, during his term of lodgment, taught Weichmann a cipher interesting enough for the boy to use in transposing Longfellow's "Psalm of Life." Had the boy but known it, this Mr. Spencer Howell was a Confederate spy, and that cipher was used far more often in getting secret information to Richmond than in transposing such innocent phrases as "Life is real, life is earnest and the grave is not its goal."

For other visitors, brought home by his friend John, Weichmann had had less regard—that "Rev. Mr. Wood" for instance, and the squat, unbathed gnome, Atzerodt. He wondered a little, too, at John Surratt's many absences from the boarding-house, but it was explained to him that John was busy with oil and cotton speculations. Now and then his friend and those visitors hurt Weichmann's feelings a little by edging away from him to talk, or by shutting the doors between them. Once he had gone into John's room to find them toying with knives and pistols. Mrs. Surratt had explained that the pistols were necessary for John's protection, since his land business took him to wild parts of the country. Again he had found a false moustache on a bureau and thought it funny when the Rev. Mr. Wood had claimed it.

In March, John, Powell, and Booth had come stamping into the house one night, whipping their boots and glowering. Coupled with newspaper reports that a plot to kidnap Lincoln had failed, this circumstance aroused Weichmann's suspicions, and he took the matter to an office-companion, a Captain Gleason at the War Department. Gleason advised him to say nothing and to watch, adding that what he had seen had probably no connection with the rumors. For a time Weichmann did watch, but against all his suspicions he balanced the obvious kindliness of Mrs. Surratt and the absurdity of thinking anything wrong of his old school friend John.

By April the boy had dismissed his doubts.

The fourteenth day of April, Good Friday, came, and Weichmann, a devout churchman, was let out of office early, with the other clerks, for the holiday. At home in the lodging-house, Weichmann was asked by Mrs. Surratt to go down to the livery stable and hire a horse and buggy to drive her out to her old home at Surrattsville, thirteen miles east of town, where she had a business engagement with a certain Mr. Nothey. Eager for the trip, the boy assented and drove her to Nothey's house. The man was not at home, and Weichmann was directed to drive to the Surrattsville tavern, where the woman alighted, carrying two packages — "things of Booth's," she described them to the boy.

Inside the tavern, with Weichmann waiting outside, Mrs. Surratt gave the packages to her tenant, John M. Lloyd, with instructions to have them ready when called for that night, or so Lloyd swore. Then she returned to the buggy and set out for Washington. As they jogged through the April twilight, they suddenly came out upon a hill and saw the capital lying below them bathed in the jubilation-fires with which the city was still celebrating Lee's surrender.

"I'm afraid all this rejoicing will be turned into mourning and all this glory into sadness," Mrs. Surratt said.

"What do you mean?" asked Weichmann.

"After sunshine there is always a storm. The people are too proud and licentious and God will punish them."

Home, at dinner, Mrs. Surratt showed the boy a letter from her son John in Montreal, where, she said, he had gone on business. The door-bell rang. Louis started for it, but the woman said "No," that she would answer it herself. Afterward Weichmann remembered that a man's footfalls had entered, then after a time of silence, had gone away. Finishing his dinner, Weichmann went into the parlor. Mrs. Surratt was gloomy.

She told her beads and asked the boy to pray for her intentions.

"I can't unless I know what your intentions are."

"Pray anyhow!"

She grew more nervous, and soon hurried Weichmann, her daughter Annie, her younger sister Olivia Jenkins, and another roomer, Miss Fitzpatrick, off to bed. A little after dawn the door-bell jangled and Weichmann, the only man in the house, answered it.

"Who's there?"

"Open up! We're detectives!"

The boy struggled with his pants. Mrs. Surratt came and peered down over the banisters.

"Open the door!" she said. "I expected the house to be searched."

When Weichmann threw back the door it seemed as if two thousand people were outside.

He gasped, "What does this mean, coming at this time of night to a widow-lady's house?"

An officer thrust a cravat under his nose.

"It means that this is Abraham Lincoln's blood! John Wilkes Booth has assassinated him, and John Surratt has killed Secretary Seward. Haven't you heard of it?"

Weichmann held up his right hand, so he said, and cried, "So help me God, I haven't heard of it before this minute, but I see now what so many secret meetings around here *do* mean."

He finished dressing while the detectives searched the house, and, as they left, advising him to report at military headquarters in the forenoon, he plead earnestly with them for his friend, John, citing the letter just received from Montreal to prove that it must have been some other who had assailed Seward.

As he shut the door on them he heard Annie Surratt cry, "Oh, Ma, just think of that man Booth being here an hour before the murder."

Those footfalls had been Booth's!

"Annie," Mrs. Surratt answered, "I am resigned. I think that John Wilkes Booth was only an instrument in the hands of the Almighty to punish this proud and licentious people."

The next day Weichmann appeared at military headquarters and was hustled promptly off with detectives to Canada to hunt John Surratt, whom the War Department believed to be conferring with the representatives of the Confederate government who had crouched on this neutral territory during the war.

As nothing of John Surratt could be found in Canada, the party had returned to Washington, Weichmann discovering there that Mrs. Surratt had been in prison since Monday night. From that day until the trial, the boy had remained under government protection — or was it government surveillance, as his critics hinted?

It was not alone the fury of defense lawyers that raged around Weichmann through the conspiracy trial. Religious controversy had reared its head to make the boy's way a hard one. Stanton, among his other freaks of imagination, had conceived the notion that the conspiracy to kill Lincoln had been manned by Catholics. Himself fanatically anti-Catholic, he had jumped to this conclusion when his detectives had brought him the news that, among the accused, four were members of the Catholic Church — Mrs. Surratt, her son John, Michael O'Laughlin and Dr. Mudd. Whether Stanton believed it or not, at least one of the judges, Gen. T. M. Harris, believed that J. Wilkes Booth had recently left the Episcopal Church to become a Roman Catholic.

No evidence other than this hearsay was ever produced to substantiate this claim, and in time it passed on into that mass of myth and legend that was to enshroud almost every act and actor in the black aftermath of Lincoln's assassination. But at the conspiracy trial, the religious issue was burning just under the surface, occasionally, indeed, breaking through into the testimony. That Powell was a Baptist, Herold an Episcopalian, Atzerodt a Lutheran, and both Arnold and Spangler of Protestant families, did not deter Stanton and Holt from their purpose of fixing the crime upon their religious rivals. And Louis Weichmann, Stanton's chief witness, was a Catholic.

No sooner was he to come to the stand than the issue arose. To match the bigoted anti-Catholics who took up Stanton's absurd cry, were bigoted Catholics to charge that Weichmann was a traitor to his faith, a renegade, helping to crucify an innocent woman because of her religious beliefs.

There is no evidence that the Military Commission, other than General Harris, paid any heed to this religious issue. All were officers of character and bravery, and had served with "Phil" Sheridan, the Irish Brigade, and the thousands of Catholics who had worn their own Lincoln-blue uniforms.

Stoutly did the War Department's prosecutors defend Weichmann against the charge that he was a diabolical liar. That he had contradicted himself on a few insignificant details was admitted, but the presence of minor errors in a story so long, the attorneys said, only proved that the major truth had not been rehearsed or fabricated. To establish this point, it was cited that the trivial discrepancies between the Gospels did not disprove the truth of the Christian religion.

Far afield did the trial run. Whether the accused were guilty or not guilty became of secondary importance to Stanton. The men he was after were the Confederate leaders in general, Jefferson Davis, Jacob Thompson and Clement C. Clay, the Confederate commissioners in Canada, in particular. The trial, he hoped, would prove that these diabolical "traitors" had planned the assassination of Union government-heads in order to win, through stealth, the victory that had been denied them on the battlefield. He wanted the trial to show that these "rebels" had organized their band of killers from the ranks of Southern sympathizers, The Sons of Liberty, a secret society of Secession partisans in the North, and from Catholics who were supposed to favor the Confederacy.

To give the Secretary what he wanted, Sanford Conover, an "informer," was brought to the stand by detectives to tell of strange and marvelous things that linked the authorities in Richmond to the conspiracy. In time Conover was exposed as a fraud of the most barefaced sort, but during the trial he seemed immensely important.

Everything converged against Mrs. Surratt. The newspapers condemned her from the start, describing her as "hard-faced," "brazen," "an Amazonian of undaunted mettle," "defiant," and "with a pair of cold, clear, devilish gray eyes that would make her a good stage landlady, ready to look after her own interests and to get all the money she could from her customers."

For her, witnesses appeared testifying to her good character, and explaining that she could not have recognized Powell in the dim light of her home that night when the detectives asked her if she knew the muddy gutter-man who had just entered. It had been because of her bad eyesight that she had failed to recognize him, they said. Her daughter Annie came to the stand distraught and sat nervously tapping her feet on the floor and looking around the court-room, asking, "Where's Mamma? Where's Mamma?"

There was no defense for Mrs. Surratt if the commission believed Louis Weichmann's story and, since it dovetailed with that told by John M. Lloyd the tavern-keeper, the vote was unanimous for her conviction. Five of the officers, however, signed an appeal for mercy, and attached it to the official verdict for Judge Holt to show President Johnson.

On Wednesday, June 14, the last witness was heard, and the arguments of counsel began. For the government John A. Bingham, of the masterly invective, summed up in a speech that ran for six days. The orations of both forces lasted two weeks, the commission found all guilty as accused on June 30, and on July 5 President Johnson approved the findings of the court, paid no heed to the recommendation of mercy, if indeed he saw it at all, doomed Mrs. Surratt, Powell, Herold, and Atzerodt to death, and fixed Friday, July 7, for the hanging. Dr. Mudd, Arnold, O'Laughlin, and Spangler escaped with imprisonment.

The day after the news had been flashed to the country, trains for Washington were jammed with the curious and the morbid.

It was to be the biggest hanging America had ever had.

19

THE FOUR WHO WERE HANGED

THERE WERE FOUR to be hanged but because one was a woman, Christian Rath, the hangman, could find nobody to dig the graves. All of the prison employees flatly refused. Rath stamped up and down the corridors of the jail, rubbing his head. Things had started badly.

At daybreak on this seventh of July, 1865, he had gone out into the prison-yard to test the new rope he had bought for the hanging. Crowds had stared at him through the tall, iron fence. Even at this early hour the morbid and curious had begun to pack the streets around the penitentiary to see what they could of the day's ceremonies. Ignoring them Captain Rath, who was all business, had marched straight to a tree, with a sack of shot across his shoulder and a rope in his hand.

Up in the tree he had tied one end of the rope to the sack and the other to the limb upon which he sat; then, edging well forward to eye the jerk, he had shoved the sack into space.

And when the bough broke, as it did in the prison-yard as well as in the nursery rhyme, down had come baby, cradle and all—the captain alighting upon his head. As he picked himself up all dirt and morning dew, guffaws and whoops of glee had risen from the mob at that tall, iron fence. Yes, things had started badly.

The rope might be stout enough, the gallows up and ready, after yesterday's carpentering, but here it was nearing eight o'clock, the hanging due around noon—and not a grave dug. Captain Rath hurried into the prison-office to see Lieutenant-Colonel McCall, who was in charge of the military guard. Could he get a detail of soldiers to do the digging? He was told to ask for volunteers.

Addressing the regiment, Rath asked for a hundred helpers, some to man the spades, some the traps, some the coffins, some to bind the hands and feet of the condemned.

"And every man will get a drink of whisky when the thing is done," he concluded.

Every soldier in the regiment stepped up. All morning the carpenters were hammering at the gallows-tree, out in the enclosure behind the prison, adding finishing touches to the strong, simple affair whose upper beam, onto which the ropes were tied, rose some twenty feet above the ground and whose platform was midway of this height.

By 11.30 the traps were ready for the test which Rath was to give them with weights, one under each of the two wide doors in the platform floor. Rath ascended the steps, noting that the four graves were ready and yawning between the scaffold and the high penitentiary wall upon which the blue-coated soldiers were lined, rifles in hand.

A thousand infantrymen were scattered about the jail-yard and to this number were constantly added newspaper men and such other civilians as could secure the prized tickets of admission. No government officials were to come to the hanging, and no high army men except Generals Hancock and Hartranft, who were in charge.

One newspaper man, as he entered the yard, looked at the four nooses dangling and the four graves gaping with their raw, red earth and blurted out, "My God, they're not going to hang all four, are they?" People everywhere in the United States were asking that too.

It was the woman people were wondering about: Mrs. Mary E. Surratt. At the announcement that President Johnson had doomed her to the gallows a great clamor for her pardon or reprieve had arisen, and at the very moment that the reporter stood aghast at the sight of her waiting grave, her lawyers were asking the Supreme Court of the District to save her with a writ of habeas corpus, arguing that her trial and conviction by a military body had been unconstitutional.

In the face of President Johnson's suspension of the right of habeas corpus in the case, the court was helpless. Johnson's answer to prayers and pleas was an adamant statement, "She kept the nest where the egg was hatched," his reference being to the Surratt house where Booth had assembled his plotters.

In the streets and hotels of Washington, which were packed with people talking about the woman, speculation upon her fate furnished the sole topic. Nobody seemed to think or care about the other prisoners. Rumors ran through the crowd saying that she had been sentenced, she had been reprieved, she had been given "life" instead.

Even some of the Radical leaders, those rulers of the nation, felt that it was going too far to hang her. "Bluff" Ben Wade, himself, blurted out to listeners, "It's a damned outrage and everlasting disgrace if she's allowed to hang." Another of the Radical chieftains opposed it, too, Thaddeus Stevens, who did not swallow Stanton's story that Jefferson Davis and his associates had inspired the conspiracy. "These men are no friends of mine," he said. "They are public enemies and I would treat the South as a conquered country and settle it politically upon the policy best suited to ourselves. But I know these men. They are gentlemen, and incapable of being assassins."

But, in Washington, Johnson, with Stanton stiffening him to his work, was firm.

To the door of the White House came streams of petitioners for the woman, among them, Mrs. Stephen A. Douglas, widow of the loyal Democratic Senator from Illinois. She could get no further than the rest. Annie Surratt, sobbing, penetrated to the President's door and cast herself against the two men, both Radicals, Preston King of New York and Senator Lane of Kansas, who stood there shoulder to shoulder against all supplicants. All the forenoon, however, Johnson's private secretary kept a fast horse hitched to a buggy outside the White House door on the bare chance that the President might change his mind.

The rattle of the drops, as Rath tested them in the prison-yard, told the newspaper men that the government had not weakened; the woman must die. And the telegraph, clicking off its bulletins to the gaping country, told everybody that all four were to hang.

One of the drops refused to work at the test, and Rath fussed about the platform among the swinging nooses directing the carpenters as they hammered and sawed. At the next test both doors worked perfectly, although with a hideous rattle that echoed in the lifeless air — it was brazenly hot in the enclosure. Deathly hot in the prison, too; hot where the condemned sat with their families — such as had families — and with their confessors, which all had.

There was but one cool place in the whole penitentiary grounds, it seemed, the grave under the floor of a neighboring warehouse, where John Wilkes Booth, like the old John Brown whom he had helped to hang years before, lay now "a-moldering in the grave." Cool down there and silent, except for the dim echoes of wails and commands that went through the premises. Lonely down there, too, for in that day's crowds not a soul, unless it was Dr. Porter, the jail physician, even knew that Booth was sleeping inside the prison-walls. Indeed it is doubtful if ten men in the whole Republic that day had any idea whatsoever of where the dark actor's body lay, so stealthily had it been hidden by Stanton.

Through the cells of the condemned, there was wailing, terrible and long. Seven sisters hid David Herold with their embraces. A nephew of sixteen had spent the night with Davy in his cell, for company.

On his last night and last day, Herold had laughed and joked lightly with his soldier-guards, weeping only when his clergyman, preparing him for Jesus, wept. As soon as the preacher had stopped his gentle pieties, Herold had turned as though in relief to the soldiers, ready to jest once more. "He seemed more butterfly than man," wrote one reporter.

Annie, sobbing recklessly, clung to Mrs. Surratt, who wavered between collapse and resignation, sometimes mastering herself, at others sinking back in feeble moans. Her jailers had pitied her ever since those first days of her imprisonment, when she had tried to starve herself to death. Dr. Porter, assigned to the task of preserving the conspirators for the trial, had talked kindly to her, telling her that unless she ate he would have to feed her forcibly, and when she became tractable, the surgeon allowed her to choose her own food.

A clod-like creature, miserably dressed, cried beside Atzerodt, who hunted in his Bible for the verse, "Be sure your sin will find you out." She was the woman with whom he had cohabited, minus benefit of clergy, in those days when he had lived wretchedly at Port Tobacco, cesspool of the Potomac, making carriages and relaying information to the Confederates across "No Man's Land" between the lines.

Coolest of all the four, as noon came, was Lewis Powell — and gamest too — perhaps not so much game as indifferent. His was the poise of a carnivorous beast on the bottom of his cage, just before the crowds come trooping into a circus-tent. He listened casually — if indeed he listened at all — to the prayers of the Rev. Mr. Gillette of the city, who had come to minister to this strange Baptist from Florida. No relatives came to comfort Powell and it seemed he needed none.

Rath, the jailer, never dissembled a fondness for this Apache; like all military men, he rated Powell higher than the other conspirators. Soldiers understood Seward's assailant. He had tried to kill an enemy. Between his sixteenth and twentieth years he had learned how to kill enemies — or to be killed by them. On the night of April 14, he had still been at war, and what he was getting now was what one got in war times. That was all. So he waited calmly in the hot cell while the preacher prayed.

Further on down in the tier of cells lay the four prisoners whom Captain Rath did not have to hang — Spangler, Mudd, Arnold, and O'Laughlin. Of these Spangler, at least, did not know his fate. From his cell he had seen the preparations for the execution, and he expected to be called. Now, as the weeping and farewells were heard in the corridors outside, the champion crab-fisherman of the Potomac wondered why there was no confessor in his cell. So he wept and howled as the final hammers rang on the gallows out in the yard.

None of the reporters bothered with these four, knowing that their departure for prison would come later. They did not belong in today's story. Around the death-cells clustered the newspaper men, peering in at the condemned and their confessors. Among them scurried Captain Rath, pretending to be busy with arrangements. In reality he was maneuvering for time.

The appointed hour, one o'clock, had come, and the death-march was due, but neither Rath nor his commanding officers, Generals Hancock and Hartranft, wanted to hang a woman. They were going to delay the thing as long as they could, hoping against hope that a reprieve might come. Finally they could decently wait no longer. Orders were orders and General Hartranft directed the march to form. Outside, two thousand people stood packed together in the stifling enclosure, half of them civilians, many of whom raised umbrellas against the burning sun.

At last the back door of the penitentiary swung open and the woman appeared, her black bombazine dress glistening in the scorching light, her veiled head drooping, and her knees sagging so that one of the two Catholic priests, who flanked her, had to lift constantly at her arm to keep her from falling. The other priest held an umbrella over her head. Behind her came four soldiers; then Lieutenant-Colonel McCall, who was to bind the woman's hands and skirts on the scaffold. For the occasion McCall had purchased a new straw hat with a ribbon on it, and the headgear shone in the sun as the officer stepped out of line to let the parade go by.

Next followed Atzerodt, still gibble-gabbering, a strange white nightcap pointing upward from his head and giving him, more than ever, the appearance of some fantastic troll from the Black Forest of his native Germany. As Atzerodt shambled along, a Lutheran minister prayed at his side.

Next came four soldiers.

Then Davy Herold. Poor Davy, self-conscious, flustered now, chattering helpless nothings as his Episcopalian clergyman kept step with him, praying.

Four soldiers.

Powell, alias Payne! The Visigoth entered the arena, his head bare, his low-cut undershirt displaying his magnificent neck. Across the yard his eye turned, hard and steady. It noted one thing — McCall's new straw hat. With a quick, cool gesture Powell lifted it from the officer's head and put it upon his own. He had borrowed a hat to be hanged in.

The procession mounted the steps and ranged itself across the platform. Mrs. Surratt had the post of honor on the right.

Sharing her drop was Powell. Herold and Atzerodt had the other trap between them.

The condemned took chairs. Mrs. Surratt swayed against the priests. Herold trembled. Atzerodt kept muttering, "Good-bye, shentlemans." Powell eased back in his chair and looked up, calm and curious, at the rope. His eyes were unwinking.

General Hartranft read the order of execution, Mrs. Surratt kissing the crucifix repeatedly. Hartranft concluded and motioned the clergymen to say their last prayers.

That done, the prisoners were motioned up to have their arms pinioned, and as Powell arose, a wandering little gust of wind, coming whimsically to life in that lifeless heat, whisked off the new straw hat and sent it zig-zagging down among the soldiers. Powell was peering after it, gesturing to the blue-coats to hand it back to him, when the executioners began binding his arms. He was still following its progress from hand to hand as he lifted his chin to ease the rope around his neck, such a gesture as a man gives in a barber's chair. And by the time the hat had come back to the gallows, it was too late. The white hood was ready, and Powell motioned "Never mind." It had not fitted him well, anyway.

McCall, bareheaded, gently removed Mrs. Surratt's bonnet and replaced it with the hood, the woman whimpering as the death-cap hid her eyes, "Don't let me fall! Hold on!"

Deftly the Colonel pinioned her arms and tied a strip of cotton cloth around her skirts, below the knees, so that they would not fly up when her body flew down. Then he slackened the rope about her arms, when she pleaded faintly that it hurt.

Atzerodt, squatting and weaving back and forth, like a little blind bear, mumbled brokenly inside his hood. Herold slumped in fear.

Back and forth behind the four went Captain Rath, adjusting the ropes and still "stalling" for time. As he fingered Powell's noose he whispered in through the cap, "Powell, I want you to go quick," and tightened the knot at the giant's ear. From out of the bag came Powell's voice, matter-of-fact, "Captain, you know best."

Everything was ready, and everybody but Rath. General Hancock had not appeared. Rath knew his general was waiting at the outer prison-door for sight of a possible messenger with a stay for Mrs. Surratt. The minutes dragged through the sweltering heat. Then the back door opened and Hancock strode out, stern of face, nodding to Rath, "Go ahead!"

Rath spoke out, loudly, in the silence, "*Her,* too?" Hancock nodded again. The soldiers on the platform all drew back to be sure their feet were not on the trap-doors.

Rath clapped his hands twice; the little German, in muffled voice, howled "Oh! Oh! Oh!" The soldiers, down below, whacked with their axes, the props flew out, the doors with their burdens flew down, and a crash jerked back and forth between the walls, echoing.

The four were hanged.

✩ ✩ ✩ **20** ✩ ✩ ✩

SHARKS AND CATS

OF THE CAST which J. Wilkes Booth had assembled so hopefully, five, including himself, were now dead. Booth, the star-tragedian of the melodrama, lay under a warehouse floor, and the others, Mrs. Surratt, the leading lady, Powell the "heavy," Atzerodt, the low-comedian, and Herold, the juvenile, slept in a row beside the prison wall.

That might reasonably have ended the fears of Edwin M. Stanton, the war minister who had dreaded the plotters so keenly. But it did not. There were still four cells in the penitentiary to be emptied, four of the fearsome band left to be handled —Arnold, O'Laughlin, Dr. Mudd and Spangler, who had been incidental characters in Booth's comedy-cast, and who now lay wondering what their sentences would be.

Beyond the mere notification that they were "guilty" they had heard nothing of what the Military Commission had found in their cases. That was a secret held by President Johnson, or by the War Department, or by both, and where these sentences should be served lay in Johnson's hands.

Considering their cases in the days that followed the hanging in the prison-yard, Johnson decided that he would send the four of them to serve their terms at hard labor in the penitentiary at Albany. This fact should be announced to the prisoners on July 17 and they should be started for their destination that same day. But on the fifteenth, two days before the appointed time of departure, Johnson changed his mind, deciding that the four prisoners should be sent to Fort Jefferson instead.

Fort Jefferson, most cruel of government prisons, lay on the Dry Tortugas, arid, sun-cooked islands a hundred miles off the mainland of Florida, the thought of which was almost as horrible to government guards as to prisoners.

Who caused this sudden switch in the President's plans is not a matter of record. However, there can be little doubt that it was Stanton. He was known to regard the four remaining conspirators as representatives of the treacherous South. He had toiled outlandishly to prevent the expected rescue of Booth's body and of the persons of the four who had been hanged. And from what was now to happen to Arnold, O'Laughlin, Spangler and Mudd it is evident that the War Department feared that vengeful friends of the condemned men would stage a sudden jail-delivery in their behalf.

On the seventeenth of July the prisoners were led out into the jail-yard and arrayed before General Hartranft, who read them the findings of their judges and the sentence of the President — hard labor at Albany. Not a word of the terrible Dry Tortugas. Midnight came — the hour when Booth's body had been hidden twenty days before — and hands shook the sleeping prisoners. Voices said "Get ready," and soon the four men were being hustled down under guard to the wharf where a ship waited with engines steaming. Through the night the steamer made its way to Point Comfort, where the prisoners were transferred to the gunboat *Florida*.

Commodore Budd of the ship was handed sealed orders and told to steam straight out to sea for four hours, then to open his orders and obey them. The *Florida* bore off eastward. If there was no legal way to strangle the four villains, there was a way to spirit them off from all imaginary danger of rescue.

On board the ship the officers knew that something was up.

This was not the road to Albany. They guessed that they were bound for Concord, where many government prisoners were held. When, after four hours' sailing, Budd opened his orders, he swung the ship's nose southward, and the prisoners, who were exercising on the deck, understood in a flash what that meant — the Dry Tortugas. Arnold despairingly said they were being sent to hell.

"Hell" loomed on July 24 and anchoring off the bare, baking island, the *Florida* transferred her convicts into the sweltering pile of masonry and turned her nose home. From the Dry Tortugas there was no danger of escape.

Around Fort Jefferson ran a wide, deep moat filled by the sea, and in it lived ten man-eating sharks that the government kept as guardsmen extraordinary. Wise officers saw to it that these sharks never grew fat nor lazy from over-feeding and every so often, by way of testing the appetites of their pets and, at the same time, displaying a healthy warning to the convicts, they threw cats to the man-eaters. Rarely if ever did the sharks let a cat touch the water.

Behind the moat the prisoners took up their lives. Dr. Mudd was by chance assigned to a cell upon whose door some waggish guest of other years had painted "Leave hope behind who enters here."

The legend seemed expressive enough until some time in 1868, when yellow fever broke out in the fort, carrying off soldiers and prisoners in daily squads. The sand-keys all around the fort were spotted with graves. When the last surgeon was dead, Dr. Mudd offered his services. The remaining officers gave him authority, and he began by enlarging all casements to let in the air. Then he set to work like a wheel-horse and soon had the epidemic in hand.

As danger passed, the officers of the fort signed an appeal to President Johnson asking that the heroic doctor be pardoned, and on February 8, 1869, a month before he was to turn over the White House to the newly elected President, Ulysses S. Grant, Johnson signed the papers for Mudd's release, following three weeks later with the order that the other prisoners be also freed.

Home they came, all but Michael O'Laughlin, one-time casual livery-stable hand of Baltimore, who lay in one of those sand-key graves that the yellow fever had filled.

Back in Maryland, Dr. Mudd took up his shattered life, and to him in 1871, broken, too, crept Spangler, who, thanks to the Dry Tortugas, had come to love him as a dog loves its master. In the friendly home the one-time champion crab-fisherman of the Potomac died in 1879, the doctor following in 1882, each leaving a sworn statement of innocence — statements that went unread, however, by a world which shuddered and shrank whenever it thought of those monsters who had plotted martyrdom for America's saint.

✠ ✠ ✠ 21 ✠ ✠ ✠

"THIS IS TO CERTIFY—"

As THE SOLDIERS, on July 7, 1865, cut four corpses down from the gallows-tree in the Washington penitentiary yard, the head of her who had been Mrs. Mary E. Surratt fell broken-necked upon her breast.

"She makes a good bow," chirped a bystander.

One of the officers in charge rebuked him, for it was no time to be flippant about Mrs. Surratt.

The "widow-woman's" ghost was abroad in the land, a ghost far more real than that wraith of hers which was soon to be seen haunting the lodging-house on H Street. There, where staring crowds daily assembled, Annie, the orphaned daughter, was packing up to move away. She had waited with a casket at the prison-gate, begging for her mother's body until officers had told her that it was useless. Stanton had decreed that all four criminals must sleep in pine boxes by the jail-yard wall, with only a little white fence around to mark the graves — no headstones — the only identification being a name on a slip of paper put inside a glass bottle beside each body.

With nothing more to wait for, Annie Surratt sold the lodging-house. Business men said it was worth $10,000, but Annie, selling in haste, received only $4,600 as she hurried away. The bargain did the purchaser no good, however, for within six weeks, he too, was gone, his nervous system reputedly shattered by what he had seen and heard. So said the Boston *Post*, which went on to chronicle how other tenants came and went in swift succession, swearing that in the dead of night Mrs. Surratt walked the hallways clad in her robe of death.

There was no imagination, though, about the ghost that stalked after President Andrew Johnson. The dead woman became, all too soon, a living force in the worst shambles that ever beset American politics, the quarrel between Johnson and the Radicals.

After Lincoln's funeral had passed, and the crowd of Senators and Congressmen had gone from Washington, Johnson began to get himself in hand. Under the racking spasm of fear which had gripped them all in those first days after the assassination of Lincoln, Johnson had gone over, body and soul, to the Radicals, agreeing with them that the South had engineered the crime and must, therefore, be punished. But the fever passed rapidly from the hard-headed Tennesseean, and the native clearness of his head began to assert itself.

With the rejoicing Radicals back in their home towns awaiting the assembly of Congress in December, Johnson could think for himself. Also Secretary of State Seward, his head still in the steel frame, came creeping back into the Cabinet meetings to woo the new President subtly away from the policy of harshness toward the South. Polished and humane, Seward had sympathized with Lincoln's merciful plans of Reconstruction, and now he began to urge Johnson back to his predecessor's path, away from the road that the Sumner-Stevens-Wade clique had charted.

From their homes the Radicals watched the turn of events with rage, but not with the old despair that had beset them when Lincoln was in the saddle. They were stronger now than when the gawky, soft-hearted rail-splitter had been alive. Let Johnson revive the Lincolnian policy all he wanted; he would get nowhere, for, this time, the "avengers" had the voters. Lincoln's death had ironically played into the hands of his enemies, solidifying the people into a phalanx of revenge which the Radicals could control.

So the "bitter-enders" bided their time, watching Johnson stray further and further from their counsels, like a calf taking rope with which to strangle itself. Johnson, warming to his benign work, listening to the tributes which the South, as well as Northern Democrats and conservative Republicans, heaped upon him for his magnanimity, pardoned ex-Confederates in shoals, appointed provisional governors to rule the Southern States with tolerance and kindness, ordered the assembling of the late "rebels" in conventions, and restored civil liberties right and left. For the sake of making the return of the South sane and easy, Johnson seemed to have forgotten the negro, ignoring the promises which the anti-slavery Northerners had been making to the black man. Old "Thad" Stevens in Pennsylvania, watching Seward coax Johnson further and further away from a stern peace, growled, "What a bungler Powell was!"

Through the South and across the surface of the North a growing chorus of praise for Andrew Johnson blew like a breeze. In the depths a storm was brewing, the fierceness of which not even its brewers suspected. On the first Monday of December, 1865, it broke.

When the Congress convened, many Senators and Congressmen from Southern States presented their credentials. They had been elected under Johnson's easy terms of Reconstruction, and were anxious to take the seats they, or their comrades, had vacated in 1860. But "Thad" Stevens, clenching his iron fists, banged the door in their faces. Organizing the House of Representatives like the czar that he had come to be, now that Lincoln was gone, he had the clerk omit all Southern names from the opening roll-call. Behind him, ranged a committee of thirty Radicals, and with them he dominated the body beyond any question. The Senate allied itself to his program, and the South quickly learned that Reconstruction was eventually to be in the hands of the national Legislature, not those of the Chief Executive.

"Forty acres of land and a mule" must be given each ex-slave, Stevens decreed, and although he never quite brought this dream into existence, it told his policy. In his fondness for the negro Stevens was sincere. When he came to die, three years later, he had a colored preacher baptize him. There was earnest passion, as well as sadistic pleasure, in him when he declared that the slaveholding aristocrats must see their property divided up among their former chattels.

Under his lash the "bitter-enders" gleefully wrecked all of the preliminary work Lincoln had done to restore the South, and particularly did they gloat over the defeat of Johnson's effort to carry out his predecessor's "Louisiana Plan," by which only a handful of negroes were to be placed upon civil equality with Southern whites.

To complete the overthrow of Lincolnian mercy, the South came blundering into the situation with an attitude that discouraged even those Northerners who were disposed to be generous. The late Confederates had not been wise in the selection of those Congressmen and Senators whom Johnson had allowed them, as restored States, to elect for their Washington representatives.

Here, in December, 1865, there appeared as duly elected law-makers, men who had eight months before been doing everything in their power to destroy the government which they now sought to share. Here were four ex-Confederate generals, several of Jefferson Davis' Cabinet, and some sixty other "rebel" leaders, asking to be seated when they had not yet even been so much as accepted back into the Union as citizens.

The South, in its zeal to regain representation in the government, had overplayed its hand with something of the same haste in which it had dashed out of the Union to start the war. To send up to Washington in 1865 legislators who were not eligible for office and who had not yet been allowed to take the oath of allegiance, was only one more certain way of defeating the cause of conciliation.

As an instance, here was Alexander Stephens, but lately Vice-President of the Confederacy, asking to be sworn in as Georgia's Senator. That he would be loyal, and an adornment to any legislative body in the world, was not the question. He had come too soon. Misrepresenting its own repentance, the South played foolishly into the hands of the Radicals.

That the Southern people were prepared now to accept the

nation as supreme over the States and to be loyal to the Union, was apparent to Andrew Johnson, as it was to level-headed men like General Sherman, who knew how helpless were the defeated populations. It touched Johnson's heart to see the Southerners, their property gone, toiling and struggling while so many of their former slaves idled luxuriously. Nothing more need be feared, least of all from the Confederate veterans. They wanted no more war and no more politicians on either side stampeding war issues their way.

To protect his late enemies Johnson did his best. He gathered Lincoln men around him and fought for the old program, but his cause lacked now the brain of Lincoln, which had known so well how to sway the voters. Instead of meeting Stevens and the Radicals with slow, cool devices which they could not fathom, Johnson fought them with their own weapons, abuse, defiance and epithet — and was worsted. To the Northern people, still sore from the war wounds which Lincoln's death had reopened, the propaganda of Stevens was convincing. "The South is still defiant," said the "avengers." "It has seduced Johnson to its cause and is about to combine with Northern 'Copperheads' to rule the country, wipe out its State debts and take charge of the government, achieving by political strokes the victory which it has lost on the battlefield." Believing this, the Northern voters rushed to Stevens' support, and backed the Radicals as they put through a system of Reconstruction which gave the vote to all negroes, placing ex-slaves in Congress itself and fastening iron oppression upon the Southern people.

The fight between the President and Congress, which was now overwhelmingly Radical, came to a climax when Johnson tried to oust Stanton from his Cabinet. Stanton, who had been carrying water on both shoulders — passing as a Johnson man in Cabinet meetings and as a Radical in his conferences with Sumner and Stevens — wouldn't resign. He barricaded himself in the War Office and defied his chief. It was the technicality for which the Radicals had been waiting and on March 5, 1868, they brought impeachment proceedings against Johnson, failing only by a single vote of accomplishing so drastic a move.

Here it was that the ghost of Mary E. Surratt got up and

walked. The "avengers," who had so thirsted for "rebel" blood in 1865, now, paradoxically, charged Johnson with having "railroaded" Mrs. Surratt to the gallows. On the floor of the impeachment trial they declared that Johnson had cruelly turned down the plea for mercy which five of the woman's judges had signed. Johnson replied that he had never seen such a paper, that Stanton and his tool, Judge-Advocate Holt, had secreted from him this recommendation. Judge Holt, now with the Radicals, as might be expected, said that the President lied, that the petition of the judges had been attached to the findings and that Johnson had seen it and been deaf to it. The few Cabinet members who cared to be quoted agreed with Holt.

Johnson cried that his enemies were trumping up old lies in their desperate attempt to ruin him. The "avengers" answered that Johnson was trying to wash blood off his hands in an effort to rally to his support the Catholic vote and the legions of former Copperheads who had decried Mrs. Surratt's hanging.

Suddenly the question of the "widow-woman's" guilt was blazing across the land again, and all word-feuds came to rest sooner or later upon the name of Louis Weichmann, the boy who had testified so fatally against her at her trial. Newspapers argued about him. If he had told the truth on the stand, she had been guilty. If he had lied, she had been innocent. Everything hung upon his word.

To make matters worse for the boy, the temper of the country was changed. A revulsion of feeling had set in the moment Mrs. Surratt was hanged. Those who had bayed for her death felt ashamed and anxious to find a scapegoat to blame for the tragic mistake — for, whether she was guilty or not, it was a mistake to have hanged her, felt the Republic.

Champions of the dead landlady published the charge that Weichmann, shortly after the hanging, had broken down and confessed that he had lied to save his own life from Stanton's men, who had strung him up by the neck until he had promised to tell the stories they wanted told. This purported "confession" was immediately branded by Weichmann as a falsehood, and to his support came Major A. C. Richards, the military police official of Washington who had taken charge of the boy when he had appeared at headquarters on his own recognizance. Weichmann had not been coerced, said Richards, he had not held back. He had simply told what he knew. Nevertheless, the tale of Weichmann's "recanting" feverishly went the rounds.

The full force of the attacks upon the boy came in June, 1867, when John H. Surratt, the hanged woman's son, was placed on trial before a civil judge and jury in the District of Columbia for his part in the assassination of Lincoln. As in the trial of Surratt's mother, one of the chief government witnesses was the open-faced Weichmann boy and, as upon that other occasion, the defense tore at his testimony savagely.

John Surratt, it appeared from other government witnesses, had been in Washington the day of Lincoln's assassination, leaving town either just before or just after Booth's deed. But the jury, which was made up of four Northern men and eight Southerners, accepted Surratt's own statement that he had been in New York City that night, headed for Canada with messages and money which Judah P. Benjamin, Secretary of the Confederate States, wanted delivered to his agents there. Not a thing of the plot to kill the President had he known, Surratt maintained. He said that he had broken with Booth weeks before and had withdrawn from the abduction-plot, in which he admitted he had been involved.

Into the trial came the religious question, burning brighter than ever, for Surratt, guilty or innocent, had hidden for nearly five months in the homes of various Catholic priests in Canada while the trial of his mother raged in Washington. Evidently playing upon the sympathies of these clergymen and crying "persecution," he had persuaded them to help him, in his dyed beard, strange spectacles and short-tailed Canadian coat, to get on board the steamship *Peruvian,* which lay in Quebec harbor, Liverpool-bound.

Flimsy excuses he had for fleeing while his mother lay in peril, the facts seeming to be that he deserted her, either justifying himself on the ground that she would somehow escape hanging or that his return would be of no help.

From Liverpool, Surratt made his way to Rome, where he enlisted in the Papal Zouaves under the name of John Watson.

In April, 1866, he was recognized by another American private of the guard, Henri Ste. Marie, who had been introduced to Surratt at Saint Charles Academy in 1863.

As Ste. Marie told it, Surratt had admitted his guilt in the murder-plot readily enough, expecting that his confession would remain in confidence. Ste. Marie, however, passed the word along to the United States minister in Rome, who began a long-winded correspondence with Washington. By November the government was ready to act, and the ambassador, Rufus King, asked the papal authority, Cardinal Antonelli, for the right to extradite the suspected man. Although there was no treaty covering such a request between the United States and the papacy, the Vatican ordered Surratt's arrest, which took place on November 7 at the town of Veroli, where "Zouave Watson" was on leave.

Surratt was desperate, and when they led him out of jail the next morning for the trip to Rome, he sprang over a balustrade into a thirty-five-foot ravine, landed as by a miracle unhurt on a narrow ledge part way down, and made off ahead of the pursuing troopers. Circling and dodging, he made his way to Naples, where he convinced the British consul that he was a Canadian, wrongfully held in the papal regiment, and coaxed the diplomat to send him across the Mediterranean to Alexandria. His description had preceded him, however, and on November 27 he was arrested at the Egyptian port by the American consul-general.

As John H. Surratt's trial wore on through its sixty-two days of Summer, the question of his mother's guilt rose up anew, for into the testimony was introduced the diary of J. Wilkes Booth that had been taken from his body by the secret-service men at the burning Garrett barn in Caroline County, Virginia. It was the public's first knowledge that such a diary had existed, Stanton and Holt having kept it from being introduced as evidence in the trial for conspiracy of 1865.

Brought out now, two years later, it was declared, by the dead landlady's partisans, to prove amply that she had been an innocent woman. Counsel for John H. Surratt read with emphasis the opening lines of the diary, presumably written on the day of the assassination: "April 14, Friday, the Ides: Until today nothing was ever thought of sacrificing to our country's wrongs. For six months we had worked to capture, but our cause being almost lost, something decisive and great must be done. . . ."

This, said counsel, proved that neither of the Surratts knew of anything except the plot to kidnap Lincoln. The assassination, they argued, was wholly Booth's private idea, as his diary maintained. Just how much the diary proved was a point for debate, since it was admitted that Booth had written most of it while fleeing from Union troopers, a time in which he might reasonably be expected to clear his accomplices from suspicion if it could be done. Any defense that he might have made for his fellow conspirators in such a time was useless as evidence, said Surratt's prosecutors. Furthermore, anything that Booth might have said about the case during his flight must of necessity be viewed in the light of his character; it was his nature to be chivalrous and gallant toward women, and like him, to claim all the credit for the assassination.

Defenders of Surratt also noted that several pages had been torn from the diary, and they charged that Stanton and Holt had ripped them out because they would have cleared Mrs. Surratt. The War Department's defense to this accusation was the statement that the pages were gone when detectives took the book from Booth's body.

With such charges and counter-charges the trial of John H. Surratt came to an end on August 11, 1867, with the jury reporting that it could not agree. Eight of the jurors had been born in either Maryland, Virginia or the District of Columbia, and voted for acquittal. Four were natives of the North, and so voted for conviction. The trial was declared no trial, and John H. Surratt was held over to be brought to justice once more. Months later, however, he was liberated on bail and never brought back for a second trial, the government despairing of ever convicting him in a civil court of law where jurors must be picked from a population still strongly sympathetic with the old cause of Secession.

As a free man Surratt basked for a while in the favor of his mother's partisans, and tried lecturing for a living. Once was enough, his premier performance at Rockville, Maryland, boring his audience so acutely that he never tried the experiment again, and eventually he passed from public view, settling into a trivial clerkship of some description in Baltimore,—back where he had started, at a level that suited him far better than did the political melodramas of J. Wilkes Booth. He was a mild and contented auditor in that time when prosaic death took him in 1916.

In one field, though, he kept lively enough. His hatred of Weichmann knew no bounds, and he was forever fomenting trouble for his old school friend, setting hot-heads to accuse the boy in the newspapers and to repeat his charge that Weichmann had been one of the original kidnaping conspirators. The tale of these attacks upon Weichmann is not wholly one of newspaper broadsides. Friends of the dead woman carried things to a more desperate pass; so the sisters of Weichmann, Mrs. C. O'Crowley and Miss Tillie Weichmann, said in 1926, when they related the story in their home in Anderson, Indiana.

"Pa took us to church that Good Friday that Lincoln was killed," Mrs. O'Crowley said. "And we heard a sermon on 'The Passion of Christ.' As we were coming out Pa said to Mother that he felt a kind of presentiment, and the next morning we read that Lincoln was dead. Then Pa read, too, that Lou was arrested and he caught the next train out of Philadelphia for Washington and saw Lou and the officers. They told Pa Lou wasn't in it and was only helping to clear it up.

"After the trial Lou came home to Philadelphia and went to work as a reporter on the *Globe*. There was a lot of talk about Mrs. Surratt, and once some ladies stopped my sister and me and made ugly remarks about our family helping to hang a woman. We were little bits of girls and it frightened us.

"Pretty soon they started worse than talk after Lou. He got letters attacking him, and he got letters from Cabinet officers and big generals thanking him for having told the truth.

"One evening, as he was walking home from work, a neighbor woman screamed to him to run. A man was following him on the other side of the street and began to run as soon as Lou did. The woman held the door open and pulled Lou in just as the man fired. The bullet stuck in the door. Another time he was sitting in the second-story window at home reading when a revolver went off across the street and the bullet hit the window sill and fell down into a flower-bed where a little neighbor girl was playing.

"The government detectives investigated and kept watch after this, but it got on Lou's nerves, not knowing when he left home whether he'd ever come back. Mr. Stanton and the government men looked out after Lou and got him a job in the Philadelphia custom-house where they could protect him better.

"Once Mrs. Surratt's daughter Annie, sent for him to come to a certain address there in Philadelphia to translate some foreign letters for her. Pa wouldn't let him go, but the detectives said for him to go ahead, they'd be on hand. They told Lou to go in the house and to break a window-pane at the first sign of anything wrong.

"He went up the steps and in the half-open door. The house was empty. On in further was a folding door and through the crack in it he saw somebody peeking. It looked like Annie Surratt. He backed out, but by the time the detectives got in, whoever it had been was gone.

"Another time, along in the early seventies, a knock came at our door one evening and a woman asked for Lou. Pa said he was upstairs. 'Come on in and I'll call him.' She said she'd wait out there. Pa said he wouldn't call Lou unless she came in. She started away and Pa followed her. Down at the next corner on Sixteenth Street she got into a carriage which was standing there with several men in it. Pa saw by the lamplight that she had a man's boots on.

"Lou had to go back and testify all over again in 1867 when they caught John Surratt and brought him back for trial. That made it worse, for when the jury, which was full of Secessionists, disagreed, John started attacking Lou and kept stirring up trouble as long as Lou was in Philadelphia.

"When the Democrats got in power, Lou lost the job he'd held in the custom-house for seventeen years. Mrs. Surratt's friends were behind it, Lou knew. The government wouldn't protect him any more, so he came to Anderson, Indiana, where

our brother, Father Weichmann, had a parish. Father Weichmann had been persecuted by the Secessionists, too. They never
missed a chance to harm any of us. Lou started a business college
and taught shorthand, but he was always terribly nervous.

"What they had said and done was always on his mind. He
could never get over it. He had done what was right and got
only persecution for it.

"He'd walk up and down this floor here and say over and
over again, 'I don't see why she should get into that trouble, a
good-hearted woman like she was.' He said that to my sister
and me just the day before he died.

"Lou always believed that Mrs. Surratt was just fascinated
by Booth, simply carried off her feet. Booth got her into it, and
all of them tried to use Lou as a catspaw. Lou thought Mrs.
Surratt tried to fix evidence on him so that she and John could
go free when the thing would come out.

"From that first night when the detectives poked that cravat
with Lincoln's blood on it right in his face, Lou was sure she was
guilty. It opened his eyes. He never suspected her before it
happened and he never doubted her guilt after it happened."

With such a background Louis Weichmann became, in his
lifetime, a legendary figure in Anderson, Indiana. Even there he
was not free from gossip, for Indiana had been a State of
divided sympathies in war-time, owning enough Copperheads
and Secession-sympathizers to hinder the Union authorities in
their work of voting funds to equip loyal forces in the field. To
these disloyalists, after the war, Weichmann was a target for
whispers. He had sworn a woman's life away, they said.

"See how nervous he is?" they would ask. "He looks and acts
like a guilty man, if ever any man did."

Weichmann, as he paced the streets of the corn-town, those
long lonely years, did act like a man with something on his
mind. Union men, rock-ribbed Republicans of the neighborhood,
explained it, defending him, "He is nervous from the terrible
experience he had. He did his duty like a man and was hounded
for it."

Whatever it might be that worried Weichmann, he kept it
to his family. Mystery clung to him. He didn't mix in a town

where every one mixed. He talked to few people, yet when he did it was with a culture and a courtesy that dignified him. His pupils — there were never many in the little business college he conducted — respected his honesty, his gentility and amazing ability to speak eight languages as well as to teach shorthand. Yet they said that they never knew him, that he was always uneasy and far away. His shy reserve warded off the questions which nosey people were dying to ask him, and he found a bulwark of protection in the hearty, witty personality of his brother, Father Weichmann — "that fine man," as even the Ku Kluxers of Anderson still remember him.

People might be polite to him and respect him, but there was no hope for Louis Weichmann to find peace. He had been caught in that mass of myth that was rising to hide Abraham Lincoln and most of the actors in the drama of his assassination and its epilogue, the trial of the conspirators. Strange fate, it was said by the superstitious, had caught almost all of the chief actors in the drama of Lincoln's assassination.

Mrs. Lincoln, they pointed out in awe, had died pitifully in her sister's home at Springfield, Illinois, after years of insanity. Little Tad had died just before he reached manhood. Both of Mrs. Lincoln's guests in the theater-box, that fatal night, had perished tragically. Major Rathbone and Miss Harris had married, only to be claimed by what must be an evil spell when the Major, going suddenly crazy, had killed his wife, then himself. Laura Keane, the actress, had felt her career blighted by the tragedy. Concerning Booth there were many stories, one that he had shot himself in the burning barn, another that he had escaped altogether and was wandering the world with no place to lay his head in safety, another that he had been killed as the government described, but that Boston Corbett, the Union sergeant who had shot him down, had gone insane and been consigned to a Kansas madhouse.

Two Northern office-holders, Preston King of New York and United States Senator James S. Lane of Kansas, who had stood shoulder to shoulder and kept Mrs. Surratt's daughter Annie from invading President Johnson's private office with her wailing appeals for her mother's reprieve, had both died by their own hand within a year, King walking off a New York ferry one night with his pockets full of shot, Lane putting a bullet through his head on the plains of Kansas.

For twenty years after the execution of the conspirators the priest, Father Walters, who had walked to the gallows with Mrs. Surratt, kept publishing in newspaper after newspaper the mad story that all nine of the Union officers on the commission that had tried and condemned the prisoners, had died violent deaths, most of them driven to suicide by remorse for having hanged an innocent woman. It did not stop this fiction to have seven of the officers in 1892 declare that they were alive and happy, and that the two who were missing had passed on comfortably of the disease known as "old age."

Even Capt. Willie Jett, the Confederate officer who had helped Booth on his flight, was said to have perished miserably. And Stanton, the "mad incorruptible" himself, was so commonly believed to have slashed his own throat with a razor in 1869 that his friends had to deny the thing publicly again and again. The rumor ran that he had killed himself in repentance for the ferocity with which he had prosecuted Mrs. Surratt. In Washington, D. C., in 1928, John P. Simonton, the veteran of two-score years in the War Department office, remembered how this tale was whispered around the town.

"After Stanton's death I kept hearing that he killed himself," said Simonton, "and one day a man came into the office on a matter and in course of conversation told me that he was a friend of the undertaker who had handled Stanton's body.

"He said that he had gone with the embalmer to the Stanton home and found that the family had bound up the dead man's throat very high with a white cloth. He had heard that Stanton had cut his throat and wanted to look and see if it was true, but he couldn't, for there was a woman always standing by the head of the bed watching.

"This man said he tried to look as disinterested as he could, and stood with his eyes fixed on the window as though he was unconcerned. He waited for his chance and pretty soon the woman was called out into the hall by another woman. He could see her, out of the corner of his eye, watching him closely as she left the bedside, and he kept on looking out of the window just as unconcerned as before. But the minute she disappeared, he tiptoed to the door, saw her walking down the hall with her arm around the other woman, talking, and he hurried to the corpse and turned down the cloth about Stanton's neck.

"There it was — his throat was cut from ear to ear."

Such a tale, told in 1869 and repeated, was reinforced by the newspapers, which on the day after Stanton's funeral stated that "only a few friends saw the face of the deceased." While they hinted nothing of suicide, they unwittingly sped the legend on its way. Surgeon-General Barnes, who attended Stanton, publicly denied the story in 1879, declaring that Stanton had suffered from almost every disease known to man unless it be small-pox. Asthma and head-pains had tortured him for years, his lungs were affected, and he died of congestion of the heart, said the army doctor who was with Stanton when he died. At the deathbed, too, were Stanton's wife, children, servants and clergyman, Dr. Starkey, all of whom backed Barnes' denial. Affidavits from Barnes and two servants branding the story as a lie was published in the Boston *Herald*, April 22, 1879, and laid responsibility for the "absurd and malicious" tale at the door of Richard Taylor, former Confederate general, who had hinted the thing broadly in his book, *Personal Experiences of the Late War*. Evidence was against the legend, but nevertheless it fitted itself into the crazy mosaic which the myth-makers were building, for whoever spoke of Stanton after his death, spoke of him in relation to Lincoln. In eulogy of him George Alfred Townsend, writing in the Chicago *Tribune* on December 30, 1869, said:

"While the President [Lincoln] jested, the Secretary of State gave dinners and the Secretary of the Treasury had ambitions for himself, Stanton was the one man alive to the fact that bloody rebellion was to be gashed, stabbed, fought, and humiliated."

In its old Copperhead hate of all Republicans, the Chicago *Times*, on December 25 of that year, was still sneering at Stanton, "The Great Energy."

"It was not creditable," said the *Times*, "to the President [Grant] and Congress that Stanton was a justice of the Supreme Court when he died, and there are good men who think they recognize the hand of a Providence guarding the Court just as there are good men who thought they recognized the hand of Providence in the murder of President Lincoln."

Stanton, who had given his life like any soldier to the Union, was soon bundled in a cocoon of myth — that myth that said that all great actors in and around Lincoln's death were doomed to tragedy. So it is not strange that people in an Indiana corntown whispered that Louis Weichmann, chief government witness at the famous Lincoln-conspiracy trial, walked the streets in fear of a violent end. Among the ex-Copperheads of Anderson it was said that Weichmann never turned his back upon a door, that he never sat between a lamp and a window and that in his breast he carried a derringer in readiness for that day, coming sometime, somewhere, when John Wilkes Booth, the escaped assassin, would hunt him out and revenge Mrs. Surratt. That Weichmann dreaded Booth is unlikely, for according to his sisters, he believed the actor dead. Neither is there evidence that he went armed, at least in his later years.

Louis Weichmann died naturally enough to disappoint the superstitious, but for all that, he was old and broken far beyond his sixty years, when, on June 2, 1902, the end came. He knew that his soul was drifting out of the window where the night-air, fresh with fragrance of young corn, drifted in. He called for a paper, his two sisters brought it, he dictated a statement, signed it, they witnessed it. What he wanted written had nothing to do with property, nor with money — nevertheless it was a bequest, a bequest, as he phrased it, "to all truth-loving people."

He was testifying again about Mary E. Surratt as he lay by the open window. This time he was before a new Court, and what he had to tell, now, was of even greater weight than had been his testimony in May, 1865, for death-bed statements are better than sworn testimony, the legal men say, arguing that no man will send his soul climbing up through the stars to God weighted down with a lie.

He testified again and died. His sisters folded up the paper and put it away. Their brother had wanted silence for himself; let silence keep his last words, too. Time, however, eases hurts, and the other day, sitting in the room where he had died, out in the west end of Anderson, grown now to be a clanging city of factories, these two aged women told in a word what their brother's dying testimony had been:

"When he was dying he asked us to get a pen and paper and told us to write: 'JUNE 2, 1902; THIS IS TO CERTIFY THAT EVERY WORD I GAVE IN EVIDENCE AT THE ASSASSINATION TRIAL WAS ABSOLUTELY TRUE; AND NOW I AM ABOUT TO DIE AND WITH LOVE I RECOMMEND MYSELF TO ALL TRUTH-LOVING PEOPLE.'

"Then he signed it 'Louis J. Weichmann' and died.

"The doctor when he filled out the death-certificate put down in the space after the word 'cause' just 'extreme nervousness' — that was all."

✭ ✭ ✭ 22 ✭ ✭ ✭

PHANTOM FOOTSTEPS

WHETHER LOUIS J. WEICHMANN DID or did not hear the phantom footsteps of J. Wilkes Booth following him through the Indiana corn-town is, after all, of no particular importance to the existence of the popular belief that Lincoln's assassin evaded justice. Out of that black welter of primitive emotion and superstition that followed Lincoln's assassination came a great American myth, rising very naturally on the wave of supernaturalism to spread across the land.

It had begun, as all myths begin, with some basis in fact, and it had been fed with crazy melodrama. The Union soldiers had killed a man, certainly, in Caroline County, Virginia, on the night of April 26, 1865. No mystery about that. The War Department had told the breathless nation that the man was J. Wilkes Booth. It had buried a corpse, sure enough, but was it Booth's?

From the day that the corpse had been brought down the Potomac to Washington, with people on the streets of the capital denying that it was the assassin's, millions of Americans believed that the real Booth was out and gone, skulking across the land in romantic wanderings, hiding under this or that alias, undisturbed by the law.

Had the United States Secret Service palmed off an innocent corpse on the nation, so that it might fraudulently collect the fifty thousand dollars reward that had been hung up to quicken Booth's pursuers? For two generations many Americans answered "Yes." Lumberjacks, sailors, brakemen in freight cabooses, cowboys around the wagons, farm-hands in the twilight of hot midland days, have answered "Yes," telling each other the story with ever-increasing detail.

Not all the believers in this folk-tale have been simple folk. Some shrewd minds have been convinced that it is true. Most American cities have had at least one capable citizen, usually an aged lawyer, whose hobby it was or is to prove that Booth evaded his pursuers. J. P. Simonton, for two-score years and more an expert on evidence in the Judge-Advocate's office of the War Department itself, searched the question through and through, lavishing years of his life on its most minute details, and when he left the service, honorably discharged because of his years, he still believed that the man whom the government killed and buried was *not* J. Wilkes Booth. In 1928, weary of the mad tangle and exhausted with the complexities of the thing, he gave up the chase. It must have been Booth, after all.

Official history has tried to outlaw the story of Booth's survival. Most pompous encyclopedias of national biography omit Booth altogether, as though to strike his name from man's memory, as the ancients erased the name of the youth who burned the temple at Ephesus. But out in the folk-mind of America, Booth has lived and still lives mightily, the story of his escape fattening on the silence of the War Department. Not once, among all the rumors and questions that champions of the mystery-tale have fired at it, has the War Department recognized that such a legend exists. It takes the position that it was right in 1865 when it announced that it had in hand Booth's freshly-killed body, and it will argue the question no further. In its secret archives are the left boot which Booth abandoned on his flight, when he halted to have his broken leg put in splints. There, too, it keeps the revolver which was taken from the man whom the cavalry killed twelve days after in the burning barn. It owns the affidavits of the detectives and soldiers who brought the body back, claiming that they recognized their prisoner as Booth from photographs which they carried. Investigators may study these, but the War Department itself has never pushed them toward the public. It stands to its guns: the body was Booth's.

In this official silence, superstitious minds have seen something deep, dark and mysterious. Even historians of note — at least one who is perhaps the greatest — has seen "something queer," something unexplained, in the attitude of the government toward the assassination of Lincoln and the handling of his alleged killer. Perhaps the believers in the escape of Booth may have been right when they said that all the persons who recognized the body in the 1865 autopsy were suborned witnesses, puppets under the thumb of a government which was in a frenzy to hide the body from the sight of men. Perhaps the War Department was so desperate to obliterate all memory of Booth from the nation's history that it rushed the wrong man to a secret grave.

For sixty-three years Booth's ghost, a will-o'-the-wisp, has stalked the Republic, no witness sufficiently impartial and free from suspicion having been found to swear that he looked upon the disputed corpse and knew it either to be or not to be J. Wilkes Booth.

No other mystery has lived so long nor so strongly in the Republic. Twenty men have been said to be the fugitive Booth in disguise, and their claims have come, one after another, to the tomb of Abraham Lincoln in Springfield, Ill., where the custodian, Herbert Wells Fay, patiently lists them and waits, with a philosophical smile, for more. Books have been written to prove the cases of several among these claimants. Reputed relatives of the assassin keep working their way into print with the story that Uncle John got away and lived, on funds supplied by the family, for years after his "official" death.

The mystery began with the belief that there was "something wrong" in the ease with which Booth escaped from Washington on the night of April 14. It deepened in the comic-opera stealth with which Stanton and his secret-service *poseurs* in late April handled the corpse of the man who had been killed in the burning barn.

However, such happenings, suspicious though they might be, were not enough, in and of themselves, to have produced a national myth. They were by no means strong enough to have established the very general belief that Booth had never been caught at all. And by all the laws of probability they would have been soon forgotten except for the fact that they were caught up in the hysteria that surrounded everything touching the martyred Lincoln.

The man who was said to be Booth was tucked into his secret grave on the night of April 27 in Washington while Lincoln's funeral was nearing the climax of its tempestuous journey, and scarcely a month later the rumors, suspicions and fancies had grown so common that newspapers were discussing them.

By June the myth had boiled up out of the folk-mind into print. Booth had been seen in the South, on ships bound for Mexico, or for South America, and columns so widely dissimilar as those of the St. Louis *Democrat* and the Buffalo *Courier*, for instance, gave the tale ample space. The Richmond *Examiner*, reviving the legend of the American pioneer clergyman who had been believed to be the missing French Dauphin, son of Louis XVI, whom the Parisian terrorists beheaded in 1793, was saying in its columns, "We may never know if the Rev. Eleazer Williams was Louis XVII, but we know Booth escaped."

The tale had fattened so rapidly by July, 1867, that Dr. John Frederick May, who had identified the body at the *Montauk* inquest, felt it necessary to make emphatic denial that he could have been wrong when he said, "That man is Booth."

Dr. May, who had been leisurely enough about obeying Stanton's order to aid in the autopsy back in 1865 — it took two commands to bring the surgeon aboard the ironclad — was now quick to fight the whispers of suspicion. But the very form of his testimony now added to the suspicion rather than cleared it up.

Some two years before the assassination of Lincoln, the doctor said, he had cut a tumor from the back of Booth's neck, warning him to keep off the stage until the wound healed. Booth, who never heeded orders from anybody, kept on playing and one night in a spirited love-scene with Charlotte Cushman was hugged so realistically by the emotional actress that his wound was reopened. Under Dr. May's care it healed, but left a large and jagged scar, and it was for this mark of his scalpel that the surgeon was to hunt upon the corpse that lay upon the *Montauk*.

"The cover was removed from the body," said May, in telling of his experience, "and to my great astonishment revealed a body in whose lineaments there was to me no resemblance to the man I had known in life. My surprise was so great that I at once said to General Barnes (Surgeon-General of the United States Army whom Stanton had sent to the inquest), 'There is no resemblance to Booth, nor can I believe it to be that of him.' After looking at it a few moments I asked, 'Is there a scar upon the back of his neck?'

"He replied, 'There is!'

"I then said, 'If that is the body of Booth, let me describe the scar before it is seen by man,' and did so as to its position, its size and general appearance so accurately as to cause him to say, 'You have described the scar as well as if you were looking at it.' The body being then turned, the back of the neck was examined and my mark unmistakably found by me upon it. And it being afterwards, at my request, placed in a sitting position, standing and looking down upon it, I was finally enabled to imperfectly recognize the features of Booth. But never in a human being had a greater change taken place, from the man in whom I had seen the vigor of health and life to that of the haggard corpse before me."

The surgeon's testimony failed to convince those who did not want to be convinced, particularly when, a little further down in his statement, he fell to discussing his examination of the *right* leg of the corpse that lay before him on the *Montauk*. It was the right leg that was broken, he said.

Now, by the word of the government itself, it was the *left* leg that Booth had broken in his jump from the theater-box on the night of the murder, and for a surgeon to note that the mysterious body had a broken *right* leg either proved one or the other of two things, the skeptics said: it proved that the body was not Booth's at all, or it proved that Dr. May was too careless an observer to be credited with any authority in the matter of the scarred neck.

Charles Dawson, the other civilian at the inquest, remembered that he had recognized Booth by the tattoo-marks "J. W. B." on his hand. From behind his desk at the National Hotel, Dawson said he had seen Booth sign the register many times and had once remarked to the actor, "What a fool you were to disfigure that pretty hand in such a way," pointing to the blue initials.

On board the *Montauk*, Dawson had found the tattoo-marks on the dead man's hand, correctly enough, so he maintained.

If Dawson told the truth, then the corpse that had been viewed at the inquest was Booth's beyond question, for J. Wilkes did have those tattoo-marks, and they had been seen upon him by Virginians during his flight. But Dawson's story failed to silence people who believed him to be, like the soldiers and detectives, too much under Stanton's thumb to be trusted.

Similarly, the doubting ones would not accept the troopers' account of Davy Herold's admission that Booth had been his companion in the burning barn. As he had crawled out of the blazing shed to surrender, Herold had told Lieutenant Doherty that he didn't know who his bed-fellow was. "He said his name was Boyd," Davy added.

According to the testimony of his captors, however, Herold had broken down on the way back to Washington, and had admitted that his comrade had been Booth rightly enough. Officially, Herold's latter statement was accredited, but the skeptics scouted it, asking if Davy had not changed his story under pressure.

Suspicion thrived, and it was not long before the Louisville *Journal* was publishing open charges that "General Baker and his associates had wilfully conspired to swindle the United States Treasury" and that "there are three men in the United States who have seen J. Wilkes Booth since what purported to be his mortal remains were dragged by those infuriated bloodhounds into Washington. He was recognized through his disguise on the twenty-seventh of April, 1865, on board a vessel which carried him far beyond the reach of supposed avengers. Again he was seen by a gentleman in the month of September, 1865, and there is a young man in this city today who saw him no longer than August, 1866, and conversed with him."

During 1867 the *Journal* continued its "revelations," publishing a letter from a Professor Frazier of Bombay, India, who told how a certain Captain Tolbert, a privateer, had won bets from dubious travelers by taking them to see the "real" J. Wilkes Booth where he was hiding on some island in Oriental seas. This tale zigzagged across the Republic.

So much newspaper discussion had arisen by 1869 that President Johnson decided to dispose of all rumors and to allow the assassin's brother, Edwin, to bury the disputed corpse in the family lot, a privilege which the Booths had been requesting for many months. On February 15, 1869, government employees dug up the body that Dr. Porter had buried under the arsenal-warehouse floor on the midnight of April 27, 1865. With it came up the bodies of the four Lincoln conspirators who had been hanged. Waiting relatives claimed all of these corpses except Powell's. His the government took to a Washington cemetery.

The time had come to settle once and for all the rumors about J. Wilkes Booth's fate. Now the murderer's family could dispel the mystery by identifying the body. But Edwin, conscious of the family's shame, tried to keep the exhumation and reburial secret, and bungled the identification most tragically. He could not bring himself to look upon the body, and remained outside the undertaker's rooms — one report had it that he waited in Ford's Theater, of all places — while the pine box was opened. Friends acted for him in examining the body and agreed, so it was reported, that the body was that of J. Wilkes Booth. But who these friends were and what proofs they found were not detailed to the curious public. Briefly it was announced that J. Wilkes' dentist had identified the body by certain fillings in his teeth, but who the dentist was remained a secret. Nothing systematic was set down for the public's eye, nothing more definite than the receipt of the body by the Greenmount Cemetery in Baltimore, where slept old Junius Brutus Booth and others of his brood.

To make matters more perplexing, the Baltimore *Gazette* was soon claiming that one of its reporters had been present at the exhumation and had noted that the body had a broken *right* leg and that no bullet-wound was visible upon it. This reporter denied one of General Baker's assertions, made in 1867, namely, that army surgeons had removed from the dead Booth's neck vertebrae which had been shattered by the Union bullet. No vertebrae were missing in this exhumed corpse, said the newspaper man.

Historians and scholars might say that the reporter had let his fancy run away with him in his morbid excitement, or that he had lied, or that he had simply made a mistake as had Dr. May, but the plain people who believed the myth only saw it as new evidence that Booth had never been caught.

Under such circumstances it is no wonder that, before long, various dark-haired, pallid men who walked with a limp, began to be pointed out as J. Wilkes Booth.

In the '80s devout ladies of Richmond, Virginia, sitting in their pews at Monumental Church, would thrill strangely as they looked up at their minister, the Rev. J. G. Armstrong, standing in the pulpit and giving the devil his regular Sunday flogging. Pastor Armstrong's eye was black, his raven hair was long, his sermons were dramatic and he dragged one leg as he walked. Many a Virginia lady's thoughts, as she listened, would not be touching God, or the devil either. Instead she would be saying to herself, "I wonder if he really is J. Wilkes Booth."

In Atlanta, where the Rev. Mr. Armstrong later preached, and in other Southern cities, the whispers followed him around. After a bit there was a story that Edwin Booth, seeing the dominie watching him from a theater-box one night in Atlanta, was so startled by the man's resemblance to his brother that he arranged a private interview after the show. Rumor had it that Armstrong wore his hair long in the back to hide a tell-tale scar. All claims evaporated when his history was examined after his death, in 1891, but there are still simple folk in the South who hold to them in fond romance.

Sometime in the late '70s a drunken saloon-keeper of Granbury, Texas, confessed to a gaping boy from Memphis that he was the genuine J. Wilkes Booth, and related a detailed story of how Vice-President Johnson had put him up to the assassination of Lincoln, furnishing him with the password, "T. B. Road," so that he might escape through the Union picket-lines, and promising him a pardon if ever he should be caught. The saloon-keeper, known to Granbury as John St. Helen, a ruffian of sportive instincts, made much of a scar on the back of his neck, and convinced the greenhorn traveler that his tale was true, although the townspeople of Granbury remembered that he had acquired the scar by a knife in a brawl at his groggery.

The youth, Finis L. Bates by name, grew up to be a lawyer in Memphis, and dallied with the tale. In 1903, while touring the Southwest on business, he read that a man claiming to be Booth had committed suicide in Enid, Oklahoma. Arriving at the frontier town, he found it in a state of delighted fervor over the romance, and exhibiting the suicide's body with pride. Through its newspaper it was crying to the world that here was the escaped hero-villain, although its people had known the fellow as David E. George, a drunken morphine-fiend. Twice at least in his life George had declared that he was not the innocent house-painter that he seemed to be, but the real and genuine J. Wilkes Booth. Both confessions had been made while he was bedfast from drugs, a fact that did not hamper the credulity of Finis L. Bates in the least. The lawyer, looking upon George's remains, jumped to the conclusion that here was his great informant of Granbury, Texas, a quarter of a century before, John St. Helen. The two men, he declared, were one, and that one — Booth. Whereupon Bates brought the suicide's body back to Memphis, where it rests today, owned by the Bates' heirs, often exhibited across the South and Southwest in its mummified state at ten cents or twenty-five cents a look, and occasionally offered for sale to the Lincoln Monument custodian, to Henry Ford, or others.

Bates, now long since dead with his pathetic dreams, wrote

the claims of John St. Helen and David E. George into a curious book which he called, *The Escape and Suicide of John Wilkes Booth, or the First True Account of Lincoln's Assassination, Containing a Complete Confession by Booth, Many Years After His Crime.* This book, read by thousands and thousands of eager-eyed believers in the folk-story, fanned the smouldering mystery flame briskly in the years following its publication in 1907. Bates had interviewed soldiers who had taken part in the pursuit and had trailed sentries who had been on the Navy Yard bridge the night Booth passed them, spurring out of Washington, and his conclusions made, for uncritical readers, a convincing story of the charges that "higher-ups" had been implicated. Also Bates' book gave to the population which cherished the escape-tale the one concluding proof it craved; it named the man who had been killed in the burning barn in place of Booth — a Virginian named Roddy.

Being a lawyer, Bates marshaled his evidence cleverly — probably sincerely, too, for his wistful eagerness indicated derangement rather than deceit. Even those rationalists who doubted the stories of St. Helen and George, were puzzled by his explanation of how Booth fled the Garrett farm. As this version went, Booth struck off through the woods at the sight of pursuing soldiers in the neighborhood, and worked his way westward to safety. A Virginian of the community, Roddy by name, had been assisting the fugitives, and had been sleeping in the barn with Herold when the troopers came and shot him down. In his pockets Roddy was carrying some of Booth's effects, which had slipped out of their owner's coat by accident and which Roddy had picked up.

The publication of this book was followed by a flood of pamphlets that supported its claims, interviews from self-styled relatives of Booth who "verified" it, statements of persons who insisted that this or that portion of it was known by them to be true.

In Oak Harbor, Ohio, a certain John Murphy used to swear that John Wilkes Booth once stopped all night at his house while fleeing to Canada. In the Southwest there grew up one of the wildest of all variants of the story, the explanation that Booth owed his escape from Union troopers to his membership in a powerful fraternal order, which spirited him away rather than see him hanged.

Soon Booth's skull was on simultaneous view in different side-shows and carnivals across the country. Col. James Hutton, veteran theatrical manager of Chicago, and himself a relative of the Confederate cavalry-leader General Forrest, found five of the assassin's skulls so exhibited in the year 1925. Hutton, too, insists today that his family, once powerful in the Confederacy, shares with two or three other Southern clans the secret of where Booth is buried, a secret which will never be disclosed.

This legend that Booth does not sleep in the family burial-lot in Greenmount Cemetery, Baltimore, has had ardent champions. Many Union veterans, aged and dramatic, have claimed that they were among the four infantrymen whom Dr. Porter employed to bury secretly the body which the two Bakers brought into the old arsenal grounds at Washington that midnight of April 27, 1865. Most of these mysterious old men have died refusing to tell what was done with the body, and their secrecy and their narratives, which conflicted at many points, only served to convince more and more people that there was indeed "something queer" about the United States government's handling of J. Wilkes Booth.

Another story, occasionally told past the turn of the century, was that the government held Booth's skeleton in the National Museum at Washington, which for a time was the remodeled Ford's Theater of tragic memory. Evidently this was a confusion of Booth with Charles Guiteau, murderer of President Garfield, for that assassin's skeleton was at the Museum rightly enough.

Pure fancy, utterly free of fact, has loved to linger around everything connected with Booth. Even the firearm with which he was said to have been shot, was, not long ago, preserved near Bowling Green, Ohio. It was a rifle, which the villagers awesomely admired in this Ohio town whose name, by a curious coincidence, is the same as that of the Virginia hamlet hard by the Garrett farmstead, while as a matter of fact it was with a six-shooting revolver that Boston Corbett did the actual killing.

As late as 1924, editions were being printed of a curious book which argued that Booth, as a secret convert to Roman Catholicism, had killed Lincoln in obedience to the demands of Jesuit plotters. Under the confident title of *The Suppressed Truth About the Assassination of Abraham Lincoln,* one Burke McCarty, styling himself "ex-Romanist," revived, in this tract, the many tales current in 1865 — one that Booth had gone to a "residence opposite the Cathedral in Baltimore" and joined the "Knights of the Golden Circle," secret pro-Southern society. This was significant, McCarty thought, and added, among other more figmentary "proofs," a statement purporting to have come from Rear Admiral George A. Baird, U.S.N., who, on November 29, 1921, declared that he had been on board the *Montauk* when Booth's body was identified, and that he had seen naval officers take a small Roman Catholic medal from the dead man's throat. This medal, said Baird, was kept for years with other Booth souvenirs in the Judge-Advocate's office in Washington, but that when he asked to see it in 1895 it had disappeared.

Collectors of Lincolniana might list McCarty's "revelations" under their library headings of "Crank Lincoln Literature," and historians might unanimously dismiss it as merely comic, but the "ex-Romanist's" book was to be handed around significantly in the near-illiterate sections of the Republic during the flare-up of religious antagonisms as late as the political campaign of 1928.

So widely had the mystery of Booth's fate spread at the beginning of the twentieth century, that trained investigators, literary explorers, began to examine it to see if it was worthy of credence. If they took the statements of the troopers and detectives who saw the man killed at Garrett's barn, and if they added the verdict of the autopsy-committee as old records preserve them, then there was never any mystery. If they examined all the claims of the pretenders to Boothdom, as did F. L. Black of Detroit, they found them transparently false. But not one eye-witness, sufficiently impartial to be above suspicion, could they find to prove that the body as viewed in 1865 was, beyond question, that of Lincoln's murderer.

In the Summer of 1928 a myth-hunter came to Virginia chasing the old, old story. By chance some octogenarian of this section where Booth had played and died, might have new evidence on the question of the assassin's survival.

"See E. V. Valentine," everybody said.

To the Valentine home in Richmond many myth-hunters have come whenever ancient fact seemed lost in the jumbled prints of phantom footsteps. In his late eighties Valentine is razor-keen on myriad details of the past. As a sculptor he led a cosmopolitan life, carving scores of celebrities in marble, and knowing the private lives of the great and the near-great as few Americans have known them. His studio in Richmond is now a civic exhibit, and his mind a gallery of biographical and historical portraits.

"Did Booth get away?"

The patriarch repeated the question, musingly, as he sat looking out over the city where the twilight was beginning to hide the long elms of the avenues and the stone Confederates who are forever riding across the thoroughfare.

"I never say 'Yes' to that question and I never say 'No,' for I have no evidence. But there is one man still alive who can solve that question. He has never talked about it, and I'm not at liberty to give you his name. He's a reserved man, and not one to come out and say what he knows. In 1865 he stood over the body that lay on Garrett's porch and looked down into its face, and he knows whether it was John Wilkes Booth lying there or not."

Valentine was silent for a time, the ember-end of his traditionally long cheroot brightening and fading as he rocked in the Virginia dusk.

Then he spoke again, quickly. "It's time that Booth mystery was cleared up, one way or the other. It's time this friend of mine talked. I'll tell you what I'll do: I'll ask him to tell what he saw. You call me tomorrow and, if I have him persuaded, I'll give you his name and where to find him. One thing you can count on, if he tells you anything it will be the truth. You can count on that."

People in Richmond are pretty apt to do what the sculptor-patriarch, Valentine, asks them to do — he is that kind of man — and on the morrow which he had promised, his voice came like a young man's, "See Mr. William B. Lightfoot at 1717 Hanover Avenue. He's the gentleman I told you of and he'll tell you what he knows."

Soon William B. Lightfoot was telling it in the parlor of his home.

"I was just back from Appomattox a few days when it happened," he began. A tall, florid man he is, like Valentine in his late eighties, a little anxious now to be done with the past and to get downtown to his insurance office, where he spends his days. "I'd been in Company B of the 9th Virginia Cavalry, Gen. William H. F. Lee's brigade, and I'd come home with my horse from the surrender — Grant let us keep our horses — he was a gentleman, sir — a great man.

"My home was in Port Royal in Caroline County, and I was eating breakfast when I heard talk about some shooting up at Garrett's farm, four miles away. I hurried up there and saw Union cavalrymen all around and a man lying on the porch. I edged up and looked at him; he'd been dead, they said, about an hour. Blood had run from his wound all over the porch where he was lying. I didn't get into the talk or make any inquiries, only stood and listened. You see I still had on my torn Confederate uniform and had my parole in my pocket and I didn't want to be too prominent in front of those Union soldiers whom I'd been fighting not much more than two weeks before. They'd been all over the country for days, picking up any lame man and questioning him.

"But I was close enough to hear what they said and they were all saying that it was Booth dead there on the porch. I stayed around until Doctor Urquhart was brought up from Port Royal and had pronounced the man dead. Then the soldiers wrapped the body in a blanket and put it in Ned Freeman's wagon — Ned was a negro laborer about a quarter of a mile down the road. I followed the wagon back to Port Royal and saw it cross the Rappahannock over to Port Conway on the other side and go off toward the Potomac. Then I went home.

"You want to know if that body was Booth's? Well, I'll tell

you; I never saw Booth in real life, but I knew his picture; had seen it many, many times, for he was a great stage favorite in Richmond before the war and his photographs, like those of other actors, were to be seen everywhere. I would have recognized him from his photographs and, sir, I did. I knew him right away, and never thought of it being possible that it could be anybody else. The dead man on Garrett's porch was John Wilkes Booth.

"Another thing; I knew the Garretts. Richard Garrett was an honorable man and he never had any doubts, after the killing, that the fellow had been Booth. The man who was killed was the same man who had come to his house begging shelter two days before. As a notary public I took down Garrett's story when he put in a bill to the government for the barn the soldiers had burned. He lost his case.

"And there was always one queer thing about that barn. The center post, against which Booth was leaning just before they shot him, didn't burn. Next day everything was burned up but it. It stood up there, sir, all blackened but still sound, mighty strangely, in all the ashes."

✡ ✡ ✡ 23 ✡ ✡ ✡

"THE GLORY-TO-GOD MAN"

IN ALL THIS LUDICROUS-TERRIFIC AFTERMATH of Lincoln's assassination there is one sunbeam — Boston Corbett, the mad hatter. Insanity had a peculiar focus upon Washington, D. C., in that month of April, 1865, and many a later historian would have gone mad among its tangles but for the occasional appearances among the yellowing pages of Corbett the Clown.

School children get to see none of his antics. He is to them merely the briefly thrilling sergeant who revenged Lincoln by shooting John Wilkes Booth. It is only those dull drones, the scholars, who have known Corbett in his full stature as "the Glory-to-God man."

His parents had named him Thomas P. when he had been born to them in 1832. The event had taken place in England, but by the time the boy was seven years of age the family had emigrated to America, settling in Troy, New York, so he grew up an American.

In Troy he learned the trade of hat-finisher, and speedily became a journeyman, at least he is recorded as having worked in Albany, New York, Richmond and Boston. It was while he was in New York that he married — evidently very young — and met sorrow, his wife dying in childbirth with her infant daughter's body already cold beside her. The young husband took to liquor for solace, went to Boston to work and was headed down-grade when the religious workers converted him.

On the streets of Boston one night he stopped to listen to street-evangelists and was saved. Under the preacher's words Corbett saw himself revealed as a sinner. His fondness for hard liquor loomed as a gaudy crime; his soul swam up before him as a precious thing, demanding sacrifices, and, with the great news on his lips, he marched to the mourners' bench and joined up for life.

Choosing the Methodist Episcopal Church, he cast about for a Christian name under which to be crowned, saying that Christ had given his disciples new names when he called them, and now he, the convert, must follow the example. He thought and thought about this, and finally, wishing to honor suitably the city of his rebirth, he settled upon the name "Boston." The "Thomas P." disappeared, and Boston Corbett he became.

His life now had a purpose — Reform.

Great days set in. Every evening when the sun went down he struck off, full of supper and glory, to help the street-evangelists with their salvage. But instead of helping, he nearly ruined them. They found it impossible to be heard above their new convert's shrill exultations. His ecstatic shouts of "Come to Christ" and "Glory to God" drowned out everything else, and at length, harassed too far by their prize, the street-preachers blessed him and convinced him that it would be better for him to carry on alone.

He nearly ruined Samuel Mason, Jr., too — Mason being his

employer at the time. Hat-finishing in those days was a matter of coördinating hands. The workmen sat in long rows, passing hats from hand to hand as each man did his bit. All day Boston Corbett sat in such a line — or rather *had* sat in such a line, for after his conversion, nothing could keep him in place very long. Whenever one of his comrades dropped an oath, a wish for a drink, or any careless obscenity, down Boston would go on his knees and up would go Boston's voice in interminable prayer. Naturally, the hats had to wait until he was back in the chain once more. Naturally, too, Samuel Mason, Jr., began to teeter on the brink of bankruptcy, and he was not to be saved until, like the evangelists, he had blessed his workman and let him go.

Eight years later, when Corbett had become a national hero, Mason's daughter was shown Corbett's latest photograph. She said, "They must have cut his hair in the army, for when he was here, he wore it like Jesus Christ, long and parted in the middle."

It is 1858 before anything is recorded of him again. Between July 16 and August 18 he is down on the books of the Massachusetts General Hospital as receiving treatments for "self-castration." Two street-walkers had ogled him horribly and unbearably one night as he prayed from his soap-box and, crying out that his usefulness to the world must not be wrecked by "bad thoughts," he leaped off his perch and broke for home, where he mutilated himself.

For the next three years Corbett wandered through Eastern cities preaching, finishing hats and spending his income on religious tracts which he gave away on the streets. Righteousness flared in his soul and prompted him to reform things right and left wherever he went. In Richmond, Virginia, he attempted to convert the South from the sin of holding slaves, and was speedily chased out of town. In a New York hat-factory on Broadway he worked for an employer who bought old hats, reblocked them to look like new and sold them for $5 each. To Boston this was immoral, since the hats were worth no more than $3.50 apiece as he estimated values, and he shook the dust of so sinful a place off his shoes.

For the South in the growing political crisis he had righteous anger, and when the storm broke he was one of the first to respond to Lincoln's call for Union volunteers, enlisting on the twelfth of April, 1861. A little before, he had nearly caused a panic among the ladies of his church by declaring in a religious harangue that he was going to enlist and shoot men on sight.

"I will say to them, 'God have mercy on your souls'—then pop them off," he had announced.

As a private in the 12th New York Militia he was soon in uniform, but not even the loss of his Messianic haircut or the rigorous drilling could down his illusion of saving the world by grace, and in a few days his comrades were calling him "the Glory-to-God man." Night and morning he prayed in his tent, despite the jeers of his comrades.

On one of those days of drilling in Franklin Square, New York, Colonel Butterfield, commanding the regiment, burst out in uncontrollable profanity at the awkwardness of his recruits. Boston Corbett stepped forth from the ranks and saluted. The officer must have gasped.

"Colonel, don't you know you are breaking God's law?" asked the private firmly but kindly.

"Take him to the guardhouse," howled Butterfield.

That, however, seemed no punishment for the Christian martyr, for the baffled colonel could hear the prisoner within shouting hymns with fervor. Ordered to stop his racket, Corbett only sang the louder. Butterfield sent him word that he would be liberated if he would apologize for having insulted his superior officer. Corbett told the messenger to say to the colonel, "No, I have only offended the colonel, while the colonel has offended God, and I shall never ask the colonel's pardon until he himself has asked pardon of God."

In the face of such determined logic there was nothing for the officer to do but turn the prisoner loose, and Corbett came up smiling with the Good Book under his arm and announcing in tones that rang, "I had a good time in there with my God and my Bible."

He was always a problem to his superiors, and he spent many of those early days in the guardhouse, wearing a knapsack loaded with bricks as a punishment for insubordination. As he paced his jail-beat, Testament in hand, he preached and cried out against swearing, intemperance and the like, and called upon his wild companions to "seek the Lord."

Toward the close of his first enlistment he announced that his time would expire on a certain date at midnight. His officers explained that the records showed the date to be several days later. Corbett made no reply, but when his chosen midnight came, he walked coolly off sentry-post and began packing up his things in his tent. Arresting him, his officers held a court-martial and sentenced him to "death for desertion." Before the date of execution Colonel Butterfield appealed to Lincoln, who pardoned him. The next day he reënlisted, in fact he reënlisted three times before the war was done, for in spite of everything in his record, colonels were glad to get him. He was a hell-cat in battle.

Colonel Mosby, the Confederate raider, who was considerable of a hell-cat himself, met Corbett once and admired him. It was in June, 1864, when Corbett was a member of the 16th New York Cavalry, that he was cornered with a squad of men by Mosby at Culpeper Court House. Those of his companions who had not been shot down escaped, and soon no one faced the foe but the emasculated zealot. He refused to surrender and put up such a single-handed fight that he held twenty-six Confederates at bay. When his ammunition gave out, he was for clubbing his foes, and would have been shot down by the gray riders if Mosby, relenting, had not struck up their rifles and told them to bring him the brave fellow alive. Before them all the dare-devil colonel complimented Corbett — and sent him to the dubious reward of Andersonville prison.

Corbett credited God with the showing he made, describing the incident later: "I faced and fought against a whole column of them, all alone, none but God being with me to help me, my being in a large field and they being in the road with a high board-fence between us enabled me to hold out as long as I did. They finally had the fence torn down, then closed around me when my pistol gave out, giving me no more fire. I was captured by them and sent to Andersonville, Ga.

"There God was good to me, sparing my life while another and myself lived to return out of fourteen men of my own company. But, bless the Lord, a score of souls were converted right on the spot where I lay for three months with no shelter. Many others were converted, for meetings were held in different parts of the 'bull pen.'"

Andersonville was not to be for him the death-trap that it was to so many Union captives. In that sink of despair he worked like a Christian in the arena of Rome, as chipper as ever, preaching, exhorting, saving souls in the caves where gaunt prisoners sold each other rats for food. His courage waxed rather than waned, and in a few months he escaped, only, as luck would have it, to be speedily recaptured by bloodhounds. Now the strain began to tell on his health and he was drooping when, on November 19, 1864, five months after his capture he was exchanged by his captors as worthless.

But there was no downing the man. Even the chronic diarrhea that wasted him could not keep him out of the fighting, and after a resting-spell in the hospital at Annapolis, and a mere thirty days' furlough, he was back with his regiment in Washington, joining it just before Lee's surrender.

Sick, ravaged by the horrors of his prison, he nevertheless toiled for the Lord, writing to his pastor in February: "Do try and lead him [an acquaintance] to Jesus. Brother Irvine is here with me and we often kneel together and besiege the throne of grace and bless God. He makes us happy in His love. We do not forget our pastors and churches and brethren and we feel that we are not forgotten by those whom we have left for awhile. Last night another brother, who belonged to our regiment, had a season of prayer with us after reading the Word, and we three were just as happy as in a Big Meeting. Brother Corbett shouted and nobody was hurt by it. Glory to God."

By April he was back at regimental headquarters applying for reinstatement, and his papers came just as Lee surrendered.

The regiment was stationed at Vienna, Virginia, twelve miles out of Washington, on Saturday, April 15, when the news came that Lincoln was killed. Like the other regiments of the Army of the Potomac, it rushed out to search and scout for the fugitive Booth and his silly-boy follower, Davy Herold, who had fled somewhere. Detachments of the regiments rode out on clues or stood guard in Washington, or paraded in the Lincoln funeral procession during the days that followed.

On Sunday night, April 23, the "Glory-to-God man" spoke at McKendry Chapel, a soul-saving center of the city. He had spoken there before, had, in fact, made a great nuisance of himself at the place more than once with his never-ending bellows, but this visit was remarkable, according to the story he told some days later, when he had become a national idol. He had prayed, he said, with great earnestness that God would not lay innocent blood to the charge of the North, but that He would bring the guilty to punishment. He had announced — so he recollected later — his assurance that Booth would be delivered into his hands as a reward for his prayers.

The next afternoon he was the sergeant of a detachment which volunteered at Major-General Hancock's call for a squad to accompany two secret-service operatives, Colonel Conger and Lieutenant Baker, on a new trail across the Rappahannock River. For ten days the hunt had been wild and fumbling. A fresh scent had been disclosed by a negro countryman, and at 2 P.M. Corbett and twenty-five troopers set out under Lieutenant Doherty to escort the detectives.

Deep in the night of Tuesday the twenty-fifth, the trail grew hot and at two in the morning the fugitives were treed in the Garrett tobacco barn. The standing order was that no one should fire without orders, the government's wish being that the desperadoes be taken alive. Lieutenant Doherty found his men so saddle-sore and weary that he assigned each one a stick, post, stone or minor landmark to be sure that they did not stray away. Sergeant Corbett's place was at the side of the building some thirty feet from it.

There were arguments through the door between Booth and the detectives, some appeals for peaceable surrender from without, and some defiances from within. Finally Herold emerged with twitters and quavers, and was bound. When it became apparent that Booth preferred to talk rather than surrender, the detectives who knew of Lieutenant Doherty's concern lest Secession sympathizers might rally in force and rescue the assassin, fired the barn.

Corbett complained to his superiors that his position, opposite a particularly large crack in the barn's sheeting, put him in danger from Booth's gun. They paid no heed.

The flames rose, popping and snapping. Smoke and flames hid Booth, revealed him, hid him again. A shot cracked above the reports of the burning wood and Booth fell. Lieutenant Baker, who had been peering in at the door, sprang inside and dropped beside the wounded man. Conger came tumbling in, crying, "He shot himself." Baker retorted, "He didn't either! The man who shot him should go back to Washington tonight in irons."

But the man who had killed Booth was not only free of irons but very full of triumph as the cavalcade started back for Washington.

God had spoken to Corbett as of old. Voices had called from the unseen, and their servant had left his post, stepped nearer to the crack, taking careful aim with his pistol resting across his arm, and had shot Booth in the back of the head — a remarkable shot, as he promptly admitted.

Conger, passing Corbett while Booth was being carried out of the inferno, asked, "Why did you fire against orders?"

Corbett, preening himself in the glare of the mounting flames, put Conger in his place by citing a higher command.

"God Almighty directed me," he replied.

"I guess He did," observed Conger, "or you could never have hit Booth through that crack in the barn."

It was as a hero that the sergeant rode into Washington. The telegraph carried his fame across the nation. His photographs were soon selling like Sheridan's, all over the North. Whenever reporters interviewed him, which was many times each day, he gave credit to God, since he had prayed for guidance as he aimed at Booth. The fact that his bullet had struck Booth at almost the same spot in the skull as that at which Booth's had struck Lincoln, proved to Corbett that the Lord had directed him. As he fired, too, he had prayed for Booth's soul.

"I always make such prayers when shooting rebels," he added.

On the witness-stand at the trial of the conspirators whom the government was trying to link to the dead Booth, the "Glory-to-God man" implied that he was superior to man-made rules. "I saw Booth make a movement toward the door," he said. "I supposed he was going to fight his way out. One of the men who was watching him told me that he aimed his carbine at me. He was taking aim, but at whom I could not say. My mind was upon him attentively to see that he did no harm, and when I became impressed that it was time, I shot him."

For this, his most flagrant insubordination, Corbett was never punished. In the face of the popular hurrah for the sergeant, the War Department could do nothing to discipline him, although his disobedience had cheated the administration out of its expectation to hang Booth as a spectacular lesson to all ex-rebels and rebels-to-be. Congress did chastise him somewhat by allowing him no more of the reward than was given to each of the other troopers. In company with the privates he received his share, $1,653.85, while Lieutenant Doherty received $5,250, Lieutenant Baker $3,000, Colonel Baker $3,750, and Colonel Conger $15,000. The remainder of the sum placed on the heads of the fugitives, $50,000 on Booth's and $25,000 on Herold's, was divided among other detectives, telegraph operators, and others who had helped to locate the trail of the fleeing pair.

In the comic scramble for this blood-money — a scramble which rocked Congress and the War Department — many demanded that the heroic Corbett be given a lion's share, but in the jockeying he was nosed out, many newspapers bemoaning the fact that he was not even promoted for his deed. To the newspaper men who kept him surrounded in those days, Corbett said that he wished no reward for having done what God had told him it was his duty to do.

"He remarked, however," said the New York *Tribune* man, "that if the government wished to reward him and would allow him to keep his little saddle horse when his term of service was over, it would be all he could wish.

"'He isn't very valuable,' he said, 'but I've got so attached to him that I would like to take him home.'"

Before he was mustered out on August 17, 1865, Lieutenant

Doherty commended him highly, declaring that "in military capacity he is second to none in the service."

Back in civil life again, Corbett, like more modern heroes of sensational trials, took to the lecture platform. Churches, ladies' clubs, Sunday schools, religious leagues, patriotic bodies, besought him to address them. But they never besought him more than once. His addresses turned into wild incoherencies on religion, and before long the patriots and even the church-folk found their curiosity degenerating into yawns.

Soon he was finishing hats again in the shop of Samuel Mason, Jr., who now looked upon his troublesome employee with patriotic eye. This work, too, failed a little later, when the style in men's headgear changed, throwing the hat-finishers out of their jobs. Corbett, returning to soul-saving, obtained the post of lay-preacher for a poor congregation of Methodist Episcopalians in Camden, New Jersey. Here he lasted a few months before his flock blessed him and shoved him on.

He is next heard from in 1878, homesteading land at Concordia, Kansas. Farming seems to have been too slow for one who had known the rush of fame, and Corbett was soon varying his toil in the field with that of the vineyards, preaching up and down the countryside as loud as ever.

For the Kansans he worked up his most ambitious lecture upon the Booth affair, and he gave it with some success, at first. Lantern slides illustrated it now, slides showing himself before the killing of Booth, after the killing of Booth, with the patriotic pistol, without it, slides of Lincoln and Tad, of four conspirators hanging by their necks, of what not.

Then the old story—the lecture vanishing in shouts of "Glory to God," people nodding in their seats, stamping out to untie their horses and be off for home across the Kansas night-roads. The Kansans, too, blessed him and shoved him on.

In the next decade Corbett was a wanderer, preaching, canvassing, fiddling about, trifling with great energy. Sometime in 1886 the Grand Army of the Republic obtained for him a door-keeper's post with the Kansas State Legislature and for a time the honor of this sufficed. But on the morning of February 15, 1887, he quietly locked the doors while the State Representatives debated and drowsed, and, without noise, drew forth two large revolvers. With his very best evangelistic voice he informed the Legislators that God demanded their lives, and promptly cut loose with both guns.

Jehovah, however, did not direct these bullets as well for him as He had that April night near Bowling Green, far away, for Corbett hit none of the frenzied solons as they tore about the room, hiding behind waste-paper baskets, trying to claw their way up smooth walls into the balcony, or butting wildly at the locked doors.

Corbett was pacified in time to prevent blood-letting; the lawmakers patted him on the back for services to the flag; the old soldiers wished him well and he was shoved on again — this time into the Kansas asylum for the insane at Topeka.

Stone walls had never a prison made to Corbett, and the man who had escaped from Andersonville could not reasonably be expected to rot in an ordinary madhouse. So it is not surprising to find him, a year and a quarter afterward, written off the asylum's books as "escaped."

On May 26, 1888, Corbett with other inmates of the madhouse had been marching along a road in the grounds when they saw a boy ride up, tie his horse to a post and wander off sightseeing about the institution. As the men filed past the horse, Corbett broke from the ranks, scrambled into the saddle and was off.

A week later he appeared at Neodesha on this horse, and finding in the town an old comrade from Andersonville days, told his story, complaining bitterly at the shameful treatment his nation had given him and adding that he was going to Mexico.

This was the last his legal guardian, Judge Huron of Topeka, ever heard of him, although in 1905 it was thought that he had been discovered in Dallas, Texas. Investigation proved that the Dallas "Corbett" was an impostor and the mystery of where the mad hatter went remained unanswered. In 1901 Osborn H. Oldroyd, the collector of Lincolniana, had traced Corbett to Oklahoma.

"Corbett has for the past four years been a traveling salesman for a Topeka patent-medicine concern," wrote Oldroyd. "His territory is Oklahoma and Texas and his headquarters and home are in Enid, Oklahoma. He is now sixty-two years old."

While it is likely that Oldroyd was mistaken as to Corbett's age, the hero having been described in his 1865 biographies as being born in England in 1832, the evidence of Corbett's residence in Enid, Oklahoma, may have been more accurate.

Enid, curiously enough, was the very town, of all tiny towns in the Southwest, where died the mysterious house-painter, David E. George, alias John St. Helen, or vice versa, who testified upon his deathbed that he was the only real and genuine John Wilkes Booth. That Corbett's drift to Enid was in any way connected with this pretended Booth is unlikely, for while George had lived for several years, according to the vague story, in and around this section of Oklahoma, it was not until mid-April, 1902, that he is reported to have breathed his claims to any living person. On that date the bibulous Mr. George was lodging in El Reno, a town not far from Enid, and, fearing that he was going to die, confessed his true name and horrible identity to his landlady and to a clergyman and his wife who were fellow roomers. Recovering, as an uncomfortable anticlimax, he had been testy about the revelation, so the legend goes, and his confidants concealed the matter, if indeed they gave it any credence. Finally the man, who had moved to an Enid hotel in December, 1902, killed himself there on January 14, 1903, repeating his gaudy tale to bedside listeners upon this occasion as he had before.

If Corbett was still alive when this hoax commanded so much gullible credence and such wide newspaper support in Oklahoma, it must have been something of a shock to have his famous deed so discounted. Probably he was dead, but even if he had been alive he would have been seventy-one, too old to have put up much of a fight against the story of the credulous Southwesterners.

One can only speculate upon his end. Myth-makers are welcome to play with it. How satisfying to them to tell a tale about Boston Corbett, the old, old man, meeting his supposed victim of a generation before on the streets of Enid, Oklahoma, and falling dead from the shock, even as he reached for his gun to kill his man again.

It is more likely that Corbett went to glory in some Oklahoma drug-store, stricken suddenly as he pinned some gaping clerk to the counter with windy threats of a righteous and awful vengeance to come.

PART THREE

ALTAR SMOKE

"The shapes arise." — WALT WHITMAN.

✣ ✣ ✣ 24 ✣ ✣ ✣

MYTHS AT THE TOMB OF LINCOLN

THERE IS NO WAY of telling just when the principal myth began.

Nobody can be exactly sure when the American people took it into their heads to start the legend that Abraham Lincoln's tomb was empty. One thing, only, is certain; the whisper has run so far and run so long that it has bobbed up every day in the year, through the 1920s, to bedevil the custodian, Herbert Wells Fay, the old-time prairie editor and collector, who presided over the Lincoln monument-tomb in Springfield, Illinois.

To this tomb there have come more pilgrims than to any other grave in the civilized world. In 1927, 134,080 persons registered in Memorial Hall, the museum room which stands at one end of the monument-base opposite the dead man's tomb. A greater number, it is true, came yearly to the burial place of Washington; over 400,000 paying admission to Mount Vernon in 1927. However, easily eighty per cent. of this army, according to "sightseeing" men of the capital, were brought by the desire to see the home, rather than the grave, of the first President. It was Washington's mansion, not his tomb, that was the shrine. In Springfield, it was Lincoln's sepulchre for which the pilgrims first inquired; his home in another part of the city attracted far fewer visitors.

"And there's never a day goes by," said Fay in 1928, "without some one — and most days, a lot of people — asking if it isn't true that Mr. Lincoln's body is missing. From every State in the Union, people come suspecting that Mr. Lincoln's corpse is gone — lost or stolen. A few years ago I got track of a Chautauqua lecturer who was going around the country telling it that nobody knew where the body was. But I never could catch up to him.

"For over fifty years people have been asking if the tomb was empty. Nearly everybody asks, quick as they get here, 'Just where is Mr. Lincoln buried?' They're all curious about that; there've been so many stories. But the queer thing is that there are thousands who don't believe he's here at all. I never let a person get away without having heard the proof that Mr. Lincoln's body is there under the catacomb floor, buried ten feet down in solid concrete, and I show everybody the photograph of the eighteen Springfield people who identified the corpse when it was put into the steel and concrete where it is today, but the story keeps on coming back to the tomb and I can't see that it gets any less for all the work anybody can do to kill it.

"Another thing, lots of people keep asking, 'Isn't it true that Mr. Lincoln's body is petrified? We heard that it had been turned to stone.' This story has been going around for years, too."

To Fay, more than to any other human being, the American people of the 1920s disclosed their superstitions about Abraham Lincoln. To him were unbosomed the myths and the fancies which the Republic had built for itself about the national folk-hero. And with the enormous increase in visitors to the monument — a number that had quadrupled in the last six years — these fantastic questions grew to such an extent that Fay arranged his exhibits of Lincolniana and his lecture to do little more than combat the suspicion that there was something wrong at the tomb.

Like a teacher he led the pilgrims from one glass case to another, pointer in hand, explaining in detail the history of Lincoln's corpse since it was brought to Springfield in May, 1865, tracing its movements, and proving by photographs and documents just where it was placed, just when it was moved and just where and when it was finally fixed for good. Seventeen times it had been moved, he told them, almost stolen once, and rehidden across the years.

There were mementoes of Lincoln that he exhibited, anecdotes he told, but with time so short and visitors so many, he had opportunity to do little beyond establish the fact that Lincoln's body was really in its tomb.

It was a tomb of questions — questions that pay no attention to answers. The greater the number of pilgrims who heard the myth dispelled, the greater the number that would come next year with the same old suspicions. Registrants in 1927 numbered 134,080; 1926 had 121,360 signers of the visitors' book; 1925 had 119,850; 1923, 94,800; 1921, 30,000 and from 1912 back to the opening of the monument in 1874 there was an estimated average of 20,000 a year.

Always these pilgrims came from all parts of the Republic, and, in the decade between 1918 and 1928 the automobile swelled the number who hail from afar. Never had Christendom seen such another pilgrimage.

And never had America had another myth quite so curious as was this suspicion, this dread, perhaps this hope, that the hero's tomb was empty. A pure folk-fancy, a story-teller's story it was, a thing only pieced together in superstition; but it is not to be dismissed on that account. It was something more than a mere creation of ghoulish scandal-mongers and backstairs gossipers.

The legend that there was something eerie and mysterious afoot at the tomb of Lincoln is one of the major adventures of the American people into folk-lore, and, as such, reveals something of the Republic's soul.

Ancient humanity could never quite believe that its greatest heroes had perished like lesser men. Always it held the thought, then the hope, then the belief, that its heroes were too precious, too wondrously made, to sink into dreamless dust like the clay of ordinary folk. Worms might take dead commoners, but not superhuman captains. So it was that the German peasants said that Barbarossa was not dead, only sleeping his sleep of centuries under Kyffhauser Mountain, waiting, in miraculous preservation, for the time when they would have need of his sword again. Charlemagne, in legend, had not left his Franks forever; he would reappear when needed. Holger Danske drowsed under the Kronborg Mountain at Helsingör, ready for the Scandinavians to call. Dietrich von Bern, Moses, King Arthur — the list of heroes with immortal bodies is long.

Not so many years ago, Breton villagers would handle roughly any one who doubted their beloved faith that King Arthur was still alive, "dozing in Avalon, watched by waiting queens." Mystery and miracle must hide the passing of the great man.

Such folk-forces were playing about Abraham Lincoln in April, 1865. Morbid curiosity about the body of Lincoln was avid and eager from the moment his death was announced, and before the slain President was halfway home, on his sixteen-hundred-mile funeral, gossip had involved the newspapers, the undertakers and officials in a discussion over the condition of the body. The New York *World* tossed to its public an item which was eagerly read and eagerly reprinted:

"No corpse in the world is better prepared, according to appearances. Three years ago when little Willie died, Doctors Bryan and Alexander, the embalmers, prepared the body so handsomely that the President had it twice disinterred to look upon it. The same men in the same way have made perpetual these lineaments. There is no blood in the body; it was drained by the jugular and sacredly preserved. . . . All that we see of Abraham Lincoln is a mere shell in effigy, a sculpture."

The scientific debate as to just how much of the dead man's body was being brought back to Springfield was still going on when he came on May 3 to his old home town.

He arrived to find two graves waiting. One grave stood on a little hill close to the heart of the town. The other waited at Oak Ridge Cemetery, the new burial ground two miles out in the prairie woods. The people of Springfield wanted Lincoln to sleep on the hill. When the telegraph had told them that their fellow townsman was dead in Washington, they organized to bring him home.

And when their delegation in Washington sent word that Springfield would have the President's body, leading citizens purchased a hill, known as the Mather Block, now the site of the State Capitol, and put men to digging day and night. On May 1, when the oncoming funeral had reached Chicago, the grave of masonry yawned ready. Suddenly, however, came the news that Mrs. Lincoln had countermanded this plan and had decreed that the body must sleep in Oak Ridge Cemetery, two miles out of town.

Springfield knew Mrs. Lincoln of old; knew her erratic nerves, her wild, sudden rages of temper. It was not prepared, however, for so strange a caprice as this seemed to be, even though it had read that the poor woman had collapsed the night of the killing and had lain distraught while her elder son, Robert, came West with the funeral party.

Springfield wanted to be gentle with the suffering widow, and telegraphed Stanton that Mrs. Lincoln's wishes would be respected. Privately it hoped, nevertheless, that she could be persuaded to change her mind. Opinion was so strongly in favor of the downtown tomb that when the mourning train arrived at the depot, communication was again opened with Mrs. Lincoln in Washington. Robert Lincoln waited for his mother's word, while Illinois, in massed hysteria, wept and orated over his father's bier. On the fourth of May came the funeral, and a reporter telegraphed the Chicago *Tribune:*

"The funeral was to leave the State House at 11 A.M. and at ten o'clock the matter was still in the air. Then Robert Lincoln heard from his mother and Oak Ridge was chosen."

To the receiving-vault of the cemetery Lincoln was carried, and beside him were lain the bodies of two infant sons; one, Willie, who had died in the White House in '62 and whose little casket had ridden at the foot of his father's big coffin in the funeral car, the other, Eddie, the baby, who had died in Springfield when his father was a circuit lawyer and whose body was now exhumed and brought from another graveyard.

"Rest in peace" said the preachers, the newspapers, the Republic. In Washington it was remembered how Lincoln, five days before his death, had, on board the *River Queen,* read from *Macbeth* to a circle of guests:

> *"Duncan is in his grave;*
> *After life's fitful fever he sleeps well."*

It was his new grave, however, that held fitful fever for Abraham Lincoln. Neither the East, which had once ridiculed him, nor his fellow townsmen, who now worshiped him, would let him sleep. Eastern friends of Mrs. Lincoln kept urging her to bring the body back to that vault under the Capitol dome in Washington. The citizens of Springfield, banding themselves into the National Lincoln Monument Association, went calmly ahead with their plans to bring the dead man over to the tomb of their original choice on the Mather Block. That grave was kept ready. Over it, once they had filled it, Springfield people planned to erect a grand monument.

With her nerves already jangled, the widow read in the newspapers of Springfield's determination. Immediately she threatened to bring the body back to Chicago if the monument was not to be situated at Oak Ridge Cemetery. Her efforts to carry off her husband's remains would be "violent," she said. Nevertheless, the association persisted and the widow countered with an ultimatum: They must agree in ten days to build the monument at Oak Ridge, or she would take the body to Washington and place it under the Capitol dome. Oak Ridge, she declared, was where her husband would have wanted to sleep. Referring to that walk in the Virginia graveyard by the James in April, she said that he had once told her to bury him in a quiet, secluded place.

Mrs. Lincoln in the summer of '65 had moved to Chicago, and delegations from Springfield went up to interview her. She would not see them, and at length Springfield surrendered, although its hope for a downtown monument never quite vanished and, indeed, reappeared determinedly thirty-four years later. With as good grace as it could muster, the city turned to Oak Ridge, and began building a temporary vault for Lincoln.

Seven months later this new resting place was ready and, on December 21, 1865, the casket was borne to the door. Six of Lincoln's old friends wanted to see that the body was safe, and a plumber's assistant, Leon P. Hopkins, made an opening in the lead box. (Leon P. Hopkins. Remember him! He is to enter again — and again — into the history of this leaden coffin.) The six friends looked in, nodded their heads, and the casket was closed and entombed.

Here it waited five years while sculptors competed with monument-designs and committees took popular subscriptions for the structure, ground for which was broken on September 9, 1869. Behind the vault on the hill, hammers chinked on stone and hoisting-engines groaned, and then, on September 19, 1871, hands lifted the coffin out. Leon P. Hopkins opened it once more, the same six friends peeped in, nodded; it was closed and carried to the half-finished cenotaph. In the catacomb, which had been completed in advance of the rest of the monument, were five crypts, one of them already filled. Two months before, Lincoln's son Tad, who as a tongue-tied youngster had captured the country's heart with his lovable incorrigibility in White House days, had died at eighteen in Chicago, and had been carried to the monument. With their father's body came, also, the little corpses of Willie and Eddie, who had died young enough to sleep, now, together in one crypt. The center niche in this death-cupboard was for Lincoln, but he did not occupy it without interruption. It had been seen that the mahogany casket in which he had been brought from Washington was breaking up, and the committee substituted for it an iron coffin, a curiously ill-fated iron coffin, into which the inner coffin of lead was transferred.

Finally, in this new receptacle, the dead man lay down to sleep for three cool years while the hammers went on chinking and the engines groaning around him. On October 9, 1874, reverent hands drew him forth again, this time to be placed, with formal state, in a marble sarcophagus that had been built in the center of the semi-circular catacomb, down in front of the crypts.

But the fitful fever burned on. The iron coffin was too long by inches for its new home, and a new outer coffin — a red cedar box — was brought. As the undertaker and a worker lined this with lead, they peeked into the lead casket just to satisfy themselves that Lincoln was really there.

Duncan seemed, indeed, to be in his grave at last, when on October 15 the monument was dedicated. Money had been raised for the groups of statuary which were to rise at the four corners of the structure. Confusion seemed over.

In reality it had only retired to attack from a new direction. Ghouls!

✦   ✦   ✦   25   ✦   ✦   ✦

THE "CONEY" MEN

IT WAS IN THE TOWN OF LINCOLN, county seat of Logan County, Illinois, that a detective by the name of W. D. Longnecker, nosing about in the Springtime of 1876, came upon a plot to steal the body of Abraham Lincoln from its tomb just outside the neighboring city of Springfield.

As Longnecker caught the threads of the conspiracy, it seemed to have been formed by a citizen of Lincoln, Benjamin F. Sheridan, who proposed to take the corpse from the monument and hide it in a field of young corn, where the growing grain would conceal it every day more securely.

Knowing how horrible the idea would certainly be to the people of Lincoln, Longnecker said nothing about his discovery and merely went on watching and waiting, and, no doubt, rejoicing when the plot gave every sign of having been abandoned. He might never have mentioned the thing at all if events of that Autumn had not reminded him.

(That Abraham Lincoln, himself, might have preferred to sleep, lonely, in a field of young corn instead of in the marble

sarcophagus among staring crowds, was not in the mind of anybody in 1876.)

As a matter of fact the plot to rob Lincoln's grave had not
been abandoned; it had merely been more carefully concealed,
and although the names of W. D. Longnecker and Benjamin
F. Sheridan passed from all connection with the conspiracy,
the scheme itself progressed.

Unsuspected by the villagers, there were living in Lincoln
members of the cleverest counterfeiting gang that ever plagued
the United States Secret Service in those lawless years that
followed the Civil War. "Big Jim" Kneally's coney men made
their headquarters in the corn-town, where no hounds of the
law would be likely to sniff them out.

("Coney men" was the nickname given all counterfeiters by
their enemies, the detectives, in the '70s.)

Big Jim himself was not often in the nest, preferring the
safer atmosphere of St. Louis, where no Illinois sleuths would
be about to note his familiar face, but the Logan County town
was an ideal refuge for his "shovers," those bland and amiable-
looking fellows who slipped out on trips across the country,
shoving bogus currency across counters to gullible merchants.

Through the Springtime of 1876, however, few of the
"shovers" had been busy. Paralysis was settling on the gang.
Their supply of counterfeit notes was running low. For almost
a year no new bills had been supplied them, since Ben Boyd,
the master engraver, had been caught at his workshop in Fulton, Illinois, and sent to State's prison at Joliet on a ten-year
sentence. Nowhere could Big Jim find an artist to take his
place. The only hope lay in getting Ben Boyd out from behind
the bars.

To accomplish this, Kneally had worked out a plot — obviously the same scheme that Longnecker had scented, then
lost. Kneally would have his men steal Abraham Lincoln's
body, the most precious possession of Illinois, and then, with
the sacred corpse in his hands, he would negotiate for Ben
Boyd's pardon. The return of Lincoln's body would be the
price of the convict's freedom.

Late in June Kneally made a move, sending five of his men

into Springfield to open a saloon, pose as innocent barkeepers and make preparations for the theft. The rôle was a difficult one to play, what with all the free liquor at hand, and soon one of the coney men, very drunk, babbled the dark secret to a "parlor-house" madam whose establishment he was enjoying. He whispered to her that she could look for some extra excitement on next Fourth of July. While she and the rest of Springfield would be shooting off fireworks on the eve of the holiday, he and his companions would be out at Oak Ridge Cemetery loading Lincoln's coffin onto a wagon, and late that night they would be hiding the corpse under a certain bridge two miles up the Sangamon River.

The story was too thrilling to keep, and the parlor-house madam told it to the chief of police and several other Springfield gentlemen besides, so that when the confiding saloon-keeper awakened the next morning his secret was all over town. Naturally he and his companions disappeared.

Big Jim Kneally, however, was not done. He merely shifted the center of his activities to Chicago, where at 294 West Madison Street he owned a saloon, The Hub, a plain, drab and apparently harmless place, with a bust of Abraham Lincoln over the bar. His man, Terrence Mullen, of harmonious drabness, and with the conventional walrus moustache of the day, ostensibly owned The Hub, dispensing liquor to workingmen in the front room and maintaining a secret club-room for coney men in the back.

To this haven, sometime in August, came one of the Kneally gang, Jack Hughes, on tiptoe. For two years Jack, excellent "shover," had been flitting about the country, one jump ahead of the secret-service operatives who had indicted him in 1874 for palming off worthless five-dollar bills upon the trusting merchants of Washington Heights, a suburb of Chicago.

It seemed particularly cruel to hound Jack, for his technique had been a gentle and homely one — one that matched his sad, patient eyes and long, honest whiskers. Of a morning Hughes would start out with only one counterfeit note nestling in his pocket — one bad bill among a lot of good ones. Half a block behind him, as he ambled down the street, would come trailing along a boy whose pockets bulged with bogus notes, and when Hughes would turn into a store, this boy would come up and stand at the doorway peeking in. Jack's custom was to make some trifling purchase and offer the fraudulent note in payment. If the clerk accepted it without question, the boy would stroll down the block and have another counterfeit bill ready for Hughes when he had caught up.

If, however, Hughes was questioned in the store, the boy would scamper off for some distant rendezvous, leaving Jack to apologize, glare angrily at the bad bill, and substitute sound currency for it.

Such tactics had proved fool-proof until the Washington Heights incident sometime in 1874, and it was from prosecution on that case that Hughes was still fleeing when he came to The Hub in 1876 and heard from Mullen in the back room that Kneally wanted Lincoln's grave robbed as soon as possible.

Neither Mullen nor Hughes seemed to feel quite up to so desperate an undertaking as this — counterfeiters being notoriously weak on crimes of violence — and both of the coney men soon welcomed into their plot a hardier criminal, who had, since earlier in the Summer, been patronizing the saloon. This newcomer was Lewis C. Swegles, confessedly the champion graverobber of Chicago and vicinity. "I'm the boss body-snatcher of Chicago," was the way he put it, adding that it was he who supplied most of the cadavers to the medical schools of the city.

Such a story was plausible enough in 1876, when graverobbing was a nation-wide horror. Illinois, like many States, had no law against the stealing of bodies, although it had a statute against the selling of corpses. Under these conditions medical colleges were in a desperate fix, since they had to find cadavers for their classes to dissect. There was only one thing to do, buy bodies from men who came to the back door at midnight with mysterious sacks which they exchanged for so much money down and no questions asked. Ghouls had become the terror of rural communities, and friends and relatives of bereaved families patrolled cemeteries for nights after burials, shotguns in hand.

With grand tales of his exploits in this field, Swegles established himself as a trustworthy soul in the eyes of Mullen, but before Hughes found time to estimate properly the new comrade, secret-service men swooped down upon The Hub, on the night of August 30, and arrested Jack on the old Washington Heights' charge. Bail soon had Hughes back, however, and he bent himself to the task in hand.

Together the two counterfeiters concluded to test Swegles before admitting him to their plot. First they proposed the robbery of another grave. How would he like to go in with them on stealing the body of a certain rich Mr. King, lately dead in Kenosha, Wisconsin? Swegles wanted to think it over, and was back the next night saying "No," that Wisconsin had a law penalizing ghouls two years. It wouldn't be safe.

This convinced Mullen and Hughes that the fellow was shrewd and practiced, and they thereupon unbosomed themselves of the great secret. Swegles, listening, was eager and helpful. The plot took form.

The three of them would creep up to the Lincoln monument some night, pry open the marble sarcophagus, lift out the coffin, transfer the body to a wagon, and drive northward to the Indiana sand-dunes. In that primeval wilderness, where the wind would wipe out all traces in the shifting sand, and where only the lonely lake and its waterfowl would see the ghouls come and go, they would hide the body.

Swegles agreed to everything but the number of men involved. The theft would be harder than they thought, he said, and added that he'd better bring on a famous criminal friend of his, a certain Billy Brown, about whom they had heard him talk so much. Brown would handle the wagon while the three others dismantled the tomb. So it was decided.

One more individual should be included, said Kneally's men, a counterfeiter named Cornelius, who would negotiate with the State for the ransom price. That was also agreed.

When Cornelius joined them, the diplomatic program was perfected. First of all, they would get a London newspaper from a foreign news-stand over on Dearborn Street — the rarer the paper, the better. Out of it they would tear a piece and take it with them to Springfield, where they would carefully leave it beside the rifled casket as they made off with the body. Detectives, finding the torn scrap of paper, would cherish it as a clue. Meanwhile the remainder of the paper would be hidden in The Hub, stuffed up inside the hollow bust of Lincoln that stood over the bar.

Once the corpse was secreted in the wild sand-dunes, Cornelius, armed with the London newspaper, was to approach the State authorities and suggest that he could secure the return of Lincoln's body for a price. When asked for some proof that he represented the ghouls, Cornelius would produce the paper, to which the detectives would fit their fragment and see beyond doubt that Cornelius was the accredited spokesman, as he claimed. So by late October everything but the date for the attempt was complete. Haste was imperative.

On the fifth of November, Mullen, Hughes and possibly one other member of the Kneally gang, name unknown to history, met with Swegles in his Chicago home for a final conference upon the moot question. Some one suggested that the night of the coming Presidential election would be an excellent time to strike, and the more they discussed this, the better it seemed.

No Presidential campaign since the Lincoln-McClellan contest of 1864 had been so bitter or so furious as that of 1876. For the first time since the Civil War, the Democrats had a chance. Even Springfield, the home of the first Republican President, might swing over to the opposition only eleven years after his death.

Ever since the Northern voters, massing behind Thaddeus Stevens and the Radical bloc of the Republican party, had elected Ulysses S. Grant President in 1868, the Democrats had been nationally helpless. In 1872 their curious candidate, Horace Greeley, had won only 66 electoral votes, all Southern, while Grant had captured 272 electors and a popular majority of 750,000 votes as well.

Grant's second administration had given the Democrats hope at last, for while the hero of Appomattox Court House was still as modest and as unsmirched as ever, his party had piled up a record of graft and corruption that had driven his followers by the tens of thousands into the arms of the Democrats, who with a New York reformer, Samuel J. Tilden, at their head, were firing the prairies and the cities in 1876 with their clamor for a national house-cleaning.

The stubby little man who had so captured the heart and imagination of the country when he accepted Lee's surrender, had been bogged in the strange, new mire of politics, where double-tongued supporters failed to obey him as his soldiers had done. Now, as the Presidential campaign marched on, he was on the side-lines, back where he had belonged all the time, with Sherman and Lee, who had both scorned politics as something undesirable after the clean fire of war.

The Republicans, with Rutherford B. Hayes as their figurehead, fought desperately to stave off the reform-wave by reviving the North's memory of those bloody hours when the Democrats had opposed Lincoln's conduct of the war. Feverishly they recalled the dark days when all Democrats had been said to sympathize openly or secretly with the Confederacy. Through the campaign of '76 "the bloody shirt" cracked its tails like rifle-fire in the winds of Republican oratory.

The election would be close; Northern States seemed willing to forget something of their war grudges and to listen to promises of governmental reform. The Southern States, even with "carpet-baggers" and "scalawags" — Northern political adventurers — assisting the negroes to rule their governments, might amass enough white voters to win for Tilden. The work of disenfranchising the negro had begun. Southern nightriders had commenced the intimidation with which they were eventually to secure again the reins of their local governments, and it was expected in '76 that the "lily-whites" of the South would carry Democracy high.

In bitterness and chaos the campaign was raging that day, November 5 — two days before the election — when the ghouls met in Chicago to fix a time when they would break into Abraham Lincoln's tomb.

That every city and town would be packed on election night with surging crowds waiting for the returns was certain. In Springfield, Illinois, everybody would be downtown till late, milling about the telegraph offices and political headquarters.

The Lincoln monument, over two miles out in the woods, would certainly be deserted. There, ghouls could work for hours, if necessary, undisturbed.

The night, too, would be ideal for carrying the body away. At midnight the roads would hold plenty of sleepy farmers jogging homeward. In this traffic, one more wagon with a long sack in the back would never be noticed, and with the election in doubt for days, there would be plenty of time to reach the sand-dunes in safety. So election night was chosen as the time to strike.

"It was considered," said Swegles afterward, "a damned elegant time to do it."

With that decision, the plotters parted, Swegles, Mullen and Hughes agreeing to meet the next night and to leave for Springfield on the nine o'clock train, Swegles promising to have the fourth man, Brown, with him.

"Billy Brown had better not sit with us," Swegles suggested. "Four men together might attract attention. I'll put him in the car behind. And in Springfield, too, he'd better keep away from us. He'll steal a horse at some hitch-rack during the election excitement and have the rig at the tomb when we're ready for it."

However, as the train pulled out the next night, Mullen and Hughes wanted to have a look at this Billy Brown. Swegles agreed, and told them to sit still in their seats while he went back into the rear car and walked their accomplice past them, which he did, the two counterfeiters agreeing that the new man looked all right. As Brown, after the examination, disappeared into his coach, the three chief plotters made themselves comfortable for the night. So far, so good.

But Billy Brown was hanging onto the back steps of the train waiting for it to slow up for a crossing on the outskirts of Chicago, and when this point was reached, he slipped off easily and turned back to the city. Billy Brown was none other than Officer Nealy of the United States Secret Service, and in a little while he was at headquarters, where he was received with no particular surprise. So far, so good for the Secret Service, too!

On that same nine o'clock train that was steaming for Springfield were a half-dozen other operatives of the Secret Service,
commanded by the district chief himself, Tyrrell. They were
in the coach ahead of the three ghouls — *two* ghouls would be
a more accurate way to express it, for Lewis C. Swegles, the
body-snatcher, was not a ghoul at all, but a "roper" instead. A
"roper" in the '70s was precisely what a "stool-pigeon" was
later on, an informer, and from the first day that he had entered
The Hub that summer he had kept the Secret Service informed
upon everything that went on therein. Swegles, posing as a
body-snatcher, had been originally sent to Mullen's saloon by
his chieftain Tyrrell to watch for Jack Hughes, and it had been
his tip that had brought about the arrest of Jack on August 30.
Seeing that he was unsuspected by his Hub friends, Swegles
had remained on the job to see what else he could discover about
the Kneally gang, and, as luck had it, his pretended skill in
grave-robbing had brought him stumbling upon another matter
— the scheme to rob Lincoln's grave.

Tyrrell directed his man to go on with this conspiracy, and
informed Robert Lincoln of the danger that threatened his
father's corpse. Robert, at thirty-two, was a Chicago lawyer,
embarking upon that curious career which was to make him
Ambassador to the Court of St. James's and president of the
Pullman Company and, as such, target for the satirists who
were later to point out the irony of his position when the negro
porters agitated for higher wages. The father had freed the
blacks, these disrespectful wits declared, and the son was now
a party to their exploitation.

Whatever confusions Robert Lincoln may have met in later
years, he faced this threat against his father's grave with prompt
action, summoning Edward Isham, his law-partner, and Elmer
Washburne, lately head of the United States Secret Service,
who was now home in Chicago working for an appointment as
chief of the city's police. Washburne, further urged to the task
by Leonard Swett, a prairie circuit-riding friend of Abraham
Lincoln, headed the body of Pinkertons and private detectives
which Robert Lincoln assembled to prevent the theft.

Together they laid this trap: Swegles was to accompany the

ghouls to Springfield, and, while assisting in the robbery, was to signal the detectives, who would be hiding in another part of the monument and who could catch Mullen and Hughes red-handed. Billy Brown was to see that the party was actually off on the nine o'clock train and to report that fact to headquarters, from where Washburne and another party of detectives would follow in the morning. Tyrrell, the chief, and his operatives were to go down on the same train with the ghouls that night.

Everything went smoothly to the very hour of the attempt. In Springfield, Tyrrell conferred with John T. Stuart, Lincoln's former law-partner and the moving spirit in the National Lincoln Monument Association, Stuart quickly advising the custodian of the monument to assist in the trapping of the ghouls.

It was all very clear what they were to do. When night came, the detectives would hide with the custodian in the museum room of the monument, Memorial Hall, which stood on the opposite side of the cenotaph-base from the catacomb wherein Lincoln was buried. There they would wait until Swegles, who would be working with the ghouls, would come past their door whispering the signal, "Wash." Then they would swarm out with drawn revolvers and capture Mullen and Hughes with the coffin in their hands.

While this trap was being laid in Stuart's law-office during the afternoon, Swegles and Hughes walked out to the tomb, scouting, while Mullen remained behind to steal an axe from a woodpile behind a saloon.

To Hughes, walking casually about the monument, the theft must have appeared simple. Only a little iron gateway with a tiny padlock guarded the catacomb. Inside stood a marble sarcophagus, which the axe would pry open with ease. Back to town went Hughes, confident of success.

Dusk comes early in November, and at five o'clock the day was darkening when the first Pinkerton arrived at the monument with a note for Power, the custodian, from John T. Stuart, who ordered his employee to put out the lights and to wait with the detective until the main body of operatives should come. Together in the twilight the two men waited, and at 6.40

Tyrrell, Washburne, and their forces arrived, the Pinkerton identifying each man as Power admitted him.

With flash-lights Tyrrell explored the place. In behind the Memorial Hall, where they were assembled, stretched a black, damp labyrinth winding through the foundations of the monument to a rear wall which served as backing for the catacomb where Lincoln lay. Against this wall Tyrrell stationed a detective to listen for the sounds of the ghouls. Then Tyrrell returned to the museum room, where the party was crouching in darkness watching the glass door ahead. At a word from the secret-service man, all took off their shoes and those who had revolvers made them ready.

Waiting and straining, they stood. At length when complete blackness had come, the bulls-eye of a lantern shone at the door, moved about inquiringly, seemed satisfied and went away. It was the ghouls, who moved off around the massive bastions of the monument, Mullen carrying the axe and a sack into which Lincoln's body was to be transferred from the leaden casket.

A file made short work of the padlock, and soon Mullen's axe had pried the marble lid from the sarcophagus, the three men standing it up against the crypts in the rear of the semi-circular catacomb — crypts in which slept Lincoln's little boys, Willie and Eddie.

To Swegles was given the lantern, and he was stationed at the rear of the sarcophagus to light up the scene as Mullen and Hughes lifted out the heavy casket. As they toiled, Swegles chafed. The time had come for him to give the signal, but how was he to do it? If he set down the lantern and went out, the ghouls would probably put a bullet in his back. Nothing to do but wait. The chance came. Mullen, with the casket half out of the dismantled sarcophagus, decided that it was time to bring up the spring-wagon which Swegles had assured them was waiting in the ravine below with Billy Brown at the reins.

"Go get it," said Mullen to Swegles, and the roper was out and down over the brow of the hill in darkness. Once out of sight, Swegles raced in a semi-circle around to Memorial Hall, and whispered the watchword "Wash" in at the door. At that moment the detective who had been listening against the brick wall in the labyrinth made his way to the museum room with the word that the ghouls were at it.

"Come on," whispered Tyrrell, and with drawn revolvers the band rushed out and around the monument to the catacomb. The gateway was ajar, the coffin half out, but the ghouls were gone.

Out of the catacomb the detectives came, scattering to search the premises. Flustered and floundering, one of the Pinkertons snapped the cap on his pistol by mistake and the "pop" echoed loudly in the night.

The moon was coming up, and as Tyrrell dashed about the base of the monument, he saw against its radiance, the heads of two men staring at him from around the corner of a massive group of statuary. He whipped up his pistol and fired. A shot answered, and, bullet for bullet, he fought it out with them in murderous hide-and-seek around the masonry. Suddenly one of them called, "Is that you, Tyrrell?" They were two of his own men.

The jig was up, Tyrrell, glad that it was over, if his report to Chief Brooks in Washington meant anything. In it he said, "It was one of the most unfortunate nights I have ever experienced, yet God protected us in doing right."

Without the comic pistol-play they might have caught the ghouls, for Mullen and Hughes had only walked off one hundred feet or more to await the return of Swegles with the spring-wagon. They had suspected nothing, but out of precaution had withdrawn to a tree where they could stand unseen by any chance passer-by.

After a few moments, they had seen a movement at the catacomb door and had started back, thinking that Swegles had returned. But as they approached the tomb a pistol cap had snapped, many dark figures had appeared against the brightening radiance of the eastern moon, and the ghouls had raced away, down through the ravine, shrieking curses as they ran.

"Shoot, you———, you'll never hit us now," one of them howled, and hearing the howl, a drowsy street-car conductor on the line that ran near-by, started, then pricked his ear as shot after shot rang out up on the monument hill further on.

Chicago and Illinois heard of the raid next day. The Chicago *Tribune*, featuring it even above the news of the crucial election, "smashed the story" on page 1.

"HORRIBLE
"Dastardly attempt to steal the
bones of the Martyr-President"

— screamed headlines of a size unwonted in that day of restrained journalistic make-up. Then followed the story, palpitating, outraged.

But the city, the State, and the nation did not believe it. The *Tribune's* rivals, the *Times* and the *Inter-Ocean*, ignored the story. In a day or so the *Inter-Ocean* did mention it, only to charge that the whole affair was a hoax concocted by Elmer Washburne in order to get himself the position of Chicago's chief of police.

On the streets it was freely charged that the whole affair had been staged for one political reason or another. It was incredible, people said, that detectives should have herded themselves in a little room where they could see nothing and hear nothing while waiting for desperate criminals. Fingers of suspicion were pointed at Swegles by doubters who said that all the work that had been done at the sarcophagus could easily have been performed by one man.

The Democratic *Times* made charges more serious, declaring that the Republican party had desecrated the grave of its dead founder in order to make it appear that the Democrats had descended to vandalism in their supposed hatred for Lincoln and the Union. "Grantism," the campaign expression for ruthless corruption, had done the deed to make political capital for the Republicans, said the *Times*, and on November 10 one of its editorials declared:

"It has been suggested that the design had been conceived some weeks ago and that the robbery was to have been perpetrated long before election that it might be published to the country as a Democratic outbreak of hatred

to the memory of the murdered President. Certainly the
partisans of Grantism cannot murmur if this atrocious design is fastened upon them by common consent, remembering the hardly less baleful measures they have adopted
during the latest years of their lawless dominion. It is
hardly baser to despoil Lincoln's grave for political capital than to summon the legions, who died to perpetuate the
Union, in the maligned cause of its continued disruption.

"Explanation is needed to neutralize the vague suspicions now abroad."

On November 18, however, the vague suspicions were well
cleared up, for then it was announced that Mullen and Hughes
had been caught. The two ghouls, fleeing from the tomb, had
gone to the home of Hughes' relatives near Lodi, Illinois, returning to Chicago in a week to find their old friend Lewis C.
Swegles awaiting them, with tall tales of his narrow escape and
puzzled wonderments as to how the detectives had got wind of
their raid. Even then, Mullen and Hughes did not suspect "the
boss body-snatcher of Chicago." On November 17, however,
they began to awaken, for the Secret Service came for them
both and locked them up, while Swegles went free.

As the news of this capture was read, the next morning,
Illinois and the nation realized that the *Tribune's* story had
been true. Disbelief gave way to horror. Among the negro
populations the story was received with ghostly terror, the ex-
slaves declaring that the Confederates had tried to carry out
"their oft-repeated threat to scatter what was left of Father
Abraham to the four winds."

Letters poured in upon the newspapers, laying the guilt to
various agencies. Some said that The Knights of the Golden
Circle, that war-time secret society of Northerners who sympathized with the South, had raided the tomb. Others insisted
that the despoilers were hirelings of the Southerners who had
collected and administered the John Wilkes Booth Fund — a
notion that had had its origin in the belief that the dying Confederacy had hired Booth to murder Lincoln.

With loyal Illinois in a temper that was heightened by the

national confusion, punishment for Mullen and Hughes would have been most certainly severe if the law had permitted. Two days after their arrest the ghouls were in a Springfield jail heavily guarded, and on the twentieth they were indicted — but only on a minor charge, that of conspiring to commit an unlawful act, no other accusation being allowed under the faulty laws.

As has been said, grave-robbing was no crime in Illinois, and the prosecution, for all that it was bolstered up by high-priced Chicago lawyers sent down by Robert Lincoln and Leonard Swett, could find no grounds for prosecution except the weak one of conspiracy. It was for having conspired to steal a coffin, the property of the National Lincoln Monument Association, that the two men were indicted by a grand jury which was purposely composed of Democrats, so chosen by the prosecution to dispose of the wide popular belief that the attempted theft had been a Republican political hoax.

Rumors of "trumpery and shenanigan" swept Springfield while the jury held its sessions, and did not die even when the jurymen voted a prompt indictment. Continuances and changes of venue wore the case along to May 28, 1877, when it came to trial with the defense lawyers arguing that the Chicago *Tribune* had entered into a conspiracy with Elmer Washburne to stage this rescue of Lincoln's body so that the heroic Washburne might win appointment as head of Chicago's police department.

Washburne, defending himself with proof that Swett, unconnected with the *Tribune*, had invited him into the case, disclosed for the first time that a *Tribune* reporter had accompanied the detectives to the tomb and had witnessed the adventures there. He had not "tipped" the *Tribune* to the story, he said, and who had done it was not revealed in later days.

The case against Mullen and Hughes was complete, thanks to admissions found in letters that the two had written to friends, and on June 2 the jury took the case, being advised that the maximum penalty under the law for such an offense was five years. On the first ballot two jurors were for the maximum, two of them for two years, four for indeterminate sentences and four for acquittal. After a few more ballots it was agreed that the criminals should serve one year. Which they did — in Joliet.

(The value of Abraham Lincoln's coffin, which they had tried to steal, was set, by the undertaker who sold it, at seventy-five dollars.)

☆　☆　☆　**26**　☆　☆　☆

THE LINCOLN GUARD OF HONOR

WITH INCREDIBLE QUICKNESS the story of the attempt to rob Lincoln's grave passed into the realm of outlawed legend.

After that first flurry of excitement, the Chicago *Tribune* itself dropped the matter for a time, as though realizing that in its enterprise it had offended the respectable readers, who saw nothing but horror and shame in the whole business. Later on, the *Tribune* did return to the thing for a recapitulation of the case and a justification of its own course in publishing news so shocking. It proved that its story had been true, then it, like the other papers, became silent.

Power, the custodian, wrote a book about the affair, but few read it. Magazines and newspapers ever after shunned the story.

A wall as though of secrecy speedily arose about the incident, and, quite naturally, served to set the myth-makers and the superstitious tale-tellers to saying that there was "something wrong," something suppressed about the whole matter.

To heighten further the sense of mystery felt by the masses, officials of the tomb adopted an air of stealthy secrecy toward all pilgrims who came to the tomb, open-mouthed, to ask questions about the robbery-raid. From 1876 to 1878, John C. Power, the custodian, gave ambiguous, evasive answers to all who prodded him on the matter. Poor man, he was in a desperate predicament, secretly trembling as people stared at the marble sarcophagus, asking him if he was sure the body had been safely returned after the ghouls had had it out. Desperate predicament indeed — for the sarcophagus *was* empty.

Queerly as it may sound, this was what had happened: On the morning of November 8, 1876, when Springfield heard that ghouls had broken into the monument the night before, John T. Stuart rushed out to the tomb with stone masons, and replacing the casket in the sarcophagus, restored the marble work. But he couldn't sleep. Night after night he tossed, fearing that the grave-robbers would come again. Six days after the raid he sent for Power and told him that the body must be hidden somewhere outside the tomb.

Power, gathering other members of the National Lincoln Monument Association, decided to secrete the corpse in that cavern with labyrinthine passage-ways that lay between Memorial Hall and the catacomb. They would steal Lincoln's body themselves!

That afternoon Adam Johnson, Springfield marble-worker, with his men, waiting until they were sure no one was looking, lifted Lincoln's casket out of the sarcophagus, covered it with a blanket in a dark corner of the catacomb, carefully re-cemented the marble lid back in place, and removed all trace of their act. Once before the body had been half out of the tomb, now it was out altogether.

When night came, Power, Johnson, and three members of the executive committee of the Association stole out to the tomb, and, straining and staggering under the load of five hundred pounds, carried the casket around the base of the obelisk through Memorial Hall and into the labyrinth, where they laid it among the odds and ends of boards left by the builders.

Next day Johnson stealthily made an outer coffin, and Power set to work to scratch out a grave in the dirt floor. It was slow work for the custodian, what with the necessity of keeping his job secret from the visitors who came constantly to the tomb, and with the water that kept welling up in the shallow hole that he was digging. At last he gave it up and covered the coffin with lumber, and Lincoln slept for two years under a heap of boards in a cellar, while pilgrims from all over the world stared, wept, mourned and pondered over his sarcophagus at the other end of the monument. More and more of these pilgrims, in the two years, kept asking questions about the theft — questions full of suspicion. The gossip about the ghouls had been a fascinating morsel and was running far.

In the Summer and Fall of 1877 the myth took on new impetus. Power, devoted to Lincoln's memory and sorely harassed by the secret, excusably gave it wings. Workmen arrived at the monument to erect the naval and infantry groups of statuary, for which the necessary funds had been so laboriously collected. Their work would take them into the labyrinth, where, Power feared, they would find Lincoln's coffin. The scandal would be out.

Power faced the situation, calling the workmen together, swearing them to secrecy and showing them the casket. They promised to keep silent, but within a few days everybody in Springfield, so it seemed to Power, was asking him if it was true that Lincoln's body was out of the tomb. The workmen had babbled, and poor Power was equivocating, quibbling, ducking, and evading in a miserable attempt to hold his secret without telling a lie.

Naturally the scandal took wings, and in the year that followed flew from mouth to mouth, nobody knows how far across the country. People gave it new attention in November, 1878, when newspapers told them that the body of A. T. Stewart, great merchant of New York, had been stolen and held for ransom. The news put Power into a panic and he rushed to the monument committee, urging that Lincoln be more securely buried. He was told that he must get new blood to help him, since the committeemen were old and had disabled themselves carrying the heavy coffin that night two years before. Power promptly selected two friends, Major Gustavus S. Dana and Gen. Jasper N. Reece, tried Unionists, and with them chose three more, Edward S. Johnson, Joseph P. Lindley and James F. McNeill. By night of this day, November 18, the six men were at work digging Lincoln a grave in the far end of the labyrinth, up against the back wall of the catacomb. Cramped for elbow room, stifled by bad air, they gave up the job by midnight with the coffin barely covered with damp earth and the traces of their activity unremoved. Power was to finish this next day.

A rush of visitors to Memorial Hall interfered, and it was two days later that the arrival of a mysterious and anonymous postal card, warning him not to be alone at the tomb, prodded Power into action. Conferring with Dana and Reece, he proposed digging Lincoln up, since the postal card might mean another attempt at theft. The spades came out and the work began. When it was half-done, one of the three noticed a strange softness in the ground near by and sunk his implement into it. Something grated loudly, and feverishly the men dug at this new spot. An iron coffin appeared. They chilled. Some one must have taken Lincoln's body from its coffin, hidden it in this strange casket, and buried it there to be returned for at some later time. But when they had the lid off this iron box it was found to be empty.

Puzzled, the three men turned back to their original task and satisfied themselves that the coffin which contained Lincoln's body had not been disturbed. Reburying it, they reported their discovery of the iron coffin to the monument committee, which calmed them with the news that it was the casket which, in October, 1874, had been discarded as too long for the sarcophagus. The bothersome postal card proved meaningless also and was put down as a practical joke. But out of the fiasco came an idea. The six friends would form a brotherhood to guard the secret of the tomb and supplement the work of the Monument Association. Younger men should be included, they agreed, and Noble B. Wiggins, Horace Chapin and Clinton L. Conkling, all of Springfield, were added in 1880, the official date of organization being set on the birthday of the dead Lincoln.

The Lincoln Guard of Honor, they called themselves, and had badges made. Springfield saw the badges for the first time at Mary Todd Lincoln's funeral in July, 1882. The poor woman had died, a lunatic, in the home of her Springfield sister, Mrs. Ninian Edwards, and her body was carried out of the very door through which she had come, forty years before,

as a bride on the arm of a penniless circuit lawyer. At the ceremonies the Guard conducted itself so mysteriously and offi-
ciously that people wondered about it. And at the tomb, when
her corpse was slipped into its crypt next her little boys, the
spectators were whispering questions to each other about the
nine men with the badges who stood so watchfully and silently
at the door of the catacomb.

What was being concealed? There must be something up.
Maybe those stories about Lincoln's corpse being gone were
true after all.

After the funeral, Stuart of the monument-committee told
the Guard that Robert Lincoln, the only surviving son, wanted
his mother's body hidden with his father's, and at 10 P.M.,
July 21, the guardsmen, on cats' feet, slipped the widow's
coffin from the crypt and once more went staggering around
the monument in the night with a double-leaded casket. By
two o'clock in the morning the wife lay buried by her husband
and back to town the burial party tottered, exhausted, Captain
Chapin limping weakly on the peg-leg he had won at Chicka-
maugua.

Pilgrims increased as more prairie years slipped along, looking now at two empty tombs. New crowds journeyed to see the
memorial when it was completed in 1883, eighteen years after
it had been commenced. More questions, too, came with the
years and Power, in his history of the monument, admitted
testily that suspicious visitors badgered him incessantly.

"There has not a day passed," he wrote, "but the custodian
has been called upon to parry the prying question of one or
more who have had a hint, before coming, that the body was
not in the sarcophagus. To all such he has invariably said, 'We
put it back there the second day after the attempt to steal it,'
which was strictly true. If they questioned further, he would
say, 'I suppose you wish to know if there is not further danger;
if so, I can assure you that it is absolutely safe.' To any further
questions he would say, 'If I were to explain what precautions
have been taken to make it safe, it would not be so any longer,
and I would prove myself unworthy of the confidence reposed
in me.' Then he was accustomed to dismiss the subject and vis-

itors generally were satisfied, but whether they were or not, he would stop and let them do the talking. This, in substance, he was to do over and over for years."

The myth grew on such evasions until in 1886 the Monument Association, either to stop the rumors or to ease their anxiety for the corpse, decided to give Lincoln decent burial. Contracts were let for a strong tomb of brick and mortar, and in April, 1887, the new home for the wandering corpse was ready. Letters counselling secrecy were sent to members of the Guard of Honor and the executive committee of the association, asking each to be at Memorial Hall in the monument on April 14 to witness the exhuming and reburial of Mr. and Mrs. Lincoln. Again secrecy failed, for on the morning of the fourteenth, Springfield read the letter and the details about the Guard of Honor, with its purpose, in one of the local newspapers. Some one had talked.

The press, nevertheless, was kept out of Memorial Hall when the two groups of secret-holders met around the caskets that had been brought out from the labyrinth. Eighteen persons who had known Lincoln filed past his casket, peeping into the square hole which plumbers had cut in the face of the lead coffin.

Twenty-two years had passed, to the day, since John Wilkes Booth had shot the man whose body lay now exposed, but the face of Lincoln had changed but little; darker, somewhat, more like the bronze face of the statue that stood on the monument above, yet still the same gaunt, strange features about which people disputed in Salem, in Springfield, and in Washington, calling them repulsive, plain, homely and beautiful.

After the last man had identified the corpse, Leon P. Hopkins, the plumber's assistant, soldered the lead square back over the hole, thinking to himself that he was the last man ever to see the face of Lincoln. The Guard of Honor lifted the casket, other hands lifted Mrs. Lincoln's, and both bodies were carried around to the catacomb, where they sank into the brick-and-mortar vault, "there," wrote Power, "to sleep for all time."

Another burial at the tomb; another whisper to seep out over the land.

Power's estimate of "all time" was not to be fulfilled. Within thirteen years Lincoln's body was out of the tomb again. In 1899, the Illinois legislators were informed by Governor Tanner that the monument must come down and be rebuilt from the foundations, since it was settling unevenly, cracking up around that everlasting vault of Lincoln's. A committee investigated and, in its minority report, out stalked the old, old ghost of the proposed grave in the Mather Block. Springfield's wish to have Lincoln sleep on the hill near the heart of town had never died. Both majority and minority reports of the legislative committee agreed that the monument as it stood would soon become a ruin. Earlier in the session, the House of Representatives had resolved that the monument's "crudity and insecurity" reflected discredit upon Illinois, and now a minority demanded that a newer and greater memorial should be placed "not in a cemetery among the dead," but in the center of Springfield. Economy, however, came to the aid of Oak Ridge, and the majority report was adopted, calling for the dismantling of the monument and its rebuilding on new foundations to an additional height of twenty feet.

So again Lincoln was moved — wandering, restless corpse. The Guard of Honor placed the dead man, with his dead widow and his dead young, in another temporary vault near by, there to wait amid the familiar chink of hammers and groans of hoisting-engines, until February, 1901, when the crypts in the new structure were ready. The bodies of the widow and the little boys went into the crypts, where they remain to this day, while Lincoln's rested temporarily (fateful word) in a crypt while workmen dug out a new vault under the floor of the catacomb. Robert Lincoln told the monument officials — they were State executives now, Illinois having taken over the tomb in 1895 — that he wanted his father's body placed this time so that it could never be moved again. He suggested a way, and gave the seven hundred dollars necessary to carry it out. He had seen a new device used in the burial of George M. Pullman, the Chicago capitalist, a steel cage placed about the coffin, while over, around, and through it was sloshed cement. Such a vault was ready for Abraham Lincoln, ten feet down, when the latest of the man's interminable burials began.

September 26, 1901. Only three of the Guard of Honor were left. They came. Thirty people, in all, some of them State officials, some townspeople, crowded Memorial Hall. Once more Leon P. Hopkins, the plumber, who had for fourteen years been calling himself the last man to see Lincoln's face, opened the casket, this time unsoldering his own soldering. Thirty Springfieldians passed by, peering down into the hole. J. C. Thompson, one of the survivors of that group, remembered in 1928 how he had approached the casket.

"As I came up I saw that top-knot of Mr. Lincoln's — his hair was coarse and thick, 'like a horse's,' he used to say — and it stood up high in front. When I saw that, I knew that it was Mr. Lincoln. Any one who had ever seen his pictures would have known it was him. His features had not decayed. His face was dark, very dark and brown — his skin was swarthy in life. He looked just like a statue of himself lying there."

The identification was absolute, but instead of scotching the myth, it merely gave new impetus to the old suspicions that there was something queer about the tomb. The body had been moved again, so it was said. Where there were so many queer, half-secret things happening, there must be something wrong.

And even more weirdly, it rekindled the companion-myth that had begun when the body was brought westward in 1865 — the fantastic notion that there was something supernatural about the body itself. Newspapers then had said that the body was embalmed in "extreme rigor" to withstand the fourteen-day exhibition tour. They had called it "a shell," "an effigy," "a statue." They had recounted Secretary Stanton's sudden order that Photographer Gurney in New York break the plates he had made of Mr. Lincoln in his coffin, since Mrs. Lincoln had complained that the pictures showed her husband's face to have a "most unusual expression."

Strange it would have been if ignorant minds, under the hysteria of the time, had not twisted these morbid terms into a fancy that the coffin held Lincoln not at all, only a statue of the man.

So, today, when pilgrims from all parts of the Republic ask Herbert Wells Fay, the present custodian, "Is Mr. Lincoln's body petrified?" he answers them gently, remembering those long-gone facts and the times, since then, that parties of identification have likened the dead face to the bronze statue.

"No, no," he replies. "Mr. Lincoln's body was only extremely well preserved, and that was all. He had but little flesh. All the arts of embalming in that time were used, and the body has remained all these years in an air-tight casket."

This myth, however, is only a minor one, attaching itself to the main superstition that the body is gone altogether. Ignorant imagination does not believe in a statue so much as in a miracle.

But there were no phantoms in the mind of Leon P. Hopkins, the plumber, as, on September 26, 1901, with his men, he soldered the lead square back over the gaping hole. Nor was he troubled with wonderments over the myth-making habits of mankind as he saw the coffin lowered into the new grave, with workmen sloshing in mortar and more mortar until the dead man slept, as he sleeps today, fast at last in the heart of a great boulder of cement and steel.

Mr. Hopkins was thinking, with pardonable pride, that he was, after all, the last man to look upon the face of Abraham Lincoln.

✣　✣　✣　27　✣　✣　✣

THE DREAMS OF A PROPHET

BETWEEN THE HEAD of Abraham Lincoln's coffin and the Liberty Bell, as the President's funeral rested in the city of Philadelphia, April 22 and 23, 1865, stood a wreath, and although it was no larger nor finer than hundreds of others that had been brought into Independence Hall for the President's funeral, it held its place of honor there from Saturday afternoon until after midnight on Sunday, as the crowds jammed past the bier. Nobody could remember who had handed it in; wreaths had showered upon the historic room since long before the funeral train had arrived.

However, it was not the wreath itself that won such distinguished position, it was the legend it framed: "Before any great national event I have always had the same dream. I had it the other night. It is of a ship sailing rapidly."

Nothing else — nothing else was needed. The words lay there, like the dead face so near them, for all passing eyes to see, and if any there were in the inching line to question what the legend might mean, there were plenty of fellow mourners, before or behind, to explain. The tale of Lincoln's dream that had foretold his tragic end had already gone over the country. Newspapers had printed it immediately after his assassination, and the people had seized it. And now the newspapers were to print it again, describing the incident of the funeral wreath in Philadelphia.

The wreath presumably withered and went to the dust-heaps of the City of Brotherly Love when the funeral pageant had crushed its way onward to other towns, but the story of Lincoln's dream proved everlasting. Biographers of the man lingered over it, orators grew dramatic with it, superstitious folk took it as evidence that the sad, herculean hero was supernatural, and even Americans who fancied themselves as rationalists cherished it as an instance of Lincoln's superiority in mystic ways.

Coming when it did, and living as it has, this story of the dream has been one of the reasons — many though they are — for Lincoln's deification in the Republic. It helped make him the American god.

It will be recalled what the dream was; that dream Lincoln described to his Cabinet on the afternoon of Good Friday, April 14, 1865, a few hours before he met the accident of assassination. When Grant, who was his guest that afternoon, had worried about Sherman, down in North Carolina, Lincoln had said that he felt everything would be all right since he had had, last night, the dream which always came to him before important events in the war — the dream in which he was in a mysterious vessel "sailing toward a dark and indefinite shore."

For a President of the United States, in a time like the Civil War, to dream that he was sailing rapidly toward an unseen shore was certainly not remarkable. Most of his waking hours, across four years, were spent in wondering where the Ship of

State was going. But no such simple explanation was made by the authors, reporters, and orators who dwelt upon the incident with emotional awe in the years that followed Lincoln's death.

Cabinet members, who had heard Lincoln narrate it, told the story as having been weirdly significant, and the morsel passed on into the stream of popular emotion about the martyr. From the funeral time, when it was woven into the wreaths and mottoes with which the people decorated their homes and floats, it progressed, being woven into the Lincoln-myth as an instance of Lincoln's strange nearness to the Unknown.

It made him seem as clairvoyant in his dreams as in his waking hours at the White House desk, when he had been tirelessly guiding the nation through the storm.

In time, the story of the dream changed in the telling. That Lincoln thought he was foreseeing Sherman's victory was forgotten; all that stuck in the minds of romantic people was the eerie fact that Lincoln had dreamed his ominous dream just before his death. Around the world went the story. Charles Dickens used to bind his listeners to their chairs as in a spell when he told it, once fascinating so practiced a fictionist as George Eliot with his version "of President Lincoln having told the council on the day he was shot that something remarkable would happen because he had just dreamt, for the third time, a dream that had twice before preceded events momentous to the nation. The dream was that he was in a boat on a great river all alone, and he ended with the words, 'I drift — I drift — I drift.'"

Perhaps the story had come to Dickens in this newly poetic form, but not likely. Those additional elements of mystery, the interjection of the "third time is the charm" element of folklore, and the melodramatic "I drift" ending, appear to have been, more probably, the artistic touches that the most resourceful story-teller of his time would have worked out as he handled the theme.

The dream-tale went to heighten the folk-feeling that there had been something "other-worldly" about the man and his death, and before Summer had fairly succeeded the Springtime of his passing, other stories of Lincoln's premonitions were adding their weight to the forces that so surely elevated him to the American Olympus.

Harriet Beecher Stowe, who would herself soon be saying that the Lord had directed her to write *Uncle Tom's Cabin*, announced that Lincoln, sitting in his slippers and unbuttoned vest, his hair every which way, had once confided to her his certainty that death was near. The busy little woman, always a great visitor, had gone to the President a few months before his end and had, in the course of conversation, asked him if he did not feel relief at the signs of early peace.

"No, Mrs. Stowe," he had answered, "I shall never live to see peace. This war is killing me."

Mrs. Stowe's brother, Henry Ward Beecher, the vacillating evangelist, who had by turns ridiculed and supported the President and who, now that Lincoln was dead, lauded him fulsomely, came forward to say that Lincoln had known all along that he would not survive the war; that he had put his whole life into the conflict and known that when it was over he would collapse.

As early as July, 1865, John Hay, one of Lincoln's private secretaries, officially stamped as truthful the stories of the late President's sense of foreboding disaster. John Hay was a man of honor (although in time swallow-tailed coats and long dinners at the Court of St. James's would turn him into a snob, ashamed of his prairie youth), and when, in *Harper's Magazine*, three months after the assassination, he described Lincoln's superstitions, he was believed. Lincoln had told him, he said, of an evil omen that had appeared as long before as when he had lived in Springfield.

"It was just after my election in 1860," Lincoln said, "when the news had been coming in thick and fast and there had been a great 'hurrah boys,' so that I was well tired out and went home to rest, throwing myself on a lounge in my chamber. Opposite to where I lay there was a bureau with a swinging glass in it, and looking in that glass I saw myself reflected at nearly full length; but my face, I noticed, had two separate and distinct images, the tip of the nose of one being about three inches from the tip of the other. I was a little bothered, perhaps startled, and got up and looked in the glass, but the illusion vanished. On lying down again, I saw it a second time, plainer if possible, than before; and then I noticed that one of the faces was a little paler — say, five shades — than the other.

"I got up and the thing melted away, and I went off, and in the excitement of the hour forgot all about it — nearly, but not quite, for the thing would come up once in a while and give me a little pang as though something disagreeable had happened. When I got home I told my wife about it and a few days after I tried the experiment again, when, sure enough, the thing came back again; but I never succeeded in bringing the ghost back after that, though once I tried very industriously to show it to my wife, who was worried about it somewhat. She thought it a sign that I was to be elected to a second term of office and that the paleness of one of the faces was an omen that I should not see life throughout the last term."

Another Middle Westerner who had followed Lincoln to Washington came forward, too, in these years directly after the assassination, to intensify unwittingly the supernaturalism with which the dead hero was coming to be so widely regarded. Ward Hill Lamon in Danville, Illinois, had been a sort of resident-partner of the circuit-riding Lincoln, joining forces with the Springfield attorney when court came to Danville. Lincoln knew Lamon as a hearty, rollicking, and fearless fellow and when the time came to go East for that 1861 inauguration, took him along for protection; Lamon, whose two guns and bowie knives might be depended upon if any of the countless threats of murder should prove to have been grounded well.

In Washington, Lamon was made Marshal of the District of Columbia, a perfunctory title attached to the social factotum of the Executive Mansion. But while Lamon was presenting visitors to the President on state occasions he was also watching for assassins. Talk of killing Lincoln increased rather than ebbed with the years of civil warfare, and Lamon in 1864 was worried, although he could never persuade Lincoln to adopt the precautions he deemed necessary. In December of that year Lamon, becoming offended by Lincoln's indifference to his warnings, made vain attempts to resign his position, charging that "you do not appreciate what I have repeatedly said to you in regard to the proper police arrangements connected with your household and your own personal safety. *You are in danger.* . . . Tonight, as you have done on several previous occasions, you went unattended to the theater. When I say unattended, I mean that you went alone with Charles Sumner and a foreign minister, neither of whom could defend himself against an assault from any able-bodied woman in this city."

Lincoln would not accept Lamon's resignation, and the testy marshal continued watching over his charge, and watching so carefully, that it is reasonable to suspect that if he had been on duty the night of April 14, 1865, the President might not have been murdered. But as things were, he was in Richmond, Virginia, on an errand for Lincoln that evening when his two guns were needed most.

When Lincoln was gone, Lamon came home with the body and remained in Illinois, trying to write his chieftain's life and failing miserably at it, not because his work was faulty but because it angered people who read it. To Lamon, Lincoln was human, real, a creature of virtues and faults, a cunning lawyer and politician, an intellectual, rather than saint. Naturally this and the double vision in the mirror, adding that the President a romantic creature of mythical perfections, divine in heart.

But for all his hatred of sentimentality and myth, Lamon fed the fire of superstition that people were kindling about the name of Lincoln. He verified John Hay's account of Lincoln and the double vision in the mirror, adding that the President had been haunted by the memory of this strange thing even after he had gone to the White House. Also, he said that Lincoln in his dreams, both as boy and man, had seen himself rise to a great height and then fall.

One time, said Lamon, Mrs. Lincoln attempted to joke her husband out of a dark mood, and had been answered in slow and measured tones, "It seems strange how much there is in the Bible about dreams. There are, I think, some sixteen chapters in the Old Testament and four or five in the New in which dreams are mentioned, and there are many other passages scattered throughout the book which refer to visions. If we believe the Bible, we must accept the fact that in the old days God and

His angels came to men in their sleep and made themselves known through dreams. Nowadays dreams are regarded as very foolish and are seldom told, except by old women and by young men and maidens in love."

And when Mrs. Lincoln asked him if he believed in dreams, he answered in that slow evasiveness with which he always refused to cross any Fox River until he had come to it.

"I can't say that I do, but I had one the other night which has haunted me ever since. After it occurred, the first time I opened the Bible, strange as it may appear, it was at the twenty-eighth chapter of Genesis, which relates the wonderful dream Jacob had. I turned to other passages and seemed to encounter a dream or a vision wherever I looked. I kept on turning the leaves of the old book, and everywhere my eye fell upon passages recording matters strangely in keeping with my own thoughts — supernatural visitations, dreams, visions, etc."

"You frighten me," cried Mrs. Lincoln, usually on nerve's edge. "What is the matter?"

Gradually she drove him into telling of his dream.

"About ten days ago," he began, very slowly, very sadly, "I retired late. I soon began to dream. There seemed to be a death-like stillness about me. Then I heard subdued sobs, as if a number of people were weeping. I thought I left my bed and wandered downstairs. There the silence was broken by the same pitiful sobbing, but the mourners were invisible. I went from room to room; no living person was in sight, but the same mournful sounds of distress met me as I passed along.

"It was light in all the rooms; every object was familiar to me; but where were all the people who were grieving as if their hearts would break? I was puzzled and alarmed. What could be the meaning of all this? Determined to find the cause of a state of things so mysterious and so shocking, I kept on until I arrived at the East Room, which I entered. Before me was a catafalque, on which rested a corpse wrapped in funeral vestments. Around it were stationed soldiers who were acting as guards; and there was a throng of people, some gazing mournfully upon the corpse, whose face was covered, others weeping pitifully. 'Who is dead in the White House?' I demanded of one of the soldiers. 'The President,' was his answer. 'He was killed by an assassin.' Then came a loud burst of grief from the crowd, which awoke me from my dream. I slept no more that night; and although it was only a dream, I have been strangely annoyed by it ever since."

Lincoln had been at times pale as he narrated his dream, said Lamon, and had come back gravely to the thing on other days, once concluding a reference to it with Hamlet's "To sleep, perchance to dream! Ay, there's the rub."

Lamon it was, too, who told of Mrs. Lincoln, distraught with horror after the murder of her husband beside her in the theater-box, finally saying as her first coherent exclamation, "His dream was prophetic."

"Prophetic" was the word. Some of the clergymen had called him a prophet as early as April 16, 1865, when his death was the Easter Sunday topic from almost every pulpit in the land, and with the years, as his stature became more and more apparent, the word rang out with such increasing frequency that it became at last a litany for the Republic. Multitudes of Americans came to think of Lincoln as people of biblical times thought of their dead leaders — the inspired of God.

Col. W. H. Crook, Lincoln's White House body-guard, shared this view. It had been as a member of Washington's police force that he had been attached to the Executive Mansion staff in January, 1865, and when he was told that his duty would be to protect the President's life, he had been awed, he said later, in describing his emotions. He remembered how he had felt as he realized that he was to guard "the life of the man who had been raised up by the Lord God Almighty to preserve the Union as surely as Moses had been raised up to lead the people of Israel through their trials and tribulations until he brought them to the threshold of the Promised Land."

Crook, too, in his writings and interviews, told the public that Lincoln had had his death revealed to him in dreams. As his nightly duty, Crook sat outside the President's bedroom, watching, watching all night long, constantly turning his head to see that no danger approached, scorning to read so much as a newspaper lest he be not ready for the great emergency should it come.

On the fourteenth of April, Crook was on day-duty and during the afternoon, as he told it, Lincoln had talked with him about dreaming three nights hand-running of his own assassination, a statement that stirred Crook to earnest entreaty that the President should not go out to the theater that evening as he planned. When Lincoln said that he must go to please his wife, Crook begged to be taken along as a guard in the theater, but the President said "No," adding that he couldn't afford to have his guard work day and night too. It was then that he gave what Crook, afterward, saw to be the prophetic sign of death.

Lincoln's habit had been to use the words "Good night" to Crook as he went from his office to his bedroom each night, but on the evening of the fatal day, according to the emotional body-guard, Lincoln had turned at the door and had said significantly, "Good-bye, Crook."

"It was the first and only time that he neglected to say 'Good night' to me," said Crook in telling it, "and the only time he ever said 'Good-bye' to me. I thought of it at the moment and, a few hours later, when the news flashed over Washington that he had been shot, his last words were so burned into my being that they can never be forgotten."

Crook told his readers that Lincoln on his last evening had said that he believed the men who wanted to take his life would do it.

"More than this," he continued, "I believe Lincoln had some vague sort of a warning that the attempt would be made on the night of the fourteenth. I know that this is an extraordinary statement to make, but the chain of circumstances is at least an interesting thing to consider.

"At a Cabinet meeting Lincoln spoke of the recurrence the night before of a dream, which, he said, had always forerun something of moment in his life. In the dream a ship under full sail bore down upon him. At the time he spoke of it he felt that some good fortune was on its way to him. He was serene, even joyous over it. Later in the day, while he was driving with his wife, his mind still seemed to be dwelling on the question of the future. When I accompanied him to the War Department he had become depressed and spoke of his belief that he would be assassinated. When he returned to the White House, he said that he did not want to go to the theater but must so as to not disappoint the people. . . . To me it all means that he had, with his waking on that day, a strong prescience of coming change. As the day wore on, the feeling darkened into an impression of coming evil."

As the biographies of Lincoln began to rain down upon the American people so unendingly, with historians and novelists combing the past for new facts about the man, other details cropped out to convince the credulous that the hero had been destined all along for a sacrificial end.

The more superstitious biographers delighted to quote the revelations that Lincoln was purported to have made concerning his approaching doom to a certain Father Chiniquy who made occasional trips from the midlands to Washington with warnings of assassination. To most men who begged him to be careful about exposing himself to supposed murderers, Lincoln had been casual, often humorous, laughing fears away. But to the Rev. Charles Chiniquy, as the clergyman declared in after years, Lincoln had unbosomed himself most amazingly, saying:

"You are not the first to warn me against the dangers of assassination. My ambassadors in Italy, France, and England, as well as Professor Morse, have many times warned me against the plots of murderers. But I see no other safeguard but to be always ready to die, as Christ advises it. . . . Now I see the end of this terrible conflict with the same joy of Moses at the end of his trying forty years in the wilderness. . . . Yes, every time that my soul goes to God to ask the favor of seeing the other side of Jordan and eating the fruits of that peace after which I am longing with such an unspeakable desire, do you know that there is a still but solemn voice which tells me that I will see those things only from a long distance, and that I will be among the dead when the nation, which God granted me to lead through those awful trials, will cross the Jordan and dwell in the Land of Paradise where peace, industry, happiness,

and liberty will make every one happy; and why so? Because
He has already given me favors which He never gave, I dare
say, to any man in these latter days. . . . Moses died for his
people's sake; Christ died for the whole world's sake. . . .
Now would it not be the greatest of honors and privileges bestowed upon me if God in His infinite love, mercy, and wisdom
would put me between His faithful servant Moses and His
Eternal Son Jesus, that I might die as they did, for my nation's
sake? . . .

"It seems to me that the Lord wants me, as He wanted in the
days of Moses another victim — a victim that He has himself
chosen, anointed, and prepared for the sacrifice, by raising it
above the rest of His people. I cannot conceal from you that my
impression is that I am the victim. So many plots have been already made against my life that it is a real miracle that they
have all failed. But can we expect that God will make a perpetual miracle to save my life? I believe not."

To men familiar with Lincoln's reticences, absence of orthodox Christian belief and characteristic manner of speech, these
disclosures were far more Chiniquy than Lincoln. In Springfield,
Lincoln's old friends of the circuit-riding days snorted their
disbelief that Lincoln had ever said anything like that to Chiniquy.

Obviously, the unbalanced imagination of the clergyman had
led him to expand some simple remarks of the President into a
metaphysical monologue which, though it retained, in all likelihood, some of Lincoln's words, misrepresented him wholly.
That phrase "perpetual miracle" had the ring of Lincolnesque
humor, but the egotistical tone of the speech was entirely foreign
to the President, who although he felt himself to be more
capable than anybody else in almost any given group, never let
listeners know it. Nevertheless the pious and not dishonest
fraud of the clergyman went on its exulting road.

As the mass of Lincoln-literature grew with the years, it became evident that woman's intuition had felt the disaster im-
pending. His wife has sensed it. So, it seemed, had his step-
mother, Sarah Bush Lincoln. Between his first election and inauguration he had gone down from Springfield into southern

Illinois to see her, and the old, old lady had embraced him with deep emotion. She would never see him again, she said, for she felt that his enemies would assassinate him.

"No, Mama, no," he had comforted her. "They'll not do that. Trust in the Lord and all will be well. We will see each other again."

At about that same time, when Lincoln was waiting for March and the fateful journey to the White House, there had come to Springfield in the army of congratulation Hannah Armstrong, at whose table the lanky young Lincoln had eaten many meals, and whose son William had been freed of a murder-charge when the lawyer, Lincoln, had proved that the prosecutor's witnesses were wrong when they said that they had seen the murder by the light of the moon. An almanac in Lincoln's hands showed that there was, at the fatal hour, no moon high enough in the sky to make such a view possible.

Hannah described her visit to Lincoln in his office. "Well, I talked to him for some time and was about to bid him good-bye; had told him that it was the last time I should ever see him —something told me I should never see him again; they would kill him. He smiled and said jokingly, 'Hannah, if they kill me I shall never die another death.' I then bade him good-bye."

As America combed Lincoln's past to find details with which to feed its worshipful hunger, it came upon many tales of his dreams, both good and bad. Of the happy dreams there was one that adjusted itself well to the growing belief that Lincoln had loved the common people with something like divine attachment.

Lincoln, as he told it, had dreamed about walking through a great crowd and hearing some one say, "He's a common-looking fellow!" To the speaker Lincoln had turned, replying, "Friend, the Lord must have preferred common-looking people, he made so many of them." The anecdote thrived in American lore not so much for its humor as for its epitomizing of Lincoln's humanity.

Items of his superstitiousness grew. Once he had telegraphed from the White House to his wife in Philadelphia, "Put Tad's pistol away. I had an ugly dream about him." From Springfield he had taken his son Robert to Terre Haute to have the boy treated for dog-bite by the mad-stone which was kept there in awesome veneration. In 1831, he had visited a "voodoo" doctor in New Orleans, and while he was President he had liked to talk to weather-prophets and rain-makers.

Spiritualists, soon after his death, set up the claim that Lincoln was one of them, citing the times he had allowed séances in the White House. That Lincoln allowed such things is very probable, but that he did it in any credulity is improbable. When death had taken Willie, his third son, as it had Eddie, his second, he was almost insane from grief. Some biographers say that he was, at this hour, almost as inclined to suicide as he had been after the death of Ann Rutledge, a sweetheart, in his younger days. It was only when the dead Willie's face came to him in dreams that he abandoned his despair. No dreams came to help his suffering wife, and it seemed that her sanity would go. He thought of many things to bring her relief, among them spiritualism, and he brought practitioners into the White House to hold their séances. In these dark hocus-pocuses Mrs. Lincoln found comfort, and Lincoln let them go on for a time, careless of whether the intellectuals of the capital thought him addle-pated or no.

In the end it was his own voice rather than the whispering trumpets of the mediums that brought steadiness to his wife's mind. Taking her by the arm, one day, he led her to a White House window and showed her the insane asylum in the distance. She would have to be taken there, he said, unless she quit grieving so wildly. Mrs. Lincoln obeyed.

Instances like this, as the American people read them, seemed typical of Lincoln's genius for management. Hadn't he guided the electorate much as he had handled his own wife, persuading them, coaxing them, saving them with sweet rationality? He had preserved the Union by a wisdom that appeared superhuman in all that bloody confusion and racing excitement of war. He had foreseen "the irrepressible conflict" and had managed it, when it came, with a success that, as people remembered it, looked to have been miraculous. His speech had been so clear when other men's had been so hysterical, his thoughts so lofty when lesser men had been frothing and ranting around him, and his brain had kept so cool in all that time of fever, that the American people, reading of him, saw the aureole of a prophet around his head. It was like a prophet to foresee his own fate as well as the destiny of his country. Lincoln had been so melancholy, it was said, because he had known that he was marching to his doom. The sorrows of his soul became as famous as the sparkings of his sense of humor.

It was unorthodox ever to remember that Lincoln's sadness might have arisen from natural causes. In his lifetime Lincoln had been recognized by plenty of his associates to be weary of all the death and strife of war time, despondent over the sufferings of the common people, for whom he genuinely cared. But once Lincoln was in his tomb, it became the national fashion to believe that the great leader on his heights had been saddened by the mysterious revelations that were sent him from the Beyond.

So providentially had he come, and so inexplicably had he been taken away in the hour of triumph, that the Republic felt that it couldn't account for him at all unless it were to believe that he had been brought by supernatural powers on an errand of sacrifice.

In Springfield, Illinois, sat a gaunt, free-thinking man like Lincoln, William H. Herndon, who saw this strange deification happening to his dead partner. Herndon, of the law firm of "Lincoln and Herndon," loved Lincoln and the truth as he knew them both, and when he saw the myth-makers turning his friend into a bloodless, hopelessly unreal effigy of maudlin sentimentality, he rose in his wrath to denounce them as fictionists. The sight of politicians and preachers who had assailed or belittled Lincoln in life, now posing as idolaters of the martyr, spurred him to make one grand effort to keep Lincoln, the Man, for America to look at in the years to come. To him, the real Lincoln was great enough to command all the respect that the Republic could ever give; why allow him to be changed into a being impossibly good, sickeningly saccharine? Herndon wrote and Herndon talked, and although his *Life of Lincoln* was the most truthful biography of that early period, it offended ro-

mantic souls by its realism and was, like Lamon's life of the dead
President, a financial failure.

So long as Herndon described the presentiments which Lincoln had had of his sad end, his biography of the martyr was
welcome. It satisfied the national desire to find that Lincoln's
own partner knew the prophet to have felt, for years, that he
would reach a high place and then be stricken down. It seemed
very moving and very true to find Herndon reporting that
Lincoln had felt deep sorrow at leaving Springfield to go East
for his inauguration "because of his feeling, which had become
irrepressible, that he would never return alive."

But when Herndon suggested that the reasons for Lincoln's
melancholy lay in the realm of the natural rather than the supernatural, an outcry of protest arose. It outraged the idolaters to
read:

"Lincoln's melancholy never failed to impress any man who
ever saw him or knew him. The perpetual look of sadness was
his most prominent feature. The cause of his peculiar condition
was a matter of frequent discussion among his friends. John T.
Stuart (a former law-partner of Lincoln's and one of his closest
Springfield friends) said it was due to his abnormal digestion.
His liver failed to work properly — did not secrete bile — and
his bowels were equally as inactive."

Lincoln had been careless of his food and of his eating, said
Herndon; he ate what was set before him, absent-mindedly. He
slept badly. He had trouble with his erratic, storm-brained wife.
He was forever sad over "the knowledge of his own obscure
and lowly origin." He had been superstitious, but, for that
matter, so had the great majority of the pioneers with whom
he had been reared and of whose blood he was.

Poor Herndon, having told what rational truths he knew,
waited for the clouds of cloying incense to clear away, and for
the myths to disappear. His answer came. From all parts of
the Republic he heard, in dismay, a strange and fearsome cry
rising, "Atheist! Atheist! Herndon's an atheist!"

THE HOLIDAY OF DEATH

IT WAS IN THE WILD DELIRIUM of Abraham Lincoln's funeral — with seven million Northerners crushing, sobbing, and fainting as the catafalque went by — that America's Memorial Day was born. Fourteen days of morbid frenzy around the bier of the martyred President were enough to prepare the Republic for an annual Holiday of Death — a day of processionals, flowers and lamentations for dead warriors.

Coming at the end of four years of war, Lincoln's funeral gave the Union population an opportunity to express, *en masse,* the sorrow and grief that it had been accumulating all along as the death-lists grew. Dramatically, the funeral touched off the pent-up passion of a people to honor, most signally, their war dead. Between the day his corpse left the White House and the day it came to rest in the Illinois prairie, Lincoln became the symbol of a nation's grief, "the sacrifice on the altar of Freedom" as so many orators told the people.

For days — and for years — that funeral hung like a passionate, grieving memory over the North, an experience violent enough to prepare the folk-mind for the spontaneous appearance later on of a great annual holiday whereon every man who had died for his country in that same crisis might be mourned as his commander had been.

But it was not even a matter of weeks, let alone years, before this aching wish of the people to honor their war dead was to appear. On the very day that Lincoln's travel-worn body lay in the Court House at Chicago with the funeral woe reaching its climax, the first memorial services for dead Union soldiers were being held in — of all places — Charleston, South Carolina, where the divided house of the Union had caught fire four years before. It was in the city which had fired the first shot at Federal soldiers that the first flowers were laid on Yankee graves.

The author of this observance was James Redpath, war correspondent for Horace Greeley's New York *Tribune* on Sherman's march to the sea. In March, with the end of the war visible, Redpath was released to become superintendent of the freedmen's schools in Charleston. He loved the South, despite the fact that he had battled with his pen and printing-press for the anti-slavery cause in "bleeding Kansas." As a wandering printer, before the war he had known and liked Charleston and now, among the ashes of Secession's nest, he was to hold the first Union Memorial Day. He had been occupied in organizing schools and orphan asylums for the ex-slaves when the news came that Lincoln had been assassinated. Nowhere was this news so stupefying as to Union soldiers. They idolized Lincoln with a unanimity unapproached in any other class. And in the Army of the Tennessee — the backbone of Sherman's flaming raid — this was acutely true. They were Westerners; so was Lincoln.

No matter how often their field commanders might be changed, blaming Lincoln, the Northern armies marched on singing songs to "Father Abraham." In defeat they cursed their generals, the War Department, the politicians, but not Lincoln. Even the Democrats and Copperheads, when they were drafted into blue uniforms, softened toward the President once they were in the field.

There was good reason for this. Lincoln missed few opportunities to favor soldiers, allowing none to be shot for falling asleep on sentry duty and pardoning them wholesale with the excuse that it was hard for country boys to break the habit of going to bed at sundown. Lincoln habitually sided with the private soldier in a court-martial, and the freedom with which he turned condemned men loose drove army disciplinarians nearly insane. Toward the common soldiers Lincoln was instinctively a father — perhaps more of a mother than a father, lavishing a woman's sympathy upon them in hospitals, visiting them in camp and field, addressing them whenever opportunity offered.

It was the natural way of his heart. Also, it was characteristic of the profound political astuteness of his brain. The soldier-vote was undeviatingly loyal. Even while vast populations at home were crying for the political overthrow of Lincoln, the butcherer of their boys, the boys themselves were begging for furloughs which they might spend in going home to vote for the President's policies, and when the news of his assassination had come, they had been frantic. Four years of killing had not hardened them against a death like this.

Redpath undoubtedly shared the soldiers' views. Around him were the colored people, to whom Lincoln was already a god. "Marsa Lincoln, he walk de earth like de Lord," they said.

Each day brought news, belated but eagerly read, of the mountainous funeral that the War Department was giving Lincoln. The news came that the cities of the North were honoring the traveling corpse with everything that imagination could devise, parades, decorations, mottoes, and flowers, flowers, flowers. The services had been both profane and beautiful.

Never before had the Republic been so near morbid insanity and never before, so the superstitious said, had April bloomed so sweetly. To the millions who saw the hand of the supernatural in all the events of that straining time, it seemed indeed as though God had loosed the very forces of Nature in one explosion of blossoms with which to decorate Lincoln's bier.

From the moment the coffin left the White House until it sank into the Illinois prairie grave, it was blanketed with flowers. The funeral car was a wilderness of blooms, with new wreaths and bouquets showering in at every stop; it traveled under arches of flowers that spanned the railroad tracks. The hearse-wheels rolled on roses, floral floats studded the long parades that followed, blossoms were wound in the manes of the horses that drew it. All night, in State capitols and city halls, committees watched to snatch away the coffin-flowers at their first sign of wilting and to replace them with even larger bouquets.

From the windows of the creeping train, the funeral party could see heaps of flowers beside mock graves on hillsides where people were staging tableaus of grief as the black train went by.

The Springtime added its emotion to the hysteria of the moment. Walt Whitman, brooding over the spectacle, described it in his ode to the Lincoln funeral train, beginning:

"When lilacs last in the dooryard bloom'd,
And the great star early droop'd in the western sky in the night,
I mourn'd, and yet shall mourn with ever-returning spring.

Ever-returning spring, trinity sure to me you bring,
Lilac blooming perennial and drooping star in the west,
And thought of him I love.

☆　　☆　　☆

Over the breast of the spring, the land, amid cities,
Amid lanes and through old woods, where lately the violets
　　peep'd from the ground, spotting the grey débris,
Amid the grass in the fields each side of the lanes, passing the
　　endless grass. . . .
Passing the apple-tree blows of white and pink in the orchards,
Carrying a corpse to where it shall rest in the grave,
Night and day journeys a coffin.

☆　　☆　　☆

Here, coffin that slowly passes,
I give you my sprig of lilac."

Something of this same shuddering ecstasy that Whitman
saw and felt, necessarily came down over the telegraph to Redpath in Charleston. In these days the Abolitionist, talking to his
colored listeners in the Presbyterian church where he was holding school for overflow classes, suggested to the ex-slaves that
they decorate the graves of the Union soldiers who had died to
make them free. On the edge of town was the Federal cemetery,
where thousands of Northerners lay buried. Like wind this idea
went through the colored population. A day was set, May 1,
and Redpath was amazed when between three and six thousand
persons, their arms full of flowers, marched to the graveyard behind the muffled drums and marching soldiers that the Union
authorities had contributed to the occasion. Droves of negro
children staggered along under their bright burdens, singing
"John Brown's Body."

News of this observance came North through the army and

spread as the soldiers, mustered out, passed to their homes through the Summer of '65. A tiny seed the idea was, but it fell on ground that had been harrowed into fertility by the Lincoln funeral ceremonies.

The story of the flowers on the soldiers' graves blended simply and dramatically into the Northern people's memory of the flowers that had stormed down to hide the martyred President's casket.

For thirty days after Lincoln was put into his tomb, the funeral mourning remained draped across the houses of the North—and in Springfield longer than that. Crowds in excursions came to look at the receiving-vault in Oak Ridge Cemetery where the corpse, guarded by ropes and armed sentries, awaited Mrs. Lincoln's distraught decision as to where her husband should be permanently buried. All summer Union soldiers, as they were mustered out, journeyed to the tomb to see where their commander slept.

Across the fields from Springfield, in another Illinois town, Decatur, the Grand Army of the Republic, an organization of Union veterans, was forming. Within twelve months after the assassination, this fledgling G.A.R. had moved headquarters to Springfield and was growing rapidly. Slowly it outgrew its rival associations of veterans and conquered its internal wranglings, so that it had twenty departments and wide strength when in January, 1868, General John A. Logan, the histrionic, part-Indian warrior-politician of Illinois, became its commander in chief.

On the fifth of May, Logan stirred, if not surprised, his followers with a general order designating the thirtieth of May as a day for all members to strew with flowers the "graves of comrades" who had "died in defence of their country during the late rebellion." He hoped that such ceremonies would be kept up from year to year and that always the Republic would "garland the passionless mounds with the choicest flowers of Springtime."

Many of the departments and posts seized on the idea with alacrity, others debated, doubting whether such an observance was wise. Within and without the organization it was feared that such a holiday "would unnecessarily keep alive war-time bitterness and foster animosities that should be buried in oblivion."

It was said that money had better be spent on maimed soldiers than on music and flowers for the dead. Nevertheless, arrangements for the day went ahead, and all objections were lost in the tremendous outpouring of people when May 30 dawned. Business houses closed their doors, factories shut down. Farmers and their families journeyed to the nearest celebration. The people had only been waiting for such an opportunity. Parades, speeches, salutes of musketry, decorations of graves with flags and avalanches of blossoms, adorned the occasion. Excursions piled crowds into the larger cities again, as they had during the Lincoln funeral. A national holiday had been born, even if the government was never to declare it so. If Washington wouldn't, the States would, and the Northern commonwealths rapidly made it legal, with the Southern States joining, differing only in the date. North and South Carolina named the tenth of May, anniversary of "Stonewall" Jackson's death, and all the rest of Dixie, April 26. Kentucky, Tennessee and Missouri adopted the Northern date.

There have arisen, since that day sixty years ago, many claims as to the origin of Memorial Day, commonly called "Decoration Day." Some had it that Logan got the idea from the occasional decoration of their comrades' graves by Confederate soldiers during the war. Others said that General John J. Murray of Waterloo, New York, had told Logan of his leadership of a group of ex-soldiers to Union graves on Sunday, May 22, 1866. Adjutant-General Chipman of the G.A.R. insisted that he had given the idea to Logan around the first of May, '68, passing on to his commander a letter in which a Cincinnati member suggested that the G.A.R. adopt the old German custom of scattering flowers on the graves of the dead each Springtime. Down in Cincinnati it was declared that Comrade T. C. Campbell, afterward quartermaster general of the order, had headed a delegation of veterans taking flowers to the cemetery in the Spring of '67 and that the idea originated there.

Mrs. Logan declared that she had prompted her husband to issue the order, having herself borrowed the thought from the memorial services which she had witnessed in Richmond, Virginia, in the Spring of the year 1868. Richmond had been decorating the graves of its war dead beautifully, and she had suggested to the general that he institute such concerted action in the North.

Through the South live still more numerous claims to the inauguration of the custom. On July 15, 1906, it was declared by the Richmond *Times-Dispatch* that while New Orleans, Columbus, Georgia, Portsmouth, Virginia, and Richmond all believed themselves to be the pioneers in the celebration, Warrentown, Virginia, had observed the ritual first, holding services over the grave of a Confederate hero, John Quincy Marr, on June 1, 1861.

Richmond, on May 10, 1866, began the first of its yearly decoration ceremonies organizing the Oakwood Cemetery Memorial Association to adorn the graves of Confederate dead and hang the city with flags. Columbus, Georgia, put flowers on its soldiers' graves with appropriate speeches on April 26, 1866, the anniversary of Gen. Joseph E. Johnston's surrender to General Sherman — last gasp of the Lost Cause. A call for an observance of this day had been sent broadcast over the South some weeks before by the Ladies' Aid Society of Columbus, which had independently decked the cemetery with flowers in the Spring of 1865. Miss Lizzie Rutherford had suggested this event, and is remembered for it in Columbus, at least, as "The founder of Memorial Day."

Montgomery, Alabama, has claimed that it observed the same day, April 26, 1866; Columbus, Mississippi, has said that it held a celebration on April 25 of that year; Fredericksburg, Virginia, appointed the tenth of May, 1866; Petersburgh, Virginia, garlanded its war cemetery on May 26, 1868, and Camden, Arkansas, remembered that it had begun its annual decorations in November, 1866. Confederate graves in Charleston, South Carolina, were strewn with flowers in the Spring of 1866, a year after Redpath's procession had been held over Union graves.

Always there has been a dispute over where and when the day began. Always this dispute will go on, because the day itself came from nowhere — everywhere. The greater the number of claimants for its birthplace, the plainer the proof that the Republic was aching vaguely with eagerness to speak its grief after four years of killing. The funeral of the war's greatest figure pointed the way.

Each little fugitive decoration of graves across the land, each individual call to action, was a spontaneous outburst of the sentiment that had been crystallized at the burial-drama of Lincoln.

Over and over again in those first official celebrations held by the G.A.R. in 1868 and 1869 could be seen the nation's attempt to reproduce the pomp and tearful grandeur of Lincoln's funeral. Many of the busts of Lincoln, arches, mottoes and trappings that had been preserved from the funeral displays of three years before, were brought out for the first Memorial Day. Placards quoting Lincoln, picturing him, naming him, lamenting him, were common in cemeteries. Special bouquets for the "great martyr of Liberty" were frequently laid at the gates of cemeteries while veterans and their families spoke and fired salutes over the flowery graves of their dead comrades. Bands in many parades played their favorites from those ninety funeral marches that had been written to Lincoln in 1865. Choirs sang as they had beside the funeral train. Girls in white paraded as they had at Lincoln's obsequies.

Empty hearses, filled with flowers, rolled at the head of many processions. The same "catafalco" — mammoth hearse — that had carried Lincoln's body so high above the heads of the onlookers in New York City was brought out, covered with flowers, and drawn through the streets on the city's Memorial Day in 1869.

At the Springfield, Illinois, holiday in 1869 the Rev. Dr. George T. Allen dwelt on Lincoln's mystic spirit hovering over the Union. "None but the Saviour of man has had a more important mission on earth or filled his destiny better than Abraham Lincoln. If there be anything in foreordination, God predestined him before the foundation of the world to be the saviour of his country. . . . Abraham Lincoln's name is now as immortal as if Gabriel had dipped his fingers in the sunbeam and written it in letters of living light across the cerulean arch of heaven."

Where the G.A.R. ceremonies of 1868 had seen the people of twenty-seven States throng to "the heroes' graves," the Memorial Day of 1869 saw thirty-one States adopt the custom, with an estimated increase of three hundred per cent. in attendance. This, too, in the face of the fact that the day in 1869 fell on Sunday, and its observance met with opposition from many clergymen. Two out of five ceremonies that year were held on Monday, May 31, in deference to the ministers, and spirited veterans exchanged criticisms with the parsons in private — sometimes in public. At the monster services in Cleveland, Judge D. K. Carter prayed that the Lord would forgive the ministers for having said that the G.A.R. was desecrating the Sabbath, and into the Grand Army's headquarters in Washington, to which city they had been transferred, came scores of complaints about the dominies from local chapters of the organization.

The Memorial Day of 1869 was marred, too, in at least one cemetery, by the floods of anti-Southern wrath which the Radicals had stirred up in the North. Since the Winter of '65, when Thaddeus Stevens had wrested the control of Reconstruction out of the hands of the Executive and placed it in the vengeful hands of Congress, hatred had been burning brighter and brighter between the two sections. General Grant who, unfortunately for himself, wore no more that mussy uniform with three silver stars on the shoulder, had been President since March 4, '69, — sitting in a chair which did not allow him the freedom of his old war-saddle. Under his nose in '69 the G.A.R. used Memorial Day to flout the ex-Confederates. At the national graveyard in Arlington, marines were stationed over Confederate graves to prevent any Southern roses from falling thereon. Adjutant-General William T. Collins of the G.A.R. replied to the resulting criticisms in the press by declaring that the troops had been placed in the cemetery "to prevent any such unseemly act as the designed decoration of those [Confederate] graves, to effect which, it is well known, there was a purpose on the part of persons whose every sympathy was, and still remains, with the 'Lost Cause.' Our refusal to decorate rebel graves marks no hatred of their occupants or friends, but our undying hostility to the ideas for which they fought and died."

It was obvious that Grant, who was not at that time a member of the Grand Army of the Republic and who had, moreover, spoken out against organization of soldiers into political bodies, was ignorant of these antics in the graveyard, and the acts were never repeated. On the same day, the Union soldiers helped decorate the graves of Confederates who had died in prison and been buried at Alexandria, another suburb of the capital.

Memorial Day, '69, was enlivened, too, by the spirited denial of the G.A.R. commander in chief, John A. Logan, that his organization was in politics. At Duquoin, Illinois, he defended the Grand Army, saying that it was not banded together to advance any man or any party, and that its decoration of graves was anything but a move for self-aggrandizement, as was being loosely charged about the country. Orator that he was, and fiery as he certainly must have been upon this occasion, he was not widely believed, for the G.A.R. had most assuredly been in politics. The Radicals of Congress had captured it, as they had captured the nation.

At Appomattox Court House the Union army had been prepared to go home and be spiritually as well as physically at peace with the South. It had fought hatred and spleen well out of its system. But when the assassination of Lincoln gave the Radical politicians of the North an opportunity to revive the ancient charges that the South was morally debased, the soldiers felt their old sores smart once more.

In the Federal ranks were hundreds of thousands of men who had been Northern Democrats before the war, and, as such, companions in party organization with Southern Democrats. As between the "black Republicans," Abolitionists of the North, and the slaveholding Democrats of the South, these men had, up to 1860, chosen to side with the Southerners. In the campaign of 1860, as in 1854, and further back than that, they had listened with contempt to the enemies of slavery assailing Southerners as degenerate beasts. They sympathized with slavery, feeling that even if it was wrong, which they doubted, it was no issue for bloody war.

But disunion was another matter. When the Southern States seceded, the majority of Northern Democrats stood like a wall for the Constitution against States' rights. The greatest of them, squat, huge-headed, golden-voiced Stephen A. Douglas, Senator from Illinois, whom Lincoln had defeated for the Presidency in 1860, had tossed aside all jealousy, and with a modesty that glorified him, had offered to serve the Union in any character, however small, that Lincoln might select for him. On the inauguration-stand that first fourth of March when Lincoln had arisen to take the oath of office and had looked around for a place to lay his hat, little Douglas had reached out quietly and simply and held the "stove-pipe" till Lincoln was done. A few days later the "Little Giant," as the prairies knew him, had gone into the West haranguing his old Democratic followers, coaxing them, persuading them, thrilling them to the support of his conqueror, Lincoln. And he had kept on his flaming crusade until he went down, exhausted by his efforts, and died on the third of June, three months after the guns of Sumter, a greater loss to Lincoln, by far, than the battle of Bull Run in July.

They had the Douglas attitude, these Northern Democrats who had worn blue uniforms through the war, an attitude very different from the stay-at-home Democrats who hampered the Union cause with their Secession sympathies, crying for peace at any price, helping Southern prisoners to escape, voting against supplies for the loyal troops in the field and opposing the draft.

To "Douglas Democrats" such Radicals and Abolitionists as Sumner and Stevens and Wade had always been mere partisan bags of wind, but when they heard the news that the Confederacy had killed Lincoln they wavered. Perhaps the Radical Republicans were right. Home they came after the great mustering out in the Summer of '65 to join, in large part, the Republican party, and thus to support Sumner and Stevens and Wade. Those among them who had entered the army in their 'teens, too young to have had previous political affiliations, were almost universally Republican at the war's end, sworn enemies of the Democratic South.

For the political campaign of 1866 the soldiers speedily organized. The "Boys in Blue" they called themselves or "Sol-

diers' and Sailors' Leagues." Their purposes were twofold;
one to back up the Thad Stevens Radical party that was supporting stern Union Reconstruction principles against the too lenient
Andy Johnson, the other to get jobs for soldiers.

Northern soldiers had been badly swindled on the latter score,
no doubt of that. When the North had needed volunteers desperately, the politicians and statesmen had gone up and down
the country promising the soldiers that when the war was over,
nothing would be too good for them. "Fight now. Save us,"
these blandishments ran, "and when you come back the office-
holders will be glad to step out and let you have the plums."

Foolishly the warriors had believed all this, but when, after
Appomattox, they came gleefully back to claim their rewards,
they found that the politicians had forgotten their promises.
Smoothly the job-holders explained that the veterans should be
content with all their glory; they were heroes now, romantic
heroes, and had better enjoy their fame and leave practical
politics to those who understood it.

Naturally the soldiers organized and, largely backed by sympathetic civilian voters, frightened the politicians half out of
their wits and got much of what they had wanted. Loosely knit
together as they were, these clubs of "Boys in Blue" either
evaporated after the '66 campaign or went bodily into the
rapidly growing Grand Army of the Republic, which had something more durable to support, rituals, secrets, mystic grips and
passwords — it was a lodge.

Gen. John A. Logan, himself a Northern Democrat who had
come out of the war a Radical Republican, had not been scrupulous about keeping the Grand Army of the Republic free from
politics in the first years of its existence. As a member of Congress from Illinois he had rushed furiously to the support of
Stanton and the Radicals in their battle with President Johnson,
and, as commander in chief of the G.A.R. — whose headquarters
were now conveniently in Washington, he even pledged the
order to warfare on the streets of the city if they should be
needed to curb Johnson's will.

Johnson, fighting wildly against the Radicals, had kicked
Stanton out of his Cabinet. Stanton would not go, maintaining

that Johnson wished to have him out so that he could use the War Department to set the defeated South up in all its old political arrogance once more. Sober, conservative men, in that hour, feared that another civil war was upon the nation, and General Logan, sleeping with Stanton in the War Department building, standing guard like a ferocious walrus, his great black mustachios bristling, whispered to the war minister that the G.A.R. was outside patrolling the night, ready to defend him in case the President should bring out troops to oust him from his office. It was true; G.A.R. men were waiting to break out secret stores of arms and ammunition to the membership if the thing came to battles and street-barricades.

Such political dabblings almost wrecked the veterans' organization — that and an over-dose of jingoism. Under Logan the order was elaborated into a comic-opera troupe. In addition to the mystic signs and secrets, a system of three grades was instituted. Upon joining, a candidate was kept for two months in the Recruit class, from which he could, by a favorable two-thirds vote, be lifted to the higher grade of Soldier. Following this he waited six months, and by the same vote became a Veteran and eligible for office. Separate rituals, signs, grips and passwords were used in each grade.

Naturally, all this was a load of mumbo-jumbo that weighted the order down. Warriors who had been mustered into the army all too easily thought it was silly to wait two months, then six months more, before qualifying for a veteran's rank, and in a few months the membership had shrunk from an estimated total of 240,000 to less than 25,000.

The tremendous enrollment of the order in Indiana too, vanished altogether about this time, for it had been organized as a sort of political machine for the stalwart Union Governor Oliver P. Morton, and had collapsed for want of firmer bonds.

Through the next decade the Grand Army of the Republic did little more than hold its own in membership, although it was laying the foundations for the enormous revival to come by turning more and more of its attention to securing help for wounded soldiers, homes for the destitute, and pensions for veterans in general. By 1881 its relief-work had become famous, and membership in its ranks became attractive to more and more of the veterans.

Moreover, the political campaign of 1880 had shown that the soldier-citizen was coming into his own. Maj. Gen. James A. Garfield, the Ohio Campbellite, had been elected on the Republican ticket for President against Maj. Gen. Winfield Scott Hancock, the New Jersey Quaker whom the Democrats had nominated. Each had been a heroic figure in the war, promoted again and again for gallantry. Predominantly the soldier-vote as a whole was Republican, the G.A.R. vote being even more generally so, but men in blue uniforms had paraded for Hancock in all the great cities.

Such situations were not infrequent in local as well as national political campaigns, and each of the great political parties wooed the veterans lavishly with promises of jobs and higher pensions. The Republicans nevertheless held their sway and reaped the reward as the G.A.R. swung into its crescendo of "joiners" through the '80s. Where there had been a pitiful handful, probably less than 20,000 in the middle '70s, there were 85,856 in '81; 145,932 in '83; 269,684 in '85 and 354,216 in '88.

Memorial Day had not, however, relied upon the prosperity or decline of the Grand Army of the Republic. It had been from the first a tremendous thing, and it grew prodigiously whether States made it legal or not, and whether the G.A.R. was heavy or light in its official enrollment. It was a people's holiday, with no one to fight it now as a few had done in '68 and '69. In those years Democrats had, in places, rebelled against the holiday on the ground that it was nothing but a mask for Republican rallies. Copperheads, here and there, had belittled the day as a trumped-up pretense behind which militaristic propaganda was being spread.

As far back as 1865, there had been occasional charges that the size of Lincoln's funeral was a publicity-device of the Republican party. The La Crosse (Wisconsin) *Democrat*, viciously anti-Lincoln, had snarled in the midst of the funeral woe: "From the hour of his taking-off, the obsequies, mourning and processions were heartless stage displays, mere clap-trap and buncombe under cover of which Democrats were murdered, printing-presses gutted, mobs rampant and the devils in hell given liberty to work their diabolical will on earth."

The common council of Wayne, Michigan, refused to attend the '69 services because they would not let the G.A.R. leaders "use them to give respectability to a training-day pow-wow." One well-known lawyer of Wayne declared that "he would give twenty-five dollars to decorate a rebel's grave, and would like to erect a monument to J. Wilkes Booth as large as the wood-piles around the depot, composed of the skulls of Union soldiers."

But no power on earth could keep the Grand Army of the Republic from rising to power in the land. It had hitched its wagon to a myth, more potent than any star. The "boys in blue" whose sacrifices were annually dramatized in the Holiday of Death, became, very soon, part of the Lincoln-legend. Bound together by fraternal ties, by oaths and lodge secrets, they slowly welded themselves into a unit that marched on for patriotism, for better citizenship, for the Republican party, and for higher pensions. To neglected and crippled veterans it hurried justice, for the old soldier who fell on hard times it brought aid, for the widows and orphans of warriors it bought food, shelter and clothing. It was human, too, in the use it made of its voting-power to compel the constant elevation of pensions from the government, an elevation that brought in unavoidable scandals at which the politicians winked patriotically. It organized its sons into a subsidiary organization, The Sons of Veterans, its wives and daughters into the Woman's Relief Corps, and both of these bodies, like the parent organization, were three hundred and sixty-four days of the year indistinguishable from the other lodges and fraternal bodies which so amply met the American demand for society, for charity and for an excuse to dress up and be seen.

But on that three hundred and sixty-fifth day, when it marched behind bands that blared and under flags that fluttered, the G.A.R. was a symbol to the North not only of the Union and of heroism but of something far more real, to every on-looker, than either of those ideals, something that he only felt without realizing, something that would be with him when the Union and heroism were both forgotten — Death.

As time went on into the new century, the nation was apt to smile at the thought of the pathetic eagerness with which the old soldiers would gather in the front rows of the churches on Memorial Day to hear visiting orators pay them romantic praise in resounding imitations of Robert G. Ingersoll's best formula for tributes. As when, for example, in the 1900s Senator James Watson spoke in the Methodist Church of Pendleton, Indiana, such unforgettable sentiments as these:

"You, who wore the blue, are heroes immortal, and in your ears ring the tributes of a grateful Republic. In the graveyard on the hill rest your gallant comrades whose memory we honor today with garlands and tears.

"But (with lowered voice, made musical) where sleep the Unknown Dead? They sleep in tangled swamp and pathless wood. And there where the hand of man ne'er cometh may Nature bloom her sweetest today, there may the wild rose shower down her petals in profusion, etc., etc."

The type is familiar.

During the year, between modern Decoration Days, the G.A.R. would seem at times selfish and childish. Sophisticated generations planning on the orgy of picnics, moonlight excursions, baseball games, automobile-racing holocausts, prizefights and dances, would think of the old veterans on parade as of little boys playing soldier. The America which had never felt wounds would laugh at ancient scars, but the laughter always sounded dangerously like weeping on Memorial Day, for then the veterans weren't carpenters, or lawyers, or millionaires, or "bums" any more, but youths of The Army of the Tennessee or of The Army of the Potomac, or of the Cumberland, their eyes sharp under their rakish hat-brims, their tassels of gold cord dancing, the street above and on either side bright with banners, and the band playing "John Brown's body lies a-moldering in the grave, as we go marching on."

To those who could see it — and they were never many — there always rolled at the head of any Memorial Day parade — the phantom hearse of Lincoln.

✭ ✭ ✭ **29** ✭ ✭ ✭

"THE SHAPES ARISE"

However much Abraham Lincoln believed in democracy, the
American masses, in the half-century following their war-Presi-
dent's death, did not seem to believe in themselves — at least
not that section of the folk that toyed with the whisper that there
had been something irregular about the birth of Lincoln.

As the people heard their religious and political orators rival-
ing each other in limitless tributes to the dead commoner, and
as they read the unrestrained eulogies that biographers, essayists
and poets heaped upon the martyr, they began to wonder how
so great a man could possibly have come from their ranks. It
seemed too marvelous to have been true. How could a man of
the stature of the nation's savior have arisen from a stratum as
"undistinguished" as he, himself, had declared his ancestry, to
have been?

It was natural to wonder how so unpromising a backwoodsman as Thomas Lincoln could have begot so superhuman a son
as Abraham. Many minds, both illiterate and literate, fell to
doubting the relationship, and soon there was a feeling abroad
that the hero must have had some author more plausible than
"Tom," who was reputed to have been shiftless and dull. In-
evitably there grew the myth that Lincoln's real father had
been some greater man.

Myth had whispered such things about the folk-heroes of the
Old World. The common people of older civilizations had refused to believe their greatest leaders born of ordinary wed-
lock. Jupiter, himself, had supplanted numerous husbands in
Mediterranean countries in order that such friendly supermen
as Hercules and Castor and Pollux, all patron saints of the
people, might be born. Likewise the greatest of gods had substituted himself for the coarser and often-erring Philip, King
of Macedon, so that Alexander the Great might be brought into
the world. One of the Titans had begot Prometheus, who was
sacrificed for Man. It is an old and common myth-form, this

belief that some male of supernatural powers visited an earthly woman and begot a marvelous child.

There had been, previous to Lincoln, various attempts on the part of the American masses, in certain sections, to fit local heroes to the ancient pattern, as for instance in the case of Thaddeus Stevens, that political enemy of the President from Illinois. As he rose to political power in Pennsylvania, fighting magnificently for more and better public schools, Stevens became a champion of the common people, however much he may have come, in later years, to doubt their wisdom. And the masses, cheering for him, began to say that he had sprung from some loins far more distinguished than those of his shoemaker father. His mother, they said, had been of a superior type, and his real father was none other than the brilliant Count Talleyrand of France, who had paid a visit to America about the right length of time before Stevens' birth in 1792.

However, the myth about Lincoln's paternity began not among his idolaters but among his enemies. Through the vicious political campaigns of 1860 and 1864, Lincoln was not only scouted by his enemies as a boorish incompetent but as an illegitimate mongrel as well. Through the South, which hated him savagely, this charge that he was a bastard flew like wildfire. To give it credence were North Carolinians, old neighbors of the candidate's mother, who swore that the story was true. Although it never quite worked its way into the political literature of the day, this tale was part of the "whispering campaign" of both elections, and was remembered well by men of the time.

Then in 1872, when the deification of the murdered President was swinging into its full stride, there appeared the *Life of Abraham Lincoln* by his friend Ward Hill Lamon, which gave further impetus to the story.

Said Lamon: "Abraham Lincoln was born on the twelfth of February, 1809. His father's name was Thomas Lincoln, and his mother's maiden name was Nancy Hanks. At the time of his birth they were supposed to have been married about three years. Although there appears to have been but very little sympathy or affection between Thomas and Abraham Lincoln, they were nevertheless connected by ties and associations which make the previous history of Thomas and his family a necessary part of any reasonably full biography of the great man who immortalized the name by wearing it."

Lamon's insinuation that Thomas, whom he further described as an idling, thriftless rover, short and stout whereas his son was tall and thin, was not Abraham's father, went far in its day, and drew the fire of educated and "respectable" spokesmen of the North.

Rumors had it that the dead President's friends bought up as many of the Lamon books as they could find and burnt them. While this is a doubtful story, it is true that the Lamon *Life* was a failure, and the author never produced the second volume, in which he had planned to describe Lincoln's life in the White House. Failure or not, the book brought the whisper of Lincoln's illegitimacy out into full voice.

Then in 1889 William H. Herndon's life of Lincoln in three volumes appeared, setting down the tale plainly for all to read. It was evident that Herndon, puzzled by his inability either to prove or disprove the story, had fallen back upon the scientific method of stating both sides and putting the matter up to the reader.

In a footnote on page 5 of Volume I, where few could miss it, Herndon said: "Regarding the paternity of Lincoln a great many surmises and a still larger amount of unwritten, or at least unpublished, history have drifted into the currents of western lore and journalism. A number of such traditions are extant in Kentucky and other localities. Mr. Weik [a Greencastle, Indiana, youth who assisted him in writing the *Life*] has spent considerable time investigating the truth of a report current in Bourbon County, Kentucky, that Thomas Lincoln, for a consideration from one Abraham Inlow, a miller there, assumed the paternity of the infant child of a poor girl named Nancy Hanks; and, after marriage, removed with her to Washington or Hardin County, where the son, who was named 'Abraham' after his real, and 'Lincoln' after his putative father, was born. A prominent citizen of the town of Mount Sterling in that State, who was at one time judge of the court and subsequently editor of a newspaper, has written a long argument in support of his alleged kinship, through this source, to Mr. Lincoln. He emphasizes the striking similarity in stature, facial features, length of arms, notwithstanding the well-established fact that the first-born child of the real Nancy Hanks was not a boy but a girl; and that the marriage did not take place in Bourbon, but in Washington County."

Legends about Abraham Inlow or "Enlow," as the true father of Lincoln, broke out in many quarters of the Southern midlands, and Lamon in his *Life* told a story of Thomas Lincoln having hastened out of Kentucky into Indiana with his family as the result of a savage fight he had fought with Enlow — a fight in which he had bitten off the end of his opponent's nose.

Herndon and Lamon found, among pioneer acquaintances of the Lincolns, many stories of the lack of sympathy between Thomas and Abraham Lincoln. The elder had knocked the boy "Abe" off of a fence for asking strangers too many questions about the big world. Countryside rumor had it that father and son didn't like each other, and, indeed, publication of Abraham Lincoln's few letters to his father in later years indicated that the son regarded Thomas as a weakling.

About his father and his ancestry Lincoln was always reticent, dismissing his forbears as "undistinguished" and their history as being nothing but the "short and simple annals of the poor." To John L. Scripps, one of his campaign biographers, he confided some facts that he did not want published and which Scripps mysteriously took with him to the grave.

To add to the legend appeared the news that Lincoln himself had doubted his legitimacy and had hunted in vain for legal proof of his parents' marriage. After his death sufficient records of the event were found in a Kentucky court-house where Lincoln had never searched, but this discovery, in itself, did not dispose of the gossip that Nancy Hanks had played her husband false with some more heroic man, who in due time became the father of her baby. Such a story was added to the mass of popular myth.

Abraham Enlow was not the only individual named as Lincoln's father. In fact, there were three Abraham Enlows mentioned, one of North Carolina, another of one part of Kentucky and an Abraham Inlow of another blue-grass section. Andrew Marshall, foster-son of Chief Justice John Marshall, was credited in one thriving tale. So was Martin D. Hardin, a Kentucky notable.

The thing grew more pretentious as John C. Calhoun, the South Carolina statesman, was given the honor, and still more heroic as Henry Clay, the Kentucky hero, was crowned with Lincoln's authorship. William D. Kelley, a Philadelphia Congressman, observed publicly that he had noted more than a passing resemblance between Lincoln and Clay.

The extremes to which folk-dreamers went in ascribing greatness to Lincoln's parentage is evident in the ridiculous story that Patrick Henry, who died in 1799, ten years before Lincoln's birth, had been his father.

In 1899 a North Carolinian, James A. Cathey, published affidavits from a dozen or more old settlers who affirmed that it had been common gossip in their neighborhoods that Abraham Enlow was the true parent, and that he had paid Thomas Lincoln well to marry the hired girl, Nancy Hanks, and to take her and the baby out of the country so that Mrs. Enlow might give her promiscuous husband rest.

For the latter half of the nineteenth century these stories were passed from mouth to mouth among the people. Valiant Republican orators and professional spokesmen of God assailed the illegitimacy-theme with furious bellows and outraged epithets, but with no facts to prove the thing false. Idolaters of Lincoln fought the legend with nothing more logical than the savage accusation that Lamon and Herndon and all others who spread the story were "liars," "drunkards," "infidels," "ingrates," or "scandal-mongers."

And the more they stormed and railed the wider spread the whispers.

Not until the 1920s, when the tireless Lincoln-researcher of Oak Park, Illinois, Dr. William E. Barton, amassed so exhaustively the evidence for and against the bastardy tale, did Lincoln's friends combat rumor with anything but idiotic "shushings." Barton and another careful historian, Louis A. Warren, once of Kentucky, later of Indiana, each independently examining records and trailing myths, produced sufficient evidence to satisfy most critical readers that Lincoln had been legitimately born, and that no evidence of his mother's immorality existed.

But by that time the story had been thriving for sixty years and had become fixed in the folk-mind of the country as part of the great Lincoln myth — the folk-fancy that there had been something marvelous about their hero's conception as well as about his life and death. The presence of so many reputed fathers proved one thing — the folk-tale tellers agreed that Lincoln's genesis had been too wonderful to have included so drab and dull an author as squat Thomas Lincoln.

Myth was busy, too, with Nancy Hanks Lincoln herself, just as myth had always been busy with the mothers of dying gods in older lands and times. Young America cut its traditions to the ancient pattern. As soon as Lincoln was dead, there began an attempt on the part of sentimental writers and orators to canonize Nancy Hanks, many rapturous eulogists, indeed, hesitating not at all to link the backwoods woman to Mary, the mother of Jesus.

Upon Lincoln's frank declaration of the love-debt he owed his mother, his idolaters built strange fantasies that carried the young woman almost as far out of the human realm as they bore her son. Lyric tributes, romantic imaginings, were wreathed about her memory. She became a dream creature — a madonna.

Phoebe A. Hanaford, one of her most ecstatic literary worshipers, was widely quoted by romantic speakers and writers as an authority, and her epitomizing of the sainted heroine was in its way the expression of millions of myth-loving American hearts.

She said, "Abraham Lincoln's mother, noble and blessed woman, was his inspiration. She was determined that her son should at least learn to read his Bible; and before God called her to dwell with the angels, she had the satisfaction of seeing him read the volume which he never afterwards neglected. Abraham's mother might have said, as did Mary, the mother of Jesus, 'From henceforth all generations shall call me blessed.'"

The Rev. D. D. Thompson sounded the same superstitious note when he declared, "Nancy Hanks seemed at times as if looking far away, seeing what others did not see."

In many—perhaps a majority—of the books and speeches touching Lincoln's mother, it was characteristically suggested that she had been spiritually superior to her husband and nearer than most mothers to the divine. That she had been a sad, hard-working, capable, Bible-loving pioneer was agreed by people who had known her, and that her mentality was above that of her community and husband was obviously believed by her son. But that there was anything mysteriously sacred about her was not believed until her son had been deified by the masses.

Nancy Hanks had died when her son was nine and her place had been taken by a step-mother, Sarah Bush Lincoln, who came to have almost as much emotional hold upon the growing boy as had his real mother, and whose influence upon his education and character was by no means to be overrated, although the old, old lady in after years said humbly and sweetly, "My mind and his went together, what little I had."

Lincoln's conviction that he had inherited his mentality from his mother led eventually to a dispute that proved to be a hurricane tearing through the clouds of myth that surrounded his memory. In talking to his partner, Herndon, one day in 1850 as they drove in a one-horse buggy through Menard County to court, Lincoln had said that he thought he had come by his mental traits and ambition through his mother, who had inherited them from her father, a well-bred Virginia planter who was not married to her mother.

When Herndon, in 1889, published this confession from his friend, a horrible fracas of words arose in the Republic. Patriots and religious advocates swarmed into print and onto the rostrum maligning Herndon for having called Lincoln's mother illegitimately born—"base-born" was their word.

Delvers into the records discovered that Nancy's mother, Lucy Hanks, in her youth had been named by a Harrodsburg, Kentucky, court for suspected immorality, and from old settlers, who had known her, it was learned that she had been a wild,

high-spirited girl in whom the tides of life beat a little too
strongly for the narrow limits of frontier life. She was no
weakling. For two generations there was no other important
truth about the question. On the evidence Herndon's story held.
He was no liar. But, scorning evidence, many preachers and
sentimental biographers tore at the story tooth and nail, trying
to drown it in sanctimonious attacks that only served to popu-
larize it the more.

In the 1920s Louis A. Warren, the afore-mentioned searcher
into the records of Lincoln's paternity, discovered certain facts
that led him to suspect Lincoln of having been mistaken about
his mother's illegitimacy. There was strong reason for believing, he contended, that Lucy Hanks was not a Hanks at all,
that instead she was the widow of a dead Hanks boy, that her
daughter Nancy was regularly born, and that the "well-bred
Virginia planter" was a phantom. Warren could not prove this,
he said, but he had established an explanation that was as well
substantiated as that other story of Nancy's unconventional
birth.

No such regard for honest evidence ruled the bulk of the
literary and platform "authorities" previous to the day of
Warren and Barton. Revelations of the most visionary sort
came to many zealous worshipers when they undertook to describe Nancy in those nine months before her baby was born.
Prenatal influence, in which the hand of God was plain, became the theme of Ervin Chapman, lecturer, evangelist, tem-
perance-exhorter and one-time superintendent of the Anti-
Saloon League, when, in 1917, he touched the peak of myth-
making frenzy in his book, *The Latest Light on Lincoln*.

Chapman, who declared in the preface that he had begun
and completed the book under the promptings of the Divine
Spirit, painted Nancy Hanks as a radiant and ethereal creature,
walking the hard prairie paths as if suspended in rapt mysticism
during the months when her child was stirring in the womb.

"Moses owed his greatness to the calm confidence in God
during the months immediately preceding his birth," said
Chapman. "The marvelous fidelity of Jeremiah during a period

of darkness and despair when kings were false and enemies were victorious is explained by Jehovah's declaration, 'Before thou camest, from the womb I sanctified thee.'

"Elizabeth, the mother of John the Baptist, when informed that her devout life was to be crowned with motherhood, retired to the seclusion of the hills of Judah and there for months quietly communed with God and was filled with the Holy Ghost."

By way of polishing off that "atheist Herndon" for his wicked slurs upon the name of Lincoln and his mother, the inspired Mr. Chapman added a description of the idyllic love-affair between Thomas and Nancy Lincoln in the seraphic swamps of Illinois. "Into this garden of God's own planting, into this Paradise of connubial felicity, the serpent in the guise of loving loyalty entered and cast its breath of scandal upon the stainless names of the most highly favored of American mothers and sons."

Chapman, too, berated another writer on Lincoln, who, although admiring the martyr with religious adoration, nevertheless had declared him "to be a weird and mysterious being who came into the world against convention." "Others," Chapman said, "regard the advent of Abraham Lincoln upon the scene of human action as something outside the chain of natural cause and effect."

Down in Kentucky, Austin Gollaher, an aged native, seemed to agree with this view of the hero's nativity. His story of Lincoln's birth was more in accord with the mythical pattern of hero-worshipers of all times than with the less wondrous stories of Lincoln's own relatives.

Gollaher, in the latter half of the nineteenth century, was fond of relating glowing tales of his boyhood intimacy with young Abe, how they had played and talked together like another Jonathan and another David, and how he had once saved his companion from drowning. It was on the birth of his chum, however, that he grew most eloquent, telling how Nancy Hanks Lincoln, alone with her little daughter, Sarah, in a wretched and freezing cabin, had given birth to a baby boy while the worst blizzard in anybody's memory raged outside.

Nancy, Sarah, and the baby, "a long eel-like string of flesh," as Gollaher described it, would all have perished if Isom Enlow, a neighbor, had not by accident blundered into the cabin, as he wandered the woods blinded by the storm. Raising the pitifully thin blankets, the frontiersman looked at the infant's blue face, upon which was "the imprint of death," and immediately fell to chafing the tiny figure. By dint of his warm hands and some melted turkey-fat which he carried to oil his gun, but which he now dribbled into the baby's mouth, the backwoodsman saved Lincoln's life.

Gollaher recalled that the neighbors had always thought Abe a wonderful child, which was not what the neighbors told William H. Herndon when he went among them collecting data for his life of Lincoln. The boy, they told Herndon, had been a curious, quizzical fellow, awkward and gangly, much more prone to read or to talk than to work. There was something mystically unique about the love that existed between Nancy Hanks Lincoln and her son, said Gollaher, so much so that the people round about said that "God came down to the world that February morning and went with Isom Enlow."

"Somebody asked why God did not quiet the storm," Gollaher used to say to J. Rogers Gore, a Kentucky newspaper man who loved to listen to the old man's yarns and who later published them in his *Boyhood of Abraham Lincoln*. "But the folks replied by saying 'The mysteries of God cannot be understood, and we shall not try to understand them.' It was just the Master's way of doing things. I reckon He wanted to give to the world an example of what a baby born under such conditions could do for the people. Had Abe been born somewhere in a big, fine house, it might have been lots harder for God to have kept selfishness out of his heart."

That there had been no blizzard on February 11 or 12, 1809, and that the birth of the baby was no more remarkable or miraculous than that of any other pioneer baby of the time, was to be established by records of the days in question and by the testimony of relatives of the family who were present. But such prosaic facts were not welcomed by hero-worshipers.

The very site of the cabin where Lincoln had been born had

gone up in myth-smoke almost before his body was cold. Fifteen locations for it were pointed out at one time or another, and three States, Kentucky, North Carolina, and Tennessee, put forth rival claims for owning the hero as a native son. Those seven Mediterranean cities that declared themselves Homer's birthplace were eclipsed by the American Republic.

Nor did the final location of the cabin-site near Hodgenville, Kentucky, by the Lincoln Farm Association in 1906 complete the matter. After the "original" Thomas Lincoln farm had been purchased and the "original" cabin installed in a magnificent memorial structure, owned by the United States government, the aforesaid Louis A. Warren — he with the troublesome enthusiasm for fact — came forth to prove, pretty clearly, that the farm did not include more than a third of what Thomas Lincoln had owned and that the sacred log-cabin, itself, was only two-thirds of it there.

Warren's discoveries clashed with the myth, and the book in which he published them was not welcomed by the masses, perhaps for the reason that it took away something of Lincoln's lowliness. According to Warren, little Abe did not grow up in quite such dramatic squalor and wretched poverty as had been popularly believed. His father had owned three hundred and forty-eight and a half acres of land, and the home cabin was as big and stout as the neighbors' — far better than that weazened, tumble-down affair which was cherished in such sentimental pathos by the nation.

Legends about the sacred logs of the cabin kept bobbing up after their discovery. Some stories had it that the timbers had been juggled with those of the original Jefferson Davis cabin, others had it that they had all been burned in a blazing box-car. Experts disproved both tales, but in their time they were popular myths, typical of the extremities to which the folk-mind had gone in imagining sorrow, disaster, pathos or drama for everything associated with the memory of Lincoln.

In still another line of traditional myth-manufacture did the idolaters labor over Lincoln. Just as ancient and mediaeval legend-weavers remembered their national heroes as beautiful creatures — fairer of face and body than ordinary men — so such fanciful dreamers as Ervin Chapman toiled to prove that Lincoln had not been awkward and homely, as his contemporaries agreed. "He was as refined as Lord Chesterfield," Chapman cried.

Gutzon Borglum, the sculptor, was quoted by Chapman as seeing Lincoln's physical beauty: "Lincoln's face is infinitely nearer an expression of our Christ-character than all the conventional pictures of the Son of God. That symbolic head with its long hair parted in the middle and features that never lived is the creation of artists. Lincoln's face is the triumph of God through man and of men through God." That the rail-splitter was "splendidly proportioned" has been repeated over and over by Lincoln's eulogists. Such frenzied lengths of hero-worship had been growing through the years and had captured the popular mind.

One of the reasons for the failure of Lamon's life of Lincoln was the painstaking and starkly human description of the man as Lamon, through almost daily contact across four years in the White House, not to speak of intimate associations in Illinois, had seen him.

"Mr. Lincoln was about 6 feet, 4 inches — the length of his legs being out of all proportion to that of his body. When he sat down on a chair, he seemed no taller than an average man, measuring from the chair to the crown of his head, but his knees rose in front and a marble placed on the cap of one of them would roll down a steep descent to the hip. He weighed about a hundred and eighty pounds, but he was thin through the breast, narrow across the shoulders and had a general appearance of a consumptive subject. Standing up he stooped slightly forward; sitting down he usually crossed his long legs or threw them over the arms of a chair as the most convenient mode of disposing of them. His head was long and tall from the base of the brain and the eyebrow, his forehead high and narrow but inclining backward as it rose. The diameter of his head from ear to ear was six and a half inches and from front to back eight inches. The size of his hat was seven and one-eighth. His ears were large, standing out at right angles, cheekbones high and prominent, eyebrows heavy and jutting forward over small, sunken blue eyes, nose long, large and blunt, the tip of it rather ruddy and slightly awry on the right-hand side; his chin projecting far and sharp, curving forward to meet a thick, material lower lip which hung downward; his cheeks were flabby and the loose skin fell in wrinkles or folds. His hair was dark brown, stiff and unkempt, complexion very dark, skin yellow, shriveled and leathery; countenance haggard and care-worn, eyes hollow, long, sallow, cadaverous face; his whole air, his walk, long silent reveries broken at long intervals by sudden and startling exclamations as if to confound an observer who might suspect the nature of his thoughts—showed he was a man of sorrows—not of today or yesterday but long-treasured and deep—bearing with him a continual sense of weariness and pain.

"He walked not from heel to toe but set the whole foot down at once and lifted it all at once, awkward but powerful."

As Lincoln mounted to his post of folk-god for a Republic which had become far more rigorously Christian than that first greater leader of its masses, Thomas Jefferson, had intended, it became irksome to have men who knew Lincoln recall the martyr's absence of orthodox faith.

The likening of Lincoln to Jesus, which had begun in many pulpits on that "Black Easter" Sunday two days after the assas-sination, had become intensified with time. Religious people, listening to the parsons who strengthened the similarity year by year, had an obvious longing for something that would reconcile Lincoln the man with the ideal. They recognized that history proved the preachers accurate in their word-pictures of Lincoln's love of honesty and mercy. They wished that so good a man could be discovered to have been a devout Christian. That would make everything simpler.

They found deep and earnest pleasure and the stirrings of romantic awe in sermons such as that which the Duluth *Herald*, in February 5, 1909, quoted from a local Baptist divine: "On the fourteenth day of April, 1865, died a martyr to his cause, the man whose blood was shed for the Union of his people and for the freedom of a race, Abraham Lincoln. It was Good Friday, the darkest day of tragedy for America. On the same day years before, Christ had suffered death on Mount Calvary. Both lives began in humble huts. Joseph was a carpenter. Thomas Lincoln was a rough carpenter. Both Christ and Lincoln were reformers, maligned and abused. Like Christ Lincoln had been calm and meek and patient. The sins of man rested on both. Like the Man of Nazareth, Lincoln realized that he was not come to send peace on earth but a sword. Both were killed as a sacrifice for man."

But they found greater satisfaction in such statements as that which the Rev. E. O. Cole uttered in the First Methodist Church of Chillicothe, Missouri, on the same day: "In his youth Lincoln was a freethinker and a skeptic, but on the battlefield of Gettysburg, he found Jesus Christ and lived and died in Him."

They had listened for a generation to sentiments such as those the Rev. T. Harley Marsh of Champaign, Illinois, uttered at this same nation-wide celebration of Lincoln's centenary in 1909:

"Like Christ he was God-sent and as Christ steadfastly set his face to go up to Jerusalem, so Lincoln left Springfield to assume the Presidency."

However, it was for something more concrete concerning Lincoln's faith that devout Americans craved. Even in 1865 this popular wish had been recognized. The first full *Life of Lincoln*, written by J. G. Holland, had attempted to give the Christian Republic the thing it wanted to hear. Holland, in the course of describing Lincoln's life in Springfield, related an incident that gratified pathetically hungry souls.

Lincoln, so he said, had gone in 1860 from his office into the neighboring quarters of Newton Bateman, State Superintendent of Schools, and had discussed the puzzling enmity of preachers and religious folk toward his Presidential candidacy. He had wept over the situation, and had told Bateman, "I know there is a God and that He hates injustice and slavery. I see the storm coming, and I know that His hand is in it. If He has a place for and work for me—and I think He has—I believe I am ready. I am nothing, but truth is everything. I know I am right, because I know that liberty is right, for Christ teaches it and Christ is God."

When Holland's book announced to the world this amazing news of Lincoln's acceptance of Christianity, William H. Herndon came down out of the office above which still swung the firm name "Lincoln & Herndon" and went over to see Newton Bateman. Herndon did not believe that Bateman, as a man of honor, could have furnished Holland with a story so preposterous. In all his years with his partner, Herndon had never heard Lincoln speak in this way, and, indeed, knew him to be wholly of a different view, one very far from the orthodox evangelical faith that Holland so confidently described.

Bateman told Herndon what he had related to Holland, but swore him to secrecy, evidently not wishing to become entangled in the war which, it was apparent, the irate lawyer was about to start. Herndon, quickly answering Holland, and marshaling as many of Lincoln's friends as would stand to the perilous guns, gave the lie to the claim of the biographer as to Lincoln's belief in Christ. The war grew bitter, with churchmen, the nation over, accusing Herndon of every known depravity.

Nevertheless, Herndon, always a man of integrity, did not betray Bateman, although he endlessly begged the school man to release the truth. Whatever it was that Bateman had told Holland will in all likelihood never be exactly known, but certain it is that Herndon felt it to constitute full proof that the biographer had grossly exaggerated Lincoln's words.

Herndon collected the testimony of Lincoln's intimates on the matter. John T. Stuart, a former law-partner, he quoted as saying that Lincoln "when he came to Springfield, and for years afterward, was an avowed and open infidel, sometimes bordering on atheism. . . . Lincoln always denied that Jesus was the Christ — denied that Jesus was the Son of God, as understood and maintained by the Christian religion."

Other Springfield associates of his dead partner and Mrs. Lincoln herself were quoted in either or both of the Lamon or Herndon biographies as refuting the claims that Lincoln had been an orthodox Christian. The President's private secretaries came forth to say that he had not changed his religion in the White House. Herndon, furious that the Christian workers should maneuver his friend into the position of a hypocrite, fought like a prairie panther.

To those few students of history who tried to view the matter in detachment, Herndon was convincing. Although eight inches shorter and much younger, he looked like Lincoln, wore his beard the same way and was homespun in manner for all that he read and thought more like a cosmopolite than his brother lawyers of Springfield. As these detached observers saw the battle, Herndon was the brain and his opponents the spirit of the strife. On his side was Reason, on the other was Belief.

Herndon's adversaries, too, marshaled their evidence, employing social and religious pressure without stint. Ninian W. Edwards, Lincoln's brother-in-law who, in company with Mrs. Lincoln and her family, looked down upon the tribes of the Lincolns and the Hankses, entered the argument to say that a Springfield preacher, the Rev. James Smith, had given Lincoln a book to read, *The Christian's Defense,* and that the tall lawyer, after brooding over it, had said, "I am now convinced of the Christian religion."

Some of Lincoln's old friends such as John T. Stuart denied that they had been quoted accurately by Herndon when he published their statements concerning Lincoln's "infidelism." And although it is possible that they had recanted under the fire of the powerful church forces, the denials raised the logical question whether Herndon, in his zeal to save his friend's honor as a gentleman, had not quoted his authorities in language that was unconsciously too much his own.

Mrs. Henry Ward Beecher, in her old age, joined in with the fanciful tale that Lincoln, with his face muffled, had come to Brooklyn one midnight to pray with her husband after the disaster at Bull Run. The credulous swallowed this tale whole, not looking at the absurdity of a President having deserted the capital in so terrible a crisis to travel clear to Brooklyn to pray with a clergyman who was so often patronizing toward his policies.

Hoping to overthrow Herndon, the champions of Lincoln's

orthodoxy revived the story that had been current in 1865 and which had been quoted in many sermons on "Black Easter" Sunday two days after the assassination. This anecdote maintained that Lincoln, shortly before his death, had been asked by an Illinois clergyman, "Do you love Jesus?" Lincoln had replied, "When I left Springfield, I asked the people to pray for me. I was not a Christian. When I buried my son [Willie], the severest trial of my life, I was not a Christian. But when I went to Gettysburg and saw the graves of thousands of our soldiers, I then and there consecrated myself to Christ. Yes, I *do* love Jesus!"

That this sort of claim, made without giving the name of the preacher who heard it, was proven by time and fact to be fictitious or exaggerated, did not lessen the mass-feeling that Lincoln was, somehow, a religious saint. Even if there was sound evidence that he had rarely spoken of Jesus and was consistently reticent about his views of Christianity, there was no question whatsoever that he had been a God-fearing man. Few occupants of the White House had ever mentioned God so often or with such deep reverence. The romanticists and the realists both agreed that Lincoln's deism had been sincere, and in time scholars also agreed that Lincoln had been more skeptical in his prairie years than in the White House, when blood and chaos washed about his long legs. He had attended church with fair regularity in his later Washington years, although never indicating any intention of joining one.

But evidence and proof counted for little out among the people where myths were spiritual entertainment. There, the legends ran that Lincoln had been a Catholic, a Freemason, a Quaker, a Methodist, a Spiritualist, an Agnostic.

That same Reverend Chiniquy, whose weird recitals of Lincoln's foresight of assassination had proven so grateful to the superstitious, fathered unwittingly the myth of Lincoln's Catholicism. Chiniquy had, after fifty years in the Roman faith, left it for Protestantism and, active man that he was, began a wordy warfare against the Jesuits that left no accusation against them unsaid. He was answered with words and lawsuits. For his lawyer he chose that Springfield attorney whose influence over juries was so remarkable — Lincoln. Chiniquy developed a lasting admiration for the tall lawyer and traveled to the White House at least three times to warn Lincoln against murderous plots which he imagined the Jesuits were fomenting against the President.

On account of the association of the two men in the lawsuits, the rumor arose that Lincoln, like Chiniquy, was a renegade from Catholicism; that he had been baptized by Jesuit priests in Kentucky as a boy, and that he had assisted at masses. Copperheads opposing the Republican Presidential candidate in 1860, and thereafter through the Civil War, noised these rumors about, and anti-Catholics added their mite to the jumble of prejudice by saying that the church was opposing Lincoln because of his apostasy. That the Vatican, like almost all other European organizations, spiritual or temporal, favored the South as against the North, was generally believed by Union populations, and when in April, 1865, a few of the conspirators in the Lincoln assassination plot were found to be Catholics, the tale took on fresh strength.

Facts might be wholly against the story of Lincoln's Catholicism, but myths have never heeded facts, and to ignorant and prejudiced minds these indictments were a matter to be hoarded in whispers across two generations — and longer — a legacy from the days when the mother countries had been split by the Reformation, in which both Rome and its dissenters had employed politics and war.

That Lincoln had been baptized by the Kentucky Jesuits was at length proven incredible when examination showed that the priests had ceased their chief missionary labors in that State before Lincoln could have come under their influence. There was no evidence to support either the legend that the man had ever been in or been out of the faith, but myths, as has been said, paid no heed to evidence.

For the companion belief that Lincoln had been secretly a Quaker, there was more basis. He had described his ancestors as "Quakers who went to Virginia from Berks County, Pennsylvania" and was quoted as saying that he had inherited certain traits from his Quaker grandmother. In certain strict interpretations of honesty, and in his long silences, he resembled them, but he was never caught in their dream of non-resistance, never indicated any desire to join them, and was at odds with them on other points as well.

That he was a Methodist was a fancy based on the prevalence of exhorters of that creed in the prairies — nothing more. That he was a Universalist was a belief arising in some of his Springfield friends who tried to fix him into that category when his elusive unorthodoxy perplexed them beyond their powers of other classification. Spiritualists, on the strength of those few séances that he had allowed Mrs. Lincoln to have in the White House, claimed him of their beliefs.

Public speakers upon occasion declared Lincoln to have been a Freemason, pointing for proof to certain words and phrases in his speeches that could have come to him only through a knowledge of Masonry. He had joined, it was argued, in some outlying lodge in the wilderness. That his name was on no records was admitted, and, later, historians dismissed the matter because of insufficient evidence, as they did much of that endless flow of rumor that had arisen from his worshipers.

Before the turn of the century, idolatry had made Lincoln all good things to all men. His love for humanity had drawn to him such love in return, that he himself had become a faith — a religion, symbol of the destiny of the Republic, as his believers saw it, the triumph of the common man.

Only in certain sections of the South, where war memories were passionately cherished, did there live any shadow of the old hatred that had once burned against him. By and large, the South softened with the years into something of the attitude voiced by so many of their leaders the day after Lincoln's death, when they had deplored his loss as that of "the best friend the South had." But sometimes Southerners, who lived in proud isolation, clinging to romantic rememberings of the happy days "before the war," would be found still blaming Lincoln for the sufferings of battle-times, for the poverty and terror of Reconstruction, and for the negro problem of their section. To them he was always the "widow-maker," the rude, crude, callous butcher who had wrecked forever the aristocratic glories of plantation life.

For such individuals who thus died hard, the North and the great body of Southern people themselves in the new century had, characteristically, only silence, understanding how many nerves had been forever jangled in those distraught years when the Radicals reconstructed Dixie.

Typical, perhaps, of the infrequent revivals of anti-Lincoln passions in the South was that discovered in *Tyler's Quarterly Historical and Genealogical Magazine* as it came from its Richmond, Virginia, presses in January, 1928. Here some unnamed book-reviewer, presumably the editor, Lyon G. Tyler, praised a certain Landon C. Bell, Virginia historian, for having exposed "in full measure the ridiculous claims made for the leader of the Northern hosts [Lincoln] in his un-Christian attack upon the property and liberties of the Southern people. Only he yields too much in saying that Lincoln has to his credit 'many kindly, generous and magnanimous acts.'

"Where and what were these acts?

"His [Lincoln's] admirers have been challenged to state them, but beyond his patting a few negro children on the head, his pardon to some deserters, and some kindly words in his messages that meant little or nothing, they have never yet been able to mention anything that Lincoln acted or said which would give him the character of a kindly Chief Magistrate. On the other hand, a whole book could be filled with the enormities of his administration that will certainly subject it some day to the condemnation of the world, when the propaganda-spirit now so prevalent dies away. It is the weakness of propaganda that exhaustion follows — and so it will be with the Lincoln-myth."

But this curious reversion to ancient passions illustrates only the attitude of a narrowing fragment of the Southern people. More expressive of the South's feeling toward Lincoln in the twentieth century was, undoubtedly, the portrayal of his character as David Wark Griffith, the Kentuckian and son of a Confederate cavalry leader, directed it to be played in his moving picture, *The Birth of a Nation*. As Griffith dramatized the end of the Civil War and the horrors of Reconstruction, it was a sad and loving Lincoln, a poetic man of mercy toward the South, who stalked through the picture-shadows as a hero, while the great villain of the piece and author of Southern woes was Thaddeus Stevens, old, crippled and cruel.

To the American people as a whole, Lincoln's example became so immeasurable that men of all faiths and purposes sought self-justification and popular approval in claiming him to have been of their beliefs. If the religious denominations struggled for his spiritual legacy, the agnostics and rationalists wrestled with the clergymen for Lincoln's soul.

Robert G. Ingersoll, the Peoria, Illinois, politician and professional orator, who found full vent for his poetic yearnings in lectures and speeches that charmed his listeners almost out of their senses, enjoyed taunting the clergy, his deepest enemies, with the declaration that Abraham Lincoln, saint of the Republic, had been, like himself, no Christian. Ingersoll, whose sarcasm was the most picturesque that the '70s, '80s and '90s heard, used to say:

"I know what Lincoln thought of orthodox Christianity. I was somewhat acquainted with him and well acquainted with many of his associates and friends. . . . Orthodox Christians have the habit of claiming all great men, all men who have held important positions, men of reputation, men of wealth. As soon as the funeral is over clergymen begin to relate imaginary conversations with the deceased, and in a very little while the great man is changed to a Christian — possibly to a saint.

"All this happened in Mr. Lincoln's case. Many pious falsehoods were told, conversations were manufactured, and suddenly the church claimed that the great President was an orthodox Christian. The truth is that Lincoln in his religious views agreed with Franklin, Jefferson, and Voltaire. He did not believe in the inspiration of the Bible or the divinity of Christ or the scheme of salvation and he utterly repudiated the dogma of eternal pain."

Then Ingersoll, his mighty voice wooing his listeners and stirring the church members among them to disapproving delight, would go on to enumerate the intimates of Lincoln who had told him (Ingersoll) that to their certain knowledge the President was no Christian. Ingersoll would name Lincoln's law-partners, his private secretary, many Illinois friends and his wife. He would ask who had any proof that Lincoln believed in the miracles upon which the Christian religion based its existence, then he would conclude:

"Where, then, is the evidence that he was a Christian?

"All admit that he was an honest man. . . . If he had become a Christian it was his duty publicly to say so. He was President. . . . It was his duty to join some orthodox church and he should have given his reasons. He should have endeavored to reach the heart and brain of the Republic. It was unmanly for him to keep his 'second birth' a secret and sneak into Heaven leaving his old friends to travel the road to hell.

"Great pains have been taken to show that Mr. Lincoln believed in, and worshiped the one true God. This by many is held to have been his greatest virtue, the foundation of his character, and yet, the God he worshiped, the God to whom he prayed, allowed him to be assassinated.

"Is it possible that God will not protect his friends?"

Not only in the field where religion warred with agnosticism did orators struggle for Lincoln's mantle. Flaming crusaders for labor unions, for socialism, populism, communism, carried Lincoln's picture on banners and repeated his words in their harangues. They were his heirs, they said.

Prohibitionists and anti-prohibitionists took quotations from his speeches for campaign texts, and where the "drys" pointed to Lincoln's temperance activities and speech, the "wets" hung in countless barrooms framed copies of the license under which Lincoln as a young store-keeper in New Salem had sold liquor.

Corporation counsels hung him in steel engravings above the mahogany desks over which they bent in plans which would serve capitalism. School teachers invoked his influence to make their pupils cling to the drudgery of classroom toil, telling their pupils how the great man, as a little boy, had been so thirsty for knowledge that he had done his arithmetic in charcoal on a pine shovel down before the fireplace. The Republican party of Garfield, Hayes, Mark Hanna, Boise Penrose, Roosevelt, Harry Daugherty, Borah, and Andrew Mellon marched into power year after year, merging its internal battles between conservatives and liberals in the common cause of serving the "glorious traditions of the founder of our party, Abraham Lincoln." At every sizeable campaign rally of the G.O.P. from 1860 to 1928 a great portrait of Lincoln cast an approving eye over the scene.

It was a customary privilege of the Democrats in campaigns to see nothing but irony in this use of Lincoln's name by the party which they said had become "the handmaiden of special privilege and rule by the few." In at least one of these campaigns the Democratic party, feeling itself to have the unquestioned support of the working classes, "the men in the street," made a determined effort to wrest the great Lincoln-tradition away from the Republicans. Toward the end of the tempestuous struggle in the Autumn of 1928, full-page advertisements appeared in leading newspapers likening the Democratic candidate, Alfred E. Smith, to Lincoln, and arguing that the same social "snobbery" which in 1860 had sneered at Lincoln for his humble birth and plebeian manners, was now ridiculing "Al" Smith for his birth and upbringing in the slums of New York City. As Democratic editors and orators worked, they drew eloquent parallels between Thomas Jefferson, Abraham Lincoln, and Alfred Emanuel Smith—three statesmen who had believed that the common people should rule themselves.

It was the name of Lincoln that the Progressive or "Bull Moose" party of 1912 cried loudly when it sought, by rebellion from the Republican organization, to down "reactionary bosses" and win the Presidency for its idol, Theodore Roosevelt. In "Teddy," it said, lived again the policies of Lincoln. Teddy was giving the power back to the common man as Lincoln had done, and through the Fall months the movement became something very like a crusade, with Roosevelt, the histrionic, making his most telling effects with speeches about "Lincoln and me."

For its campaign song the Bull Moosers took that Union favorite, "The Battle Hymn of the Republic," which Julia Ward Howe, in Civil War times, had fashioned by setting religious words to the red rhythms of the soldiers' marching-tune, "John Brown's body."

With the bands playing music so thrilling in 1912, it seemed clear to several million voters that Lincoln's political philosophy had at last returned actually to guide the Republic.

Such spasms were soon over. It was always a welcome relief for Americans in the industrial epoch to get away from puzzling, toilsome efforts to understand Lincoln's intellectual theories of government, and to return again to that old, instinctive, heart-warming worship of his name.

✶ ✶ ✶ **30** ✶ ✶ ✶

AFTERGLOW

IN ILLINOIS it used to be said that the brown thrush was not heard at its singing for a whole year after Lincoln had been laid in his tomb.

In Illinois, politicians have told audiences that the legislators, meeting at the Capitol in Springfield, feel the strange, mystic spirit of Lincoln brooding over them, leading them to better and ever better services for his people.

At Elmhurst, Illinois, the ancient Irish flagman of the Chicago, Aurora & Elgin Railroad, gave to Carl Sandburg one morning a new and solemn version of just what it was that J. Wilkes Booth shouted after murdering Abraham Lincoln. History has understood this cry of Booth's to have been "*Sic semper tyrannis*," but the flagman had heard it differently.

"This man Booth, he shot the Prisidint, jumped down onto the stage and hallooed, 'I'm sick, sind fer McGinnis!'"

On another morning Sandburg asked the flagman how he would tell, in a few words, why Lincoln was loved so finely by so many people.

"He was humanity," said the flagman.

In all parts of the Republic are to be seen the large wooden or metal watch-faces with which jewelers and watch-salesmen advertise their places of business. Frequently people say to each other, "Do you see where those watch hands are set? At eight-seventeen! That's the hour and minute Lincoln died!"

Sometimes people have it a little differently, saying, "That's the hour when Lincoln was shot!"

And the fact that Lincoln was shot shortly after ten o'clock, and died at seven-twenty the next morning, has not harmed the myth in any way. Neither has the legend been injured by the watchmakers' explanation that the clock hands are set at 8.17 because this position allows them the maximum space for advertising their firm-names and slogans.

On the right-of-way of the New York Central Railroad, track-walkers, sand-house men, "shacks" and section-hands used to tell this ghost story of Lincoln's funeral train. So said the Albany *Evening Times:*

"Regularly in the month of April, about midnight the air on the tracks becomes very keen and cutting. On either side of the tracks it is warm and still. Every watchman, when he feels the air, slips off the track and sits down to watch. Soon the pilot engine of Lincoln's funeral train passes with long, black streamers and with a band of black instruments playing dirges, grinning skeletons sitting all about.

"It passes noiselessly. If it is moonlight, clouds come over the moon as the phantom train goes by. After the pilot engine passes, the funeral train itself with flags and streamers rushes past. The track seems covered with black carpet, and the coffin is seen in the center of the car, while all about it in the air and on the train behind are vast numbers of blue-coated men, some with coffins on their backs, others leaning upon them.

"If a real train were passing its noise would be hushed as if the phantom train rode over it. Clocks and watches always stop as the phantom train goes by and when looked at are five to eight minutes behind.

"Everywhere on the road about April 27 watches and clocks are suddenly found to be behind."

EPILOGUE

✧ ✧ ✧ 1 ✧ ✧ ✧

POST MORTEM

When the colonists in America had cut the cord that tied them to the Old World, they rang the Liberty Bell and threw their hats over the windmills. Independence was a brave and joyous thing for them to have won, yet when the shouting died, they felt a little lonely in the wilderness, realizing that in gaining their political freedom they had lost their claim upon the warm folk-traditions of the mother lands. They missed the security of all those national myths upon which a people must lean. They were spiritually homesick for the folk-lore of their race, for the ancient and friendly heroes of legend, and they honed for the protection of familiar deities who had, long before, been set up as patron saints, keepers of the national tradition.

It was one thing to have banished King George III from their lives and another to have lost King Arthur. So felt the English colonists who by the strokes of Independence Hall and Yorktown had become Americans. In freeing themselves from the modern oppressor, they had lost the legendary leader who had died like a god to save Briton peoples.

Nor did it cure this folk-nostalgia to hold up English traditions in schoolbooks and literature. Try as it might to hold onto its common share of British history and mythology, the little Republic of the United States could not be at ease about the matter. It had screamed its political defiance too earnestly, had cried "no entangling alliances" too often.

The new nation was like a child that rejoices to walk alone, but who subconsciously remembers the womb with a wishful pang.

Time did not quickly bring the young Republic the American traditions for which it yearned, for as it grew up there came pouring in upon it fresh shiploads of immigrants from other races and other lands, each group rejoicing at freedom, yet coming to miss, as had the English colonists, the household Lares of their own national antiquity.

Most of all, the new people missed the dying gods of their fathers. Each of the mother races had worshiped, in its beloved mythology, one hero brighter and more beautiful than the rest, one dear, friendly god who had sacrificed his life for the race.

If the British colonists had loved and lost King Arthur, the Teutonic and Scandinavian newcomers had given up Balder the Beautiful, and the Mediterranean immigrants had surrendered Apollo, Attis, Moses, Adonis or Osiris. And if the French arrivals were now willing to call themselves Americans —citizens of that new country where man was to be free from Old World tyrannies—they must no longer expect supernatural protection from the saving power of Jeanne d' Arc.

From the infancy of the human race, the superstitious mind of man had clutched at these tribal, racial, or national gods who watched over their chosen peoples. Man had always felt, somehow, that it would take some divine intercessor to help him through the cruel ordeal of life, some powerful friend in the skies to protect him from the dread and bitter Winter which would always be coming again, threatening starvation. Certainly the super-god who ruled over all must be angry to take bright Summertime away. Surely he must be punishing Man, in his stern and vengeful way, for some sin. Primitive people reasoned so as they saw the corn die in the Autumn and felt the first hint of terrible Winter in the winds of shortening days.

What could weak mortals do to mollify the great god's wrath? How could they coax the Almighty to let the sun come back and start the corn to growing again on the jungle-edge?

In their superstitions they slowly worked out the answer: they would sacrifice their most wonderful possession — their king. This tribal chief or king held his post by divine right — so the priests said. He was the chosen of God. To offer his life as a sign of the people's repentance would surely touch the Almighty's heart.

So came the habit of killing kings, a habit to be seen in any study of magic or religion as they run through the story of mankind.

Primitive kings, superior men that they were, soon learned how to suggest to their people that the sacrifice of a substitute would appease the angry god just as certainly as would the killing of the king himself. Soon the tribe was choosing a lesser man for the glorious rôle. For a day this common man was king. He sat on the chieftain's throne, ate what he liked, had the women he craved, and wore a mock crown upon his head. Then when the appointed holiday of death had come, the people fell upon him and cut his throat with festal honors.

The magic always worked. The sacrifice was never in vain. Sooner or later, this year or next, the corn would grow again. The days would be sure to grow longer, the trees would quiver with leaves, and the corn be shooting upward to the warming breath of Spring.

As the races grew older and tribes became nations, it became more and more customary to believe, even when the people themselves had abandoned king-killing, that the deaths of the more popular monarchs had been miraculous, mysterious sacrifices foreordained by the gods. Gradually certain dead kings were given martyrdom by the tale-tellers, and, as the legends were fattened, the dead heroes slowly rose to the stature of gods themselves. From hero-worship to god-worship is but a short step.

Around the evening fires, in cave and hut, old men retold the hero-tales they had heard in their boyhoods, and out of the mists national patron saints and deities appeared. Eventually it was natural to say that these heroes had been gods who had come disguised as men, to live awhile with their chosen people and then to sacrifice their lives in order that the common folk might regain the Almighty's favor. Often, as these beliefs developed, the friendly god came to life over and over again, dying and returning, dying and returning each year, sometimes never coming back, but never really dying either, only going away into some charming other-world to sleep and to wait until his people might have desperate need of him once more.

The myth of the dying god is one of the oldest, one of the commonest, in the chronicles of folk-beliefs. Always these martyrs have been beautiful of face and soul, kind and gentle friends of Man, pouring out their blood with patient gladness that Man may live and prosper. Osiris, for centuries, was worshiped by the Egyptians as he died each year to bring sprouts to the dormant grain. Along the Mediterranean Sea, people worshiped the beneficent and beautiful Adonis, whose death ushered in the Springtime, and when the scarlet anemone, sacred to his memory, bloomed in the mountain meadows, simple folk told each other to look—the blood of Adonis was being shed for them again.

The list of dying gods is long, and the myths about them are longer still, yet strangely alike, as Sir James George Frazer has set down in *The Golden Bough* for the curious to see. As the races grew up, they learned only to conceal partially their trust in such superstitions, not to kill their beliefs.

America, where freedom was to reign, grew up pathetically eager to repeat the ancient formula, yet never realizing that it was chained thus to the past. For three generations the new nation toiled in vain to give birth to a folk-god. Three candidates in that time it had, three men who had been heroes of the people—Washington, Jefferson and Jackson, but try as it might, the Republic could not exalt them into mythology. George Washington, most likely of the three—since he had fathered the nation—was too austere. High as the people could build his statue, he remained, in their minds, only a statue, too cold in his perfections to claim anything more than their formal reverence and sober admiration.

Thomas Jefferson, even more a friend of the common man, that noblest work of God, was not so near as Washington to godhood. For all its creed of democracy, the Republic could not fix the Sage of Monticello in its spiritual memory. The man had been too much a creature of brain, always tampering with intellectual heresy. Neither could the people exalt out of the natural world that other champion of their virtues, Andrew Jackson. Heroic he might have been, but his rages had been too human; he had been too willing to shed blood.

Besides, all these heroes had lived too long. By no stretch of imagination could their passing be construed as mysterious or sacrificial. Neither in life nor death had they touched anything that could be interpreted as miraculous.

Were the new people to be denied what all the old people had had, a national mythology of its own, packed with proud racial memories, glories, legends, gods, and dreams? For ninety years of the Republic's life it seemed that this must be true.

Perhaps there was a good reason for it. Perhaps the people of the United States despite their glorious talk about Messianic America, the land of the millennium, were not yet rightly a people. Perhaps their nation was not yet wholly a nation, conscious of its unity. Could it be said that Americans were a race wholly to themselves? — a race so clear-cut and individual that the world could say, "There goes an American," as it said, "There goes an Englishman" or a German, a Frenchman, or a Swede?

Then came the day when, indeed, the nation was born; born out of four years of civil warfare with delirium mounting over blood and grief until at the day of peace no man could be quite sane any more. Over a half-million Americans were dead in their uniforms, and thirty millions of people were so spent with suffering that their minds had become in many ways as childish as had been the minds of their ancestors on the jungle-edge so long before.

The day was 1865 — time for the dying god of America to come — and to die.

After the fashion of older dying gods in older worlds, he had come stalking up from among the people, often mocked, unrecognized for what he was until death had claimed him. It was not until Abraham Lincoln had been killed and his body shown to the people that he was understood by the American masses to have been their long-awaited folk-god. As they saw him stretched to his giant's length in the coffin, they remembered with awe how cool and strong he had seemed through those four years of terror, now miraculously ended. Remembering how he had been abused in his lifetime, and how even his friends had mistaken his patience for weakness, the people began to worship him. Seeing his body go back to the common soil amid such sobbing pomp, they understood, in a flash, that he had sacrificed himself for them. Dimly, but with elemental power, they felt that he had died out of love for the people.

Under him the nation had become for the first time one, all questions of its division settled, its unity cemented in blood. More than that, the nation was at last a great world-power. With Lincoln for leader the young Republic had defied Europe. Under him four million negro slaves had been set free. To have done what he had done, it seemed that he must, perforce, have been superhuman, a mysterious symbol, from on high, of the superiority of the American common man in whose image he had lived.

As Lincoln lay in his Springfield tomb, the national dreams, pride, hope, fear, and superstition had some one to cling to. The pattern of the American god had been filled.

So it seemed from May 1865 onward.

Myth had taken the man, irresistible forces had him, and very soon no one was safe in proclaiming that Abraham Lincoln had once been a very human creature, only partially like the god-figure whom the Republic was worshiping. The folk-mind was raptly curious to learn how Lincoln had suffered, how he had prayed, dreamed, and conquered, how he had loved mankind; it did not want to hear how he had doubted, despaired, schemed, evaded, contrived, like ordinary mortals.

It was the sad, warm heart of the new deity that America wanted to read and hear about, not that cool, tantalizingly slow brain with which Lincoln had defeated enemies of the Union within and without his own political party.

At the end of the war he had been the chief American hero; assassination had elevated him into mythology. Old gods had

died to save Man's crops in the field. This new god had died
to save Man's barns from Jefferson Davis' raiders, and the
difference between the old and the new was too small to keep
Abraham Lincoln from mythdom.

And as Lincoln made this ascent into immortality he took
J. Wilkes Booth with him.

That, too, was according to a pattern of antiquity. Most of
the gods who had died for Man had taken their betrayers
with them into the realm of legend. Worshiping multitudes in
ancient and mediaeval days awarded immortality to the slay-
ers of their gods as well as to the gods themselves. Osiris shared
his myth-heights with his slayer, an evil brother Set; Adonis,
the radiant, was believed to have been doomed by the swart
and jealous Ares, who could not therefore be forgotten; Balder
the Beautiful lifted his envious assassin Loki into the superstitions of the Germanic peoples; Dionysus gave an added
demon-stature to his killers, the grimy Titans, themselves already gods; Britons remembered with fond hatred Sir Modred,
the dark knight who had taken from them their bright-browed
King Arthur. And Judas Iscariot, in the eyes of Christians,
most terrible of all, had won eternal infamy by his betrayal of
Jesus.

Twice before the death of Lincoln was to give focus to the
folk-yearning of America, the New World had tried to create
its own evil god, some national scapegoat upon whom it might
lavish its hate. Older civilizations had had their Cains. Where
was America's?

For the abhorred honor, the Republic first nominated Bene-
dict Arnold, but since he had only been accused of betraying
the flag, he dwindled and soon was living only in schoolbooks.
Aaron Burr, the other candidate, was little better; the courts,
it was always to be recalled, had acquitted him of treason.
Furthermore, the common people could never be expected to
hate, so very much, the man who had killed Alexander Hamilton. Hadn't Hamilton called the public "that great beast"?

J. Wilkes Booth, however, was more promising material.
No matter what he had been in his lifetime, he had done one
act of demoniac infamy; he had killed America's patron saint,

and was, therefore, the Cain, the Judas, for whom the myth-wanting patriots had longed.

For this reason no proof of Booth's identity as the man who lay dead on Garrett's porch can ever be expected to lay his ghost. The legend has consistently defied credible testimony. Most scrupulous historians — perhaps all — have been satisfied that the War Department, in spite of its childish desire to play hide-and-seek with a cadaver, did bury the right man in the warehouse of the penitentiary at Washington.

There was never a thing in Booth himself to warrant the deathlessness of his name. That he assassinated a President of the United States does not explain his survival in folk-lore, for who has ever questioned or cared where Charles Guiteau or Leon Czolgosz are buried? The assassins of Garfield and McKinley were soon forgotten.

Obviously, Booth has owed everything to his victim's deification. Having made himself the folk-story Judas of America, he was soon believed to be doing what the traditional betrayers of mythology always did, wandering the world, friendless and branded with infamy.

The myth of his survival is of an age-old pattern. Ordinary death was never felt, by primitive peoples, to be punishment enough for the various betrayers of great heroes. The Cains and Judases have been too monumental in their villainies to suffer man's conventional penalties. They must always wander on, tortured by remorse, shunned by the world, to wretched deathlessness or to suicide.

Many races, many peoples, across many centuries have cherished the myth of the Wandering Jew, that servant of Pontius Pilate who dealt Jesus a blow as he was led out of the palace toward Golgotha. The legend runs that Jesus said to the man, "Thou shalt wander on earth till I return," and that henceforth the man drifted from land to land, coming down the centuries with never a grave to give him rest. He was seen here, seen there, and even as late as 1830 he was reported to be in England, wandering on.

The myth of the Flying Dutchman, too, has had countless creditors, people who devoutly believed that its captain forever sailed the seas in punishment for his sins. Likewise, there is the European legend of the Mysterious Huntsman, doomed forever to be vainly pursuing the phantom deer.

Any opportunity for suspecting that the identification of a hero's or a villain's body has been incomplete has been seized by the masses as an excuse to whisper, "He is not dead."

Lord Kitchener of Khartoum, drowning in the North Sea on a torpedoed warship during the World War, was said by Britishers to be still alive, mysteriously waiting in some German prison for release. The myth-form worked in Ireland when the peasants passed the word along that their parliamentarian hero, Charles Parnell, was not dead, as the papers said, only hiding until the appointed hour for his return. It was working when story-tellers and even newspapers of the '90s wondered if the "Mad Mullah," that fearsome African chieftain, could not in reality be "Chinese" Gordon in disguise. Gordon, the British general, had fallen in the Soudan, but the myth of his survival lived on fantastically.

In the American West there were, for years, people who would never believe that Brigham Young was dead. His death was a hoax, they said, a plot to fool his enemies, and from some safe concealment, often declared to be Mexico, he was guiding his Mormon followers.

Sometimes the workings of the old folk-fancy have taken ridiculous turns. Not so long ago it was commonly whispered that Col. William F. Cody, the Wild West hero, "Buffalo Bill," was dead, and that the circus owners had kept his demise a secret in order that business should not be injured. Creditors of the tale would point to the white-haired colonel as he rode about the ring shooting glass balls out of the air with his rifle, and would say, "That's not Buffalo Bill! That's his cousin who has been dressed up to take his place."

At other times people have said that Oscar Wilde, the English poet, did not suffer the tragic death which was reported, but, in disguise, wandered the British Isles.

J. Wilkes Booth was not a hero to the people in the ordinary sense of the word, but he was what folk-lore recognizes to be a "demon-hero," one of the many such who have been so dramatic and romantic in their crimes as to merit a notoriety that approximates heroism. The fiction-tale of his escape, supported by just enough gossip to give it the appearance of plausibility, was a gaudy entertainment in the lives of toilers in those money-grubbing days that followed the Civil War. There was fascinating mystery in the thought that the killer of Abraham Lincoln was still at large, wandering unknown through the country that he had bereft. People who felt a touch of national pride when they talked of Jesse James, the outlaw, as if he had been an American Robin Hood, felt the same pride when they shuddered over J. Wilkes Booth as though he were an American Judas.

☆ ☆ ☆ 2 ☆ ☆ ☆

SOURCES

Of the standard biographical works of Abraham Lincoln, the most useful have been those by William H. Herndon and Jesse Weik, Ward Hill Lamon, John G. Holland, Carl Sandburg, Isaac N. Arnold, Nicolay and Hay, William E. Barton and Ida M. Tarbell. Of the biographies of Robert E. Lee the most frequently consulted have been those by Fitzhugh Lee, Robert E. Lee, Jr., Long, and Maurice. Concerning Ulysses S. Grant, his own *Memoirs* and the biographies of William Conant Church, Charles A. Dana, and the views of Gen. Horace C. Porter in his *Campaigning with Grant* and his article in *Century* for September, 1897, have been drawn upon.

The biographical volumes on Charles Sumner by Walter G. Shotwell and by E. L. Pierce; on Andrew Johnson by R. W. Winston, and on Edwin M. Stanton by Frank Abial Flower and by George C. Gorham, have been used liberally, as have the memoirs of William T. Sherman and Joseph E. Johnston.

James Ford Rhodes' *History of the United States* has been consulted more often than any other one source.

The books of Dr. William E. Barton, as mentioned in the

text, are *The Paternity of Lincoln* and *The Soul of Lincoln.*
Louis A. Warren's work is *Lincoln's Parentage and Childhood.*
Sources for certain specific incidents are as follows:

Charles Dickens' version of Lincoln's dream is quoted in
The Life of George Eliot by John Walter Cross (Houghton
Mifflin, 1908).

The hiding of John Wilkes Booth's body is described by Dr.
George L. Porter in the *Columbian Magazine* for April, 1911,
and by Ray Stannard Baker in *McClure's* for May, 1897. The
identification of Booth's body is from Dr. John Frederick May's
article in Vol. XIII of the records of the Columbian Historical
Society.

Edwin M. Stanton's improbable suicide is discussed in *Anecdotes of the Civil War* by E. D. Townsend (Appleton, 1884).

J. W. Booth's behavior at the hanging of John Brown is described in Ezekiel's *History of the Jews in Richmond.*

Lincoln's actions at City Point in 1865 are pictured by the
Marquis de Chambrun in *Scribner's* for January, 1893. Clara
Morris' memory of Booth is to be found in *McClure's* for February, 1901, and the schoolgirl's story of her meeting with
Booth on the morning of April 14, 1865, is told by Jesse Weik
in the *Century* for February, 1913.

Facts concerning the Lincoln tomb at Springfield and the
hiding of his body therein are contained in J. C. Power's *The
Attempt to Steal Abraham Lincoln's Body* and in *The Building of the Lincoln Monument* by Paul M. Angle.

The statement on page 5 that Lee whispered to Grant his
request that food be given his hungry men is made by William
Conant Church in his *Ulysses S. Grant*, N. Y., 1926. As editor
of the *U. S. Army and Navy Journal,* Church knew many of
the surviving witnesses, after the war. General George H.
Sharpe who, as Assistant-Provost-Marshal-General at Grant's
headquarters, took the parole of Lee and his staff at Appomattox,
declared in his eye-witness account of the surrender in *Annals
of the War*, Philadelphia, 1879, "There was one moment when
there was a whispered conversation between Grant and Lee
which nobody in the room heard."

Certain brief changes were made, for the 1940 edition, in the texts of Chapters XIII and XIV dealing with the illegitimacy of John Wilkes Booth and the nature of the pistol wound he received in the South. New evidence brought to light by Stanley Kimmel in *The Mad Booths of Maryland*, Bobbs-Merrill, 1940, has clarified points hitherto in question.

A fuller and more detailed examination of the evidence on Lincoln's responsibility for the surrender terms given Confederates by Grant and Sherman, and particularly on Sherman's understanding of them, is contained in Chapters 50, 51 and 52 of the author's *Sherman: Fighting Prophet*, Harcourt, Brace & Company, 1932.

A list of books read and not otherwise listed, is as follows:

LIFE OF EDWIN BOOTH, William Winter (Macmillan, 1893).

LETTERS OF EDWIN BOOTH, Edwina Booth Grossman (Century, 1894).

VAGRANT MEMORIES, William Winter (Doran, 1915).

ELDER AND YOUNGER BOOTH, Asia B. Clarke (1882).

POLITICAL RECOLLECTIONS, George W. Julian (Jansen, McClurg, 1884).

JUDICIAL MURDER OF MARY E. SURRATT, David Miller DeWitt (Murphy, 1895).

HISTORY OF THE U. S. SECRET SERVICE, Lafayette C. Baker (Baker, 1867).

REMINISCENCES OF THE ASSASSINATION OF LINCOLN, J. E. Buckingham (Darby, 1894).

ASSASSINATION OF ABRAHAM LINCOLN, Osborne H. Oldroyd (Oldroyd, 1901).

ASSASSINATION OF LINCOLN, E. W. Coggeshall (Hill, 1924).

DEATH OF LINCOLN, Clara E. Laughlin (Doubleday, Page, 1909).

ASSASSINATION OF LINCOLN AND HISTORY OF THE CONSPIRACY (Hawley, 1865).

LIFE, CRIME AND CAPTURE OF JOHN WILKES BOOTH, George Alfred Townsend (Dick and Fitzgerald, 1865).

ASSASSIN'S DEATH, George Alfred Townsend (Dick and Fitzgerald, 1865).

THE GREAT CONSPIRACY (Barclay and Co., 1865).

UNWRITTEN HISTORY OF LINCOLN'S ASSASSINATION, Orra L. Stone (Smoot, 1908).

REMINISCENCES OF WILLIAM M. STEWART (Brown-Neale, 1908).

MEMORIAL SERVICES AT THE SOLDIERS' GRAVES (Government Printing Office, 1868).

NATIONAL MEMORIAL DAY (Government Printing Office, 1869).

ASSASSINATION OF ABRAHAM LINCOLN AND THE TRIAL OF THE CONSPIRATORS, Benn Pitman (Government Printing Office, 1865).

TRIAL OF JOHN H. SURRATT (Government Printing Office, 1867).

HISTORY OF THE GRAND ARMY OF THE REPUBLIC, Robert B. Beath (1889).

GRAND ARMY OF THE REPUBLIC, Oliver M. Wilson (Hudson, 1905).

CONSTITUTIONAL VIEW OF THE LATE WAR BETWEEN THE STATES, Alexander H. Stephens (National Publishing Co., 1868).

JEFFERSON DAVIS, William E. Dodd (Jacobs, 1907).

SHORT HISTORY OF THE CONFEDERATE STATES OF AMERICA, Jefferson Davis.

STATESMEN OF THE OLD SOUTH, William E. Dodd (Macmillan, 1911).

LINCOLN OR LEE, William E. Dodd (Century, 1928).

ASSASSINATION OF LINCOLN, T. M. Harris (1892).

SCRAP BOOK, Vol. XI, April 1924, Mildred Lewis Rutherford (Athens, Ga.).

FROM MANASSAS TO APPOMATTOX, James Longstreet (Lippincott, 1866).

THE DIARY OF GIDEON WELLES (Houghton Mifflin, 1911).

LEE'S DISPATCHES (Putnam, 1915).

LINCOLN AND HERNDON, Joseph Fort Newton (Torch Press, 1910).

THROUGH FIVE ADMINISTRATIONS, William H. Crook (Harper and Brothers, 1909).

✣ ✣ ✣ 3 ✣ ✣ ✣

INDEX